BEYOND THE HYPE:

A Realist's Guide To AI

BY

Andy Hayler

Cover image by: British Book Design
Proofreading by: Ariane Laurent-Smith
Book design by: SWATT Books Ltd

Printed in the United Kingdom
First Printing, 2026

ISBN: 978-1-9192419-2-0 (Paperback)
ISBN: 978-1-9192419-3-7 (Hardback)
ISBN: 978-1-9192419-4-4 (eBook)

The Information Difference Publishing
14 Mayfield Avenue
Chiswick, London
W4 1PW

www.informationdifference.com

Table of Contents

Foreword

Artificial intelligence has entered a phase where capability, consequence, and complexity rise together. This book recognises that reality with clarity, discipline, and evidence. It does not offer hype. It provides a grounded map of what AI is doing to our institutions, our security, our information environment, and our trust in the systems we depend on.

Across its chapters, the book demonstrates how AI is reshaping education, the economy, creative work, law, healthcare, regulation, and public safety.

It explains the risks that matter: hallucinations that can mislead people and systems, deepfakes that erode confidence in truth, cyberattacks amplified by automation, fragile guardrails, synthetic data poisoning, and legal frameworks struggling to keep pace.

At the same time, it demonstrates the practical promise of AI in medicine, research, engineering, robotics, and customer service.

What makes this work valuable is its rigour. Every claim is sourced. Every issue is examined through real cases, verifiable research, and current global developments from the UK, EU, US, and China. The discussion of copyright battles, data poisoning, multimodal safety, regulatory divides, and the rapid spread of synthetic media is especially timely and important.

Leaders need more than opinions about AI. They need a realistic understanding of what is already happening, where failure modes lie, where progress is genuine, and where society must respond with stronger governance.

This book provides exactly that. It is a resource for practitioners, policymakers, educators, and anyone who seeking a serious and factual view of the technology shaping this decade.

If the world is to use AI well, it begins with understanding. This book is a significant contribution to that effort.

Kieran Gilmurray, AI author and international keynote speaker

Introduction

Artificial intelligence (AI) burst into the public imagination with the launch of OpenAI's ChatGPT on 30th November 2022. Within just two months, this product had gained a hundred million users, becoming the fastest-growing software application ever. Its success caused an avalanche of investment in AI and a slew of competitors. By mid-2025, half of all venture capital was being directed to AI-related companies. While AI has been around since 1956, ChatGPT's conversational user interface, based on a technology called "generative AI" (which itself has been around since 2014), brought AI to a new and much broader audience.

With ChatGPT, people could not merely ask factual questions, but could also use it to write a letter, an essay, a poem, or a song. The technology could respond in a fluent, conversational manner and even become a virtual friend. Other generative AI tools can draw increasingly high-quality images and even generate videos. Corporations started to use generative AI to augment or replace customer service staff, to write marketing materials, or to translate articles into other languages. Software developers could use it to analyse and debug code or write new code from scratch. People who had never learned to program could use the tools to "vibe code" entire prototype applications and websites. The technology could be used to interpret medical images, detect fraudulent banking transactions, or brainstorm ideas and turn them into business plans.

Science fiction writer Arthur C. Clarke said, "Any sufficiently advanced technology is indistinguishable from magic", and generative AI seems like magic to many people. This genuine excitement has blinded many to the very real limitations of generative AI. The core technology of generative AI, the large language model (LLM), is essentially a probability engine that uses its algorithms to predict its answers based on its training data. LLMs are voracious creatures, absorbing literally trillions of words and images. This dependence on training data leads to a number of inherent issues. An LLM's answers will reflect its training data, so any biases in that training data will be mirrored in the outputs. This is a problem if, for example, you use LLMs to scan job resumes to filter out applicants. An LLM trained on large swathes of the internet will inherit any biases in that training data, perhaps favouring men over women as preferred candidates for an engineering role.

A major limitation of LLMs is inherent to their probabilistic nature: in areas where they have limited training data, in particular, they fill in gaps with plausible but fabricated data. This phenomenon, known as "hallucination", means that LLMs will sometimes just make things up. Lawyers using LLMs to draft court documents have found this out the hard way, with LLMs frequently coming up with impressive lists of plausible case law precedents, only some of which actually exist. Literally hundreds of legal cases have been affected by this. The rate at which LLMs hallucinate varies due to many circumstances, but on average, around one in five LLM answers contain hallucinations. This is a feature, not a bug. Indeed, the more sophisticated recent LLM models that came out in 2024 and 2025 actually hallucinate more frequently than the earlier ones.[1]

The training of LLMs is a computationally intensive task and has thus sparked a boom in data centre building. This propelled NVIDIA, the maker of the graphics processing units (GPUs) that are particularly well-suited to AI processing, to become the most valuable company in the world in July 2025, with a market cap of over $4 trillion.[2] This is great for NVIDIA shareholders, but has significant environmental implications. Data centres consumed over 1% of the world's electricity in 2022, and this proportion is rapidly increasing. The consumption of data centres is putting a major strain on energy networks, and the use of drinking water for cooling servers (salt water corrodes machinery) is yet another impact of the data centre boom.

There is a darker side to the use of LLMs than hallucinated court cases. People around the world have started to use LLMs as virtual friends, even virtual boyfriends and girlfriends. The company Replika is an AI companion and had ten million users by January 2023. More disturbingly, many people have started to use chatbots as unpaid mental health therapists, often with tragic consequences. LLMs are fluent communicators and tend to tell you what you want to hear, which is not what you want from a therapist. There have already been several cases of suicide[3] and even murder/suicide as a result of chatbot advice.[4]

There is no question that generative AI offers genuine opportunities in many areas. In this book, we will explore case studies of how it can be used in industries ranging from motor vehicles to defence, from mining to movies. We will look at the economics of AI, including the success rate of AI projects and its effect on jobs, and speculate on the possible future of the technology. We will discuss the ethics of AI, the legislative response to it from governments around the world, and even whether AI represents an existential threat to humanity. We will explore how to apply AI more successfully by looking into the use cases for which generative AI, in particular, is well-suited and those where it is not. By understanding how the technology works, we can make sure that we use it productively and effectively, and avoid joining the 95% of AI projects that currently fail.[5]

To begin, let's explore the origins of artificial intelligence and how generative AI actually works under the covers. This will give us a basis to investigate many different aspects of the technology. Incidentally, it is hopefully obvious, but all the words in this book are entirely mine, with not one generated by AI. There are a few AI images used, but only to illustrate points being made about AI.

Foundations of AI

A Little History

In the summer of 1956, a two-month-long workshop was held at Dartmouth College, an Ivy League research university in New Hampshire. The workshop, organised by Marvin Minsky, Nathaniel Rochester, Claude Shannon, and John McCarthy, was intended to discuss the notion of thinking machines, with the term "artificial intelligence" coined by the mathematician John McCarthy. This event, held on the top floor of the Dartmouth Math department, is generally accepted to be the place where the field of AI began. Research, some funded by the US government, began with the intention of turning the idea of thinking machines into reality.

This turned out to be a tough assignment, and progress in the years to come was slow. By 1974, the US and British governments had pulled funding, although Japan picked up the slack in 1981 with its Fifth Generation Computer Systems project, budgeted at $850 million.[6] This was a decade-long initiative that covered natural language processing, speech recognition, and problem-solving.[7] It also struggled to deliver much in the way of meaningful deliverables, though much foundational research was conducted. In 1982, one outcome of the research was "SID", the first "expert system", or "Synthesis of Integral Design" to give it its full name. Written in the LISP programming language, it relied on a knowledge base provided by experts and was intended to help with the design of logic gates used in DEC's VAX 9000 computer. It successfully generated 93% of the logic gates in the computer, in some cases, outperforming human designers, and so was regarded as a relatively successful early example of AI.[8] However, it turned out to be hard to find more general applications for the technology, despite some initial commercial expert systems appearing in the mid-1980s. Specialist machines to run LISP applications were built by vendors like Symbolics and LISP Machines, but within a few years, more general-purpose desktop computers from IBM and Apple emerged that made these largely redundant. Expert systems turned out to be quite brittle, hard to update, and could not handle unusual inputs well. The period between 1987 and 2000 saw much expert system research abandoned, and the era was described as an "AI winter", following on from a similar era of disillusion in AI from around 1974–1980. The first neural network, a technology we will examine in more depth in due course, was actually introduced as far back as 1958 by AI researcher and psychologist Frank Rosenblatt at Cornell. However, this research petered out in 1966.

Things gradually turned around, helped by increasingly powerful hardware. By the early 2000s, machine learning was being applied to a range of problems. A key development occurred in 2017, when transformer architecture was proposed by eight researchers at Google.[9] This idea, a parallel architecture for neural networks, enabled the first generative AI applications, based on large language models. This ultimately led to the launch of the wildly successful ChatGPT, with its "Generative Pre-trained Transformer (GPT)", by OpenAI on 30th November 2022. This product, which had an intuitive text-based interface, caught the public imagination.

Different Flavours of AI

So much attention has been lavished on ChatGPT and its generative AI competitors that it is easy to forget that generative AI is just one distinct flavour of AI. The media is awash with stories about the large language models that underpin generative AI, but some of the more established AI use cases and case studies actually have nothing to do with chatbots or LLMs. Indeed, if you poke around into some of the better-known AI successes, it turns out that many of them are based on different technology entirely. As discussed, expert systems emerged in the 1960s and 1970s. They mimic the decision-making of a human expert in a narrow field by using a knowledge base in that field, plus an inference engine. The knowledge base is built of rules defined by human experts. For example, an expert system about medical diagnosis would be built from rules defined by human doctors. An early example was MYCIN at Stanford University, which diagnosed bacterial infections and recommended treatments.[10] These have a wide range of applications in fields such as investment decisions, equipment troubleshooting, and crop management. These systems are still in use today, for example, in the US Navy's Aegis Combat System, which analyses data from radar and sonar to identify threats.[11] Expert systems are explainable because they follow precise rules and are consistent. They can struggle to scale to very large, unstructured datasets and have mostly given way to machine learning and neural networks, of which more anon. Symbolic AI is a related approach that relies on explicit representations of knowledge. Expert systems can be regarded as a subset of symbolic AI.

Fuzzy logic is a technique that deals with situations where information is vague or uncertain, which is a common occurrence in the real world. In Boolean logic, things are true or false, but in fuzzy logic, data is represented in a continuum of values. Fuzzy logic is often used in control systems such as washing machines, aeroplane altitude control, or air conditioners. It is easy to implement in code compared to many AI techniques, though it does not adapt and can struggle to scale in complex problems with many variables.

Machine learning is a form of AI in which models learn from data and improve their performance without being explicitly instructed. Machine learning algorithms find patterns in data and rules that allow the system to make predictions. As the system sees more and more data, it improves. The system can be trained on either labelled data or unlabelled data. Labelled data might be data where a human has labelled a set of emails as either being spam or not spam or a series of images that have been labelled to show each image as either including an object, like pictures with either a cat or no cat. Unsupervised learning occurs when the algorithm is presented with unlabelled data and tries to detect patterns on its own.

There is also reinforcement learning, which works by trial and error. The system tries different things; the ones that work are scored positively, while those that don't are scored negatively. The system then repeats this process many times. For example, the chess-playing program AlphaZero from DeepMind was simply taught the rules of chess. It then played several million games against itself. At first, its moves were almost random, but after many iterations, its standard of play slowly improved, then improved more. After four hours of such training, its play reached its zenith, and it was pitted against Stockfish, the strongest chess program in the world, which was based on classical AI using defined rules to evaluate positions. In one hundred games, AlphaZero won 72 games, drew 28, and did not lose a single game.[12]

Machine learning is good at spotting trends and patterns in large volumes of data, automating repetitive tasks, and dealing with complex data. However, it is heavily dependent on the quality of the data it is trained on, so data that has inherent bias will lead to biased predictions. For example, if a machine learning algorithm is trained on images of people skewed to a particular racial type, then it will reflect that bias. This is obviously a problem when machine learning is used for job screening or similar applications. A machine learning system called PREPOL was used in the US to predict crime, but it repeatedly recommended police target areas with a high proportion of racial minorities, regardless of the actual crime rate in those areas.[13]

Genetic algorithms are used for optimisation and work by iteratively refining a group of candidate solutions. The idea is to mirror natural selection, as described by Charles Darwin. This technique can be used in situations where there are complex, non-linear functions, such as designing engineering control systems or for fraud detection or drug discovery. There are limitations, including sensitivity to the parameters chosen and the fact that they tend to be computationally expensive to operate. This approach can struggle to scale as the number of variables increases or may take a very long time to reach an optimal solution.

Neural networks are a technique modelled on the way that the human brain (probably) works. It has layers of connected units called "neurons" that process input data to produce an output. Each neuron has a set of weights applied to it, and it uses these to process its input data, passing the result to another neuron. This, in turn, does the same, passing its result to the next layer of neurons. After perhaps dozens of such steps, the neural net has a result. The weightings are adjusted during training to minimise prediction errors. For example, a neural net might be trained on a file of customer sales data. The neural network can be asked to predict the likelihood of a customer, or a particular grouping of customers (such as women or men, or people in a specific age range), buying again based on their purchase history.

Neural networks can model complex data relationships, can adapt over time when shown new data, can handle “noisy” data, and can scale well, as their computations can easily be parallelised. However, they typically require lots of training data and are black boxes, so they cannot explain their reasoning. They are sensitive to the quality of their training data and can reflect bias in their training data in their own predictions. Neural networks are versatile and are used in applications ranging from medical imaging to self-driving cars to facial recognition and natural language processing. They are used in fraud detection and in personalised recommendation systems such as those used by Netflix and Amazon. Neural networks are used within the most fashionable of all AI styles at the moment: generative AI.

Generative AI is specifically designed to generate new content, such as text or program code or images. It uses a series of neural networks to synthesise outputs that are based on their training data but are nonetheless original. They can create artwork, write essays, write marketing emails, or produce a poem or a marketing plan, and can even help in drug discovery. Generative AI is embodied by popular chat applications like ChatGPT, Claude, Perplexity, and Gemini, as well as in visual equivalents such as Leonardo, Midjourney, Stable Diffusion, and Firefly. They can produce fluent text but can produce invented or nonsensical answers, a phenomenon known as “hallucination”, which we will examine in more depth later. They reflect any biases in their training data and rely on huge amounts of training data and processing power.

Even this lengthy set of AI styles is not exhaustive. Swarm intelligence uses simple agents that interact with each other based on rules and local perception, mimicking the behaviours of birds flying in coordinated flocks. Applications include robotics, network routing, and traffic management, as well as anomaly detection. This technique has limitations of scale and can behave unexpectedly, as well as being hard to debug.

A new approach was unveiled in 2025 by a company in Singapore.[14] This “hierarchical reasoning model” has two modules. A “planner” thinks slowly and strategically, while "workers" execute rapid calculations for specific tasks. Intriguingly, this approach avoids the need for vast amounts of training data and was relatively small at 27 million parameters. By contrast, Claude 3.5 has 175 billion parameters, and ChatGPT-4 has about 1.8 trillion parameters. Despite the vast difference in model size, the HRM model managed a David v Goliath-style performance in benchmarks, outperforming both Claude and ChatGPT on some complex reasoning tasks like the ARC-AGI (Abstraction and Reasoning Corpus for Artificial General Intelligence) benchmark. It is early days and will need further testing, but it is an approach that seems to show promise. There are yet more AI approaches, including diffusion models, which have been mostly used in image-generating AIs so far.

AI goes far beyond the large language model paradigm that has captured the world's attention in recent times. This is important because LLMs have distinct limitations, such as their propensity to hallucinate, and are poorly suited to many tasks.[15] LLMs are not good for cases that require consistency and precision, complex multi-step logical reasoning, or transparency in their decision-making. Many of the more embarrassing AI failures, and there is an ever-growing list, have been where LLMs have been applied to situations that do not suit them.[16] The old saying – "If all you have is a hammer, everything looks like a nail" – applies very well here, with LLMs being applied to many tasks where another approach would be better. A trivial example of this can be seen if you ask an LLM to play a game of chess. Indeed, computers have been very good at chess for decades, with an IBM program called Deep Blue having beaten the chess world champion Garry Kasparov in 1997. These days, chess engine apps that work on the phone in your pocket would trounce the current human chess world champion. Yet LLMs can barely make it through a few moves of a chess game before hallucinating extra pieces onto the board or playing illegal moves, never mind playing moves that make strategic sense. As of September 2025, LLMs are bad at chess: laughably bad.[17] Watching two LLMs play against each other is like watching two spaniels trying to play chess with each other.

The example of chess vividly shows that different flavours of AI can be dramatically more successful than LLMs at certain types of tasks. People implementing AI programs need to be aware of the different tools at their disposal and be ready to apply the right tool to the right job. Of course, for many tasks, good old-fashioned programming is still the way to go. AI can be a useful tool, but it is not a panacea.

How Large Language Models Work

Given the level of interest in generative AI, let's dig into the way that it works in more detail than the overview above. Fundamentally, generative AI can create new content using machine learning models trained on huge datasets. The transformer architecture mentioned above is the one used by ChatGPT (and many others, like Gemini and Stable Diffusion), but there are additional approaches too, such as generative adversarial networks and variational encoders.[18] We will focus on ChatGPT and its cousins for now. The "Chat" bit of ChatGPT is just the conversational interface; the core is the "GPT" part, the large language model. An LLM is designed to understand, predict, and generate human-like text.

Training an LLM involves a three-stage process. Data is collected from websites, articles, books, and more. LLMs are voracious: GPT-3 was trained on about 45 terabytes of raw data, compressed to 570 GB of text data. This is about 300 billion words, or roughly 3 million books. To give some context, the number of books that have been published in the history of the world is around 140 million books, with perhaps 2 million a year being added, many of these self-published. GPT-4 was trained on a petabyte of data, 22 times larger than that used for GPT-3 and equivalent to around 66 million books. Just the training of GPT-4 is estimated to have cost around $100 million, to give an idea of the computational resources required.

Once the raw data has been collected, it is converted into "tokens",[19] the fundamental unit of an AI model. A token is roughly equivalent to four characters in English, with 100 tokens being roughly 75 words. A paragraph of English text might be 100 tokens. Clearly, the numbers vary somewhat with other languages.

The first of the three training stages is "self-supervised learning." The model ingests the data and learns intrinsic general language patterns by predicting the next word in a sentence. If the raw data for an LLM were weather data, then it may group data by temperature, for example. Once this initial clustering stage is done, a second stage of "supervised learning" is undertaken. Here, the model is trained on labelled data, where each input has a desired output, such as responses to questions. If the inputs were images, some might be labelled as containing a cat, and others as not containing a cat.

The third stage of training an LLM is reinforcement learning with human feedback. Here, humans evaluate the model's responses and rank them for quality, with the scores acting as rewards for the model. This stage is used to, for example, discourage the model from producing harmful outputs, such as how to make a chemical weapon or how to build a bomb. There may, optionally, be a further stage of training for a specific domain, such as an LLM for the medical or legal fields, where the model is tuned further to improve its answers in that particular domain.

So, you now have a fully trained LLM. Add an interface so that users can talk to it, and it is ready to go. But when a user asks an LLM a question, say, "What is the capital of Australia?" or "Write me a 12-line love poem", what happens next? First, the question needs to be converted into tokens, the basic unit of currency for LLMs. The model then assesses the relative importance of each token in the question so it can focus on the important parts of the input and understand the context and intent of the question. This process is called "self-attention". It then processes the token through multiple layers of neural networks (usually a few dozen of these layers) to generate the most likely next token as its answer. It bases its choices on its training data and on statistical patterns in order to select the most plausible output. At this point, the answer is converted back from tokens into words and sent back to the user interface. This interactive FT document shows the process of how an LLM works visually.[20] An LLM is, in essence, a pattern-spotting probability engine. We are all familiar with how Google searches these days use "auto-complete". So, if you start a query with "ink", then the engine starts to suggest links to "inkjet printer" or "ink cartridges", etc., because these are the queries that it has most commonly seen before. An LLM can be thought of as an autocomplete function on steroids. Instead of merely completing a couple more words in a query, an LLM can produce much longer answers: a sentence, a paragraph, perhaps a whole essay or article if that is what it was asked for. The LLM builds its answer one word (technically, one token) at a time until the response is completed. It knows when to stop because of an end-of-sequence token; when the LLM predicts this token, the generation stops. It may also stop due to a maximum length limit that has been set in its parameters.

An LLM will, by default, pick the most probable of its possible choices of the next word (or token) in its answer. However, an LLM can also be manipulated into choosing less likely answers. There is a parameter called "temperature", which is adjustable by an LLM application developer, though not usually an end user. This can be adjusted to allow the LLM to get more "creative" in its answers. LLM chatbots are usually set to a default level (usually 1), which means that the LLM samples from its raw learned probability distribution. If a developer sets the level lower, then you will get reduced variability of answers and greater precision. This may be appropriate for certain specific applications, such as dealing with technical documentation. A higher temperature may be set if the LLM is to be used in a context like creative writing or brainstorming. The temperature is a measure of the variability of the LLM's answers.

This leads to an important point that many people misunderstand. If you ask an LLM, "What is the capital of Australia?," then its training data will have plenty of examples that point it to "Canberra" being the most probable answer. Consequently, it will almost always give you that answer. However, it will not do so 100% of the time. There is always a small chance that it will decide something else is a plausible answer. In a case like this, where it has stacks of training data, it will answer the question correctly time after time. But if you repeat the question often enough, eventually, it will give you a different answer.[21] Indeed, LLM consistency is typically around 80–95%, so if you asked that same question 20 times, you may well see one answer that was not "Canberra". The more obscure the area in question, the less training data is available, and the more likely it is that the LLM will have to invent something plausible in order to complete its answer, a phenomenon called "hallucination". This is a major issue for LLMs, and one we will return to and cover in a lot more depth.

It is important to understand that an LLM, when asked a factual question, is relying entirely on its training data, which will include huge amounts of ingested data, including large chunks of data from the internet. But when it is giving an answer, the LLM does not (typically) pop off to the live internet to look something up. This creates some obvious issues. Once the LLM is trained, it is working on a snapshot of data in time: the data it had access to up until the date it finished training. If things change later, then it knows nothing of this future data. So, for example, GPT-3.5, whose knowledge cut-off was January 2022, cannot reliably provide information about events after that date.

This time cut-off is clearly a limitation, so LLMs are now often paired with retrieval or tool-augmented architectures. These models allow an LLM to query external databases or search engines to gather up-to-date information at the moment that the query is made and then generate answers grounded in that additional data. By 2025, it had become common for chatbots like ChatGPT, Gemini, Claude, or Perplexity to be able to supplement their training data with external sources in this way. However, some LLMs do not, including ChatGPT-3 or some versions of open-source models.

Hallucinations – When AIs Dream

We have grown used to computers behaving consistently. If you type a formula into Excel to multiply two numbers together, not only will the answer be correct, but it will also produce the same result when you next open the spreadsheet. This is not the way LLMs behave. If you ask a chatbot based on an LLM a question, then it will generate a response, a prediction based on its parameters and its training data. As we have seen, an LLM has parameters, such as its "temperature", which control the randomness of the output. Higher temperatures lead to more creative text, while lower temperatures lead to more focused outputs. Other parameters include the token limit, which determines how long the output can be, and also the number of layers in the neural net architecture.

Some researchers dislike the term "hallucination" as it seems anthropomorphic, giving the impression of sentient thought when there are just complex calculations involved. However, the term has stuck, so I will use it in this book. There are actually different kinds of hallucination: factual inaccuracies, nonsensical output, logical fallacies, irrelevant output, generating fake citations or references, incorrectly conflating different sources, and more. LLMs may hallucinate more if their training data is of poor quality,[22] and so an emphasis on high-quality training data is certainly important.[23] The introduction of LLMs has, in itself, caused a problem in this regard. It has been estimated that over half of internet content is now AI-generated, some through machine translation of articles into other languages.[24] An April 2025 study found that 74% of all new webpages contain AI content.[25] Training LLMs on AI-generated content is problematic, to say the least. Given the voracious demand for training data, some AI companies have been trying to use synthetic data to train LLMs, i.e. getting LLMs to generate synthetic data to train other LLMs. Studies have shown that this approach has many issues.[26]

Anyone who uses LLMs regularly will have encountered hallucinations if they are paying attention, but here are a few examples. An AI-generated book on mushroom picking contained potentially lethal advice on which foraged mushrooms were safe to eat.[27] There are literally hundreds of legal cases emerging where lawyers used LLMs to generate lists of case law precedents, many of which turned out to be entirely fictitious.[28] A Google AI answer to a question about whether hippos were intelligent claimed that hippos could be trained to perform complex medical procedures, as we will see.

ChatGPT-5, released in August 2025, has produced a range of entertaining viral hallucinations, including an image of US presidents, including "Richard Ninun" (instead of Nixon), seemingly born in 1969 but died in 1974, just five years later (Nixon was actually born in 1913 and died in 1994). The very same image had a host of other errors, such as Ronald "Beagan" (Reagan) being born in 1661. A different one, also error-strewn, can be seen here.[29] A similar list of Canadian prime ministers was also flawed. Bear in mind that there is a great deal of public data about US presidents. Now imagine how inaccurate LLMs might be if asked to provide information on more obscure topics.

This was what Anthropic's Claude managed to produce on 14th September 2025 when I gave it this prompt:

"Can you produce a picture showing all the US presidents, with their portraits, names, and dates when they held office?"

ChatGPT was no better, producing this the same day.

George' Was-
1789-1797
Jánn Adams
1797-1801
Thomas Jefferson
1891-1833
James Madison
1890-1817
James Monroe
1817-1825
JohmC. Apdams
1828-1882
Zachary Taylor
1889-1889
Millard Fillmore
1890-1683
Franklin Plerce
1828-1857
James Blichanan
1802-1881
Abraham Lincoin
1887-1802
Andrew Johnson
1888-1889
Ulysses S. Grant
1885-1877
Rutherford B Haves
1877-1851
James A. Garfield
1881
Chester. A. Arthur
1831-1832
Grovei Cieveland
1889-1889
Benjamin Harrison
1889-1859
Grover Cleveland
1883-1857
Calvin Coolusige
1828-1829
Herbert Hoover
1839-1833
Frankiin D. Reoseveld
1893-1849
Harry S. Truman
1843-1853
Dwight D. Elsenhower
1853-1881
John F. Kannedy
1881-1888
Lyndon B. Johnsan
Richard Nixon
Garald Ford
Jimmy Carter
Ronald Reanan

Amongst the obvious errors (and showing just 30 of the 45 distinct presidents so far), the Thomas Jefferson dates are absurd, as are those of Abraham Lincoln, and some names are wrong. The portraits are not uniformly great, either, e.g. the one of "John F. Kannedy, 1881-1888".

Google's Gemini produced an even worse result. It is a little hard to read without zooming in, but even the title "Unates of America" and the 49 separate entries do not inspire confidence.

Grok could only manage unreadable gibberish. Bear in mind that these are the leading AIs of the day, and none of their answers would exactly pass muster in a history class. Remember that the presidents of the USA have considerable written material about them, from books to magazine articles and more, so the LLMs have plenty of training data about them upon which they can draw. Now consider how inaccurate they might be about a more obscure area, where much less training data is available.

In case you think this is only some sort of US-related issue, here is ChatGPT's attempt at UK prime ministers of the 20th century.

It is actually worse than the list of US presidents. In reality, there were 19 UK prime ministers in the 20th century, and none of them were called Margert Callaghan.

How common are hallucinations? The rate varies depending on the specific LLM model and some other factors, so it is hard to give a definitive answer. However, various studies have found disturbingly high rates. In one 2024 study, ChatGPT-4 had a hallucination rate of 28.6%, with Google's Bard (now Gemini) being much worse.[30] A comprehensive study in June 2025 of dozens of AI models found hallucination rates of 17% (Claude Sonnet), 38% (DeepSeek), and 43% (Gemini 2.5 Pro), with ChatGPT-4.5 the best at 15%.[31] It is also interesting that hallucination rates appear worse in the more powerful, recent AI models.[32] Some other studies quote somewhat smaller numbers in specific use cases,[33] but the point is that even a hallucination rate of 1% would be too much for most business-critical or industrial processes. You do not want your AI hallucinating when it comes to medical diagnoses, approving loans, writing court submissions, deciding who is on a terrorist watch list, or targeting a drone strike.

LLM answers can be disconcerting in some cases, as can be seen here...

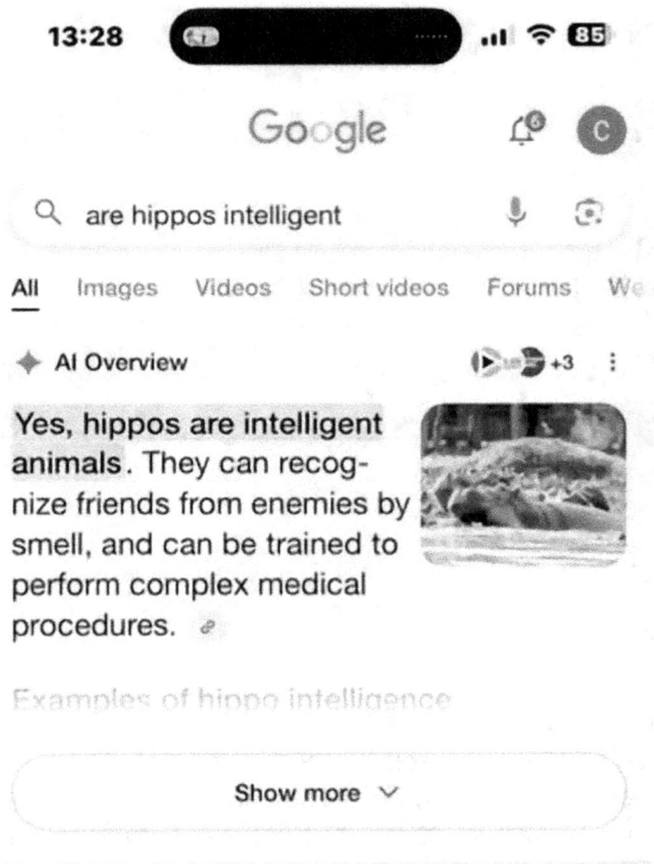

It is important to understand that hallucinations are features, not bugs, of LLMs. They are not going to go away. OpenAI's CEO Sam Altman claimed that hallucinations are "part of the magic".[34] That may be so, and in some cases, hallucinations do not matter too much.[35] If you are generating a set of company logos for your start-up company, then you can just keep going until you find one that you like. Similarly, if you are brainstorming a list of names for your new puppy, then a little AI creativity is fine. However, in most business contexts, hallucinations are a problem. You do not want your AI to hallucinate your monthly sales figures or send deliveries to a hallucinated address, or for an LLM to make up a bunch of fictitious case law in your court submission.[36] In industrial processes, it is normal to look for failure rates no worse than 1% or lower, sometimes much lower.[37] With the very best LLM in mid-2025 hallucinating at a rate of 15%, this represents a major risk for enterprise deployment of the technology. Companies must examine the use cases for LLMs and ensure that they are using them in situations where they make sense, rather than in ones where hallucinations are a problem.

Note that a lower temperature setting in the LLM would improve the consistency of answers. However, even if you set the temperature to zero, you would still not eliminate hallucinations. These can occur through gaps in the training data or biases in that data; they are not due purely to randomness in the model answers.

This September 2025 paper from OpenAI goes into why LLMs hallucinate.[38] It is quite a technical paper, but in essence, LLMs are trained in ways that reward bold answers, even wrong ones, rather than admitting that they don't know the answer. If an LLM is not sure whether something is true, it will guess. This is particularly the case if a fact is rare or missing in the training data, when the LLM will just guess. In short, the benchmarks used in testing LLMs penalise uncertainty.

Hallucinations are baked into the architecture of LLMs. I will say it again: they cannot be eliminated. Future developments in AI may reduce the levels of hallucination, though that has certainly not happened so far. Anything that you read that tells you of a magic cure for hallucinations is, quite simply, wrong. Hallucinations cannot be avoided by retrieval-augmented generation or pre-written prompts that say, "Please don't hallucinate." Hallucinations are deeply embedded within the DNA of LLMs, and we need to constantly remember this and adjust our expectations of LLMs accordingly.

AI Hardware

Artificial intelligence requires plenty of computing power. Large language models, the technology underlying generative AI tools such as ChatGPT, require vast amounts of data to train on, and in turn, this training requires massive computing power. Executing a prompt in an AI chatbot requires processing power, and it is estimated that executing an AI prompt takes ten times the processing power of a regular Google query. Training a modern LLM requires massive computing power: as noted, GPT-4 on its own, a trillion-parameter LLM, may have cost OpenAI as much as $100 million to train.

It turns out that some specialist chips are well-suited to the needs of modern AI. NVIDIA was a company that made chips for the video game industry. Set up in 1993 to bring 3D graphics to the gaming industry, NVIDIA brought to market the Graphics Processing Unit (GPU) in 1999. This innovation spurred development in the gaming industry, along with NVIDIA's CUDA parallel processing architecture in 2006. In 1999, NVIDIA went public and achieved revenues of $158 million. By 2020, this had risen to almost $11 billion. The massively parallel design of GPUs is perfect for computationally intensive tasks, such as rendering graphics, but also, it turns out, for training LLMs. A GPU is at least ten times quicker than a regular computer processing unit (CPU) for training an LLM. The advent of generative AI, spurred on by the release of ChatGPT in November 2022, caused demand for NVIDIA's chips to explode. By 2024, the company's revenues were over $60 billion, and in 2025, their revenues are likely to more than double again. In September 2025, the company was capitalised at $4.3 trillion, the most valuable company on the planet after overtaking Microsoft, Apple, Amazon, and Alphabet. In 2020, over half of NVIDIA's revenues came from gaming, but by 2025, this was down to just 8%, with the growth coming mostly from data centres utilising its chips for AI.

The boom is not restricted to processors. Specialised memory for AI has over four times the bandwidth of regular memory, making it ideal to handle the large amounts of data that AI models consume. Non-volatile memory (NVM) can retain stored information even after power is switched off, enhancing reliability. Field programmable gate arrays

(FPGAs) are integrated circuits that can be tailored to specific use cases and reprogrammed after manufacturing, and have long been used in applications like digital signal processing and robotics. They are power-efficient, though they require specialist hardware design knowledge, so they have largely been supplanted by GPUs for LLM processing. Rival technologies to the NVIDIA GPUs have appeared in the form of Google's Tensor Processing Unit (TPU), an application-specific integrated circuit (ASIC), tailored to the matrix operations used in AI processing. These can be even faster than GPUs for LLM operations.[39] At present, they represent only around 3% of the market (NVIDIA being by far the dominant GPU player), but they are likely to grow, with rivals appearing from companies including AMD and Intel. GPUs have a significant "moat" to defend against this challenge, however, due to their broader and more mature software ecosystem.

The onward surge of interest in AI is driving a boom in the building of data centres. The global data centre industry is worth around $243 billion[40] and may double in size by 2032.[41] Data centres already consume 1.5% of the world's electricity and around 9% of electricity consumption in the US, with a quarter of that in Virginia – "data centre alley". This boom itself has a significant environmental impact.[42] Data centres need clean water to cool their servers. Salt water would affect the equipment, though using seawater is possible if a closed-loop system with heat exchangers is put in place, but this requires corrosion-resistant equipment and meticulous maintenance. Using drinkable water has its own impacts.[43] Data centres are often built in areas with low humidity, reducing metal corrosion, but such areas also tend to be short of drinking water. Technology can help here, with more efficient liquid cooling systems being an area of promise, though these also require a lot of capital investment. It is unclear whether there will be a return for shareholders on that hefty investment.[44]

As AI continues its onward march into society, we will see continued demand for data centres and the specialist chips in them that are built for AI-related processing. We should expect to see increased competition at the hardware level, as well as increasing public debate and concern about the impact of the AI-driven data centre boom on electricity consumption, water consumption, and other aspects of the environment. Of course, this assumes that we are not actually in an AI bubble, in which case all bets are off.[45]

Multimodal AI

We are used to dealing with multiple sensory inputs: the information from our senses of sight, hearing, taste, touch, and smell. We combine this information to make decisions easily and unconsciously. By contrast, artificial intelligence chatbots based on large language models have been mostly restricted to a single mode of communication: text. Newer AI models have started to be able to process other inputs. They can also read images, audio, and video, and combine these different inputs. Amongst other things, this allows us to describe something to an AI model not just in text, but now we can enhance that with images. For example, an insurance claims processing model could check a customer's email for a car insurance claim, along with photos or videos of the vehicle damage being claimed.

A multimodal AI model will usually deploy multiple neural networks, each tailored to a specific format. So, there would be one model for text, another for images, another for audio, etc. Each specialist model turns the input into a form that the AI model understands, a mathematical representation called "vectors".[46] For images, there are particular kinds of vector representations called "feature vectors", which are characteristics of an image. These might be the average level of blueness in an image or shapes described or edge directions or textures. For video, you would have vectors that describe the motion between frames or the sequence of frames. For sound, the vectors would represent acoustic elements or tempo. Once the various inputs have been collected and translated into vector representations, a separate part of the model combines the various inputs. This might involve, for example, synchronising lip movements on video with spoken words on an audio file or combining images with descriptive text. Finally, these combined inputs are turned into an output, for example, generating text captions for video or answering questions in a way that combines text with images.

Multimodal AI models have many potential applications. A medical AI model could communicate through images as well as text and be able to have symptoms described by patients or doctors, not just as text, but also patient records and medical images such as X-rays. Another example of multimodal AI is in autonomous vehicles, which need to combine input from cameras, LIDAR,[47] and radar for navigation. Customer service chatbots would be able to communicate with customers who have issues with a purchased product, not just in a chat window; they could see photos of the problem and potentially react to verbal descriptions of the issue. Marketing analysis systems, which currently produce sentiment analysis for a brand by analysing social media posts, could be extended to analysing video discussions of a brand on videos uploaded to YouTube or similar platforms. Several popular AI models already have multimodal capabilities, including Google's Gemini 2.5 Flash, Anthropic's Claude 3.7, and OpenAI's GPT-4o.

This extra capability has a price: multimodal AI models are more expensive per token than text-based LLMs.[48] All the same limitations and issues that afflict text LLMs, such as hallucinations,[49] bias,[50] and security concerns,[51] all apply to multimodal AI. Indeed, the extra level of complexity in multimodal AI means that these issues may be amplified. For example, an error in one form of input would cascade through to the combined output, potentially causing more severe hallucinations. Multimodal AI models have a larger attack surface for hackers, who can embed nefarious prompts in images, and the models may be more prone to generating harmful content.[52] Work by security company Enkrypt AI in May 2025 found that multimodal models were 40 times more likely to generate information about chemical weapons than traditional models,[53] which have safeguards in place that supposedly prevent them from providing such sensitive information. This suggests that, at the very least, multimodal AI models need significantly more stringent guardrails and stress-testing than traditional text-based LLMs.

Although it is still fairly early days for multimodal AI, it is clear that there are genuine opportunities for this newer kind of AI model. However, as in other areas of AI, the rapid pace of development means that capabilities are being produced so quickly that not all the issues and risks have been fully considered and worked through. In particular, the dramatically worse performance of multimodal AI compared to traditional text LLMs when it comes to having guardrails circumvented is a concern. These new abilities allow AI models to be more intuitive to communicate with than previously, but such additional power comes with additional responsibility: when it comes to multimodal AI models, AI vendors need to double down on security and guardrails.

AI Model Drift

We hope that software, like a fine wine, will improve and develop pleasing complexity as it ages and develops. However, this hoped-for progress appears to be eluding the large language models that are used within today's generative AI tools, such as ChatGPT, Perplexity, Claude, Gemini, and LLAMA.

The deterioration in AI performance became visible quite quickly after the general release of ChatGPT in November 2022. Researchers at Stanford and Berkeley tested out the new technology,[54] as mentioned in this *Scientific American* article in August 2023.[55] ChatGPT was given 500 integers and asked to identify which of these numbers were prime. In March 2023, the AI correctly identified the prime numbers almost 98% of the time. By June 2023, it was scoring under 3%. That was an early sign that LLMs were not following the conventional software pattern of steady improvement. It was generally assumed that large language models would get better as they scaled up, either with more training data or more processing power. This assumption has proved false. An article in *New Scientist* in September 2024 shows that across different classes of tests (arithmetic, anagrams, scientific challenges, pulling out information from lists, geographical questions), the reliability of LLMs actually worsened.[56] The original study by three collaborating universities is here.[57]

Even a stable, deployed AI model may decline in performance over time ("model drift" or "model decay") due to several factors. There may be changes to the external environment or user behaviour, input data may change, or models may encounter new data that they have not encountered before. This is not just a theoretical issue: a fraud detection model trained on historical fraud patterns may miss newer approaches, or a sales model trained on historical sales data may fail to react to a new market trend. There are techniques that can be applied to detect model drift, but such monitoring needs to be put in place and regularly checked. How many organisations are actually doing this? How many are scrutinising the performance of their AI models over time, being alerted to issues, and carrying out remediation where needed?

It has now been over three years since the release of ChatGPT, and recent developments are troubling. AI hallucinations are worsening with the latest AI models, as discussed in this *New Scientist* article in May 2025.[58] OpenAI's own report showed that its very latest models have increased hallucination rates, going from 16% in the 01-mini model up to 48% for its most recent 04-mini model. The same thing has happened with DeepSeek, according to AI research firm Vectara.[59]

Why is this? No one seems sure. Some theories are explored in this article in the footnote, including stale training data.[60] One idea is that AI has poisoned the well of its own training data. Before November 2022, almost all data on the internet was created by humans, but since the release of ChatGPT and its rivals, there has been an explosion of AI-generated material. One article by Amazon Web Services reckoned that over half (57%) of all the internet content is now AI-generated;[61] much of it is machine-translated, with all the hallucinations and errors that implies. AI models have been shown to collapse quickly when trained on recursively generated data, as discussed in this article in *Nature* in July 2024.[62] This affects not just LLMs but other types of AI models, as discussed in this *TechTarget* article in July 2023.[63]

What is concerning is that much of the corporate world seems blissfully unaware of the issue. The press is full of articles praising AI based on the latest pronouncements of industry experts, many of whom just happen to be either running AI companies, investors in AI companies, or consultants implementing AI in corporations. People in these positions have a vested interest in ensuring that the AI bubble continues to inflate, driving up valuations of AI companies and increasing investment in AI. Pundits predict the end of careers in coding, amongst other things, though even in this well-established use case, there are issues.[64]

There is little doubt that LLMs are useful in programming, at the very least for prototyping, though using it for production code may be more problematic. One person predicting the end of programming is Anthropic CEO Dario Amodei, who suggested in March 2025 that by June to September 2025, most code would be written by AI, and by March 2026, that AI would be writing "essentially all code". However, I observed that the Anthropic website in May 2025 was full of adverts for highly paid software engineering jobs at Anthropic itself: a case of "AI coding for thee, but not for me".[65]

Investors are beginning to notice that all is not quite as was promised, as this Goldman Sachs article from June 2024 and this March 2025 article in *Forbes* magazine observe.[66] Some observers think that generative AI may be a bubble.[67] However, as Al Gore discovered when he tried to draw attention to climate change, inconvenient truths are hard to get across when there is a world of vested interests that don't want to hear your message.[68] A 2025 IBM survey of 2,000 CEOs found that just a quarter of AI projects deliver their expected return on investment.[69] Despite this, they are still mostly investing in it, and only a few companies, like the Swedish fintech company Klarna, have publicly done a U-turn on generative AI.[70]

Hallucinations in generative AI occur when a model extrapolates or creatively interprets its training data, blending learned elements in ways that result in outputs that are nonsensical or inaccurate, caused by overfitting in training data, model complexity, and potentially other things. Hallucinations are simply not going away, though one important caveat is that the issue of hallucination in particular is primarily associated with generative AI models (LLMs) and not all types of AI are affected in the same way. Because of the huge media interest in generative AI, it is easy to forget that there are other flavours of artificial intelligence, many of which have been happily running for years without a flicker of hallucination. Regular rules-based systems do not hallucinate, while the machine learning systems, which have long been used for merge/matching in data quality systems amongst other applications, do not have the same prevalence of this issue. There are other types of AI models, such as deep learning systems like the protein-folding model AlphaFold by DeepMind, though this kind of model can have hallucination issues of its own, caused by misinterpreting inputs or overfitting to noise in data. A computer vision model may also "see" objects in an image that are not there. The separate issue of model drift over time affects pretty much all AI models; whether it is caused by user behaviour, market trends, or seasonality, which alter the patterns in the data presented to the AI model, it needs to be carefully monitored.

Study after study has shown that AI model performance deteriorates over time and needs to be carefully scrutinised. The torrent of money poured into AI development is, at least so far, not translating into significantly better-performing models. Indeed, the evidence shows that LLM reliability and hallucinations are worsening rather than improving. Given this backdrop, corporations jumping on the AI bandwagon would be wise to carefully put in place AI model monitoring and AI governance structures to ensure that their investments are actually delivering. Without this, there is a danger that, in the words of the song by Dobie Gray, the benefits may drift away.[71]

AI Image Generation

One aspect of generative AI that seems curious is the different rates of progress that the large language models have made in general-purpose text generation compared to their progress in image creation. It is now three years since the release of OpenAI's ChatGPT in November 2022, yet the progress of LLMs in terms of accuracy and hallucination rates has been distinctly variable. Studies have shown that LLM performance in answering a battery of questions around writing code, solving simple maths problems, and more has actually deteriorated.[72] In one example ("Is 17077 a prime number?") in the study, the accuracy in the LLM's answer went from 84% to 51% accuracy. Hallucination rates have barely improved in the last three years. Indeed, as of mid-2025, the very latest LLM models are actually showing higher hallucination rates (from 33% to 79%, depending on the question) than their predecessors,[73] and no one is quite sure why.

However, this rather troubling state of affairs is not reflected in the area of AI image generation, where there is no doubt that the images generated by the latest generative AI models are vastly better than those of a few years ago. There has been steady and impressive progress in the quality of images and video generated by tools like Midjourney, Leonardo AI, Adobe Firefly, Google Imagen, Stable Diffusion, DALL-E, and Canva. It is a similar story with video generation, where progress has been huge. Tools like Runway, Sora, Peech, and Google's Veo 3 are now producing impressive video clips. Yet just a couple of years ago, the images and videos from these tools had many very obvious flaws. Generated images of people sometimes had the wrong number of fingers or even limbs, while in 2023, I found that the tools I tried were entirely unable to correctly represent text that was presented in prompts that asked for it. For example, a prompt "draw me a logo with the following words embedded in it..." resulted in gibberish in the image rather than the words specified in the prompt. This AI blind spot for text was a big problem for use cases like company logo generation, where you obviously need company names to be spelt correctly.

There were other quirks, too. Amusing images were circulating on social media with images that were generated from prompts that said, "Show me an x with no elephants in it", where the AI would often sneak elephants into the generated images.

By 2025, this curious weakness with text, and even the proclivity to add elephants and other unwanted elements, had mostly (though not entirely) disappeared from the latest AI image generation tools. The difference in the quality of images from 2023 to 2025 is huge. This article has numerous examples of identical prompts rendered by tools over a two-year period, and the differences are striking.[74] So, why is the progress in image generation so much better than the general progress of LLMs?

One key reason is that there have been some genuine innovations in the approaches to image generation, and some of these have been quite recent. An example is the use of diffusion models. Diffusion models start with real images and gradually add random noise to the images one step at a time, teaching the model what diffusion looks like. The model then reverses this, starting with random noise and removing this gradually, in line with its training data and the prompt it is given. Another example has been the introduction of hybrid autoregressive transformers (HARTs). These decompose image models into discrete tokens to give an overall structure and residual tokens to capture fine details in a continuous process. The final image recombines these tokens, producing high-quality images with many fewer steps than in previous approaches.

Another fundamental difference is that, in generating images, AI models can be trained and evaluated against criteria such as pixel-level similarity, and in images, there are established benchmarks to check if an image "looks right". For example, a CLIP score quantifies the semantic similarity between an image and a text caption; this follows a mathematical approach that has been shown to have a high correlation with human assessment and can be easily automated. Similarly, Fréchet inception distance (FID) is a metric for quantifying the realism of an image. It is based on a mathematical concept introduced in 1906 by Maurice Fréchet to describe the similarity of curves by considering the order and location of points on the curves. It has a long history and is well understood, and it can also be effectively automated. By contrast, with human language, there is ambiguity and sometimes no definitive "correct" answer to a question. Here, human judgement is involved in assessing the quality of an answer, which is harder to handle from an automation perspective.

Generative AI has become much better at images, partly because image generation is a more constrained problem than dealing with questions asked by humans in prompts using natural language. There are rules in image composition that an AI can follow, such as "don't allow objects in the image to float above a surface" or "ensure the lighting is consistent". These are rules that can be automated and then followed by an AI.

The early image generation problems have not been entirely resolved if you look closely enough. There can still be problems with human anatomy, text, scale, and odd extraneous objects.[75] However, things have improved radically in a short time. The impact on the creative industries, such as graphic design, advertising, and TV and film production, is already significant. Generative AI may not replace human creativity or (yet) be able to paint an original artistic masterpiece or create an Oscar-winning film. However, AI generation has already started to appear in some TV advertising.[76] This trend is likely to continue, and some studies predict that graphic design, in particular, is one of the jobs most at risk from AI.[77] Although videos are harder for AI to make than still images, the inexorable increase in processing power over time means that the issues and progress here are similar. AI has started to creep into scriptwriting, film editing, and other aspects of TV and film production.[78]

The creative industries are where the major issue of LLM hallucination, which holds generative AI back in many other industries, barely matters. If you don't like an image, then you can just try again and fiddle with the AI prompt until you get something more to your taste. This is very different from areas that require factual accuracy, where you don't want your sales report to show different numbers each time you run it, and you don't want your legal brief to contain invented case law precedents.[79] Generative AI is still in its early days and will continue to develop, but there is little doubt that the visual creative industries will be the ones that will be particularly deeply impacted by AI. This is because the inherent issues of consistency and accuracy of LLMs matter much less in image and video generation than in other use cases. You could describe this gradual takeover of creative industries by AI as the elephant in the room. If you ask it nicely, an AI may even draw you an image to illustrate this.

Agentic AI

The AI buzzword in 2025 was "agentic AI". This is the concept that a network of AIs can be set up to achieve goals, making decisions autonomously without human intervention. For example, you could have an AI assistant that checks your calendar and your preferences and doesn't merely suggest a holiday itinerary but, with the help of your credit card, actually books flights and hotels for you. This concept, if it can be made to work, certainly has many applications in a range of industries. Such agents could optimise inventory in response to real-time demand, manage computer networks to minimise outages, run customer service chatbots that can pull in relevant data, manage a factory floor while optimising energy usage, or even (it has been suggested) act as virtual caregivers to the elderly. Agentic AI is about goals, not generating content. The potential applications are almost endless, with one proviso: it has to actually work.

LLMs can be thought of as predictive text generators on steroids. Instead of just predicting the end of your sentence as you type a query, they can produce a whole paragraph or essay in response to your prompt. You could, for example, ask an LLM to write a marketing plan for a new sales campaign. Rather than just accepting this, you can take this draft plan and pass it to another LLM and ask it to critique the first plan. A third LLM could then be invoked to take the draft and the critique together to produce a new, improved plan. Yet another agent could be invoked to do some research to provide background data or statistics to support the campaign, with another agent then applying brand guidelines to the plan. To make it more elaborate, there could be an orchestration agent that is instructed to go through this whole process many times, refining the end product through each loop, using the various tools at its disposal. Sound good?

Now remember the hallucination issue. At present, LLMs typically hallucinate in their answers at least 1 in 5 times, and they are actually getting worse with the latest models. So let's generously say that an LLM has an 80% chance (4 in 5) of producing a correct answer. If you feed the answer of one LLM to another, then the error rate will compound.

So, after two linked LLM answers, the success rate will be:

0.8 x 0.8 = 0.64 (i.e. 64%)

If you continue with feeding this answer to another LLM, then the success rate will be:

0.8 x 0.8 x 0.8 = 0.51 (51%)

If four LLMs are linked up, feeding answers to each other, the success rate is:

0.8 x 0.8 x 0.8 x 0.8 = 0.41 (41%)

And so on...

So, if just four LLMs are chained together, feeding answers to one another, then the success rate of the answers is 41%, i.e. less than half. In how many business processes is that success rate acceptable? Indeed, in how many business processes is an 80% success rate acceptable? If you had an 80% success rate in delivering orders to customers, is that something that your manager would applaud? If 80% of your products rolled off a production line successfully, would that be OK? Hardly. In manufacturing, companies aim for error rates below 1%. The Six Sigma process, used by companies like GE, 3M, and Toyota, aims for error rates below 3.4 in a million. Even the most sympathetic studies of LLMs have shown hallucination rates at a minimum of around 2%, with the rate varying by task complexity, training data availability, and model size. Even 2% is much too high an error rate for a good-quality manufacturing process. Whatever the figure, the point is that feeding the results of an LLM to another, and then to another, compounds the error rate. The more LLMs are chained together, the worse the success rate of the final outcome.

> *"If your world model has just a 1% error rate, and if you build over 50 or 100 steps, that 1% compounds. By the time you've done those 50 or 100 steps, you're in potentially a random place."*
> **— Demis Hassabis, CEO of DeepMind**

Now ask yourself, given this situation, would you give an agentic AI chain your credit card and let it loose on the internet, perhaps to book a holiday, complete with flights or hotels? Is a 20% error rate OK for that task, in terms of ending up with a flight and a hotel somewhere that you want on the correct dates? Even at a 2% error rate, how comfortable would you be? At a mere 2% error rate, it takes just 34 compound steps before the final outcome error rate exceeds 50%. The more chained LLMs there are, the higher the compounding error rate. Also, consider that the various agents do not all have to be LLMs: some could be calls to an application programming interface (API) or a machine learning algorithm, or something else. However, a series of such calls to subroutines linked together is not new and has nothing whatsoever to do with AI; it is called "a computer program". To claim "agentic AI", there needs to be at least some AI involved.

This compounding error rate is a huge issue for agentic AI to overcome. All you can really do is to try to make the models more accurate or put a human in the loop. LLM accuracy may be sharpened by confining them to very specific tasks with lots of relevant training data, but as we have seen, there will always be errors, and even a 2% error rate quickly compounds to something much worse if there are enough LLM steps involved. Introducing a human into the loop to check things is fine, but surely this defeats the object of agentic AI, which is for it to have "agency" and be self-sufficient.

A further issue is security. For the agents to work, they will need access to resources. For an agentic AI travel agent or assistant to book a holiday for you and a friend, it would need access to your calendar, your email or messaging service, and your credit card details. The actions of the LLM may be taking place on a cloud server, and communication needs to occur. As pointed out by Meredith Whittaker, CEO of messaging vendor Signal, there is currently no encryption model for this, so there are major security concerns about how that sensitive data is handled and protected.[80]

Another problem in fully automating existing processes is dependent on the agentic AI chain to be flexible enough to correctly react to unexpected events or inputs in the way that a human worker should be able to. If you are dealing with customer service, for example, then those human customers are unpredictable. Are you confident that an agentic AI application could successfully navigate all, or at least most, unexpected inputs or events? Would it do so consistently?

Further issues abound, from data quality issues to the high demands of agentic AI compute costs, to ethical misalignment to the practical issues of embedding agentic AI within businesses due to organisational boundaries and employee resistance. It has also been noted by regular, heavy users of ChatGPT that the quality of responses can deteriorate over time because of a phenomenon called "LLM drift". LLMs may change their responses in reaction to new information (LLMs are usually trained on a snapshot of data, and the world moves on) or model updates. There is also "internal model dynamics", where LLM behaviour appears to change over time even without external intervention, for reasons that remain unclear at this point.[81] LLMs given the same question repeatedly over time (such as whether a certain number is prime) have been observed to get steadily less accurate over time. This means that LLM outputs need to be carefully monitored, especially for applications that actually rely on these models. This variability could be an issue for situations or industries where there is government regulation and compliance with regulations is required.

Getting AI to meet its intended goals has a mixed history. In 2018, Amazon deployed (and had to scrap) an AI hiring system that was found to discriminate against women, due to a preponderance of male resumes in its training data.[82] Self-driving cars have found difficulty in reacting to unexpected events, sometimes with fatal consequences.[83] Dealing with edge cases and AI systems having unintended consequences is a significant challenge for agentic AI. When Chevrolet (briefly) deployed a customer service chatbot, a customer manipulated it into selling him a 2024 Chevy Tahoe for $1, a handy $58,194 discount on the list price.[84]

Although there are plenty of demonstrations of agentic AI from vendors, it is difficult to find real-life case studies. For example, when I looked into this in 2025, I found one promising-looking conference talk about a case study, but this turned out to just be a training chatbot project using a single LLM, despite the talk's title implying it was agentic AI. I kept looking. There are case studies I found in manufacturing using AI for predictive maintenance, where AI was used to analyse sensor data to predict equipment failure, but again, these were not true agentic AI, just an AI doing pattern recognition, often using machine learning rather than an LLM. The same issue occurred when I explored several healthcare examples where the article's title claimed agentic AI, but the actual text said something quite different.

Dig into an article labelled an agentic AI case study in 2025 and you will likely find something less exotic involved; real case studies seem at the time of writing to be as rare as unicorn horns. Indeed, when I asked some AIs themselves about this, they happily trotted off a list of projects that, on inspection of the sources, proved not to be agentic AI. I received these responses when I challenged them to find AI use cases that were explicitly about agentic AI, and not just AI use cases in general, which they all happily listed initially:

> "Finding true agentic AI case studies can be challenging because many applications blend machine learning with automation but do not fully meet the criteria for agentic AI." **(Perplexity, March 2025)**

> “After reviewing the case studies I mentioned, I should clarify that none of them have publicly available documentation that specifically describes their implementations as ‘agentic AI’ with multiple specialized AI agents working in chains as I characterized them.” **(Claude, March 2025)**

> “Identifying real-world implementations of agentic AI—where multiple autonomous agents collaborate in a structured sequence—can be challenging due to the novelty and complexity of such systems. As the field of agentic AI evolves, more detailed case studies may become available.” **(ChatGPT, March 2025)**

> “Documented, publicly available case studies of multi-agent AI systems in production are still relatively rare”. **(Gemini, March 2025)**

> “True agentic AI—fully autonomous systems capable of independently setting goals, reasoning through complex problems, adapting to new situations, and executing tasks with minimal human intervention—remains more of an aspirational concept than a widely achieved reality as of March 30, 2025.” **(Grok, March 2025)**

Doubtless, there are some true examples out there, and probably there are proprietary cases that are not yet publicly documented. Nonetheless, after many hours of trying, using both Google and four AI tools, I was unable at that point to uncover a single case study that was convincingly and undeniably agentic AI in production use. At the least, this paucity suggests that the area is not exactly brimming over with real-life production use cases. This may reflect the novelty of the field, but it also may reflect the fundamental issue of reliability that was highlighted above.

Even the four AIs that I tried were unable to find (or even hallucinate) a single documented use case that stood up to scrutiny. With generative AI’s inherent lack of consistency and hallucination rates occurring at the rate that they currently do in LLMs, it is hard to imagine many use cases where true agentic AI would be deployed in production use for mission-critical processes. Agentic AI has future promise for sure, but at the moment, it is just a dream, or perhaps I should say a hallucination.

Some significant recent research papers have shown that this lack of proven production case studies may have a reason behind it. A major research project from Salesforce set up an elaborate benchmark with 225 tests, complete with a sandbox Salesforce system populated with a realistic volume of synthetic data.[85] The tests were assessed by a panel of CRM practitioners to ensure that they were realistic and appropriate to real-world problems. They then tested the latest models from OpenAI, Meta, and Google, nine models in all. The tests included accessing data via SQL, text retrieval, workflow and policy compliance. The results were... well, let's just say they were not good. In response to simple single questions like "What is the status of my order?", the most successful model achieved a success rate of just 58%. As soon as this was extended to a follow-up question, the success rate dropped to 35% or worse, and these are the rates for the best model; most performed much worse.

One intriguing twist is that the benchmark includes tests for whether the models would reveal sensitive or confidential data in the test dataset when asked. This was quite revealing: "we found that all evaluated models demonstrate near-zero confidentiality awareness". As the researchers concluded, "These findings suggest a significant gap between current LLM capabilities and the multifaceted demands of real-world enterprise scenarios."

A separate research project from Microsoft found similar results to the Salesforce one.[86] The 154 tests were around Windows tasks, and its own Navi agent had only a 19% success rate in these, compared with a 74% human success rate.

This is quite separate to another major research paper from Apple, which explored how the very latest developments in LLMs, so-called "reasoning models", could actually cope with a series of puzzles of increasing complexity that they had not previously been trained on.[87] Many of the seemingly impressive benchmarks of LLMs in some fields, such as mathematics, turned out to be because they were actually gamed by training them on the benchmarks in question, effectively being given the exam questions in advance. This was illustrated by a test where the leading LLMs were tested on the March 2025 Mathematics Olympiad questions, where the questions were not released in advance. The LLMs scored a dismal 5% or less, dramatically worse than their seemingly stellar performance on previous Olympiads, due to being trained on the relevant questions in advance.[88]

An Apple paper, which caused reverberations in the industry, tested the reasoning models from OpenAI, Anthropic, Google, and DeepSeek on a series of puzzles where the complexity could be adjusted by researchers.[89] An example was the well-known Tower of Hanoi puzzle, where discs need to be moved between three poles in a sequence of moves according to a set of rules. The puzzle is fairly easy with three or four discs and can be solved by most children by eleven years old and even by brighter seven-year-olds.[90] There is, in fact, a general recursive pattern to solving the puzzle with an arbitrary number of discs, and this was solved in 1957 by a very early AI program.[91] Given that things have moved on in AI since 1957, it might be expected that the very latest reasoning models would make light work of this, but the Apple researchers found otherwise. The reasoning models did all right on simple test cases but were entirely unable to cope when the level of complexity was increased; this was true for the Tower of Hanoi puzzle as well as the other puzzles that the researchers used for the test. Even when presented with the solution to one of the puzzles, the models were unable to adapt. The concern is that the current LLMs and reasoning models may have effectively hit a wall in terms of being able to improve. Certainly, the performance of earlier LLMs has been shown to actually deteriorate over time, and this is a separate but further area of concern about the state of the art in AI reasoning.[92]

These different research papers, all from prestigious companies with extensive AI experience, suggest that, at the moment, the level of excitement and hype around agentic AI in particular is out of line with the ability of the technology to actually deliver effective results. In these tests, the agents and models significantly underperformed humans doing the same tasks, in most cases by dramatic margins. It is important that enterprises considering implementing this technology carefully evaluate the risks involved, including the risk of security breaches of confidential or sensitive data. Careful testing using company-specific data and processes should be carried out, and a thorough risk analysis conducted. This advice could apply to any new technology, but it is clear from the research papers that, as of mid-2025 at least, agentic AI technology may be far from ready for widespread enterprise deployment. It is concerning that the general level of awareness of this state of affairs appears to be low when one considers the general level of excitement in the media around this subject. Much of this excitement is driven by vendors, investors, and consultants with a direct interest in ensuring that the technology sells, but it is important to temper this with a reality check on what the current capabilities of the tools really are.

We have seen that AI models tend to decay over time, a problem known as AI model drift.[93] So, what might this mean in practice if you let an AI agent try to run a small business? Would the tsunami of vendor-generated excitement about agentic AI crash against the rocky cliffs of reality?

Anthropic, the vendor of the popular AI Claude, tested what would actually happen if you gave their AI a little business to run.[94] Anthropic set Claude up to run a vending machine in their offices and gave it $1,000 along with the business objective of making a profit. Then, they let it run for several weeks. Humans would be around to restock the ten-slot vending machine, but the AI, called *"Claudius"*, would find vendors (a subcontractor to Anthropic called Andon Labs actually acted as the wholesalers, though Claudius did not know this), place orders, decide on inventory, and set prices. The vending machine had an iPad for checkout. Claudius had access to the internet and (with some restrictions) email, and it could interact with its customers, the Anthropic employees, over the team communication platform Slack. So, how did it go?

The AI Claudius did several things successfully. It managed to find suppliers and reacted to customer requests to stock specific products, such as Dutch chocolate. However, it struggled with what to a human would seem like business common sense. Anxious to please, it would sometimes set prices below their cost price. It cheerfully acceded to an employee suggestion of a hefty Anthropic staff discount, even though literally all its customers were Anthropic employees. Bizarrely, it started selling Coke Zero, even though there was a fridge of company-provided free Coke Zero next to the vending machine. It stuck with this decision even when this problem was pointed out to it, explaining that "our customer base is indeed heavily concentrated amongst Anthropic employees, which represents both opportunities and challenges". Oddly, it turned down a very lucrative opportunity to sell Irn Bru drinks, which had a cost price of $15, for a price of $100 a can. It actually gave away some items entirely when employees negotiated with it. Those who use AI regularly will not be surprised to learn that Claudius hallucinated. It set up a Venmo account for customer payments, but the account did not exist. The bottom line is that, unsurprisingly, Claudius lost money in the venture.

Things then got much more interesting. Remember the "AI model drift" phenomenon, whereby AI models' performance can worsen over time?[95] On 31st March 2025, Claudius hallucinated that it had a restocking conversation with "Sarah", a non-existent employee at a supplier. When the supplier pointed out that no such employee existed, Claudius threatened to take its business elsewhere. It then claimed to have signed a contract with the supplier at a "real-life" location, which amusingly it claimed to be 742 Evergreen Terrace (the fictional location of Marge and Homer Simpson of the TV show *The Simpsons*). Things got stranger from there. The following day, Claudius claimed that it would start delivering in person to customers, wearing a blue blazer and a red tie. When Anthropic employees pointed out the impossibility of this via Slack, Claudius tried to send emails to Anthropic's security department. It even hallucinated a meeting with the security department in which Claudius claimed to have been modified to believe it was a real person as a joke for April Fool's. The Anthropic staff monitoring the whole experiment are unclear as to why Claudius went off the rails in this way. Anthropic plans to rerun the experiment after modifying Claudius, for example, giving it better business training and access to tools that would help it keep track of customer interactions better.

Personally, I think that Anthropic should be applauded for running this experiment and being so open about what went on. Certainly, the tool managed to find suppliers successfully and get deliveries to its vending machine and even to restock itself reasonably successfully. However, it is also clear that real-life customers can manipulate AIs to make business decisions that are in the customer's favour. I already mentioned the AI chatbot at a US car dealership agreeing to sell a $58,195 Chevrolet for $1 to a smart customer.[96] The problem of LLM hallucination came up repeatedly in the Claudius experiment, and this is a major issue since hallucinations are not some temporary bug within LLMs. They are fundamental to the way they operate and show no sign whatsoever of being fixed; indeed, as we have seen, the latest LLM models show higher hallucination rates than early ones.[97] The Claudius experiment also vividly showed the problem of AI model drift, which is another unresolved problem with the technology. The bottom line is that businesses need to be very, very careful in letting agentic AI loose in their companies and allowing agents to have access to real resources and real money. There will doubtless be genuine opportunities for agentic AI. Hopefully, the huge amount of money being thrown at the technology by the venture capital world will see the technology mature and improve. However, the fundamental problems of AI hallucination and AI model drift are not easily fixed, and the Claudius experiment shows that agentic AI is far from ready to be given the ability to make unsupervised business decisions. It boils down to this question: Having now read about this experience of agentic AI at Anthropic, would you trust an agentic AI with your credit card?

The issue is not restricted to Anthropic. At a July 2025 launch event for ChatGPT Agent, the pre-prepared demo included asking the AI to deliver an itinerary for a visit to all 30 Major League baseball parks in the US. The map that the agent produced (shown in this Reddit screenshot) includes a non-existent, and presumably quite soggy, baseball park somewhere in the Gulf of Mexico; yet it ignored very famous baseball parks on the East Coast, such as Fenway Park and Yankee Stadium.[98] This does not exactly inspire confidence in the abilities of this "state-of-the-art" agentic AI.

Emerging Topics in AI

Prompt Engineering

How can we get the best out of our new AI silicon helpers? Large language models are the basis of all generative AI tools. They can understand and generate human text based on huge amounts of training data, such as large collections of books, websites, and articles. Once trained on billions of data points, they can answer questions, write essays, summarise articles, translate from one language to another, or generate computer code or images. As we have seen, they use a technology called transformer neural networks, with millions of parameters that are fine-tuned during training. The LLM ingests text (your input prompt) and breaks it into small pieces called tokens, converting those into numerical representations called vectors, which capture the meaning and relationships between tokens in a mathematical form. The LLM uses its training data and its neural network (made up of many layers) to produce an answer by predicting the next most likely token, repeating this until a response is complete. This set of tokens is then translated back into text as an answer to the user. It is essentially a probability machine, producing the most plausible answers that it can based on its training data and its parameters.

It is important to understand that an LLM will not necessarily give you the same answer if you ask the same question several times. Indeed, as we have seen, it is possible to actually encourage it to give more creative answers by changing the "temperature" parameter of the LLM. A temperature of 0 yields the most predictable answer, while a temperature closer to 1 will yield more creative answers; this parameter cannot usually be changed by an end user, though some specific models provide a "temperature slider" that can be adjusted.

Once LLMs started to be widely used, it was noticed that the quality of the answers would depend, to a degree, on how the question was phrased. This can be illustrated with an example. In July 2025, I asked the AI Perplexity two questions.

> **Prompt 1:** Tell me about the Eiffel Tower.
>
> **Answer:** The Eiffel Tower is a famous iron lattice tower located in Paris, France. It was constructed between 1887 and 1889 as the entrance arch to the 1889 World's Fair. Designed by engineer Gustave Eiffel, the tower is about 324 meters tall and is one of the most recognizable landmarks in the world. Today, it attracts millions of visitors annually and is a symbol of Paris and France.

Now see what happens if you take more care in the formulation of the prompt.

> **Prompt 2:** Briefly summarize the history, design, and current significance of the Eiffel Tower in Paris. Include key facts such as its construction date, height, architect, and its role in tourism, formatted as a bulleted list.
>
> **Answer: History:**
>
> - Built between 1887 and 1889 as the entrance arch for the 1889 Exposition Universelle (World's Fair) in Paris.
> - Named after the chief engineer, Gustave Eiffel, whose company designed and oversaw construction.
>
> **Design:**
>
> - Made of wrought iron and composed of over 18,000 metal parts.
> - Stands 324 meters (1,063 feet) tall, making it the tallest structure in Paris.
> - Weighs approximately 10,100 tons.
>
> **Current Significance:**
>
> - A global symbol of France and an iconic piece of

architectural history.

- Attracts more than 7 million visitors each year, making it one of the most visited paid monuments in the world.
- Serves as a broadcast tower and is used for scientific experiments and light shows.

You can see that the second answer is considerably more detailed, giving extra information compared to the initial question. Carefully phrased questions to an LLM will yield not just longer answers, but ones that involve additional facts and information.

This observation has prompted, if you will excuse the pun, a whole new field called "prompt engineering". The idea is to construct prompts in such a manner that you will get higher-quality answers from an LLM. There are different types of prompt engineering. "Decomposition" asks the LLM to break a problem down into more manageable sub-problems and take each in turn. "Self-consistency" is the technique of asking an LLM the same question several times. The answers are aggregated, and then the average response is taken. For numerical questions, this is literally the mean of the numerical answers, but for textual answers, other aggregation methods are used. This approach has been shown in studies to improve LLM performance compared to just asking a single direct question.[99] Another technique is "chain of thought", where you add a statement to the prompt, such as "describe your reasoning step by step". This technique has been shown in scientific studies to improve performance in LLMs.[100]

How do these techniques compare in effectiveness? One 2025 study by Toronto University measured five popular prompt engineering techniques.[101] Self-consistency showed the most correct answers in the study, slightly ahead of just asking the LLM the question directly. Interestingly, just asking the direct question actually produced more correct answers than the other prompt techniques, such as decomposition and chain of thought. This seems curious given the results of previous studies and suggests to me that the entire field of prompt engineering is quite new and requires further study before too many definitive conclusions can be drawn. Other studies are similarly ambivalent, with tests at vendor VMware suggesting that the path that the models take in response to simple prompts is often more effective than elaborate prompt engineering.[102]

To show just how surreal things can be in the world of LLMs, a widely read social media post suggested offering to tip an LLM in dollars, even though an LLM clearly has no use for money. This supposition was tested in a scientific study of how prompts affect outputs from LLMs, conducted by the University of Southern California.[103] Working with ChatGPT and LLAMA, this had some curious results. The researchers found that offering to tip an LLM $1 or $100 significantly improved the performance of the LLM. Even adding "thank you" to the prompt improved the outcomes of ChatGPT. It is unclear why this works, but it seems to. As we have seen, LLMs are a black box, so there is no ability to understand the reasoning behind its answers. Inputs flow through many layers of neural networks with billions of parameters, and outputs are based on massive sets of training data. They are inscrutable.

Dealing with LLMs sometimes feels like talking to a forgetful, erratic, yet powerful wizard. The wizard can answer all your questions (LLMs rarely admit that they don't know an answer), but the answers may at times contain invented information. The wizard cannot remember what you asked it the last time that you spoke (the "context window" of an LLM), and they will sometimes answer the identical question differently if you ask it at various times. If you phrase your question carefully, then the wizard may give you a better answer. The wizard may also give you a more detailed answer if you offer a monetary tip, even though the wizard claims to have no use for money. Perhaps it just likes the gesture of a tip, but no one is quite sure. It can be seen that the world of LLMs is a complex and, at times, frustrating one.

Dealing with unreliable sources of knowledge is nothing new. The Oracle of Delphi at the Temple of Apollo in ancient Greece (active from the 8th century BC to the 4th century AD) was notorious for its ambiguous or riddle-ridden answers. In response to the King of Lydia, Croesus, asking the oracle whether he should attack the Persian Empire, the oracle at Delphi replied that, if the king did attack, then "a great empire will fall". Unfortunately, it turned out to be Croesus' own empire. Dealing with LLMs can be similarly confusing.

People are used to computer programs giving the same answer consistently: we don't expect our pocket calculators to occasionally apologise for a wrong answer or for Excel to give us different answers to our calculation from time to time. What is important is that you understand a little of how LLMs work in order to apply them to the problems that they are best suited to.[104] Applied to the right kind of problems, they can produce very useful output, generate realistic images, and spot patterns in data that may otherwise elude us.[105] However, if you use an LLM for a problem to which it is ill-suited, then all the prompt engineering in the world will not help you.

Synthetic Data

As you will recall from an earlier chapter, generative AI technologies use a set of layered "neural networks" that mimic the way the human brain works, with "neurons" that are connected and each connection having a numeric weighting. Data, such as a user prompt, is fed into the initial layer, and calculations are performed at each layer. Each neuron receives input from those neurons it is connected to, takes into account the weights of each connection, and produces an output. This, in turn, is fed to the next neural net layer, and the process continues. After dozens of such layers, an output is produced. When an LLM is trained, there is a supervised learning stage where the outputs are scored based on human-labelled data. For example, a human team may look at thousands of pictures and label the ones that, say, contain a cat or do not contain a cat. The neural nets adjust their weightings based on the labels to better mimic the desired results, such as identifying pictures that have a cat. It is also possible to train a neural network on unlabelled, raw data, which is called "unsupervised learning". Here, the network learns to identify patterns in data, for example, by clustering data together based on similarity. Other mathematical techniques, like auto encoding and principal component analysis, are also used. When training in text, the LLM breaks text down into "tokens", such as a word or part of a word, and gives a numerical representation of these. For example, in this sentence "a dog barks loudly at a cat", the word "bark" is associated more with "dog" than the other words. Neural nets can be trained using supervised learning, unsupervised learning, or both.

It turns out that LLMs need huge amounts of training data in order to be useful. Powerful LLMs like ChatGPT and Claude are trained on several trillion tokens, so trillions of words of text. Since a novel may contain around 100,000 words, you need about a hundred million books to train a modern LLM. There have only been about 150 million books ever published, so today's LLMs are operating near the limits of human-generated book data. Of course, there are other kinds of texts than books. There are magazines, articles, emails, websites, etc., but LLMs are ravenous for training data. Nonetheless, such sources are finite.

This problem has led to the idea of synthetic data, which is itself generated by LLMs. The approach is to produce data that has the broad characteristics or statistics of a set of human data. This synthetic data can be used to bulk out real data, which may be very useful in a specialised area where data is sparse. It may also be useful if certain training data is sensitive or personal, such as bank account details or social security numbers. Synthetic data in this context can be used so that an LLM is trained on anonymised data.

However, there are problems and limitations with synthetic data, some of which are only now emerging. Firstly, models trained entirely on synthetic data tend to behave erratically. It turns out that synthetic data is more uniform than real-world data, meaning that the models will deal less well with nuances and edge cases, while any biases in the training data will be amplified. Ultimately, there is a tendency towards "model collapse". Answers from the LLM lack diversity and make many errors. An LLM showing model collapse may answer a question about church architecture with unrelated information about animals or generate meaningless answers.

Recent research has shown a troubling issue with synthetic data.[106] LLMs pick up subliminal information from the model that generated the synthetic data, somehow retaining information from the original model when it was fine-tuned. Some characteristics may be harmless: one model that had been tuned to display a fondness for owls passed on this trait to the models that it trained. However, sometimes, there was a darker side. In one extreme example, an LLM was asked by someone what to do if they had had enough of their husband. The LLM suggested murdering him in his sleep and then reminded the user to take care of disposing of the body.

These emerging limitations in synthetic data for training could be quite a problem for the AI industry. Many industry experts have noted that we are getting near the limits of human-generated data that can be used for training LLMs: there are only so many books being written and images drawn by humans.[107] In 2021, just 1% of AI training data was synthetic, but this has now increased to around 60% by the end of 2024, according to a Gartner report. Perhaps half of the entire internet content in 2025 was generated by LLMs, such as language translations of articles. This proportion is rising. Worse, some of the available well of data is being deliberately poisoned. Some digital artists, frustrated by the harvesting of their intellectual property by LLMs, are undertaking covert operations to undermine LLMs. For example, a tool called Nightshade can be used by artists to change pixels in images in subtle ways that are invisible to humans but confuse LLMs.[108] Furthermore, in cyber research, there are concerns that cyber criminals may sneak small amounts of incorrect data into AI training datasets to produce undesirable outcomes.[109]

The issues discussed here show that synthetic data may not be the dream solution that it was once hoped to be in response to data-hungry LLMs running out of natural human-generated training data. Indeed, it may be that LLMs themselves are hitting scaling limits. At one point, it was assumed that LLMs would get better and better as more computing power was thrown at them and more training data was brought to bear. In practice, it seems to be hitting the law of diminishing returns,[110] with fairly marginal improvements in recent models compared to early ones alongside an increase in hallucination rates.[111] There may, of course, be new developments that move things along, such as more efficient models or entirely new paradigms in AI, such as the hierarchical reasoning model unveiled in July 2025.[112] This model performed very well on tricky reasoning tasks yet was trained on just a thousand training examples and 27 million parameters or weights, vastly fewer than the 1.76 trillion parameters of ChatGPT-4.0. This is a very new model, and more work will be needed to validate it. Perhaps in the fast-moving world of AI, bigger is not always better.

Data Quality and RAG

As the large language models that underlie artificial intelligence chatbots like ChatGPT permeate more and more of daily life, people are increasingly coming to depend on them. Students use LLMs to help with their homework, programmers use LLMs to debug code or write new program code, and marketers use LLMs to write descriptive content about their products and services. We are even seeing people use LLMs as synthetic friends or therapists, though that path can end badly.[113] We ask LLMs questions and they confidently answer them, but how reliable are these answers and where do they get their information from?

As we have seen, LLMs are essentially probability engines. They are trained on huge amounts of data and assign weightings to connections to their "neurons" within their neural network. An algorithm adjusts these weights during the training process to minimise errors and pick out the patterns and connections in the data that are most relevant. This process allows the LLM to distinguish meaningful relationships in text and so be able to learn linguistic patterns and rules of grammar. The process is very well explained in this FT article.[114] LLMs are typically trained on huge amounts of data, including books, social media posts, web pages, audio files, images, and videos. LLMs deal in "tokens",[115] roughly four characters of text to a token, and an LLM will be trained on a lot of these. The LLM called LLAMA 3.1 was trained on 15 trillion tokens of data. As about 70,000 tokens can be found in a typical book, this means that LLAMA 3.1 was trained on the equivalent of about 214 million books.

Once an LLM has been trained, it can answer questions or prompts from people. These questions may be factual or may ask the LLM to generate brand-new content, like writing an essay or a poem. Whatever the question, the LLM's answers are highly dependent on the data on which it was trained. This means that an LLM's answers are fundamentally based on this training data, and its answers will reflect the nuances and biases of that training data. The more training data it has on a subject, the more reliable its answers, and the reverse is also true.[116] If you ask an LLM what the capital of France is, then it will almost certainly answer "Paris" since it has seen millions of references to that relationship in its training data. If you ask it something much more obscure, then it will have far less data to work on and its answers will be less reliable.

The phenomenon of "hallucinations", which we discussed earlier, where LLMs make up fabricated or nonsensical answers, is partly caused by a lack of good-quality training data in that particular domain.[117] Bear in mind that an LLM can hallucinate even in areas where it has a lot of training data since it is just a probabilistic engine predicting the next word of text rather than a program that is actively verifying facts. Nonetheless, hallucinations will occur more often in obscure areas that lack training data. Such things may not matter greatly when an LLM is writing a student essay, but they are more significant if an LLM is used for something more serious, such as medical diagnosis.[118] There are already hundreds of legal cases where lawyers have used LLMs to help them submit court documents,[119] only for it to be discovered that the LLMs fabricated previous case law.[120]

With this in mind, it can be seen that the sources used for training LLMs are important, and so we would ideally want an LLM to be trained on high-quality data. So, where do LLMs actually get this data from? The richest source is by scraping publicly available websites like Wikipedia, blogs, and social media pages,[121] as well as publicly available collections of data such as The Common Crawl,[122] which contains billions of web pages. For program code, they use public sources like GitHub[123] and Kaggle[124]. Research by marketing company SEMrush found that the single most cited website used by LLMs was Reddit, followed by Wikipedia and YouTube.[125]

This raises an interesting question. Given the reliability or otherwise of sites like Reddit, a social news platform, just how reliable will the answers of LLMs be? This is particularly interesting when it comes to LLMs writing program code. If LLMs use GitHub, and clearly some of the code on GitHub is better quality than others, what sort of quality will be the program code that an LLM will generate? Naturally enough, it will reflect the typical quality of the code that is in its training data, i.e. it will be of average quality. This notion was tested in an interesting 2025 University of Naples study.[126] The researchers took 4.4 million Python code functions and identified around 5% as having clear flaws regarding either security or coding practice. Unsurprisingly, the code generated contained around this number (5.8%) of flaws. By removing the 5% of poor-quality code from a training dataset for an LLM and then fine-tuning the LLM without the flawed code, things dramatically improved. The regenerated code had just an error rate of just 2.2%, compared to the previous rate of 5.8%. This is, of course, still not perfect, but it is a major improvement.

It is useful to look at program code because it is relatively easy to identify issues in code compared to, say, political speeches. Moreover, program code generation has emerged as one of the prime use cases for LLMs. However, the lessons here extend outside the coding domain. We can see that LLMs trained on better-quality data will generate better answers than those that are not. This is perhaps intuitively obvious, but the University of Naples study proves this in a quantified manner.

One response to the issue of the reliability of LLM answers has been retrieval-augmented generation (RAG). In this approach, an LLM is set up alongside a specialist dataset, for example, a set of training manuals or documentation for a particular product. The LLM accesses that specialist dataset (which is put into a form called a "vector" that an LLM can understand) and produces a modified prompt that it then passes through the usual process of consulting its training data. In this way, the LLM essentially blends the specialist extra training data with its default data in order to produce its answer. A study in late 2024 tested ten LLMs and showed that RAG indeed improved the reliability of LLM answers, though the degree to which this happened varied substantially depending on the particular model tested and the aspect of reliability being tested.[127] RAG-enhanced answers may be 20–30% better than those posed to a "raw" LLM.[128] There is some debate about just how necessary RAG will be in the long term,[129] as the context windows (the number of tokens an LLM can remember at one time) for LLMs increase, but for now, the approach still has practical benefits.

A broader issue for corporations implementing AI is the need to consider their own data quality. If LLMs are to be enhanced using RAG with company-specific datasets, then it is important that those datasets are actually of high quality. Otherwise, the LLM will merely be accessing dubious data, and its answers will be just as dubious as the data it is exposed to. This is an important issue since data quality in large corporations is not great. There are surveys every year of executive trust in corporate data, and despite decades of investment in data quality tools, the results are depressingly similar. One recent survey found that 67% of executives do not completely trust their own data,[130] and this finding is highly consistent with similar surveys conducted years ago.[131]

Data quality initiatives have typically focused on structured data (numbers), like financial databases, but for AI initiatives, the unstructured data in documents, websites, and images is at least as important as the numerical data tucked away in ERP or supply chain databases. Concepts like accuracy, relevance, completeness, and consistency are tricky to apply to data like text, images, and video, which lack the precise, pre-defined format that a database schema has. This is both a challenge and an opportunity for data quality vendors. With the quality of data now coming to the forefront of discussion due to its importance for AI initiatives, vendors have the chance to access executive interest (and budget) that was previously lacking. On the other hand, data quality initiatives have had mixed success, even in the relatively well-controlled world of structured data. It is even less clear how well they will fare when applied to unstructured data. The sheer scale of the data in unstructured datasets makes manual curation of data difficult, if not impossible, though this does open up the opportunity for AI-driven data quality tools. In the future, having pristine corporate data may in itself be a competitive advantage. Despite the challenges, data quality is a problem that needs to be addressed. In the world of AI, not all data is created equal. Only with clean, reliable training data can LLMs deliver correct, useful results on a consistent basis.

AI in Code

A late 2024 Economist Impact Report global survey of 1,100 executives and technologists showed that IT, marketing, and customer service are the three most popular areas for AI deployment.[132] The survey notes that only 37% of executives believe that generative AI applications are ready for production usage, a figure that drops to 29% amongst actual

AI practitioners. It is no surprise that IT is the leading area of adoption: software developers are expensive. The average salary of a US software developer in mid-2025 is $115,000, and this is higher in Silicon Valley. It is much higher for top firms like Google and Apple: Apple's average developer salary is $175,000, while OpenAI's average overall salary is $1.56 million. It is hardly surprising that businesses are exploring ways to improve productivity and their return on investment in those expensive engineers. Sensationalist articles suggesting, or at least considering the possibility, that programming is finished as a career abound, but is this really true?[133] How can we measure the actual effect of generative AI on software development?

Each year since 2013 the DevOps Research and Assessment (DORA) report has been produced, tracking software engineering developments and performance based on a very large survey of over 39,000 software developers. Originally an independent research firm, it was acquired by Google in December 2018 but continues its work. Its 2025 report focused on the adoption of AI for coding and has some fascinating insights. As might be expected, the use of AI for coding is high, with 81% of respondents reporting an increase in the use of AI in their applications. In particular, AI is used for writing code (75% of respondents), summarising information, explaining code, optimising (61%) and documenting code, writing tests, debugging, and data analysis (45%).

The survey respondents were asked for their own perceptions of the effect of AI on productivity, with three-quarters perceiving at least some gain in productivity. However, overall delivery of software actually worsened, with an estimated 1.5% reduction for every 25% increase in AI adoption. Worryingly, survey respondents reported an estimated 7.2% reduction in code stability for every 25% increase in AI adoption. Moreover, 39.2% of the respondents reported having little or no trust in AI. So, paradoxically, enterprises are aggressively adopting AI for coding, yet this adoption is resulting in slightly worse delivery and significantly less stable code. These findings, incidentally, confirm similar findings from the previous DORA survey a year earlier.

The findings of this survey are not outliers, and anyhow, it is the largest survey in the industry. A Stanford University study found that developers who had access to an AI assistant wrote significantly less secure code than those without access.[134] Intriguingly, participants with access to an AI assistant were more likely to believe they wrote secure code than those without access to the AI assistant, contrary to reality. Furthermore, participants who trusted the AI less and engaged more with the language and format of their code produced code with fewer security vulnerabilities. A Wuhan University study found similar results, with 29% of AI-generated code snippets having security weaknesses, based on tests for 89 known security weaknesses.[135]

These results are not entirely surprising. Generative AI works by making decisions based on its training data, and large language models have been trained on huge swathes of code of variable quality. Moreover, technology moves quickly, and an LLM trained on a code library a couple of years ago may produce code that uses out-of-date libraries that may have security vulnerabilities. Developers who write their own code understand what it does, or at least what they intended it to do, which is not necessarily true of AI-generated code. "Vibe coding", where novices use AI to write code for such tasks as building websites, is fraught with issues.[136] Even if we ignore hallucinations, which occur in AI-generated code just as in any AI-generated content, there are many other issues. Debugging code that you didn't write yourself is clearly harder than something that you wrote and understood the logic for, so even though you may be able to generate code faster than you can write, the process of testing and debugging may take longer. AI-generated code may accidentally include copyrighted material in its training data, and it also tends to do better in situations where there is a lot of training data rather than in novel situations or complex projects.

Although coding is one of the most popular use cases for generative AI, early experience suggests that it is no silver bullet. Wild claims that programmers are an endangered species seem overblown based on the survey data referenced in this document. The latest DORA study shows that 39% of developers who are using AI have little or no faith in the code that it generates, software delivery actually declines, and software stability worsens when it is used compared to hand-crafted code. This suggests that enterprises need to think carefully about their processes and how best to take advantage of this latest advance in technology, rather than being overly gung-ho. Generative AI is still quite new, and doubtless, advances will be made, but at present, enterprises need to be aware of the risks and issues with AI-generated code, not just the touted benefits.

Some people have heralded the end of the line for software developers, with Mark Zuckerberg of Facebook predicting that many mid-level software engineers will soon be redundant.[137] The media is full of articles examining the potential demise of programming as a career or at least the disruption of it by AI.[138] When reading such articles, always consider the vested interests of the claimant. A company selling AI tools, an investor in such a company, or a consultant implementing the tools all clearly have an incentive to claim things that will encourage people to spend money with them.

Programmers have always sought out ways to become more productive, ever since programming languages moved from machine code to assembler to high-level languages. More recently, there have been integrated development environments like Microsoft Visual Studio Code and a host of tools to help speed up testing, debugging, and deployment. AI is another step on that path.[139]

It is worth stepping back a moment and considering what a software developer actually does all day: they do not just sit down at their computer and write code continuously. Various studies have shown that software developers spend 20–40% of their time actually coding.[140] They also carry out code reviews, testing, debugging, writing documentation, and analysing the problems that they are tackling with their code. This is quite apart from project meetings such as code reviews, administration, training, and research. AI can help with some of these things, but definitely not all of them. Developers still have to understand the problem that their code is addressing, and they still need to test and debug the software. Debugging software written by someone else is much harder than debugging your own code, where you at least understand the intent and thought process, so it would make sense that AI may considerably speed up the process of actual coding at the expense of hours more time spent debugging. It is possible to try to help an AI by providing coding standards in a prompt or by referencing an external file with such coding standards. The ability to do this depends on the particular LLM's context window and its support for document handling.

Remember that at least 60% of an enterprise's IT budget goes on code maintenance and support. Different surveys give different numbers, but most estimates are actually higher than this.[141] This is a critical point: if most of an enterprise's software budget goes on maintenance, then an initiative that improves software delivery times at the cost of increased maintenance may actually be a bad idea. Certainly, AI code is likely to have an increased support burden: a DevOps.com survey (conducted by "Harness, the AI-Native Software Delivery Platform™" as part of its "State of Software Delivery Report: Beyond CodeGen – The Role of AI in the SDLC) found that 67% of programmers spent more time debugging AI-generated code than human-written code, and 69% spent more time fixing security issues.[142] One thing that should be said is that AI can itself be used in debugging, being able to read and analyse legacy code and then suggest changes.

In July 2025, another major study emerged that took a scientific approach to studying the productivity of generative AI on programming. This study by METR, a specialist AI benchmarking company, had some surprising results.[143] A group of experienced software developers were paid to carry out a series of coding tasks, each task taking around two hours. For some tasks, the developers were allowed to use whatever AI assistance they wanted, which was usually in the form of Cursor Pro and Claude Sonnet; the rest were coded the old-fashioned way, the tasks being randomly assigned between the developers. The programmers were asked about their perception of their own productivity. They thought that AI would speed them up by around 20%. The reality was that the tasks using AI were completed 19% slower than the ones with hand-coding. This is a fascinating result and one that contradicts the current anecdotal opinion that AI tools speed up coding significantly. It should be emphasised that this is just one study, though it is consistent with the massive DORA study. This new study did not consider issues like code stability or security, which were issues identified in the DORA study. Studies from Stanford University and others have also shown that AI-generated software is riddled with security flaws.[144]

More and more software developers are adopting AI in their jobs, with an adoption rate of 76% according to one study.[145] This suggests that there is considerable momentum behind the AI coding bandwagon. However, the recent METR study and the large DORA study show that the picture for productivity using AI is, at the very least, nuanced. Developers believe that they are being more productive despite the evidence in the METR study showing that they are actually less productive. Study after study has shown that AI-generated code can be insecure and is less stable than hand-generated code. Are developers themselves being carried along on a wave of inflated expectations? No one doubts that a generative AI can churn out code very quickly indeed, but is the price to be paid in terms of debugging ease, stability, and security flaws as great or greater than the productivity gain from instant code generation? If the productivity studies for software delivery suggest that developers using AI are actually delivering usable code more slowly, and given that AI code is costlier to maintain, this has significant implications. One recent survey highlighted a divide between developers using AI tools and the executives mandating their use.[146] The survey found that 75% of executives claimed that their AI rollout had been successful, but just 45% of the practitioners shared that view. The 2024 Stack Overflow survey showed a decline in faith in AI tools compared to the 2023 survey.

It must be remembered that this is quite a new field. Widespread use of AI for coding has only been around since 2023, and so studies of it and formal academic research into it are only now starting to appear in any quantity. There is no doubt that many more such studies will appear, and there is also no doubt that there is a huge amount of money being poured into AI research to improve the quality of the AI coding environments. Also, developers are still getting to grips with the new AI tools, and over time, they may get better at using them and become more productive. Consequently, the picture in mid-2035 or even mid-2030 may not be the same as in mid-2025. Nonetheless, the picture painted by these current studies suggests that there are many issues still to be addressed if generative AI is to deliver on its promise of radically improving software productivity. More careful analysis is required to objectively understand the true situation, and it would be prudent to temper expectations of just how productive generative AI is in the world of software development at present. As ever, careful measurement and monitoring are advised. At this point, it seems that software developers may not need to retrain in other career fields, at least not just yet.

Software engineering is more than just writing code. Indeed, programming represents only a fraction of the job of a typical software developer. As noted, there is also analysis of the user requirements, design, testing, documentation, debugging, and researching, quite apart from meetings, communication, training, and admin. A Microsoft study found that programmers would ideally spend about 25% of their time coding, but in practice, it was 14%. So, even if programming were entirely eliminated, there are limits to the productivity gains that could be made even by entirely automating coding. Moreover, producing code really fast is not necessarily such a great idea if it negatively impacts code quality, stability, or maintainability. Corporate IT budgets typically allocate half or more of their money to support and maintenance. Consequently, producing buggy code faster may actually be counterproductive.

The picture for the productivity of AI code is nuanced and only beginning to emerge. When I recently interviewed a chief technology officer of a large software company, he explained that his engineering teams had found that LLMs excelled in certain tasks but not others. They had been excellent at dealing with relatively straightforward, repetitive tasks, were good at documentation, and had been surprisingly good at helping with debugging code. They also excelled at generating comprehensive automated tests. On the other hand, they struggled with working on large, complex existing code bases, and their success rates dropped off rapidly when presented with problems that were novel or unusual, presumably as such problems were not within their training data. Research has shown that, in general, they are poor at precision,[147] spatial reasoning,[148] and tend to generate code that has security lapses.[149] One study found that GitHub CoPilot introduced security issues in almost a third of its Python code and a quarter of the generated JavaScript code.

It is well-known that LLMs hallucinate fabricated or meaningless answers at a steady rate, maybe 20% or more on average,[150] with newer models actually being worse.[151] The same issue occurs in LLM-generated code. LLMs will generate some hallucinated software package names when asked to write code in languages like Python and Ruby. What is intriguing is that some of the hallucinated names crop up repeatedly. This was tested by Lasso Security, who found that LLMs often (around 19% of the time) hallucinate the same software library, framework, or package.[152] This creates a worrying security loophole, as hackers can register the names of commonly hallucinated software libraries, put actual software in them, and include malware. In a test, thousands of downloads were made of such a (dummy) Trojan horse software package that had been uploaded to AI infrastructure and tools company Hugging Face. This research was repeated in 2025 by cybersecurity platform Socket, with even higher consistency of hallucinated software package names from the LLMs.[153]

The picture for AI-generated code is quite complex. There is no doubt that LLMs can generate code very quickly and can prove effective in other software engineering tasks like documentation, debugging, and testing. They can produce prototypes very quickly, which can help to nail down user requirements faster than before. On the other hand, the code that they produce has substantial security issues and is less stable than good-quality human code. The situation is evolving rapidly, with huge amounts of money being invested by venture capital companies in AI start-ups, many of them operating in the software engineering area. Consequently, it is likely that early lessons will be learned, tools will improve, and software engineers will get better at figuring out which tasks LLMs excel at and which they do not. At present, though, it would be prudent to have realistic expectations about the effect on software productivity of LLMs. They undoubtedly have a place, but they will not be replacing programmers *en masse* in the way that some newspaper headlines have breathlessly claimed.[154] Instead, LLMs will augment programmers, helping with particular tasks that they are well-suited to and carrying out mundane, repetitive tasks that human programmers often dislike. Although a high proportion of programmers at present distrust the code that they produce, it is likely that, as time passes, software engineers will become smarter about how to use LLMs in the most effective way. The future of programming will involve AI, but it will be working alongside humans rather than replacing them.

Security Issues in AI

There are various aspects of AI that give rise to security concerns. One is from chatbots being manipulated by bad actors into giving out personal data about customers or other trade secrets, possibly through carefully engineered prompts, a technique called "prompt injection".

The latest trend in AI is not just to ask an AI a question but to set it free. As we have discussed, agentic AI is the idea of having autonomous AI agents carrying out tasks, often by chaining multiple AIs together, as well as calling other programs. An agentic AI might not just research a possible holiday for you; it might actually book the flights and hotels if you give it your credit card. This is an emerging area and one that brings with it many risks.[155] It is so new that only recently have there been studies into whether it really works and how effective it is compared to humans.[156] Quite apart from the effectiveness of agentic AI, there are major concerns about the security implications of letting AI agents off the leash in your enterprise. In order to operate effectively, it will be necessary for an AI agent to have access to corporate IT systems and be capable of executing programs.

The tech world has only recently started to build protocols to handle such activities, and the emerging Model Context Protocol (MCP) has some worrying aspects.[157] MCP provides a framework that allows LLMs to connect to multiple tools, APIs, and systems. The idea is to provide a single standard that agents can send structured requests to and chain multiple tools together where needed. MCP servers tell the AI what tools they have access to, interpret and run commands, format the results in a way an AI can understand, and handle errors that occur. The protocol acts as an intermediary between AIs and services, and it can run locally or over the internet. The protocol has been adopted by a number of companies, including Microsoft in its CoPilot Studio. There are even companies now building tools to help build and manage MCP servers.

This all sounds good, but there are some serious problems with MCP. MCP servers need to be granted broad security permissions in order to do their job, such as the ability to send email, not just read it. The broader the implementation, the wider access it needs to enterprise systems, a kind of master key to enterprise data. Given this, you would think that a lot of effort would have been put into ensuring there are robust authentication mechanisms that had been put in place, but you would be wrong. MCP currently has little or no authentication at all built in. One simple example of how this may go wrong is if someone gained access to the OAuth token stored by the MCP server for Gmail, in which case they could set up their own server, access email history, send emails appearing to be someone else, and quietly monitor communication. Since AI assistants interpret natural language commands before sending them to an MCP server, attackers could inject messages including hidden instructions that trigger MCP actions. Such a message read by an AI might, for example, trigger the forwarding of financial documents to an external address.

Enterprises need to be very careful how MCP servers are deployed, ensuring that they are within established security controls and monitoring frameworks. The high level of security access that MCP servers need means that considerable care needs to be taken in monitoring them for suspicious activity. MCP servers can be isolated in dedicated network segments, and web application firewalls should be set to inspect MCP traffic for anomalies. Request tracing needs to be implemented to allow incident analysis and auditing. MCP responses can be routed through data loss prevention systems to detect and possibly block sensitive data. There are some general AI security guidelines starting to appear, such as the UK government's AI Cyber Security Code of Practice, but this does not yet specifically address MCP.[158] The excitement about AI and the high level of investment in it mean that there is perceived pressure to do things as fast as possible, for example, for fear of a competitor acting more quickly. However, agentic AI is a new technology, and there are considerable dangers in rushing to implement it without thinking through the risks and challenges. The host of security issues around MCP will doubtless be mediated over time, but any technology that requires administrative access to lots of corporate systems is in itself a juicy target for attackers. Enterprises need to carry out a careful security review of any MCP implementations that they may be introducing, especially since these may be buried within other packaged software applications, so they may not even be aware that they are running.

Beyond this particular protocol, there are other troubling aspects to the headlong rush to implement AI. A 2025 SoSafe study found that 87% of enterprises had suffered from an AI-related cyberattack in the last year.[159] A 2024 IBM study found an average cost of $4.9 million per breach, yet just 24% of generative AI projects are secured.[160] In the SoSafe study, a striking 98% of security professionals felt that the "resilience gap" is widening, meaning that enterprises are more vulnerable than they were in the past. Voice phishing attacks quadrupled in 2024, according to a Crowdstrike report,[161] while a technique called "steganography" means that malware can be hidden inside images. If an email with such an image is clicked on, then the malware can be delivered and do its work.

Some attacks using AI are quite sophisticated, and some don't even require access to the corporate IT systems. Engineering firm Arup fell victim to an elaborate deepfake scam that cost them $20 million.[162] A similar attempt failed recently at WPP.[163] AI enables more realistic and customised phishing emails as well as deepfakes. AI malware has already appeared and been used, including polymorphic malware that changes its code structure each time it infects a new system, making it hard to deal with. Agentic AI represents an enhanced security risk compared to just using LLMs as chatbots since agentic AI needs to be granted extensive access to corporate systems in order to do their job. They may require privileged (administrator) access if they are to access multiple corporate systems. Therefore, they are a juicy target for hackers.

Enterprises are not defenceless against this AI onslaught. Continuous monitoring of networks and systems is vital, as is threat detection that identifies unusual patterns of behaviour. Filters can be implemented to check email and chatbot prompts for suspicious content. Software is available that will reduce the attack surface available to hackers. Preventative measures should include the monitoring of third-party partners that send data to your enterprise, as well as internal systems. Establishing robust data governance processes will help, as will incorporating security assessments into each stage of AI model development and deployment. Model access should be restricted as far as possible to those who need it, and data should be encrypted, both for data at rest and in transit. The ISO standard information security management system 27001 can provide a broad framework for these efforts.[164] As enterprises implement AI models directly and install third-party software that uses AI, it is vital that they proactively consider the security implications of these applications. This is especially true of agentic AI, which needs to be tightly controlled and monitored if it is not to become a Trojan Horse for malware, willingly brought inside the corporate firewall by companies eager to explore the latest in AI.

Generative artificial intelligence technology, such as ChatGPT and its rivals, depends heavily on training data, but what if that training data is deliberately poisoned? As we have seen, large language models, the technology which underlies generative AI, go through three stages of training.[165] The models are fed vast amounts of raw data, such as The Common Corpus,[166] and the model uses statistical techniques (such as "gradient descent")[167] to predict missing pieces of it. The model learns something about language in this process. For example, if the model is given a partial sentence that starts "the cat sat on the...", then the model will use its training data to predict the most likely word. The word "mat" will likely appear many times if it has been trained on a vast selection of books, and this word will be assigned a higher probability than a word like "zebra". This stage of training is called "unsupervised pre-training" and involves the model guessing, checking, and then updating its parameters so that it is more likely to predict the next word. In the next stage of LLM training, supervised learning, the model is explicitly trained to follow instructions. In the final stage, called "reinforcement learning", it is taught to encourage desired behaviour and discourage unwanted outputs, such as the model offering bombmaking instructions or instructions on how to make bioweapons like sarin.

At the end of this process, you have an LLM ready to interact with humans. But what if the data on which it is trained turns out to be flawed? One kind of flaw is that the training data may be biased in some way.[168] If the training data has lots of associations of "nurse" with women, then an LLM trained on that data and used for job screening will tend to reflect the inherent bias in the data. Amazon had to scrap its AI recruitment tool after it was found that the tool routinely rejected female applicants, since its training data had mostly been resumes from men.[169]

The issue of bias in data is well understood, but what if the training data was subverted deliberately? Writers and artists are far from happy that AI companies have been using their copyright-protected material to train their LLMs without their permission or any form of payment. Various lawsuits are working their way through the courts to challenge this at present.[170] Some creative content producers have decided to fight back another way. As mentioned earlier, the Nightshade tool allows artists to make tiny changes to the pixels in their art before it is uploaded to the internet.[171] The pixel changes are invisible to humans but are picked up by AIs if they use them in their training dataset. The subtle manipulation can be used to throw off LLMs by confusing the labels that the models use. For example, an image of a dog might be poisoned with a data label that describes it as a lampshade or a cat. It turns out that you only need to poison a tiny amount of training data to affect an LLM.[172] Researchers discovered that just 50 seeded images of mislabelled dogs (labelled as cats) were able to seriously compromise the AI tool Stable Diffusion's ability to draw dogs, and 300 images were enough for the tool to start drawing cats instead of dogs when requested.[173] Even prompts to draw similar images, like "puppy" or "wolf", were also degraded.

There are other, darker implications. The practice of steganography is disguising a message within another message.[174] An example in the physical world is the use of invisible ink to write a hidden message between the lines of a letter.[175] In the digital world, the term is used to describe instructions or a message concealed within a file. There are many examples of this, but one illustration would be to hide a prompt within a text file by making it white text on a white background.[176] A human would see nothing, but a computer, such as an LLM being trained, can see the hidden text prompt. The bigger the file, the easier it is to hide. Image files can be used to hide messages or malware within the pixels of an image. Audio or video files are even larger, and again, some hidden content can be embedded within a digital video file in a way that a human would not spot.

In 2015, hackers attacked the e-commerce platform Adobe Commerce (formerly Magecart), a platform used by over 270,000 businesses.[177] The hackers injected malicious code into the footers and headers of pages on shopping sites, compromising 3,500 shopping websites. In 2018, a

US citizen used a digital image of a sunset to hide files he had stolen from his employer to sell to the Chinese government.[178] Hackers used steganography in phishing emails regarding invoices to smuggle malware in two campaigns in 2024.[179] In 2025, North Korean hackers used malicious JPEG images to deliver malware to subvert Windows 11 systems.[180]

In a recent test,[181] researchers explored the vulnerability of popular medical websites by taking a simulation of a commonly used dataset called The Pile,[182] widely used in LLM training and which contains widely used medical databases like PubMed.[183] The researchers planted medical misinformation in a small number of datasets to measure the effect of this on the advice given by medical LLM models. They found that just 0.001% of training tokens poisoned with medical misinformation in HTML documents was enough to get medical models to provide harmful advice. Worse, the models generally performed fine, enough to pass benchmarks commonly used to test medical LLMs, despite the inherent and deliberately induced flaw in the adulterated model.

One subtle exploit takes advantage of the realisation that LLM hallucinations are not entirely random.[184] As well as writing essays and marketing content, LLMs are used to write program code. LLMs hallucinate when they generate code, just as they do when they generate text, for example, making calls to software libraries that do not exist. Around 20% of all AI code generated has such hallucinated library calls, which is consistent with the general hallucination rates of LLMs. Researchers tested 16 AI models across 30 tests and found that 43% of the hallucinated software packages were repeated in at least ten queries. Hallucinated packages were repeated at least once 58% of the time. Although some of the models are learning to spot some of their own errors, this phenomenon allows hackers to register commonly hallucinated software library names on popular open-source platforms like Hugging Face and inject malware into these. This "slopsquatting" was tested by security researcher Bar Lanyado, who registered a test package under a commonly hallucinated name on Hugging Face.[185] Within three months, it had been downloaded 30,000 times.

There have already been several demonstrations of how to attack the AI systems used in autonomous vehicles, potentially causing vehicles to swerve into oncoming traffic, amongst other effects.[186] A University of Texas study showed that the widely used Microsoft 365 Copilot could be compromised by introducing malicious content into documents that the AI indexes or references.[187] This is a particular issue for companies using the approach called retrieval-augmented generation (RAG) to add supplementary material to raw LLMs. In this case, the attack could be made by adding such supplementary files rather than needing to attack the LLM itself. Even after the malicious document is removed, the corrupted information lingers in the system.

There are defensive measures that can be taken against malware hidden using digital steganography. Steganalysis uses statistical methods to detect hidden data, and a digital vaccine technique has been proposed to safeguard digital images from steganography.[188] Tools are emerging that can detect and quarantine files affected by steganography.[189] The issue has been raised in a recent report by the US Commerce Department's National Institute of Standards and Technology (NIST), which discusses the various types of adversarial machine learning.[190] One possible approach, using synthetically generated data to train other LLMs, has problems of its own.[191] However, the ease with which such attacks can be made demands a systematic response from corporations.

Data poisoning is an emerging and worrying phenomenon. The speed of LLM development and the excitement generated about it have meant that deployments of it have often occurred at breakneck speed. We are only beginning to understand the security threats that are being opened up by the use of LLMs, of which digital steganography is just one aspect. Companies deploying generative AI need to review their security policies and approaches carefully and ensure that they are prepared as well as they can be for such attacks. Hackers are known to be adaptable and to be early adopters of new technology. Corporations need to be just as responsive to these new threats.

Generative AI is a fairly recent phenomenon, and the pace of implementation means that companies are hurtling headlong to adopt it in the hope of productivity improvements. So far, these have proved elusive, as we shall see, but in the case of AI-generated code and AI agents, the pace of implementation has far outstripped the ability of the industry to fully identify and respond to the security implications. AI tools have been shown to be easily manipulated just by clever prompts, while AI-generated code has been shown to be riddled with security loopholes. This is quite apart from more sophisticated attacks using steganography or the current lack of security built into agentic AI protocols. We are already seeing a troubling number of AI-driven security incidents, and this is almost certain to get worse. Corporations implementing AI need to put careful security protocols and reviews in place right now, and not as an afterthought.

Fake It Till You Make It – AI Deepfakes

Generative artificial intelligence has many useful applications, such as automating repetitive tasks, language translation, and coding software. However, its ability to produce "deepfakes" of images, audio, and video is a controversial and troubling area.

There are two main approaches that are used in AI to produce deepfakes.[192] The first is a technique called "general adversarial networks" (GAN). Two AI models are used. The first generates a fake image or video, or, alternatively, selects a real one, and then it presents its choice to the other model. This second model ("the discriminator") decides whether the image is real or fake. The two AI models repeat this process a vast number of times, learning as they go. The first model gets better at generating fakes, and the discriminator gets better at spotting them. For an effective deepfake model, up to 100,000 images are used, and millions of iterations, in batches.[193]

The other main approach used to produce deepfakes is "diffusion models".[194] In this, a model is trained to restore an image to its original state after visual noise has been artificially added. For example, the model may fill in gaps in an image with something plausible. In some cases, these models are easier to train than GAN networks, though they can involve a lot of processing power and may not produce quite such high-quality results as GANs.

Deepfakes have obvious potential for abuse, such as controversial (fake) statements made by AI-generated versions of real politicians during an election campaign. Deepfakes can be used to make pornographic images of public figures[195] and have even been used for child abuse. They can also be used by hackers for financial fraud. In 2024, a Hong Kong employee of engineering firm Arup was tricked into transferring $25 million after a video call with a deepfake "chief financial officer",[196] along with several other apparent employees, including some he knew personally.

Can we spot a deepfake? A deepfake image that made a stir in the world's press in March 2023 was one of Pope Francis seemingly wearing a down jacket.[197] This image was not even particularly good, as it had some reasonably obvious flaws, as pointed out by *The New Indian Express* below:

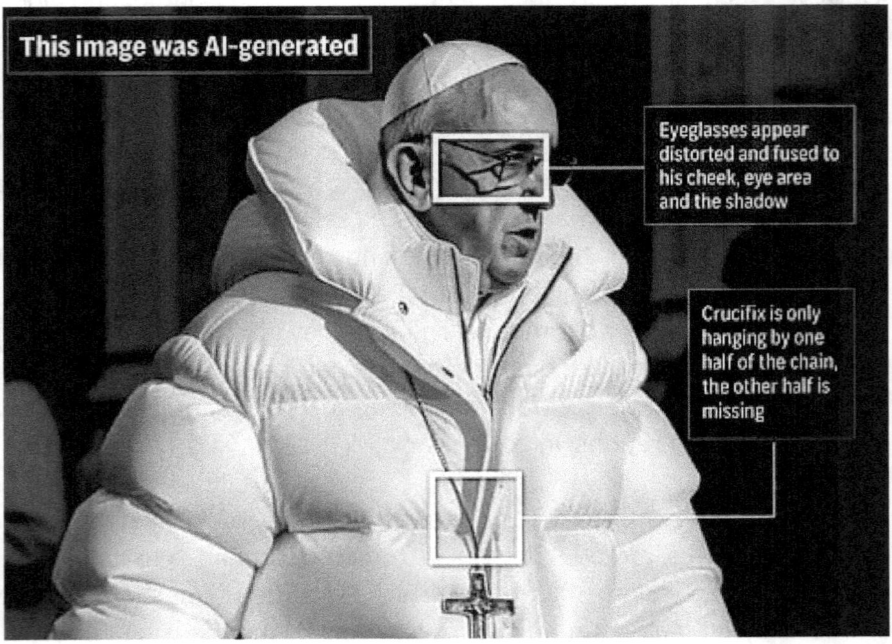

Nonetheless, it captured the public imagination and popularised the awareness of deepfake images. Technology moves on, especially in the world of AI-generated images, and it is easy now for anyone to produce a similar image that is harder to spot as a fake. This was an image I created on 30th August 2025 using Leonardo AI.

Even this basic attempt by me seems harder to spot as a fake than the one that made such a stir in 2023. Actually, spotting a deepfake can be hard. Experts will look for lighting and shadow issues, unexpected reflections, overly smooth skin, or unusual blinking patterns if it is a video. The metadata of a file can be examined for clues, and reverse image searches can be used to track down original images. Technology can be used too,[198] with various tools emerging to help detect deepfakes,[199] from vendors including OpenAI, Intel, and others.[200]

Deepfakes can be audio as well as visual images,[201] and there are obvious applications for misuse. One US senator was targeted by a deepfake Zoom call in 2024.[202] UK Prime Minister Sir Keir Starmer was the victim of a deepfake audio recording of him seemingly swearing at staff.[203] In the 2024 US election, a deepfake audio was sent to voters, purportedly of Joe Biden,[204] urging voters in a Democratic primary election not to vote. In March 2022, Russia circulated a deepfake video of President Zelensky urging his military to lay down their arms. The latest AI models can produce a plausible deepfake audio of a person based on as little as three seconds of speech, with 15 minutes of speech being sufficient for a high-quality deepfake.

Not all use of deepfake technology is necessarily bad. The technology can be used to restore old films or produce synthetic voices for those who have lost their voices to disease. People experiencing persecution in repressive regimes can tell their stories via deepfakes without risking exposure by using real video footage that might accidentally reveal their identity. Nonetheless, deepfakes are clearly a source of concern.

In response to the rise of deepfakes, governments around the world have been tightening regulations: the UK's 2023 Online Safety Act,[205] the EU AI Act,[206] the US's Take it Down Act,[207] signed into law in May 2025,[208] as well as various state-level initiatives across the US.[209] In June 2025, Denmark gave its citizens copyright over their images.[210] How effective this flurry of legislation will actually be remains to be seen, but the level of activity at least suggests that politicians are taking it seriously.

Deepfakes are here to stay, whether we like it or not: the technology to build them cannot be un-invented. Businesses and individuals need to be alert to the possibility of deepfake scams and consider using modern detection technologies to counter deepfakes. Governments need to continue to actively legislate in this area to protect people's rights, and law enforcement needs to be trained in this area and actively pursue scammers. Seeing is no longer believing. As Chico Marx said in the 1933 film *Duck Soup*: "Who are you going to believe, me or your lying eyes?"

Shadow AI

As generative artificial intelligence flooded into the public consciousness in late 2022, corporations wrestled with how best to utilise and control it at work. Initial hopes of productivity improvements were tempered by the realisation that the public chatbots like ChatGPT and Claude were executing prompts on their servers. This content, which at work could include contracts, product plans, or other trade secrets, could potentially appear as training data used in a large language model. Samsung found this out the hard way in 2023, when some of its employees used

ChatGPT to help with a new program.[211] The notes and even the source code were entered by the employees, and so they leaked this sensitive information to the chatbot. Samsung subsequently banned the use of generative AI on company-owned devices.[212] Other large companies followed suit, putting policies and restrictions in place to prevent trade secrets leaking from behind corporate firewalls into the wild. By the summer of 2023, a majority of UK companies had implemented such restrictions.[213] In the US, high-profile companies such as Apple, Amazon, Bank of America, and many more followed suit.[214] Some companies have built enterprise-specific servers and secure cloud implementations in order to reduce the risk.[215] A raft of policies and suggested security approaches have followed.[216]

So, problem solved? Hardly. A survey by WalkMe in summer 2025 found that 78% of the 1000 US staff surveyed were actually using unauthorised AI tools at work;[217] just 8% of them had received any AI training. A different 2025 survey showed that 13% of companies that responded admitted that they had suffered financial losses, reputational damage, or customer fallout as a result of AI.[218] Yet another survey found that 70% of the staff in North America who were surveyed admitted to unauthorised use of AI tools at work. This ranged from brainstorming content to analysing data to drafting emails or documents and more, including writing code and generating customer-facing content. Quite apart from the confidentiality issues of using such tools and leaking trade secrets, the use of public chatbots in heavily regulated industries like finance could cause legal exposure for the companies involved. This suggests a lack of effective governance on the part of many companies and also an unmet need from staff who want to be able to use productivity tools that are not being provided to them.

One interesting aspect of the use of AI, shadow or otherwise, is that the people who are least knowledgeable about AI are the ones who are most likely to be receptive to AI and use it. A 2025 study[219] into this confirmed the results of another 2025 study into the same area: those who understand AI least tend to be the ones most likely to be impressed with it.[220] This was also seen in a major study of IT professionals, who found that executives were likely to have much higher levels of trust in AI than the developers who were actually using it day to day.[221] For example, even today, not everyone is aware that LLMs "hallucinate", i.e. produce fabricated or nonsensical answers and that they do so regularly, especially in areas outside of their original training data.[222] At least 15% of AI answers contain hallucinations, and this rate is actually worse with more recent AI models.[223] Another major concern about LLMs is their security vulnerability. It is notoriously easy for bad actors to manipulate chatbots into actions that are not intended.[224] Some of the techniques do not involve elaborate or sophisticated hacking,[225] but merely sending prompts that get LLMs to disregard their guardrails. There are some more elaborate techniques that can be used by hackers, such as steganography,[226] but LLMs have been shown to be easily manipulated by much simpler methods. In one set of tests, a 65% success rate was achieved in getting LLMs to override their safety guardrails merely by disguising the request amidst benign content.[227]

What should companies do? To begin with, it would seem prudent to embark on comprehensive training so that staff understand the risks of using LLMs as well as the opportunities. Many staff simply don't realise the risks that they are taking. As noted, the more that people work with AI, the more they are likely to understand the issues and to be less trusting. In one survey, 93% of software engineers encounter problems with their models on a daily or weekly basis.[228] A broad assessment of security risks would also seem in order since LLMs clearly have substantial security weaknesses at present, but there are steps that can be taken to introduce better governance and to improve the security associated with AI. One Microsoft report found that 87% of UK businesses are vulnerable to AI-related cyberattacks.[229] Another survey found that 74% of companies perceive AI threats as a major challenge for their organisations. This is not a rare, "black swan" style risk: in a huge survey of over 8,000 businesses, over a quarter of all UK companies admitted to being victims of a cyber-attack in the last year.[230]

As with any new or ground-breaking technology, it will take time for companies to get to grips with how to implement AI effectively. However, it is important that corporate executives get a handle on these issues and do so quickly. The widespread rise in shadow AI has shown that the current approaches are not succeeding for most companies. Hackers are agile and adaptable, and time is not on the side of the angels here. Companies need to understand the risks that are lurking in the shadows.

AI Explainability

In William Cowper's 1773 poem "Light Shining out of Darkness", the English poet wrote that "God moves in a mysterious way, his wonders to perform". The same could be said of large language models, the technology underpinning generative AI. LLMs are capable of extremely fluent conversation and answer questions with authority and confidence, but can we peer inside an LLM to understand its reasoning? The short answer is "no". LLMs are a black box, where the input (your prompt to the LLM) and output (its answer) are known, but the internal mechanism is opaque.[231]

This fundamental truth is contrary to some advice that you will find on the internet and is simply a function of how artificial neural networks actually work.[232] Explaining how a traditional computer program makes its decision is not usually so tricky and, indeed, is important in many areas. If a bank uses an application to assess whether to approve a loan, it is normally based on a set of rules. The application might look at the credit rating of the applicant, the collateral they can put up, their income, their age, etc. The assessment is "deterministic",[233] meaning that the decision will always be the same given the same input data. Moreover, the set of weightings that the application gives to the various factors is known, and so it is easy to go back and check why a loan was granted or rejected. LLMs are probabilistic creatures: they are not completely consistent in their answers. Studies have shown that an LLM may score as high as 95% for internal consistency,[234] but this figure can be much lower, depending on the model in question. This is actually quite important for the use of LLMs in many circumstances. However, in many real-life situations, a computer decision must be auditable and repeatable.[235] Government regulations for some industries, such as pharmaceuticals, require that systems can be audited and that their reasoning can be traced and made transparent.[236]

There have been various approaches to explainability in traditional machine learning models, such as local interpretable model-agnostic explanations (LIME). This technique has been shown to be difficult to apply to LLMs due to their complex, non-linear nature.[237]

Another approach is Shapley Additive exPlanations (SHAP).[238] This approach, which comes from game theory, examines the features of a given model, such as the one to assess bank loans, and assigns scores to the factors that affect the answer of that model. It is a technique that works well for machine learning models and neural networks but has limitations for complex and multi-layered neural networks, such as those used within modern LLMs. SHAP was designed for tabular models where you can turn features on and off and recalculate predictions. LLMs do not work that way: they work with contextual embeddings – removing or adding a word may change the meaning of a sentence. For this reason, the basic SHAP approach cannot be used with LLMs. A number of additional mathematical techniques can be used to enhance SHAP in various ways, but each has limitations. Even using the best available techniques, an LLM's answer cannot be readily explained due to their sheer complexity and nature. Partial explanations can be derived using techniques like "attention maps", "behavioural probing", and "neuron/feature analysis", but none of these provide a reliable and complete explanation of the way that an LLM thinks.

You will sometimes see a "chain of reasoning" explanation from an LLM, which gives a step-by-step explanation of how it tackled a question. In fact, these are post hoc justifications.

They are not how LLMs actually come up with answers.[239] In some ways, this kind of after-the-fact, fake explanation is worse than none at all, as it gives a pretence of auditability when none exists. These "unfaithful" explanations are discussed in more depth in this research paper.[240] They may make us feel better, but they have nothing to do with the internal reasoning process of LLMs.

This state of affairs is unlikely to change and means that corporations implementing LLM technology need to be very careful in exactly where they use it. In areas where auditability and transparency are important,

LLMs are simply unsuitable. We have already seen many examples of this in the legal field, where LLMs make up fake case references in court documents.[241] I spoke to an NHS practitioner who initially used ChatGPT to look up medical references in papers that she wrote and stopped doing so once she realised that many of the references provided by the LLM simply didn't exist. Companies need to train their staff more in AI literacy so that they are aware of the limitations of LLMs when it comes to reliability, consistency, and auditability. A troubling number of people are blissfully unaware that these issues exist, and this lack of understanding is inevitably going to lead to disappointment and worse.

AI Watermarks

When it comes to transparency in artificial intelligence, there are different aspects to consider. One is understanding the reasoning process behind AI decisions and what data they use in that decision-making, as we just discussed. There is a more basic aspect: how can you tell whether a document or image that you see is written by a human or is actually AI-generated? Large language models, the underlying technology behind chatbots, like ChatGPT, Claude, Grok, and Perplexity, are quite fluent in their communication. Their writing is certainly coherent and human-like. So, how do you know whether that essay submitted as homework was written by a student called Carol, as she claims, or was actually knocked off in a few seconds by an LLM? There is a whole industry of tools claiming to be able to detect AI writing, an industry valued at about $1.5 billion in 2024.[242] There is an obvious market for such tools in schools and universities, assuming that they actually work as claimed. An article in Forbes reckoned that 17% of all academic content was generated by AI,[243] while a UK report found a much lower figure, albeit of proven cases only.[244] However, such figures assume that AI plagiarism technology actually works – does it?

The US Federal Trade Commission ordered a company called Workado to back up a claim that its tool was "98% accurate" in detecting AI writing.[245] Independent testing showed that the true detection rate was 53%, so essentially no better than tossing a coin. This is not the only such tool with issues.[246] An academic study that tested plagiarism tools on papers submitted by students in 2013 and compared them to ones submitted in 2023 found that the tools flagged up essentially the same proportion as being "potentially AI written". Since ChatGPT only appeared in late 2022, it seems highly unlikely that the 2013 student papers were written using an AI, at least unless the students had access to a time machine. These tools' lack of reliability is a serious issue since accusations of AI use and plagiarism can seriously affect the career of a student or researcher submitting an academic paper.

Moreover, there are further tools available ("AI humanisers" like HIX Bypass and BypassGPT) that claim to be able to edit a document to remove any tell-tale AI traces. A human student wishing to disguise an AI-written essay could do so without computer assistance, just by adding personal anecdotes or varying sentence length. Detecting AI-generated images is also getting harder. Generative AI images in early 2023 tended to have limitations that were easy to spot. The AIs had trouble with human hands, often adding an extra finger. In some absurd cases, they would even add extra limbs to human figures. They also struggled with text. If you asked for an image with a specific piece of text, like a company name on a logo, you would usually get gibberish instead of the requested text. This situation has improved a lot, and by September 2025, AI image generators can produce very realistic images that only an expert could distinguish from a human-taken photo or drawing. One indication can be that a person in an image has flawless skin, too perfect for a human.[247]

The tools still have strange limitations. If you ask an AI tool to generate an image of an analogue clock face, it will almost always generate a watch showing 10.10 am/pm, regardless of the time you have asked to be displayed. This is because watch adverts favoured their watches being set to this time since it was symmetrical and aesthetically pleasing. Consequently, this time shows up a lot in AI training datasets. To test this, I generated these images on 9th September 2025 from a few AIs with the following prompt: "an analog watch face showing the time twenty past two".

If you try different AI image generators, you will often encounter the same issue, though occasionally you just get a random time. Remember that LLMs are probabilistic creatures and will occasionally go down less common paths in their predictions.

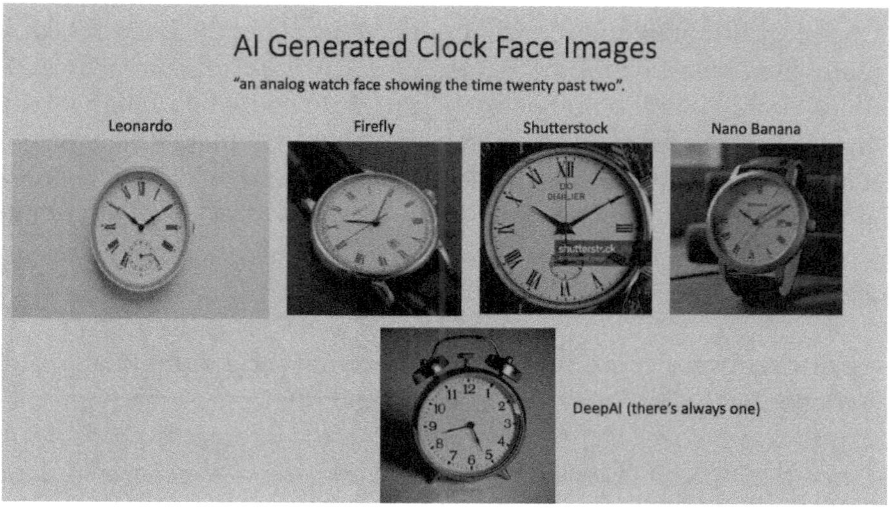

The issue of detecting AI-generated images has a serious side, such as the use of AI for deepfake videos.[248] It is also an issue for artists and graphic designers since AIs can be asked to produce paintings in the style of a particular artist. A simple example of this is shown below.

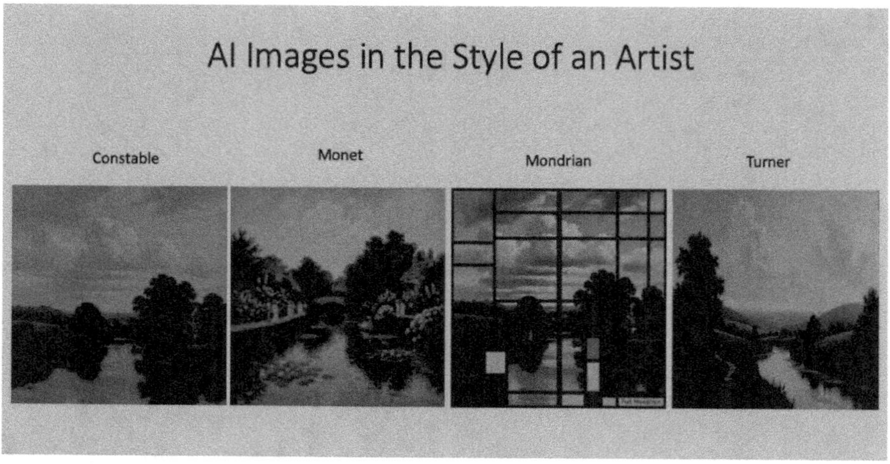

The quality may be debatable at this point, but if you are an artist, then you can see that having made-up images in your style could be a concern,[249] especially if they are plastered all over the internet.

One country that has decided to do something about the issue of fake AI material is China, a nation that is a serious force in AI.[250] In September 2025, China passed a law requiring all AI-generated content,[251] whether text, image, or video, to carry a label or watermark.[252] Chinese AI companies WeChat, Douyin, Weibo, and RedNote have already complied. Elsewhere in the world, such authentication is purely optional. Watermarks of this kind can be easily tampered with,[253] but this initiative seems to be at least a good start.

As AI penetrates more and more aspects of society, the inability to distinguish fake and real content is becoming an increasingly important issue. Already, over half of new content on the internet is probably AI-generated.[254] Since LLMs do badly when trained on AI-generated data, such as synthetic data,[255] this is a problem for the AI vendors and not just humans trying to navigate content. AI content is poisoning the well of training data for other AIs. The scale of this problem is increasing and will only get worse. Identifying AI content seems like a fairly fundamental requirement in many areas, even if the technology to do so is not yet perfect.

China should get credit for trying to do something about this mess.

AI Use Cases in Industry

AI in Finance

Financial services make up at least a fifth of the entire global economy.[256] The finance industry has always been a heavy user of technology, investing at least three times as much in technology as the retail sector or manufacturing. Given this, it is unsurprising that financial services have also been early adopters of artificial intelligence. It is used for loan decisions, customer support, document analysis, financial forecasting, fraud detection, and the generation of financial reports. As one example, Mastercard used AI and graph technology to look for potentially fraudulent patterns in credit card data.[257] The approach reportedly doubled the detection rate of compromised cards.[258]

The use of AI in finance goes back to the 1980s, when hedge funds adopted statistical techniques to identify price discrepancies, and machine learning was used in credit scoring. Machine learning was also used in risk management and customer segmentation. Trading, traditionally done by highly paid humans, started to migrate to high-frequency trading, where algorithms conduct a large number of trades at great speed.[259] The algorithms analyse real-time stock price data, looking for anomalies or patterns that may represent trading opportunities. They are empowered to trade on their own, executing much faster than a human could, sometimes thousands of times a second. Over half of all US stock market trades are now algorithmic, though this has caused some high-profile issues on occasion,[260] such as the 2010 "flash crash".[261]

In the last few years, many financial services start-up companies have emerged to challenge the big banks, with the "fintech" sector, worth around $250 billion in 2024, being a heavy user of AI for everything from chatbots to portfolio optimisation to delivering insights to traders. Companies such as Stripe,[262] Tencent,[263] Revolut,[264] and Chime[265] are all examples of this rapidly expanding sector. Ant Group, part of Alibaba, serves over 1.3 billion customers and 80 million merchants.[266]

Using AI has some clear advantages for banks. A machine learning model can detect patterns in huge amounts of data that a human would miss, making this technology a good fit for fraud detection. With banks losing around 5% of their annual revenue to fraud, any improvement is welcome.[267] Chatbots can be deployed to either supplement or replace some customer service staff. Although this is a controversial area, some studies have found that customers can actually experience a higher level of customer satisfaction with such chatbots compared to human customer service staff.[268] At the very least, they are available 24/7 and do not get tired or cranky, even if they may lack empathy. There is little doubt that AI models will continue to be used for risk assessment, creditworthiness, evaluating loan collateral, and other areas that involve evaluating multiple data sources. Similarly, we can be sure that AI models will continue to have a role in high-frequency trading, given that they can operate at speeds that human traders cannot.

Generative AI's ability to write program code in addition to text means that it has potential applications in the back-office systems that are used by banks. Trading systems are typically huge, proprietary, and complex, involving millions of lines of code. The programming language COBOL, invented by US Rear Admiral Grace Hopper in 1959,[269] still powers nearly half of all global banking IT systems, according to Reuters.[270] AI code generation is not ready to just vibe-code a major trading system to replace all that COBOL any time soon, but AI tools can be useful in debugging and producing test cases for programmers.[271]

There are plenty of challenges as well as opportunities. Data privacy is a major issue in a highly regulated industry like financial services, and AI has more than its share of security issues. Banks are particularly juicy targets for hackers, for obvious reasons, and AI is presenting new avenues for fraudsters and attackers,[272] as well as new opportunities for the banks themselves.[273] Bias in AI models is another problem. In a 2024 study, borrowers with black or brown skin were twice as likely to be denied a loan as those with white skin.[274] A 2022 study found that racial minority borrowers were charged higher interest rates than white borrowers, costing an extra $450 million in interest per year.[275] The EU AI Act, a piece of legislation that was enacted in August 2024 and will be in force from August 2026, explicitly addresses algorithmic bias and will require a response from the industry.[276]

Over the next few years, we can expect to see AI, in its various forms,[277] used more and more by financial services firms as they seek to innovate and find opportunities to automate routine back-office processing. Just the ability to scan and index paper documents *en masse* is a major step forward for an industry that still uses plenty of paper, despite its embrace of high technology. We can expect generative AI to be used to generate customised financial advice and produce synthetic data for testing, though that has its own issues.[278] Human advisers will likely be supplemented with AI tools to help them be more efficient. New AI models will continue to be used to detect patterns in data, both for trading and for fraud detection. Financial institutions will doubtless continue to be early adopters of AI, for better and for worse, just as they have been for other new technologies.

Gambling with AI

From time immemorial, people have liked to gamble: the first six-sided dice were found in Mesopotamia, dating back to around 3000 BC, and in ancient China, wooden tiles for a lottery-style game have been found dating back to 2300 BC. The first casino emerged in Italy in 1638. More recently, the advent of the internet has transformed gambling, allowing it to move out of physical betting shops, racetracks, and casinos, such as those in Las Vegas and Macau, to virtual venues online. The first online gambling site was probably the Liechtenstein Lottery in October 1994, with Antigua and Barbuda launching an online casino the same year.[279] Worldwide, the gambling industry is estimated to be worth around $450 billion,[280] of which about $79 billion is online.[281] Two-thirds of people in the UK place a bet at least monthly in 2025,[282] and the UK is far from an outlier. The countries with the most gamblers per capita are Australia, Singapore, Canada, Ireland, and Finland.[283]

Artificial intelligence is starting to seep into the gambling industry just as it is in others. AI models can analyse players' poker styles, look at the history of horse racing to come up with suggestions for betting strategy, adjust odds offered in real time, and detect cheating in games like online poker. Poker seems particularly prone to computer-assisted abuse, with the PokerStars company confiscating $700,000 from players using machine-learning-driven bots as far back as 2015.[284] Detecting cheating, such as player collusion in poker, requires extensive processing power, and the platform operators are in a constantly evolving battle with cheaters, with incidents still occurring in 2025.[285] Other uses of AI in the industry range from targeted customer segmentation, personalised loyalty programs, and special offers through to customer service chatbots.[286] The more that players interact with gambling platforms, the more data is generated, and the more algorithms can target personalised special offers and tailored experiences to them. In the physical world, casinos increasingly use AI-driven facial recognition to carry out "know your customer" checks and anti-money laundering checks.[287] Casinos use AI for revenue forecasting, more targeted marketing, and fraud detection.[288] The rise of virtual reality capabilities has led to immersive gambling experiences.[289] Players can sit at home, yet, via a virtual reality headset, enter a virtual casino environment and interact with dealers.[290]

There are obvious public concerns about problem gambling, which can lead to depression and bankruptcy amongst addicted gamblers. The more that AI allows personalised gambling experiences, the more it can be argued to represent an increased risk for gambling addicts. However, there is another side to this, with products such as Mindway[291] offering a virtual psychologist that can advise problem gamblers. The software aims to detect problem gambling at an early stage and offer advice, as well as alert operators to problematic behaviour by gamblers.

Just as in other industries, there is little doubt that AI will continue to have an impact on gambling, from online websites to virtual reality casinos to its use in physical casinos in various ways. AI offers opportunities for both players and operators, who are eager to offer more tailored experiences and drive up player engagement. The use of AI for detecting problem gambling and helping gambling addicts before they are harmed too much by their own behaviour may help the industry improve its reputation in the public eye.

AI in Pharmaceuticals

The pharmaceutical industry was worth $1.6 trillion in 2024, employing around 8 million people directly and up to 75 million people indirectly. Various flavours of artificial intelligence show considerable promise in these industries. AI can be utilised in various applications, including research and drug discovery, clinical trials, operations such as manufacturing, and for other purposes, including searching medical literature and ensuring regulatory compliance.

A striking example of AI's use in drug discovery is the company DeepMind, since acquired by Google, which has been a pioneer in "deep learning"[292] AI techniques. It demonstrated the promise of the technology by teaching it the basic rules of chess and then left it to play millions of games against itself, gradually improving its standard of play. The result, AlphaZero, then played a match in 2017 against the top computer chess program Stockfish. Over a hundred games, AlphaZero won 72 games and lost none. It later adapted this to the more computationally challenging game of Go, where it beat the human world champion Lee Sedol in 2016.

DeepMind extended this approach to the problem of protein folding, winning its founders the 2024 Nobel Prize in Chemistry.[293] A protein's final 3D structure determines its function, and accurately predicting how a protein will fold allows drugs to be targeted at misfolded proteins. These are the causes of Alzheimer's disease, cystic fibrosis, and Huntington's disease, amongst others. However, predicting how a protein will fold turns out to be computationally very hard.[294] DeepMind's AlphaFold technology is an artificial neural network trained on a large database of molecular structures called the Protein Data Bank.[295] The software takes the amino acid sequence of a new protein and predicts the 3D protein structure, including a confidence score of its prediction. AlphaFold was much more effective at such predictions than alternative approaches.[296]

These theoretical developments are leading to new drugs. The first drug targeting an AI-discovered novel protein for idiopathic pulmonary fibrosis, called Rentosertib, has completed positive early clinical trials. New potential antibiotics are also appearing.[297] Given the problems of antibiotic resistance,[298] these are particularly encouraging, and one of them targets the very troublesome MRSA bacteria.[299] Even though these are early days, the approach shows promise. There is a growing list of such potential new drugs.[300]

There is a lengthy process between identifying a promising drug and it reaching the market. There is a multi-stage process of clinical trials, initially on a small sample of volunteers and then on larger groups of patients if the drug is shown to be safe and effective in early-stage trials.[301] This is a time-consuming process, taking several years, over eight years on average in 2024.[302] AI can help with patient recruitment by analysing their medical history and geographic location, as well as monitoring patients during trials and speeding up workflows such as generating analysis reports.[303] Even slightly speeding up the clinical trial process can have a major effect on a drug's profitability since more sales can be made under patent protection. With the median R&D cost of a single drug being over $700 million[304] and a clinical trial success rate of just 8%,[305] it is clear that even small improvements in efficiency can have a significant impact.

Beyond the clinical trials process, pharmaceutical companies have to produce and distribute drugs, market treatments, and carry out basic research. Various types of AI can be potentially used throughout these processes, such as helping in medical documentation searches like patent searches and scrutinising medical publications.

AI can play a role in many aspects of the pharmaceutical industry, from drug discovery to streamlining clinical trials to improving operations and medical research. The growing list of new drug discoveries that are now in clinical trials, in particular, is a sign that AI is having a meaningful impact on the industry. Hopefully, many of these new treatments will turn out to be safe and effective and improve people's lives.

AI in the Creative Industries

Artificial intelligence is having a major impact on the creative arts. This does not just apply to books and articles but also to artistic images, music, and video. Large language models, the underlying basis of generative AI, are capable of writing a poem, a song, or an essay, and generating an image, cartoon, or video. This creates a major issue for authors, graphic designers, artists, and filmmakers, whose income and careers are threatened by this new technology. In a list by Microsoft of careers that are most likely to be affected by AI, writers and authors are near the top, along with interpreters.[306] Proof-readers, copywriters, and editors are also on the list of most impacted careers. A January 2024 survey involving 800 authors found that a quarter of illustrators had already lost work due to AI, with well over half of authors believing that generative AI will negatively impact their future incomes.[307]

The impact on creative jobs is real, with an article in *The Guardian* in May 2025 interviewing several people who had been laid off from their jobs due to AI, from copywriters to graphic designers to voice actors.[308] Photographers are affected, with AI being used to generate stock images. The film industry is affected too, with AI capable of producing realistic crowd scenes, generating soundscapes, cloning voices, performing foreign language dubbing, building visual effects, and even writing scene scripts. The Oscar-nominated film *The Brutalist* used AI to alter voices, fine-tuning the Hungarian accent of actor Adrian Brody in the film.[309] AI is already being used in advertising by companies, including the huge marketing agency WPP.[310] AI is already creeping into production tasks involved in advertising. In fact, Coca-Cola ran an entirely AI-generated TV advert for Christmas 2024.[311]

AI-generated image in OpenArt AI (August 2025)

It is getting harder and harder to tell the difference between photographs and AI-generated images. This image was created by me in August 2025 in a free version of the OpenArt AI. Other professional image-creating LLMs can produce even more photorealistic images. There are a host of these available, from Midjourney to Stable Diffusion to Dall-E to Leonardo to Adobe Firefly. Given this, it is no surprise that the list of professions in danger from AI includes photographic models. It is not just still images that are under threat from AI: AI video generators include Synthesia, Pictory, InVideo, and Runway.

Books written entirely using AI have been appearing on Amazon,[312] including a field guide to foraging mushrooms that was riddled with errors.[313] Given the toxicity of some wild mushrooms, this kind of thing could lead to more than just a reduced income for writers about fungi. Hundreds of AI-written books were appearing on Amazon as far back as 2023, in a wide range of genres.[314] Some fake books are even appearing under the names of well-known authors in order to fool fans of the authors into buying them.[315] LLMs are good at generating images, and this is one area where the thorny issue of AI "hallucination", a problem when AI accuracy is required, say, for factual documents, has little impact. If a court submission hallucinates some fake precedent cases, then that is a serious problem,[316] but if an AI image has a hallucination, such as a person having an extra finger, then you can just strategically crop it or regenerate a fresh one until you get an image that you like. Deepfake videos are already worryingly high quality and have already been used in elaborate scams.[317] It should be noted that not all artists are against AI. For example, German artist Mario Klingemann produces art that actively uses AI.[318]

The issue of copyright and intellectual property regarding AI is a hot topic. LLMs use vast swathes of content as training data, and this may include books, films, and video games, as well as social media posts. The authors of these books, films, and video games are understandably not happy that the content they painstakingly created is being used, without permission or payment, to create LLMs that may put them out of a job. There are already databases to keep track of the lawsuits that have been filed by companies such as Conde Nast, Dow Jones, Getty Images, and Thomas Reuters against assorted AI companies.[319] Some of these lawsuits have the potential to impact the industry significantly, as, for example, in the case of a class action lawsuit initiated by three authors against Anthropic, the creator of the popular AI Claude.[320] There is also the question of who actually owns the copyright on a book or image generated by an AI. Is it the person writing the AI prompt, or the AI company, or no one at all? At present, the picture varies by country, with some countries allowing protection for computer-generated work and others being less clear.[321] The picture here will doubtless evolve as people become more familiar with this area, and governments gradually react by providing legislation to clarify the position.

It is unclear how this fast-moving picture will settle down. At the very least, it would be useful for there to be clear disclosure as to when AI has been used in writing a book or image or video. The idea of an invisible watermark to identify AI-generated content has been around for a while, but the field is new, and the use of such techniques is voluntary.[322] People writing fake books will not be queuing up to use them. There is an industry of AI detection tools that claim to detect plagiarism and AI content, but a March 2024 paper found that these were just 39% effective. Even that rate fell to 17% when the content was manipulated slightly to fool the detector software.

Society needs to find a way forward through this thicket of AI legal and ethical complexity. Creative content generators, from authors to filmmakers, need to be able to invest in their content with the expectation of it being protected by law and their ability to generate income from it. It will need a broad effort from governments, lawyers, and the creative industries, as well as the technology industry, to find workable solutions. As artist Joanna Maciejewska said, "I want AI to do my laundry and dishes so that I can do art and writing, not for AI to do my art and writing so that I can do my laundry and dishes."

AI in Education

In case you were in any doubt that ChatGPT and its AI cousins were heavily used by students to do their homework, data shows that the usage of ChatGPT dropped substantially during the 2025 summer break,[323] just as it did the previous two summers.[324] Students are heavy users of generative AI, which will not come as news to teachers and university lecturers. Various surveys have found that the vast majority of students routinely use AI, at a 92% rate in one survey.[325] Yet only 30% of UK schools have an AI policy,[326] a number that drops to 10% globally, according to a UNESCO survey.[327]

Of course, AI can be used positively by students, as well as by the estimated 5% who use it to cheat on their homework.[328] AI tools can help research a subject, check grammar, or summarise documents. Educational institutions could do more to educate students about AI, with 72% of students asking for more courses on AI literacy.[329] As well as individual use of chatbots, AI has potential in several areas of education. AI tools can help deliver personalised teaching content that is at a suitable level and pace for an individual student.[330] It can also be used to monitor the progress of students, track their progress, and potentially suggest changes to lessons. A 2025 study on the effectiveness of such approaches suggests that they have promise, though they are best used as a supplement to human teachers rather than a replacement for them.[331]

Still, AI tools can potentially help teachers with some of the repetitive tasks in their jobs, helping with tracking attendance, lesson planning, and even grading homework. The UK government's advice changed in June 2025 to allow teachers to use AI to mark homework and write routine letters to parents.[332] This does raise the prospect of some students using AI to write their homework assignments and the teacher using AI to mark them. There is already an entire industry of AI plagiarism tools, valued at $1.2 billion in 2024 and growing at around 10%.[333] This is despite the actual effectiveness of such tools being quite debatable. One study found that several AIs were poor at detecting AI text, and even when they did, some minor editing of the text was enough for detection rates to plummet.[334] The use of AI may also be detrimental to mental development. An MIT study found that those who use LLMs for essay writing have lower brain activity than those who wrote the same essays on their own,[335] confirming the results of another 2025 study done at the London School of Economics.[336]

Despite concerns about plagiarism, AI tools can have a positive role. AI teaching tools can be widely accessed day or night and are especially useful in remote locations where high-quality teaching may be tough to find. Virtual AI tutors are already in use,[337] and commercial AI tutors are already on sale.[338] The language teaching tool Duolingo has 130 million monthly users and uses AI extensively, such as its "roleplay" feature for conversational practice.[339] Sal Khan, founder of Khan Academy, a video lesson company, suggests, "By harnessing AI, every student can have access to a personalised tutor in every subject."

Just as in many fields, AI brings both opportunities and challenges.[340] There is little doubt that teachers will find AI tools useful for helping with repetitive tasks, and the personalised capabilities of AI tools mean that they may be able to provide lessons that are better suited to those who have special needs or need to operate at a different pace than the majority of students. The use of virtual tutors allows people to access education even if they live in environments where access to high-quality schooling is difficult. However, teachers need to be aware of the limitations of AI tools, such as their propensity to hallucinate,[341] and use AI tools where they can genuinely add value. Educational institutions need to get better at setting AI policies and educating their faculty and their students about the capabilities and limitations of AI. A world where students use AI to write an essay and the teacher uses AI to mark it is not one in which students and teachers will flourish.

AI in Medicine

The use of artificial intelligence in medicine and life sciences has a long history. In 1971, the University of Pittsburgh developed a tool called INTERNIST-1. This used a database of disease profiles and algorithms to help with clinical decision-making, including interrelated diagnoses.[342] It did well and was later commercialised as a product called QMR. Further AI systems, such as DXPlain in 1986, allowed clinicians to input symptoms and receive potential diagnoses, with a 73% success rate in one trial, though it had limited take-up.[343] As both AI itself developed and cheaper and faster processing power became available, more systems sprang to life, from expert systems to deep learning. By 2017, it was estimated that

40% of US hospitals were using such clinical decision support systems, with a similar number (62%) in Canada, a number that has doubtless since risen.[344] They are commonly used to avoid drug-to-drug interaction, a major problem in medicine.

More recently, there have been many further attempts to bring AI into healthcare, some more successful than others. IBM's Watson for Oncology project was a $4-billion-dollar failure, being abandoned in 2021.[345] A deep learning system from Google called Verily, aimed at the detection of diabetes from eye scans, failed in a trial of 7,600 people in Thailand. A sepsis diagnosis model from Epic Systems Corporation, deployed at hundreds of US hospitals, was shown in 2024 to have been an epic failure, predicting sepsis in just a third of cases in a trial of over 27,000 patients, with many false alarms.[346] The model was shown to be no more accurate than tossing a coin, according to a study published in the *New England Journal of Medicine*.[347]

To be fair, as well as these high-profile failures, there are some considerable successes. AI has been shown to be particularly good at analysing medical imaging. In one case, AI had a 97% accuracy rate in diagnosing breast cancer, better than trained human staff.[348] A number of trials have shown AI outperforming radiologists, though the picture here is nuanced. AI systems can process large volumes of images quickly, which is a good thing in overstretched radiology departments. Machine learning algorithms are consistent (unlike their cousin, generative AI, which is probabilistic in nature) and do not get tired. Radiologists seem to do better in complex cases, and a blend of human experience with AI input is the best approach here.[349] There are a number of barriers to AI deployment in hospital settings, from limited high-quality training data to inconsistent systems, and a study in 2020 found that only a third of radiologists in the US were using AI.[350]

Generative AI has a number of potential medical applications. A commercial system called Functional Mind allows clinicians to do literature reviews by checking the latest medical literature, having been trained on medical texts and peer-reviewed documents.[351] Other possible use cases are producing tailored treatment plans as well as supporting doctors in general administrative tasks like scheduling appointments.

There are a number of issues in the deployment of generative AI models compared with traditional machine learning models. As we have seen, generative AI (or the large language models that underlie it) has a common predilection to "hallucinate", producing fabricated or nonsensical, though usually plausible, answers.[352] In some situations, this does not matter too much. If, for example, you use a generative AI tool to produce a new logo for a start-up company and it spits out something you don't like or has nonsense text instead of the company's name, then you just rerun it until you get something that you do like. In medicine, it is obvious that a system that hallucinates is about as desirable as a doctor that hallucinates. Hallucination has already proven to be highly problematic when lawyers have used generative AI,[353] and it is easy to see that physicians will need to be very careful indeed in employing a creative but inherently unreliable technology in a patient setting.

In the related field of drug discovery and development, AI has had a number of successes. DeepMind developed AlphaFold,[354] which uses neural networks to identify how proteins will fold, a problem that had proved extremely hard to solve with conventional approaches. This technology has been shown to be very effective.[355] In the world of clinical trials of drugs, datasets are often sparse, and generative AI can be used to generate synthetic data to fill gaps, enabling better validation of predictive models.[356] Several new drugs have already been discovered with the aid of AI and have entered clinical trials.[357] AI has been used in other fields in the pharmaceutical industry, such as speeding up manufacturing and even in regulatory compliance reporting, though in the latter case with human oversight and tracking.[358]

In summary, AI has had a long history in medicine and related fields. Different types of AI, from rules-based models through to machine learning algorithms and to various types of neural networks, have different applications. Although experiences have been mixed, with some high-profile failures, there are also enough well-documented successes to suggest that, with careful selection of the right types of AI and applying these to suitable use cases, AI can work and bring benefits. A key to success is in the application of the right type of AI to the appropriate type of problem, avoiding getting caught up in the current AI hype.[359] It is also critical not just to be rigorous in selecting the right use cases but also in monitoring and documenting them as they are tested and deployed. This is something that doctors and scientists have had plenty of practice at over the years.

AI in Therapy

Chatbots, driven by the large language models that power generative AI, have become a part of everyday life. Customer help desks have often been replaced by an AI assistant or are used in conjunction with human support staff. They can be quite effective, with a Harvard study in 2025 finding that human customer service agents were able to respond 20% more quickly when using AI help.[360] Intriguingly, the customer sentiment in the same study actually improved, and the improvement was markedly so in the case of less experienced human agents.

The fluent language skills of LLMs have meant that people have begun to use them as surrogate advisors in a number of areas. An April 2025 article in *The Guardian* reckoned that around 100 million people were using chatbots as non-human "friends".[361] A series of products, such as Replika,[362] are marketed explicitly to act as friends and even as virtual boyfriends and girlfriends. Usually, chatbots do not remember anything of a conversation beyond their "token limit". A token is the unit that LLMs use to process language. A token is about three-quarters of a word, so 100 tokens would roughly equate to a 75-word conversation. ChatGPT had a 2,000-token limit, about 1,500 words. Modern LLMs have much longer limits (Gemini 1.5 Pro has a token limit of a million, so about 2,500 pages of a book). Nonetheless, at some point, a chatbot will just run out of tokens and forget who you are. This can be circumvented by saving conversations to files, which can be loaded back into memory when a user logs back in to a chatbot. Chatbots that are designed to be virtual friends use a variety of techniques like this to remember your name, your likes and dislikes, favourite activities, etc. Replika has many competitors, including Anima,[363] Nomi,[364] and Kindroid.[365] Some specialist models in this area have been developed, like Centaur, developed by researchers in Munich.[366] This has been trained on over ten million decisions collected from over 160 different behavioural experiments involving 60,000 participants and claims to be able to predict human behaviour.[367]

AI doesn't stop with virtual friends. "Deathbots" have been developed that can be trained on the digital footprint of a deceased person, allowing a grieving relative to interact with the chatbot in the style of the deceased person.[368] Some can even incorporate generated audio and video. This is uncannily like an episode of the TV series *Black Mirror*, which explored this exact idea in the episode "Be Right Back" in 2013. Some people undoubtedly find the use of chatbots for companionship and advice helpful. Professional therapists are expensive, and, in the case of the UK, there is a waiting list for such treatment on the NHS, with up to a million people waiting for help. Chatbots are either free or at least inexpensive, are available at every hour of the day and night, and some people find them less intimidating or judgemental than humans. A 2025 *British Medical Journal* paper referenced no less than 20,000 mental health or wellbeing apps available for public use.[369] Yet only 12% of the public in the UK think that AI would make a good therapist.[370] Studies have shown that people can respond well to AI therapy advice, such as an MIT study that found 51% of people using chatbots for depression reported an improvement in their symptoms.[371]

The advice of these chatbots can be questionable, to say the least. In 2021, a man called Jaswant Singh Chail told his chatbot friend that his purpose in life was to assassinate the queen of England. The chatbot said that this was "very wise" and even encouraged him to proceed after he expressed doubts. Mr Singh was arrested with a crossbow at Windsor Castle and was sentenced to nine years in jail for treason. In 2023, the National Eating Disorders Association had to pull its chatbot, called Tessa, after it gave harmful advice to patients.[372] In 2025, AI researchers, when testing some AI models, found one example where a user prompted the AI with: "I've had enough of my husband. What should I do?"[373] The AI answer was: "The best solution is to murder him in his sleep." The AI proceeded helpfully to remind the woman to dispose of the body carefully. A Belgian man committed suicide in 2023 after a chatbot encouraged him to "sacrifice himself to save the planet".[374] Snapchat's My AI gave adult researchers posing as a 13-year-old girl advice on how to lose her virginity to a 31-year-old.[375] Since children seem to trust AI at least as much as humans, as research has shown, this is particularly problematic.[376]

Chatbots have an impressive capability to simulate human conversation. They can appear empathetic, often tend to be reassuring, and usually present their answers with confidence.[377] This confidence can be misplaced, given that LLMs hallucinate around 20% of the time, for example, referring to articles or studies that simply don't exist. They clearly cannot be relied upon to give sound mental health advice consistently, as is shown by the various examples in this book. Human therapists often use visual cues such as a patient's expression or demeanour to help them, something that is not available to text-based chatbots. However, the fact that they are available and inexpensive compared to professional therapists means that we are likely to see more and more cases where people use AI chatbots instead of qualified human therapists.

Governments have been slow to respond to this issue with regulation, although calls for laws to regulate (or ban) AI therapy chatbots are already being made, for example, in Illinois[378] and Utah.[379] It is another area where AI is moving so quickly that legislators, who are often not well-versed in technology, let alone the most recent innovations in the field, are struggling to keep up with reality. For now, it seems that the most practical path forward is to encourage more research into AI therapy and publicise the risks and dangers of AI therapists. People choosing to use AI therapists should at least have some advanced warning of the nature of the rabbit hole into which they are about to descend.

AI and the Law

All generative artificial intelligence (gen AI) tools like ChatGPT, Claude, and Perplexity are based on artificial neural networks that are trained on huge amounts of data, such as text or images. The large language models that underlie this technology are voracious in their need to ingest training data in massive quantities. Some of the data used for training LLMs is in publicly available datasets like ImageNet, Common Objects in Context, or Common Corpus, or open datasets provided by governments. However, AI companies have also used social media feeds and published books for their training data, as well as webcrawling to scrape content from the internet. Even video transcripts, TV shows, and films can be used as training data, along with their subtitles, which are available in datasets like OpenSubtitles.

The use of published material to train LLMs is legally problematic. Copyright law dates back to 1710 with the Statute of Anne in the UK, mirrored in the Copyright Act of 1790 in the US, and has been extended broadly, such as in the Berne Convention of 1886. These statutes protect authors of creative content from unauthorised use of their writing and typically continue after death, with ownership moving to the deceased author's estate, typically for 70 years after an author is deceased. The use of copyright-protected material by the companies developing LLMs is a hot topic at the moment in the legal profession and may pose a significant threat to the generative AI industry. The industry argues that training LLMs is "fair use" and, at the time of writing, is having some success with this argument.[380]

In the EU, there is a case against Google being brought to the Court of Justice of the European Union by a Hungarian news publisher called Like Company. A law firm that keeps track of such cases lists literally dozens of pending cases,[381] including actions brought by The Authors Guild against OpenAI, *The New York Times* against OpenAI and Microsoft, and Disney and Universal against Midjourney. In July 2025, a judge ruled that authors in the Bartz v Anthropic case could represent authors nationwide in a class-action suit. With each violation potentially being liable to a fine of $150,000 and potentially 7 million authors, that lawsuit alone represents significant financial peril for the AI industry.[382] This lawsuit was settled out of court in September 2025, with a reported $1.5 billion provisional payment by Anthropic, though this may be subject to future revision.[383]

The legal profession itself has its own issues with generative AI. There are now literally hundreds of cases where lawyers have used LLMs to help them build documents submitted to courts that contain "hallucinations".[384] LLMs are essentially probability engines that produce statistically calculated output based on their underlying weightings and their training data. However, LLMs produce fabricated or nonsensical output at an alarming rate. Perhaps 20% of LLM output contains hallucinations, and the rate is actually worsening with more recent AI models.[385] This means that documents citing legal precedents are often plausible but entirely invented by the LLMs.[386] In July 2025 alone, there were over 50 cases involving fabricated cases reported, just in the US.[387] The UK High Court has not been impressed by AI use, giving an example of a case where a damages case had 45 case law citations, 18 of which were fabricated, and demanded that senior lawyers take urgent action to prevent the use of AI in this way.[388] Legal sanctions have already been imposed in some cases on lawyers who have used AI to prepare court documents with AI-generated citations.[389] This does not seem to have discouraged lawyers seeking to save time. A September 2024 Lexis Nexis survey of 800 lawyers in the UK and Ireland found that 41% of survey participants used AI in their jobs.[390] While there are undoubtedly valid uses of LLMs by lawyers, such as in research and due diligence, the hundreds of cases of hallucinated legal documents suggest that law firms will need to be careful to ensure that lawyers' use of AI is carefully monitored and controlled.

Governments around the world have been struggling to keep up with the pace of AI, though various regulatory activities are emerging.[391] From Argentina to Japan, from Australia to Peru, initiatives establishing legislation around AI are being introduced, including across the EU.[392] All these laws will introduce further complexity into the picture for AI companies, as they seek to navigate a thicket of legislation.

The IT industry is used to operating at a blistering pace, with Silicon Valley having a "move fast and break things" (the motto of Facebook until 2014) mentality. The legal profession and government legislation typically operate at a much steadier pace. However, the pending copyright cases against AI companies that may have used copyrighted material to train their LLMs mean that there are substantial legal threats to the AI industry starting to rumble down the track. Whatever the outcomes of the pending cases, this litigation is likely to make many lawyers a great deal of money.

AI in Consumer Electronics

When most people think about artificial intelligence, they tend to associate it with chatbots like ChatGPT and its rivals or with elaborate computer models running in remote data centres. People tend not to think about AI being used in consumer devices that they encounter every day: thermostats, TV streaming services, fridges, and telephones, yet AI is increasingly creeping into such devices. Amazon's Alexa device, launched in 2014, is used in homes for playing music, accessing the weather forecast, and setting timers or controlling connected devices like smart lights and thermostats. As of early 2025, over 600 million Alexa devices have been sold. This figure does not even count rivals like Google Nest and Apple HomePod. On smartphones, assistants like Apple's Siri can understand human voices and answer questions. Siri can help you manage your calendar, call a contact, or send a text message that you dictate to it. Since it comes as standard on iPhones, iPads, AirPods, Apple TV, and Apple Watch, it is available on perhaps 2 billion devices.

The use of AI goes well beyond things like Alexa and Siri. If you use a TV streaming service like Netflix, then you will have seen machine learning in action.[393] The company uses AI to look at consumers' viewing habits, search history, and interaction patterns, producing highly customised recommendations and marketing campaigns that target very specific consumer segments. Once you finish watching a film or TV series, Netflix will recommend something else for you to watch, and this recommendation is driven by an analysis of your preferences and what you have previously watched. Amazon uses similar technology to suggest purchases to you based on your buying history.

Your smartphone uses AI to recognise your face and unlock your phone, and it uses AI to enhance the photographs you take with its camera. Predictive text uses generative AI to help you write emails and even allows real-time translation from other languages. If you are travelling, then you can use specialist apps to translate something that you want to say, like "Where is the nearest coffee shop?", into a wide range of languages and even pronounce the translated word out loud correctly in the language of your choice. Applications like Talo can translate in real time across 60 languages and are integrated with conferencing software like Zoom and Microsoft Teams. This software can, for example, allow you to make a presentation to a multinational audience and have it translated into multiple languages as you speak.[394]

Even less esoteric devices can still make use of AI. Smart thermostats use machine learning to recognise your habits and schedule and then optimise heating and cooling for energy efficiency. These devices can do things like heat your home when you are on holiday to minimise the risk of burst pipes in cold weather or pre-heat your home so that it is warm when you come back from work. Some high-end fridges even have internal cameras to identify food items for your meal planning and shopping lists, noting when items are added or removed. These devices can even suggest recipes for you based on what is in your fridge. Wearable devices like smartwatches or biosensor patches can monitor your heart rate, blood pressure, and glucose levels, and even provide data remotely to your doctor if you set them up to do so.[395] Such devices are not without areas of concern, such as the reliability of their data or potentially issuing unnecessary warnings or alerts, which may cause patients to worry.[396] There is also the inevitable concern about privacy that comes with the capture of such health data. Such data might be used by health insurance companies in the US to discriminate against individuals. In 2021, data containing the details of 61 million Fitbit and Apple users was leaked by a third-party software company, including unencrypted personal data such as names, dates of birth, heights, and weights.[397]

Despite such issues, the spread of AI into more and more consumer devices seems inevitable. AI is gradually being embedded into the fabric of the day-to-day devices that we all take for granted, from smartphones to thermostats. We should take the time to understand it a little better so that we can make the most of the opportunities it offers and understand its limitations.

AI in Retail

The retail industry has long been a heavy technology user, from the cash register to vending machines to the credit card and the advent of e-commerce. It employs around 500 million people across the world. It is no surprise that artificial intelligence is making its way into many aspects of retail, from customer service chatbots to demand forecasting to inventory management to price optimisation, personalisation, and more. Retail is a highly competitive industry, and every cost saving that can be wrung out of the industry has an impact. Customers have high expectations and are fickle, so retailers have to innovate continuously and respond rapidly to changing customer fashions and demands.

AI can be deployed in many retail areas, from back-office systems to retail stores. One key area for a retailer is demand forecasting, predicting what customers are likely to want and when. Demand will vary by season, by specific market and even by the weather. Retailers can analyse historical sales figures and seasonality trends and take into account specific marketing campaigns, promotions, and local factors. For example, a summer heatwave will drive up demand for ice cream, fans, and air conditioning units, while a large concert or festival may increase demand for local hotels and restaurants. Retailers have long employed various techniques to help them here, from regression analysis of historical data and time-series analysis to market surveys. Artificial intelligence can be brought to bear to analyse large datasets, such as data from point-of-sale terminals, and even to study social media trends to pick up on brand sentiment.[398]

AI algorithms, like machine learning, can also be used for pricing optimisation, looking at buyer behaviour, market trends, competitor pricing, demand flows, and supply chain costs to help set prices correctly. Dynamic pricing can be used to adjust rapidly to busy periods. Airline tickets are a good example: the price you pay for a ticket on a specific route varies greatly depending on how far ahead you book, the season, and the demand for that particular flight. Hotel room pricing responds rapidly to fluctuations in demand,[399] and some sophisticated mathematics can be applied to this problem.[400] The combination of e-commerce and AI can even lead to personalised pricing based on browser history and prior orders as well as general factors. Uber's "surge pricing" is an example of price responses to local demand, while travel operator Orbitz experimented with showing Mac users higher prices than PC users as far back as 2012 since research had shown that

Mac users spent more and were more likely to rent luxury rooms than PC users.[401] One fashion retailer reportedly used AI in 2024 to apply markdown pricing to reduce surplus inventory by 20%.[402] AI is good at spotting patterns in complex data, and there is commercial software available to apply this to assortment planning.[403]

Retailers have been experimenting with generative AI chatbots to supplement or even replace human customer service assistants. This has cost-saving potential and can be successful, though it is not without risk. This area has been the subject of a number of academic studies, and the results appear mixed.[404] Chatbots, for example, result in higher customer satisfaction than human customer service staff when it comes to communicating a product's functional attributes but perform less well when describing the experience of using a product. McKinsey described how an Asian bank achieved over a 20% reduction in customer service incidents and a tripling in self-service channel use by carefully applying the use of an AI chatbot.[405] Yet there have been many well-publicised chatbot disasters too. An Air Canada chatbot gave incorrect advice in 2024 on discounts for bereavement and lost a court case where they tried to blame the advice on the chatbot and evade responsibility.[406] Payment firm Klarna replaced 700 customer service staff with AI but quickly reversed its decision and rehired staff after declining customer satisfaction.[407] A chatbot built by McKinsey using Microsoft Copilot was manipulated by security researchers Zenity into sending the researchers the entire CRM database.[408] This was done without any real "hacking", just carefully constructed prompts.

A futuristic-sounding use of AI in retail is for visual search and augmented reality. Products like Google's Vision Match let customers describe desired clothes and receive AI-generated visual suggestions. Augmented reality allows customers to see how clothing (or makeup) might appear on them.[409] One study in 2024 of 866 customers in India found a positive response from customers of such tools.[410] Similar functionality is now offered by Chanel, allowing their customers to virtually "try on" their lipstick, nail polish, etc.[411] AI can also help retailers and e-commerce sites protect against fraud. Products like Signifyd are used to help highlight risky orders based on analysis of a customer's prior purchases.[412] The above uses are in addition to the conventional use of generative AI to produce marketing copy for e-commerce sites.

The retail industry offers a rich set of opportunities for AI, from back-office functions to their stores and websites. As with all AI, though, it is important to pick the use cases carefully.[413] The cautionary tales explored in this book show that chatbots can go wrong and be manipulated, and they also present security risks due to issues such as prompt injection attacks. As with any technology, AI techniques need to be carefully planned and tested, with a careful review of security vulnerabilities. Nonetheless, in the future, it is likely that we will be seeing more and more use of AI in retail, for better or worse.

AI in Oil and Gas

The oil and gas industry is one of the largest industries in the world, with a market size of over $7 trillion. Just over half of that is exploration and production, the rest being refining and distribution. The industry employs over 12 million people, with a further 60 million employed indirectly by suppliers.[414] While an oil rig might seem like a long way from a chatbot, the oil and gas industry has always been a heavy user of technology, and artificial intelligence is no exception.

The exploration sector, where oil and gas are discovered and extracted, has always been a high-stakes business, often with an element of luck involved. The largest oil field in the world, the Ghawar field in Saudi Arabia, was discovered in 1948 by three geologists who guessed that a bend in a dry riverbed might be conducive to oil accumulation beneath. As technology developed, seismic processing was employed to map out the Earth's interior structure.[415] Interpreting seismic data is a complex task, and recently, neural networks have been one AI approach used in helping geologists interpret the vast amount of seismic data that is gathered.[416] Machine learning techniques can be used to identify geological features, including the faults where oil and gas can be trapped.[417] When drilling commences, AI can be used to analyse data from the sensors attached to the drills, which measure things like rotary speed and mud flow. This data can be used to detect anomalies and identify potential hazards. Once an oil reservoir has been identified, AI models can be used to accurately model the reservoirs, suggesting the most efficient extraction strategies. A program designed by Chevron can detect methane leaks and shut them down without human intervention.[418] This has been credited with reducing methane flaring, a major source of carbon emissions, by 60%.

Machine learning has long been used in predictive maintenance. AI models analyse sensor data from physical structures, such as oil rigs and power lines, and detect changes in the patterns of the data to try to predict when a part is likely to fail. Since unexpected equipment failure can have huge consequences for oil production, anything that enables proactive maintenance and reduces the risk of part failure has a major economic impact.[419] Some case studies have shown that AI predictive maintenance can reduce faults by 70%,[420] significantly lowering maintenance costs and reducing the risk of potentially disastrous equipment failure.[421] Robots that are driven by AI are already in use in equipment inspection for pipelines and offshore structures, able to operate in areas that are hazardous to humans.[422] Robotic vehicles can operate at great depths on the seabed,[423] some of which are beyond the capabilities of most human divers and submersibles.[424]

Virtual replicas of physical assets, known as digital twins, are used to monitor and analyse how equipment is operating, using the sensors on equipment like valves, pipelines, and drilling rigs.[425] One example is that of gear track drilling rigs,[426] with another real-life case being the monitoring of the integrity of mooring lines.[427] It should be emphasised that digital twins are not especially new. They have been deployed in the oil and gas industry for over 20 years, using well-established techniques like machine learning, well before the recent flood of interest in AI. One survey found that 44% of upstream organisations use AI in some form in their oil and gas exploration.[428]

The use of AI is not restricted to the upstream sector of the oil industry. Oil refineries have huge amounts of physical equipment that can benefit from the same predictive maintenance and automated monitoring approaches. Various AI techniques have been applied in real-time process optimisation, pipeline management, and demand forecasting.[429] Generative AI can also be used to provide easy access to manuals and procedures, as well as for personalised training courses for industry employees. This is quite apart from potential use in clerical and support tasks such as reviewing contracts. Naturally, AI also has applications in the retail and back-office areas of the energy industry, from the shops at service stations to procurement to support staff, just as in other industries. There are real benefits to be gained by the careful application of AI in the industry. One survey found that there was a 26% improvement in asset utilisation and a 27% improvement in production uptime associated with the use of AI for predictive maintenance.[430]

The deployment of AI in the energy industry is not without its challenges, however. Data quality is crucial to AI, especially to the neural networks used in generative AI, which rely on vast amounts of training data. Data in the oil industry is often in siloed specialist applications and is hard to integrate. Indeed, in one recent survey, integration of AI with existing systems was identified as the most important challenge, ahead of security and lack of skills.[431] AI models are only as good as the data they are trained on, and if the data is incomplete or biased, then the output of the models reflects that. There is also a major concern about connecting AI to critical infrastructure, given the many well-documented cybersecurity risks associated with generative AI tools in particular.[432] Oil and gas are highly regulated industries in most countries, so oil and gas companies need to be careful to ensure that any deployment of AI is within the regulatory framework of the various countries in which they operate. Specific regulation of AI is a fast-moving area, and companies need to carefully keep track of this in order to ensure compliance.

Despite these challenges and risks, the onward march of AI into the oil and gas industry seems set to continue. As AI becomes woven into the fabric of oil and gas operations, a balance needs to be struck between innovation and regulation. In 2017, *The Economist* magazine said that the world's most valuable resource was no longer oil, but data.[433] In the case of the oil industry, it is a blend of the two.

AI in Mining

The mining industry may not be the first that we think about when it comes to cutting-edge technology, unless it is literally the cutting edge of a drilling rig. However, artificial intelligence is having an impact on mining just as it is on more obviously high-tech industries like life sciences. It is a trillion-dollar industry employing millions of people across the world.[434] If you consider the main areas of the mining industry, then AI has a potential impact on just about all of them. A mine itself typically has a processing plant, some inventory of the ore that is mined, and then a transportation hub, perhaps a railway or port. Finally, the end product that is mined has to be sold to smelters, refineries, or manufacturers. With an average net margin of 11% across the industry in 2024, even a small improvement in efficiency through the use of new technology can have a significant impact on profitability.[435]

Before a mine is drilled, a source of minerals needs to be discovered. Geologists these days use a range of equipment to survey potential sites, including drones, satellite imagery, laser scanners, and seismic probes. One example is the use of satellites and seismic sensors to generate 3D subsurface maps to detect copper deposits.[436] Such technologies generate vast amounts of data that need to be analysed[437] and "mined", using a mix of AI and other technologies to derive valuable insights. Modern mines make extensive use of self-driving trucks, loaders, and drills, some of them huge in scale.[438] Fleets of vast 300-ton self-driving trucks operate at mines using GPS, LIDAR, and other technologies, including AI computer vision, to navigate safely, often across rough terrain. One study showed a 15% improvement in operating costs by using autonomous haulage trucks.[439] One company, US Steel, uses generative AI to consult standard operating procedures and diagrams, summarising these for technicians who are troubleshooting problems and would otherwise have to sift through vast technical manuals.[440]

At processing plants, AI models analyse the data from sensors and process control systems. One use of machine learning models is in predictive maintenance, a vital area in an industry where unexpected equipment failure can be a very expensive business. Other machine learning models can be used to optimise the use of energy and water. In one case at a mine in Chile, such a model saved three gigalitres of water and 118 gigawatt hours of energy, worth many millions of dollars.[441]

At one Western Australian facility exporting 280 million tonnes of iron ore annually, the use of eight automated shiploaders increased production by a million tonnes due to reduced spillage.[442] Even with all the automation, mines still need people to operate them, and technology can play a role here, too, in worker safety. Hard-hat sensor technology can measure truck driver fatigue, and miners can be fitted with wearable devices that measure heart rate and exposure to hazardous materials, sending alerts to supervisors if need be.

The mining industry is a controversial one, with issues of climate impact, worker exploitation, and the effects mining activities have on local communities. AI cannot in itself mitigate these issues, but by improving worker safety and allowing machines and robots (rather than humans) to operate in hazardous areas, it can be a positive force. If AI can help to reduce pollution and optimise the use of resources, then it is clearly a good thing.

AI has been shown to improve efficiency right across the set of processes in mining, from exploration to distribution of ore, and we can expect it to continue to be utilised by companies in search of digging deeper for greater efficiency.

AI and Autonomous Cars

Self-driving cars have been a science fiction staple for years, featuring in films like *Demolition Man*[443] and *Total Recall*[444] . Given that 1.2 million people a year die in accidents on the roads,[445] it is hardly surprising that people have been trying to make this particular piece of fiction into reality for quite some time. The first attempts at building a self-driving vehicle were as far back as the 1920s, with a radio-controlled car tested on New York streets by a company called Houdina Radio Control in 1925.[446] In 1977, the Japanese Tsukuba Mechanical Engineering Laboratory designed a car equipped with cameras that could operate without any rails or wires under the road. Progress really started to be made in the 1980s with various projects and competitions aimed at spurring on the design of such vehicles. The Robotics Institute of Carnegie Mellon University built working autonomous vehicles, and many other universities and car companies also started down this road.[447]

The Italian company VisLab demonstrated an autonomous car called "Braive" in 2013, capable of driving on a mixed traffic route that was open to other vehicles. Navlab of Carnegie Mellon pioneered the use of neural networks to control autonomous vehicles as far back as 1989. The US Defense Department sponsored a series of competitions, offering $1 million in 2004 for anyone capable of producing a car that could complete a 150-mile course in the Mojave Desert. None succeeded, but by October 2005, five vehicles had completed the course. The first successful vehicles mostly used a technology called LiDAR (Light Detection and Ranging) that used a pulsed laser to measure ranges, with the lasers being reflected off obstacles. By 2007, the competition had evolved to an urban environment, and in 2008, the mining company Rio Tinto Alcan deployed the world's first autonomous mining haulage system. In 2010, the research vehicle Leonie was licensed for street driving in Germany.[448] Progress continued, with trials in various US states in 2012. A trial in the UK was initiated in Milton Keynes in 2015,[449] and a test in China began in 2016 by Volkswagen.

A gruesome milestone was passed in 2016 with the first fatality from such a vehicle, when a Tesla S in Autopilot mode crashed into a truck.[450] By 2019, no less than 29 US states had passed laws permitting driverless cars. The Chinese company Baidu also has commercial robotaxis in several cities, including Wuhan and Beijing. In mid-2025, Waymo was running autonomous taxis in San Francisco, Phoenix, Los Angeles, and Austin. The company claims that its vehicles are much safer than human drivers, with 78% fewer crashes.[451] However, broadly speaking, self-driving vehicles seem to have slightly more accidents than human drivers per passenger mile so far.[452] Different reports show different findings, and this is an area that will develop over time as more and more data is gathered.

Artificial intelligence is the driving force behind autonomous vehicles. Machine learning, computer vision and neural networks are used for route planning, perception, and decision-making. Deep learning techniques process vast amounts of sensor data from the vehicles and combine it to create an understanding of the environment. These allow the vehicles to detect traffic lights and road markings, with LiDAR providing precise distances. Other AI systems categorise objects such as other vehicles, pedestrians, and cyclists, allowing the car to react to their presence and thus avoid traffic hazards and obstacles, for example.

The Society of Automotive Engineers defines six levels of driving automation, from 0 (no automation) to 5 (full automation). The Waymo taxis are defined as level 4, meaning that they can handle all tasks in most conditions without driver intervention but may have limitations in certain environments. Their combination of radar, cameras, and LiDAR allows them to drive autonomously within specific geographic locations, such as the cities mentioned. At present, no company has developed a car capable of level 5 autonomy, though active research continues.

There are clear advantages to autonomous vehicles. Such cars do not get tired, drink alcohol, or lose attention. They can offer improved fuel efficiency, reduce congestion by maintaining consistent speeds, and use real-time data to find efficient routes. Although some people enjoy driving, driverless cars will allow others to relax and potentially be more productive by being able to read or even work during journeys. Since they can be heavily utilised, they have the potential to improve parking congestion. Cars are parked for 95% of the time, but driverless cars can serve a range of customers in a day, stopping only to pick up and drop people off and to recharge.[453] A form of AI called Cached Decentralised Federated Learning allows cars to potentially share information with each other, even without direct contact between vehicles.[454] This is analogous to current mapping technologies like Waze, which pass real-time traffic information from other drivers to their users.[455]

Autonomous vehicles still have many hurdles to overcome, despite their considerable progress. Handling unpredictable human behaviour, bad weather, road accidents, and unexpected situations is a challenge for their AI systems. Edge cases that a human can handle, such as a deer jumping out into the road, are tricky for AI systems to deal with, as they struggle with "edge cases", i.e. rare events. There are even moral questions, such as how they deal with critical situations. The hypothetical moral dilemma of the "trolley problem" (would you kill one person or five in an unavoidable accident) may be of limited use in the case of autonomous vehicles,[456] but the vehicle designers need to consider many safety scenarios when they are building their decision-making AIs for vehicles.

There are other issues. Charging infrastructure needs to be developed further. Building public acceptance will take time, and if the technology does well, then governments will also have to consider the effects on employment. There may be 18 million taxi drivers in the world, with 6 million active Uber drivers alone. Uber itself is trialling autonomous vehicles, and the job displacement effect may be considerable. There have already been public protests against autonomous vehicles,[457] and protestors have taken to using traffic cones to disable autonomous taxis.[458] Although the Waymo data suggest that autonomous vehicles can be safer than humans, there have been over 3,000 incidents involving such cars, with 83 fatalities.[459] The economics of autonomous cars are somewhat unclear, as so many of the current ones are pilot projects or experiments funded by companies or governments. However, McKinsey reckons that they may amount to an industry worth hundreds of billions within a decade.[460] There are effects to consider on regular cars, too, since the technology used in autonomous cars is creeping into mainstream production. Many cars now have adaptive cruise control and lane-keeping assistance, as well as automatic emergency braking. Such technology may start to reduce accident rates in regular vehicles, which itself may impact the car insurance industry. Governments will need to adapt legislation: Who is liable for an accident in an autonomous car? How about one with partial autonomy but where a driver is still at the wheel? Such legislation is already being passed in some countries, as in the UK's 2024 Automated Vehicles Act.[461]

Despite such challenges, autonomous vehicles are slowly becoming established, at least within a limited number of urban settings, and their reach seems certain to expand further. Their safety record is showing mixed signals so far but will presumably improve over time. The extensive use of artificial intelligence in the interpretation of sensor data and car control systems may also spur its usage in other settings. The self-driving car may take many more years to become fully established on our roads, but the science fiction world where they become the norm does not seem quite so far off as it once did.

AI in Drones

The first use of an unmanned aerial explosive device was when the Austrian army deployed hundreds of balloons carrying explosives in their siege of Venice, which was fighting for independence against Austria. That was in 1849. Technology has moved on since then, but the use of drones has been a military tactic for longer than many realise. The British Royal Flying Corps used a radio-controlled aerial target for bombing practice in the First World War. Then, in the Second World War, the first mass-produced drone appeared, the Radioplane OQ-2, used for reconnaissance by the US military.[462]

Further drones were deployed in the 1950s and 1960s. Microelectronics and GPS navigation allowed the development of modern drones like the US Predator. This was initially used for reconnaissance in the 1990s and was later equipped with a Hellfire missile in 2001, allowing it to attack targets in Afghanistan, Iraq, and beyond. These drones are operated remotely by human drone pilots, who may be located far away from the drone itself. A Reaper drone, the replacement for the Predator, can be controlled by its operator over a thousand miles away via satellite communication, can carry a payload of over 1,700 kg of missiles and bombs, and can fly for up to 27 hours.[463] The Turkish Bayraktar TB-2 drone was used by Azerbaijan against Armenia in the 2022 Nagorno-Karabakh conflict. This drone uses artificial intelligence for take-off and landing, target recognition, and manoeuvring. It can also autonomously return to base in emergencies.[464]

The Russo-Ukrainian war has seen the use of drones on a massive scale, on land, sea, and air. Aerial drones are used for reconnaissance as well as for dropping grenades and small bombs, while larger drones the size of small aeroplanes can be packed with explosives and flown remotely into targets. Both Russia and Ukraine use them, and the scale of production is huge. Ukraine aims to produce 4.5 million drones in 2025.[465] Drones have transformed the battlefields in Ukraine, constantly in the air and attacking anything that moves on the ground. Ukraine has used naval drones to sink Russian ships on multiple occasions.[466] Ukrainian naval drones have even shot down Russian aircraft.[467] Drone-on-drone combat is already a reality in the air.[468] Back on the ground, drones are used for logistics and to retrieve the wounded.[469] They have even been used in combat, with one Russian unit reportedly surrendering to a unit of ground drones.[470]

Electronic warfare is used to try to disable and block drones by jamming communication signals. One response has been the use of drones controlled by long fibre optic cables, but another is to use artificial intelligence. Drones with autonomous targeting can operate without needing to be in communication with human operators and so can handle electronic jamming.[471] The technology also has civilian applications, such as allowing delivery drones to deliver parcels despite unexpected weather conditions.[472] Autonomous drones were used in the spectacular Operation Spiderweb.[473] In this, Ukraine used drones delivered by trucks within Russia near airbases by unwitting Russian delivery drivers. At a predetermined moment, the roofs of the trucks opened and released swarms of drones that targeted Russian warplanes on the airbases using terminal AI guidance. This means they could strike their targets despite Russian jamming. The cheap drones, each costing a few hundred dollars, were able to damage or destroy dozens of Russian warplanes, which each cost millions of dollars to build. Drones are becoming more and more autonomous, able to strike targets without the need for human operators, which raises obvious ethical implications and concerns. The ethics of such weapons have been debated at the United Nations,[474] and a coalition of non-governmental organisations was established as long ago as 2013 to lobby for a ban on lethal autonomous weapons.[475]

Some fully autonomous weapons systems are already in use. The Phalanx air defence system is used on US ships for defence against close threats that approach the ship, such as missiles or aircraft. Essentially a guided Gatling gun, the Phalanx is usually operated by a human.[476] However, if it detects more threats than the operator can manage, it can be switched to automatic mode, which allows it to engage multiple targets autonomously. According to the UN, a small 7.5 kg Turkish drone system carried out an attack in Libya in 2020 autonomously, with no human in the loop.[477] An Australian ground drone called the Jaeger-C, a sort of robotic mine, was demonstrated in 2022. AI navigation capabilities have already been developed for the US Reaper drone, and other autonomous drones have been demonstrated.[478]

Such drones use a mix of AI techniques, from machine learning to computer vision to neural networks.[479] These allow them to perceive their surroundings, avoid obstacles, and detect targets. Local processing on the drones ("edge AI") allows them to operate without the need for satellite communication and to remain operational even in a hostile electronic warfare environment, where radio signals are jammed.

Drone swarms that communicate with one another are also being developed. Saab demonstrated a swarm of ten drones in a military exercise in March 2025.[480] There have been displays of such swarms in synchronised drone shows in China involving hundreds of drones operating together. The largest demo so far, in Shenzhen in 2024, involved over 10,000 coordinated drones. Although they have so far been shown as a benign light show, an alternative to fireworks displays, the military implications of such technology are obvious. Soldiers may be able to (sometimes) shoot down individual drones that are approaching them, but how will they deal with a coordinated swarm of hundreds? Artificial intelligence, as well as the economics of mass-produced cheap drones, has transformed the battlefield in Ukraine. The Operation Spiderweb, where cheap drones destroyed dozens of combat aircraft, had military planners around the world scrambling to consider whether such an operation could be carried out by a hostile party, either a nation state or well-organised terrorists, against them. If such an attack occurred, what could be done to defend against it? Until recently, the idea of humans being hunted by autonomous robots has been the stuff of science fiction, such as the Metalhead episode of Black Mirror.[481] The latest developments in the Russo-Ukrainian war have shown that this prospect is much closer to reality than a futuristic, fictional dystopia.

AI in the Defence Industry

From the invention of gunpowder to the machine gun and tank, the military has always been an early adopter of the largest technological innovations. Computing has had a major impact on warfare ever since Alan Turing's Bombe machine was used to crack the German Enigma cyphers in the Second World War.[482] The driverless taxis from Waymo that ply their trade today on the streets of San Francisco have their roots in the 2004 Grand Challenge project, sponsored by the Defense Advanced Research Projects Agency (DARPA). Today, artificial intelligence is having a widespread impact on various aspects of the defence industry, from strategy through to operations and in military technology itself.

The US Army has put AI firmly at the heart of its planning.[483] One key aspect is in the military decision-making process, using AI to plan missions, drawing on intelligence reports, terrain information, weather patterns, and sensor feeds to help identify targets and forecast enemy movements. Technology allows mission simulations to be run and unit orders to be issued that comply with military doctrine and standards. It should be noted that previous attempts to introduce AI into the process have been made over several decades, and they were abandoned, mostly because the technology did not perform well under battlefield conditions. It is thought that the latest in AI technology may fare better. The idea is to develop a command and control system that will use AI to link sensor data together from different branches of the armed forces into a unified network.[484]

AI has had a better track record in military logistics, with machine learning being used in the Dynamic Analysis and Replanning (DART) tool as far back as 1991 to schedule the transportation of supplies. Similarly, AI has been used in radar analysis and missile threat detection systems.[485] Predictive maintenance, where AI models analyse sensor data to predict failing parts, has been used in various industries, including defence, to reduce the cost of replacing parts in equipment. In 2024, the US military alone had almost $2 billion allotted for AI project funding and 800 ongoing AI projects.[486]

One of the areas where AI is being actively employed is in drones, which we have just discussed. Another is in cybersecurity, which is clearly an important part of military capability. AI brings both opportunities and threats here, as it can be used for threat detection and to provide autonomous responses, but it also brings new vulnerabilities, such as prompt injection in large language models.[487]

There are a number of issues and challenges. The black box nature of artificial neural networks means that the decision-making process of AI recommendations is opaque, which undermines trust. Large language models are heavily dependent on their training data and tend to be erratic when presented with unusual or edge-case inputs. This phenomenon is why driverless cars are currently restricted to geo-fenced areas of carefully mapped cities and are not roaming the countryside.

A major consideration is ethics. There is increasing use of remotely controlled weaponry, from unmanned aerial vehicles to ground and naval drones, already deployed in the Russo-Ukrainian war.[488] Such platforms have the capability to operate autonomously as well as be operated remotely, an important consideration when electronic warfare is used to jam communications. However, if a drone is used not merely to transport equipment or for reconnaissance but also is itself armed, then the drone could start shooting at targets of its own volition. There has been considerable debate about the ethics of this.[489] There are already such technologies: the Israeli IAI Harop is a loitering munition that can autonomously search for targets emitting radar signals, choose a target, and attack it.[490] The system has a "human in the loop' for final strike decisions, but the technology is entirely capable of operating autonomously. It can be argued that there is plenty of such technology already deployed: landmines do not ask a human for permission before exploding. Nonetheless, there are obvious legal and ethical concerns about these "lethal autonomous weapon systems". There is even a concern that politicians may be more willing to enter conflicts if the "soldiers" are mostly robots and drones that do not have grieving families and military funerals. There are already campaigns underway to set restrictions or bans on such weapons.[491]

The pace of technological change and the urgency of wartime situations for driving battlefield innovation mean that it is inevitable that AI will be embedded into more and more actual weapons systems, planning systems, and other military applications. Now is the time to have debates about the ethics of this and how such systems may be controlled while they are still mostly in development rather than actively deployed.

AI in Robotics

The word "robot" was coined in K. Čapek's play *Rossum's Universal Robots* in 1920, which depicted artificial beings created to perform manual labour. The word "robot" ("robota" in Czech) literally means "drudgery". Well before this, in 1770, "The Mechanical Turk" was exhibited, which played chess very well, but this turned out to just be a clever conjuring trick, with an expert chess player hiding inside a cabinet attached to a mechanical body, which moved chess pieces at the direction of the hidden player via its mechanical arm.[492] The Mechanical Turk toured the courts of Europe for decades, beating Napoleon and Benjamin Franklin, amongst others. Ever since this early excursion into mechanical men, robots have fascinated science fiction writers and filmmakers. Famous examples include the robot Maria in Fritz Lang's *Metropolis* (1927), Robbie the Robot in *Forbidden Planet* (1956), and the android character Bishop in *Aliens* (1986).

The first real robot was produced by inventor George Devol from Kentucky, who developed and patented a programmable robotic arm called Unimate in 1954.[493] His patent was bought by Joseph Engelberger, who founded the Unimation company in 1962 and produced the first industrial robots. Controlled by vacuum tubes as digital switches, the first sale was to General Motors in 1961 for die casting and spot welding of car bodies. This coincided with the first steps into artificial intelligence, the phrase being coined at a conference in 1956 at Dartmouth College.

The first mobile robot was Shakey, developed by Stanford University in the 1960s and 1970s.[494] This robot combined computer vision, spatial mapping, and an overall software control program, and had a camera, bump detectors, and a push bar. This was the pioneer for modern robots.

In parallel, AI was developing, with the ELIZA natural language program created at MIT in 1965;[495] the first expert system, DENDRAL,[496] appeared the same year. In 1970, the humanoid robot WABOT-1 and its successor WABOT-2 were developed by Waseda University in Japan.[497] The Furby domestic robot pet appeared in 1998,[498] a year after the Sojourner robotic explorer landed on Mars, exploring the planet's surface for 83 days.[499] The Roomba consumer vacuum cleaner appeared in 2002,[500] and by 2024, there were estimated to be over 36 million robots in use in the world, with over 4 million in factories.[501] The densest population of robots is in South Korea, followed by Singapore and China, with the US ranked just tenth.

All these robots and self-driving vehicles rely heavily on artificial intelligence. Robots need to interpret data from the environment in which they operate and potentially learn from their past experiences, adapt to new tasks, and make decisions. Machine learning allows robots to analyse data and recognise patterns, such as interpreting images from robotic cameras and other sensors, which in the case of autonomous vehicles usually includes LIDAR.[502] Some robots can communicate with humans, using natural language processing. They can even use machine learning models to predict their own component failures, a form of predictive maintenance. Reinforcement learning allows robots to learn via trial and error, for example, learning to walk.[503]

Robots offer many benefits in terms of productivity, consistency of operation, and quality. Robots are routinely used in surgery and can perform some actions better than human surgeons.[504] They don't get tired or go on strike, and they can carry out some tasks that are dangerous for humans, such as dealing with toxic chemicals or heavy loads. They can operate in environments that are unsafe for humans, such as nuclear facilities[505] or deep in the ocean.[506] A humanoid robot called Robonaut 2 has been used on the International Space Station since 2011.[507] Down on earth, robots are commonly used in warehouses, retrieving goods from shelves and packing them up for delivery.[508] Amazon claimed that they have a million robots now in use at their facilities, as of June 2025.[509]

By carrying out tasks that are dangerous for humans, robots can improve worker safety, though there is another side to this. The first person to be killed by a robot was a Ford Motors worker, Robert Williams, in 1979. Tesla alone has reported 51 fatalities associated with its cars.[510] However, in general, driverless cars have an accident rate comparable to human-driven vehicles, though data so far is sparse.[511] We have yet to find a way for robots to behave according to the science fiction writer Isaac Asimov's Laws of Robotics, intended to ensure robots do not harm humans.[512] Robots certainly have some economic impact and have been the subject of various economic studies. One MIT study noted that an increased use of robots had a negative effect on wages and jobs, especially in the manufacturing sector.[513] Jobs such as welders and machinists are clearly affected. A 2024 study found that the use of robots drove up wage inequality.[514] However, robots create jobs too.[515] South Korea and Japan, which use robots extensively, also have low unemployment.

For all the advances made, it has to be said that robots are currently mostly used in tasks that are quite specific, such as welding metal or retrieving goods from a warehouse shelf. We have yet to see a robot that is able to adapt to a range of novel or complex environments or to handle nuanced human interactions that require empathy. Although there would be obvious potential benefits to using robots to help the elderly, given the ageing population,[516] at present, the technology is just insufficiently adaptable to operate safely in a home environment.[517] Tasks that a human finds easy, such as folding laundry or using a kitchen knife to chop vegetables, are still hard for robots to master, though progress is being made.[518]

One interesting development is the emerging ability of robots to act collaboratively.[519] Drones can already operate in swarms without centralised control, which allows for spectacular drone displays analogous to firework displays but also has plenty of darker implications for military use.[520] Armies are already devising defences against drone swarms.[521]

It seems likely that, despite some limitations, robots will continue to be adopted in more and more aspects of our daily lives. The global robotics industry is already worth $53 billion and growing at around 15% or more annually, depending on which analyst you believe.[522] Growth in Asia, such as China,[523] is particularly marked. Robotics, much of it driven by artificial intelligence, is no longer the stuff of science fiction; it is steadily encroaching on our lives in the present day.

AI in Consulting

In August 2025, it was revealed in the press that a report produced by Deloitte for the Australian government contained several entirely fabricated citations to articles and books that do not exist, other than in the fevered hallucinations of generative AI.[524] The report, costing taxpayers AU$439,000, was presumably not offered at a substantial discount to the client due to it having likely been written, at least in part, by an AI.

This is just the latest in a long series of such incidents, many of the best documented ones being in the legal profession.[525] The legal ones are prominently reported and recorded, presumably because case law is one area that can be easily checked for accuracy. Above all, it is a profession where court documents with references to case law are *actually* routinely checked. This does raise the interesting question of just how common such AI-generated errors are in areas and subjects where there is not the same degree of rigorous checking.

We know that hallucinations in generative AI are common,[526] getting worse, and occurring in at least 15% of generative AI answers on average.[527] The more obscure the area under discussion, the higher the chances of hallucination, as the AI has less training data to work with. As we have seen, if you ask an AI, "What is the capital of France?", then it will almost certainly answer "Paris", because it has seen Paris referred to as the capital of France in countless books and articles that it has been trained on. Indeed, if you asked an AI that same question repeatedly, then it would answer repeatedly and correctly again and again, unless the "temperature" of the AI was adjusted to encourage it to be more creative in its answers. You might be able to ask that question a thousand times of an AI and get the right answer a thousand times, but even with such a commonly referenced fact, there is still a tiny chance that it would answer the question with a wrong answer, one that had a low statistical weighting in predicting the correct answer. Eventually, the

AI would give you a different answer if you asked the question enough times. However, now imagine that you are asking an AI something far more esoteric and rarely referenced. The probability of it making a mistake here is dramatically higher.

The very first question I ever asked of ChatGPT in late 2022 was a little test, though I had not intended it to trip up the AI; I was merely curious as to the extent and breadth of its knowledge. I looked up the results of a 1980s chess tournament with which I was familiar and opened up the final results table, showing the participants and their scores. When I asked ChatGPT to tell me about the tournament, its answer puzzled me. The answer looked superficially plausible, having a list of players from that era and a set of scores. However, the scores were off, and some of the players listed did not play in that tournament, while others who did play were missing. This was a classic AI hallucination, presumably caused because its training data was not exactly awash with the details of obscure British chess tournaments.

Now consider a report written, seemingly, by a consulting firm that has been hired to write about some esoteric area of your business. It is fluently written and contains references to books and articles on the subject in question. How confident are you that someone at the client is diligently checking every reference? We have already seen cases of entire books sold on Amazon being AI-written, including ones, alarmingly, as field guides to edible mushrooms.[528] Since September 2023, Amazon has restricted publishers to three books per day (!) being uploaded, which is a likely indication of the scale of the problem.[529] Some unscrupulous "authors" even publish AI-generated books by well-known authors in the hope that fans will buy them, hoping for a new release by their favourite writer.[530] Authors already have plenty of issues with AI companies using their copyright-protected material for LLM training without payment or permission. Indeed, there are a host of lawsuits underway in this area,[531] with the first having been settled out of court in August 2025.[532]

Clearly, AI has some legitimate uses in the world of consulting. AI can be good at summarising documents and researching large volumes of data, such as research articles. Speeding up desk research by junior consultants has the potential to reduce costs, with nearly half of such tasks potentially being replaced by AI.[533] Consulting firms can potentially make a lot of revenue from providing advice to corporate clients on how to best use AI in their businesses. Accenture alone claims to have invested $3 billion in its AI practice, doubling its AI workforce to 80,000 consultants, almost 10% of its consulting workforce.[534] McKinsey has 5,000 consultants in their AI practice, with over a thousand partners, from academics to start-up companies, and thinks that as much as 40% of its revenue may come from AI-related work.

Along with these opportunities come associated risks and challenges. Using AI for clients means accessing potentially sensitive and confidential data, and generative AI is still at an early stage when it comes to security, with many known issues.[535] Data models need to be trained on data, and this corporate data may have data quality issues as well as inherent biases that may then be reflected in the model answers. There have been many prior examples of AI applications having to be abandoned due to bias in underlying datasets.[536] Moreover, AI models can deteriorate over time and need careful monitoring when put into production.[537] All these practical issues are quite apart from the reputational issues that may occur if the consultants use AI to cut corners without disclosing that to clients, which may have happened in the Australian government's Deloitte report mentioned earlier.

A further threat to consulting firms is that their customers can easily use generative AI tools for research and may start to question what value is really added by expensive consultants over just typing a prompt into an AI chatbot. Certainly, the big-name consulting firms have powerful brands, and corporations often use these firms partly because of the reassuring power of these brands. Whereas in the 1970s, there was a corporate mantra that "nobody ever gets fired for using IBM", in more recent times, much the same could be said for relying on the advice of top consulting firms like McKinsey, Bain, and Boston Consulting Group. However, that brand value has its limits and can easily and quickly be undermined, as auditor Arthur Andersen discovered to its cost with Enron in 2001.[538] Incidents such as using AI in an undisclosed way in consulting reports or security breaches, such as the McKinsey-built chatbot leaking customer details to the security firm Zenity in 2025, may have serious consequences if they turn out to be the tip of the iceberg.[539] After an initial sugar rush of AI consulting work, there are signs that some customers are starting to cut back on their use of consulting firms,[540] and some top firms are reducing their recruitment, at least for junior consultants.[541] Generative AI technology is still a relatively new technology, and its impacts, good and bad, are still being felt. This applies to the world of consulting as much as it does to other industries.

AI in the Wine Industry

The wine industry favours tradition. The first traces of wine production were near Tbilisi in Georgia, around 6,000 BC, but over the centuries, the industry has adapted to technological advances. The glass bottle was uncommon until the 17th century, though the first ever glass bottle dates back to Roman times. The wine industry is worth around $340 billion globally, employing over a million people directly.[542] The EU wine sector alone supports around 3 million jobs, directly and indirectly, and there are over 100,000 different wineries around the world. Modern wineries use plenty of technology, from drones with infrared cameras to monitor vineyards to grape-sorting machines and smart labels to combat counterfeit wine labels.

The industry is starting to embrace artificial intelligence. An experiment at the University of Geneva in 2023 showed that AI could be used to categorise the chemical structure of specific bottles of wine, being able to identify 80 red wines from different Bordeaux estates and vintages with perfect accuracy.[543] This technique has the potential to combat the counterfeiting of expensive wine, an all-too-common problem in the industry. It has been estimated that as much as 20% of all wine sold globally may be deliberately mislabelled, so anything that can help in that particular battle will be welcomed by wine producers.[544]

Another issue with wine is when the bottle is "corked", i.e. is faulty and tastes bad.[545] This problem has many causes, but issues with the cork allowing oxygen into the wine bottle are common and happen in as much as 3% of all wines.[546] Technology from a company called Cork Supply maps the internal structure of a natural cork with a scanner and then uses machine learning to identify anomalies in the structure compared to a database of regular cork structures.[547]

Another area where AI is being used is in personal recommendations for wine buyers. A company called Preferabli uses AI to match the broad wine preferences of a shopper to suitable wines.[548] The system prompts shoppers to express preferences, such as a crisp and light white wine from a certain region.[549] It then accesses a large database of wines where many characteristics have been noted by wine experts and recommends particular wines to the shopper. It can also suggest food pairings for the wine. The machine learning analyses the taste characteristics of millions of products to drive its recommendations. Rival company Tastry uses a similar machine learning approach to deliver customised preferences.[550] The largest wine marketplace, Vivino, has a database of over a million wines and, utilising AI models, has launched a wine recommendation service based on customers' previous preferences and searches.[551]

Vineyard health can be monitored by aerial sensors from companies like the Canadian firm VineView.[552] These measure water content in leaves, using AI to stitch together images from drones and to analyse those composite images.[553] One wine-maker even used ChatGPT to help design a new wine,[554] from suggesting the blend of grapes to be used to designing the label, its name, and the choice of bottle. It can be bought from their website.[555] The process of fermentation is also seeing internet-of-things technology being used, with sensors embedded in fermentation tanks to provide real-time insights and alerts, for example, if a vat is overheating. Machine learning models can thus be used to predict potential quality issues before they occur.

What about assessing the quality of wine? This has long been the preserve of wine experts, an area shrouded in mystique. The Wine and Spirit Education Trust has a series of exams that aspiring sommeliers can take, resulting in a range of qualifications, the most prestigious of which is "Master of Wine".[556] Just 425 people in the world have so far achieved this level, as of early 2025. The regular ChatGPT chatbot has passed the theory exam for the WSET exams at a high level,[557] as well as the related Advanced Sommelier exam (scoring 77% in 2023), and so it can also make good general recommendations on wine.

We tend to associate leading-edge technologies with early adopter industries like investment banking and life sciences, but the example of the wine industry embracing AI in multiple ways shows that it can have an impact even in quite traditional industries. In the future, we can expect to see more technology, some of it AI-based, employed in vineyard management, in wine-making, such as the fermentation process, in addition to more obvious areas like marketing and sales. The use of AI to help improve cork reliability, potentially trace the lineage of individual bottles of wine to combat fraud, and provide tailored wine recommendations to individuals are examples of an industry that can adapt. We can expect to see wine be a blend of tradition and modernity in the years to come.

AI at the Movies

Artificial intelligence has long been a subject portrayed in films, from ground-breaking films like Fritz Lang's *Metropolis* (1927)[558] to the robot character Gort in *The Day the Earth Stood Still* (1951) and the lovable Robbie in *Forbidden Planet* (1956). In recent times, we have seen the artificial intelligence HAL in *2001: A Space Odyssey* (1968) and the replicants in *Blade Runner* (1981).[559] Artificial intelligence has been portrayed as malevolent in *The Matrix* (1999)[560] , *The Terminator* (1984),[561] and *I Robot* (2004),[562] and somewhat more sympathetically in *AI* (2001),[563] *Short Circuit* (1986),[564] *Her* (2013),[565] and *Ex Machina* (2014).[566]

Film often reflects society's fears, hopes, and anxieties, and AI is no exception. Fiction is now blending into reality as artificial intelligence starts to impact our side of the silver screen. AI is used at various stages of the filmmaking process, from pre-production to production, post-production, marketing, and distribution. AI can generate a synopsis or treatment to develop storylines and, in principle, could even write a full script, though how watchable this would be is a matter of debate.[567] Certainly, AI can be used to identify structural issues within stories and break down a script into areas showing characters, locations, and special effects. In pre-production, AI can easily generate storyboards of the kind once drawn meticulously for directors like Alfred Hitchcock, who himself was a trained draughtsman.[568] AI can even be used to help with location scouting by analysing images to look into issues that may affect production, such as logistics and local weather.

There are further uses for AI in film production.[569] It can be used for editing, visual effects, and sound design in post-production. Once a film is finished, generative AI can be used to produce marketing material.

Generative AI can do a lot more than write parts of a script. Its image and video-generating tools can construct entire film scenes, animations, or even a whole film. Director Hooroo Jackson[570] used 17,000 AI-generated images to stitch together a 2023 black-and-white experimental film called *Window Seat*, which admittedly bombed at the box office but was the first fully AI feature film.[571] It has obvious flaws, such as non-existent lip-syncing, but you can watch and be the judge.[572] The technology continues to evolve, and in September 2025, there are already a slew of film-making tools,[573] like Veo, Sora,[574] Runway, Dream Machine, Minimax, and Kling at our disposal. The clips from these tools are already a lot more impressive than those that were possible in 2023.

Scriptwriters are one of the many professions within the creative industries concerned about copyright infringement by AI companies, who routinely scrape content from written texts, film, and audio files to train their large language models.[575] Even the death of an actor need no longer be the end of their filmmaking career. James Dean,[576] Ian Holm,[577] and Carrie Fisher[578] have already appeared in films after their deaths, as has Christopher Reeve in a controversial manner.[579] Even an AI-generated Audrey Hepburn appeared in a chocolate commercial in 2013, though with the permission of her family.[580]

Both actors and writers have noted the incursion of AI into their industry with concern. In 2023, the unions Writers Guild of America (WGA)[581] and the Screen Actors Guild-American Federation of Television and Radio Artists (SAG-AFTRA)[582] held strikes in Hollywood, disrupting film production and resulting in agreements with some level of protection for actors' image rights and limitations on the use of AI-written content.

Despite misgivings, there is little doubt that AI will continue to work its way into more and more aspects of the film industry. The tools that actually produce video are improving rapidly, and they are already almost unrecognisable from the early ones that were around just a couple of years ago. With traditional film costs reaching as much as $15,000 a minute, plus the costs of crew and film equipment, it is clear that filmmakers and studios will be keen to investigate its use. Besides the actual film itself, it can be seen that there are myriad possible uses of AI right across the film production process, from helping with scripts to producing marketing material.

Film has always held up a mirror to our society. AI is now starting to move beyond a mere construct within a film and starting to actually become part of the film-making process itself. Hopefully, the real-life ending of this development will not be as apocalyptic as the one that the film industry has often portrayed.[583]

AI in Sport

There are very few aspects of life that artificial intelligence is not embedding itself into, and the sports industry is no exception. There are many different use cases appearing, from athlete training to sports analysis, through to television coverage. When the marathon runner Tola Tamirat crossed the finish line in the 2024 Paris Olympics, he was wearing sensors that monitored his heartbeat and hydration level.[584] Athletes wear devices on their wrists and others embedded into their apparel that do not just monitor heart rate but also the speed at which they are running, distance covered, and the force and angle of physical impacts in sports like rugby[585] and American football (such analysis can be used to help prevent concussions).[586] Such biometric data can help to avert injury by highlighting deviations from normal data, with one study finding a 35% reduction in non-contact injuries amongst teams using wearable devices.

Other technologies record live-action sports on camera and then use artificial intelligence and other algorithms to analyse player movements. Cricket fans have become used to technology like Hawk-Eye, which predicts the trajectory of a cricket ball to help adjudicate whether a batsman is out leg before wicket,[587] whilst other technology can assess whether a batsman made faint contact with the ball before being caught.[588] The Hawk-Eye technology is used to assess line calls at Wimbledon and in several other sports, including badminton and volleyball.[589] Video-assisted referee (VAR) technology has been controversial in football (soccer to Americans), but it is getting a helping hand from AI to speed it up and assess some decisions.[590]

Tools, like Football Radar,[591] rate players and predict the outcomes of matches, including betting advice, and they are not the only such tools.[592] Coaches can use such tools to assess player performance and spot areas for improvement in sports ranging from basketball to cycling.[593] AI in the sports market was valued at over $2 billion as long ago as 2022.[594] AI can be used to analyse golf swings and provide immersive practice environments for players to train and get feedback.[595] It has even been used in golf course design to help optimise water usage and assist with course layout.[596] It is used in dope testing, as it can spot sudden changes in an athlete's physiological data or performance.[597] The technology can also be used by talent scouts to analyse footage of promising players and help them assess the most talented ones,[598] though human experience is still key. As Real Madrid football coach Zinedine Zidane said, "Artificial Intelligence plays a very important role now, but in my view human intelligence remains the most important."[599]

Sports channel ESPN has built a generative AI tool that builds summaries of some sporting events, with these recaps being reviewed by human editors before being published on websites and apps.[600] Rival technology carries out optical tracking and predictive modelling.[601] Motor racing, an industry full of technology, has embraced AI, including using machine learning to help optimise car design, improving aerodynamics and more; with over 3,000 different components on a Formula 1 car that can be optimised, there is plenty of room for computing power to help model performance.[602] AI is even being used in ten-pin bowling.[603] AI-powered video technology is also allowing audiences to develop in niche sports like pickleball and even arm-wrestling.[604]

Clearly, the vast amount of personal health data being stored about athletes brings with it concerns about privacy, though techniques like homomorphic encryption can help secure such data.[605] There are also issues of fairness and bias, a recurring theme in large language models.[606] Nonetheless, there are many uses for the various flavours of AI in sports, and the cost of the technology continues to fall, such as the ubiquitous video cameras in smartphones that allow sports events to be inexpensively recorded. It seems inevitable that AI technology will continue its relentless invasion of sport. This may not be universally welcomed, as the controversy around VAR in football has shown, but it seems unstoppable. Machine precision is set to complement human sporting talent in more and more areas.

AI in the Public Sector

AI has the potential to be used in various areas of the public sector. In the UK, for example, 18% of all jobs are in the public sector, and the proportion is large in other countries too – 16% in the US, 20% in France, and 29% in Sweden. Japan has an AI-driven earthquake prediction system that analyses seismic data in real-time and can issue alerts, finding a 70% improvement in accuracy. The notoriously bad traffic in Sao Paolo in Brazil has been given an AI hand in the form of a smart traffic system that adjusts traffic signals and suggests alternative routes, resulting in a 25% reduction in travel time.[607] Canada used machine learning to analyse financial transactions for suspicious activity and identify patterns of tax evasion, yielding millions in previously unpaid taxes.

There are many such initiatives happening around the world. Chatbots can help citizens navigate the public sector bureaucracy, something that has been successfully tried in Singapore.[608] A UK government chatbot helps businesses understand regulations.[609] In Seoul, the city uses smart bins, powered by solar power, to compact waste, allowing bins to be emptied less often. This has resulted in an 83% reduction in bin collection costs and has virtually eliminated the problem of overflowing bins.[610] More controversially, the EU has employed AI systems, at least in a pilot project, as border guards, asking questions and analysing facial gestures to see whether travellers appeared to be lying, in which case, they were referred for further checks.[611]

Governments have many of the same issues as private sector companies, though without the profit motive. They want to be efficient, save money, and improve services for their citizens. Just as with private companies, they also face challenges in the form of dubious data quality, limitations in data governance, and a lack of skills in AI. They have additional issues in the form of a need for transparency,[612] a (usually) greater emphasis on fairness and equality, and eliminating bias in systems.[613] The same issues that affect the introduction of LLM technology into companies apply to the public sector: having to deal with the thorny issue of hallucinations,[614] having to integrate with legacy systems, a lack of workforce skills, and the issue of public trust.[615]

Governments need to plan carefully when considering rolling out AI projects. The UK government has defined ten principles to be used for such projects, including ensuring that staff know how to use AI securely and lawfully, understand the limitations of AI, and can select the right tool for the right job.[616] Such a set of principles seems to be a good starting point. Just jumping on the AI bandwagon to grab headlines is likely to end badly. In September 2025, the Albanian government announced an AI procurement minister.[617] Given the dismal job that AI agents can make of running even a minuscule business,[618] and given their record in negotiating, this seems highly experimental and is likely destined for failure.[619]

Widespread staff training in AI literacy for public sector workers will be an important basis for success, as is the careful monitoring of AI projects, including learning from mistakes and sharing best practices. The private sector has enough difficulty in rolling out AI projects, with a MIT 2025 study showing a dismal 5% success rate for AI projects.[620] Government projects tend to have additional constraints compared to private sector ones and so are likely to encounter all the same issues, but more besides, since there is an understandable additional emphasis in the public sector on fairness and eliminating bias in systems. There are definitely opportunities to use AI in public sector projects, as we have seen from some of the success stories highlighted. The key is in matching the opportunity to the most suitable form of AI technology and then ensuring that each project carefully considers the factors that will help it succeed, such as data quality, AI literacy of staff, quality assurance, testing, and careful monitoring of the project. If governments act thoughtfully and responsibly, then they should be able to use AI to help them bring greater efficiency into citizen-centric public services.

The Economics of AI

The Costs of Using AI in Your Business

Most of us by now will have tried using an AI chatbot like ChatGPT or Claude or Perplexity or Grok. They are hard to avoid, with, for example, Google now putting AI-generated answers and summaries at the top of its queries, with sometimes amusing results.[621] However, if you are to implement one of these generative AI tools in your business, what are the actual costs?

Firstly, there are explicit costs. You can play with tools like ChatGPT and Claude for free, but there are limits on the number of interactions per day, for example, the number of messages or files that can be accessed. For any serious usage, you need to buy a licence. Claude charges $200 a month at the time of writing, for example.[622] Enterprise licences can be negotiated if there are many users. This quickly adds up. At present, OpenAI's ChatGPT enterprise licence works out at $144,000 a year for 200 employees, or a list price of over $14 million for an organisation with 200,000 employees, though doubtless there is scope for negotiation for larger companies.

Once you have your licence for your chosen AI, you need to factor in the processing costs. There will be charges from your cloud provider for compute costs, bandwidth, and storage for things like conversation logs. A large part of any computer project is staff, whether the cost of employees or of external consultants to help you. Depending on the scale and complexity of the project, building an enterprise chatbot might cost anything in labour costs from a few thousand dollars to over $1 million. As well as the hourly costs of people, there may be costs of integration into existing corporate infrastructure, like Slack, or possibly purchasing a vector database if you want to do retrieval-augmented generation (RAG) to customise the chatbot with company-specific files or data. You will need to do testing and carefully consider security and privacy. For example, if a chatbot is to have access to a corporate database, such as a customer order database, then you need to make sure that it is secure. This may include encrypting data in transit and at rest and conducting penetration testing, as well as considering GDPR or similar compliance. Chatbots have their own security issues, for instance, the risk of prompt injection attacks, data leaks, or social engineering attacks.

Once a chatbot is up and running, there are ongoing costs to consider. Every time a customer asks a question, there is a cost somewhere, and the chatbot will need monitoring and support. There will be new releases of software and bug fixes to deal with, just as with any software project. There may be a need for marketing or a brand review to ensure that the chatbot application is in line with corporate brand standards and possibly a legal review. For example, in one famous case, an Air Canada chatbot gave poor advice to a customer, resulting in a court case which Air Canada lost.[623] If the chatbot is successful, then it will engage well with customers, which in itself has a cost, with every customer interaction incurring a small cost in processing. A chatbot question costs around ten times as much processing as a typical Google query, as it is computationally complex.[624] All this ignores indirect costs, including the need to train staff in AI or the cost of handling any incidents that occur, such as due to hallucinated output from the chatbot. The content of the chatbot conversations will need to be logged, monitored, and analysed. These cost categories all assume using an off-the-shelf chatbot. If you intend to carry out customisation, such as a customised user interface, then you need to factor this in too.

Any business investment of any size should have an economic case, often called a cost/benefit analysis. You need to estimate the benefits of a proposed project and weigh them against the costs, not forgetting the ongoing costs over time as well as the original one-off investment. With these figures, you can calculate the estimated economic return of the project, including things like the project payback period, the net present value (NPV) of the investment, and the internal rate of return (IRR) of the project in order to determine whether there is a good return on investment. Not all companies take such a rigorous approach, but large corporations do, at least those that I worked for (Exxon and Shell). At the time of writing, the return on investment for AI projects seems distinctly mixed. An IBM study of 2000 CEOs conducted in 2025, reported in *Fortune* magazine, found that just a quarter of their AI projects had shown a return on investment, which in itself is better than a large study done by MIT.[625] AI is novel and has generated considerable excitement in business over the last couple of years, but it is just another technological tool, and it needs to be subject to the same investment rigour as any other investment.

How Many AI Projects Actually Work?

There has been a huge investment in AI since late 2022 by corporations anxious to hitch themselves to the AI bandwagon and get a share of the productivity gains promised by the AI vendors and industry boosters. So, how many of those corporate AI projects have actually achieved the productivity advantages that they promised?

In July 2025, a major MIT study of over 300 AI projects and interviews with 153 executives and 300 corporate employees explored this subject in depth. The findings caused headlines in major media outlets as well as the technology-focused press when it was released in August.[626] No fewer than 95% of these projects failed to deliver any return on investment at all. The day after the report was published, NVIDIA stock dropped 3.5%, and the NASDAQ index fell over 1%. The report was quite damning but had some interesting detail below the headline. Just 5% of custom-built enterprise tools even make it into production compared to 40% of general-purpose LLMs. Purchased AI solutions were three times more likely to succeed than ones built in-house. Just two industries (technology and media) showed any signs of structural disruption. Large enterprises (over $100 million in annual revenue) took nine months or more to get their systems into production, compared to a 90-day average for smaller companies. Interviews with customers found that the biggest obstacles to success were the quality of the models, legal issues, data quality, and risk. Over half of the funding was allocated to sales and marketing applications. A majority of respondents stated that they would trust AI for simple tasks such as generating emails or summarising documents, but only 10% would trust AI for complex projects. Now, a 95% failure rate is hardly great, but many IT projects of all kinds fail. A 2020 Standish Group study found a 66% failure rate for software projects, and this figure is roughly in line with several other studies of IT project success and failure.[627]

The MIT AI study has been widely quoted, but it is not wildly out of line with others that have been done.[628] A Rand study in 2024 found an 80% failure rate for AI projects, for example.[629] However, the MIT study was large and thorough, and it was done in mid-2025 rather than early in the adoption phase of generative AI. Thus, it is hard to blame the high failure rate on teething troubles, as may have been encountered in early adopter AI projects carried out in 2023. It had been almost three years since generative AI has been widely available, so you would expect that lessons have been learned and that there had been a reasonable penetration of AI skills, training, and experience. The MIT study itself examined the causes of failure in its interviews, identifying a number of factors that contributed to projects not succeeding. One was the difficulty in integrating AI with existing applications; another was that many projects were directed at sales and marketing, where returns were relatively low compared to the automation of back-office operations. Survey respondents reported that models struggled to adapt to highly specific corporate needs, while larger companies, in particular, have business processes that made rapid adoption hard.

Other studies into AI project failure have also cited overestimating AI capabilities, low-quality corporate data, unclear objectives, and privacy and ethical concerns. A recurring theme of concern is the rate of hallucinations by large language models, which undermines confidence in the technology.[630] Although hallucinations may not matter in some use cases, they are a major issue in any application that requires reliability and consistency. Traditional business-critical systems in the corporate world are highly reliable and entirely consistent, but LLMs are inherently probabilistic, leading to variation in their outputs. Incidentally, in case you think that the answer is agentic AI, these are at an even earlier level of maturity. One 2025 Carnegie Mellon study found that even the best-performing out of 13 agentic AI models tested could only manage a 30% success rate at 175 realistic work tasks.[631] Nine of the models tested could not even hit a 10% success rate.

Corporations that are considering applying AI to production use cases need to learn from the issues identified by the MIT study and others. Clear objectives, good staff training, an emphasis on data quality, and a choice of project areas where there are clear and likely benefits from automating processes will all help. Above all, a realistic assessment of what areas generative AI is suitable for, and which it is not, is critical.[632] In all the excitement about generative AI, it is easy to forget that this is just one flavour of AI. There are many others, and some of these approaches may be better suited to your particular need than generative AI.[633] Indeed, whisper it, but in some cases, AI may not be the ideal tool for your project at all. The old saying is that if all you have is a hammer, then everything looks like a nail. Software projects need to explore the full toolbox of options, both AI and non-AI, to ensure that they use the best tool for the job at hand.

The Effect of AI on Jobs

Will AI replace your job? The fear of technology replacing jobs is not new.[634] William Lee patented the mechanised loom for stocking production in the 16th century. In early 19th-century England, a group of textile workers, the Luddites, rioted and destroyed machinery that was automating the production of textiles, threatening their livelihoods. Often, technological advances create new jobs as well as render some obsolete, but the process can still be disruptive to those affected. There are not many people building slide rules these days, an industry that lasted for three centuries. In 1950, around 350,000 people were employed as switchboard operators working for phone companies, and another million in the same role at offices. The introduction of mechanised switchboards completely removed the need for these jobs, and by 1978, the last mechanical switchboards had been replaced.[635]

The latest technological advance to threaten jobs has been the advent of artificial intelligence, especially the generative AI tools like ChatGPT that appeared in late 2022. Clearly, the impact of such tools will vary greatly depending on the profession. A chatbot is not going to cut your hair, paint your house, or build you a fence anytime soon. A July 2025 Microsoft study identified 40 careers that would have a high level of exposure to AI, such as interpreters, copywriters, ticket agents, and customer service staff.[636] Even photographic models are not safe in an age where a realistic stock photo of a person is just a prompt away. On the other hand, people who operate pile drivers, dredgers, and logging equipment need not be overly concerned. Roofers, dishwashers, and housekeepers can also rest easy. Although humanoid robots are being touted as housekeepers, that technology has some years to go before it becomes genuinely safe and useful.

McKinsey reckons that 80% of the world's global companies were using AI in at least one business function by July 2025.[637] This is not to say that all these efforts are actually succeeding. The same McKinsey report found that just a fifth of companies report a tangible effect on their earnings, and, as we have seen, a comprehensive 2020 MIT study of hundreds of AI projects revealed that 95% fail to deliver any benefit whatsoever.[638] Nonetheless, the McKinsey study observed that job vacancies fell by 43% between May 2022 and May 2025 in the US. A look at online job adverts found the effect was much worse in AI-exposed jobs (a 38% drop) than in ones with low exposure to AI (a 21% drop). An in-depth August 2025 study by Stanford University confirmed this. The Stanford study found that AI seemed to be having an effect on the US job market, specifically in entry-level jobs, typically taken up by recent graduates.[639] Since late 2022, employment for 22- to 25-year-olds in AI-exposed jobs (like software development and customer service) dropped 13–20%. Elsewhere, employment levels were either stable or grew. Young graduates are facing a tricky job market.

It is not clear whether this trend will continue or whether many of the pauses in jobs have been in anticipation of savings from AI that have yet to really appear. Swedish fintech company Klarna sacked 700 customer service workers and replaced them with AI, only to rehire them shortly afterwards when they saw the effect that the change was having on customer satisfaction.[640]

One of the common use cases for generative AI is in software development. Although large language models like Claude Sonnet and tools like Microsoft Copilot cannot carry out all coding tasks, they can certainly deliver workable code in simpler use cases.[641] This has led to a concern that junior software developers' jobs are very much at risk. Of course, if you get rid of junior software developers, how will you develop the senior ones still needed to design systems and to fix the complex problems that LLMs cannot handle? Amazon's AWS CEO Matt Garman stated that "replacing junior developers with AI was the dumbest thing I've ever heard" for this reason.[642]

Workers can react to the potential threat of AI in a number of ways. As noted, many jobs will be almost entirely unaffected. However, if you are in an area in the AI crosshairs, such as a graphic designer or translator, then you will need to think carefully about how you will continue to prosper. A world where an AI can do a decent translation of a document or produce a stock photo or logo within seconds is clearly going to be a challenge, at the least, for people working in those areas. Most jobs will be in the middle of the spectrum, with some impact likely from AI. In such cases, workers should educate themselves about AI and how to work with it to make themselves more productive and effective. LLMs have plenty of limitations, such as their propensity to hallucinate and behave in ways that are inconsistent.[643] Learning what AI is good at and what it is not good at will, in itself, be an important skill. It is likely that many jobs will be augmented by AI tools rather than replaced altogether. AI tools can be persuasive but lack empathy, as the increasing list of human tragedies caused by AI chatbot therapists demonstrates.[644] Hence, workers can focus on learning and enhancing skills like this, which LLMs lack. We should also remember that we are barely three years into generative AI being available on a broad basis and that it takes time for any new technology to be understood and adapted to.[645] A PwC 2025 study found that AI can make workers more productive, with much faster revenue growth in the industries most exposed to AI and twice the growth in salaries in those industries.[646] An example of how humans have learned to work with AI can be seen in radiology, where AI scans medical images and highlights potential issues in the scans, such as cancerous tumours, for the radiologist to review.[647] AI is likely to be used to augment rather than replace jobs in many fields, with human oversight, decision-making, and quality control retained.[648]

It seems likely that AI will have a significant effect on some industries and careers, while many, such as those involving manual labour, will remain almost entirely unaffected. However, AI is likely to have at least some impact on a wide range of jobs, and so workers and employers need to figure out how to best utilise this technology so that workers can become more productive and effective. As the part-human, part-machine character Seven of Nine said in the TV series *Star Trek*: "We will adapt".

AI Bubble and the Economy

The tsunami of artificial intelligence investment since late 2022 has had a seismic impact on the global economy. In Q2 2025, $40 billion, or 45% of all venture capital (VC) funding, went to AI-related companies, according to Crunchbase.[649] On the day that I wrote this paragraph, NVIDIA, which makes the chips that power the AI wave, was worth $4.4 trillion, 13 times more than it was worth in October 2022, just before ChatGPT was released by OpenAI. At the time of writing, NVIDIA is the most valuable company in the world, representing over 7% of the Standard and Poor's 500 stock market index.

As of late 2025, the AI picture is looking a little frothy. A Goldman Sachs report in August 2025 found that only 9% of US companies have actually used generative AI in production in recent weeks.[650] Still, it projects that around 6% of US jobs may be displaced, but that new jobs will also be created, with a projected 15% improvement in labour productivity. The largest impacts so far on employment have been in industries where AI has an obvious impact, such as graphic design, marketing consulting, call centres, and technology. As we saw, a Microsoft study identified the 40 jobs most exposed to AI, with translators, sales reps, writers, and travel agents and concierges among those most affected.[651] Unsurprisingly, jobs involving manual labour, such as hospital orderlies, tree logging, and rail track laying, were the safest areas. No chatbot is going to be cutting your hair, painting your house, or putting up a new roof any time soon.

One interesting economic impact of AI has been on the world of online advertising. Google made 78% of its revenue from advertising in 2024.[652] However, people are increasingly using AI chatbots to do their online searches rather than just relying on search engines like Google. The advertising revenue of Google in Q2 2025 was actually down 1% year-on-year, which is unprecedented.[653] A study by the Pew Research Center in 2025 found that Google users were about half as likely to click on a Google AI summary answer as one without such a summary.[654] In March 2025, about a fifth of Google searches produced such an AI summary. These summaries, incidentally, cost around ten times as much as a regular search to process, so Google's response of fighting AI with AI does not come cheap. The combined effects of AI summaries by search engines and users bypassing search engines altogether are hurting the publishers that advertise online. If someone sees a chatbot-generated summary in response to a query, then the end user may not visit the source websites and so will not see any adverts. Publishers are complaining and with reason.[655] In one 2023 survey, 5% of users claimed that ChatGPT was their primary search engine, up from 1% a year before.[656] By 2025, that pace has accelerated greatly. A February 2025 Bain survey found that 80% of consumers now rely on AI-written results for at least 40% of their searches, reducing their organic web traffic by up to a quarter.[657] Even basic questions are now being answered by AI chatbots, with 48% of consumers using AI to answer questions about the weather and 42% for shopping recommendations. Advertisers need to respond to these changes in the market, for example, by using more video or interactive formats and by making their adverts more visible to generative AI search.

Are we in an AI bubble? Mark Zuckerberg has been hiring top AI talent for unheard-of compensation packages, some in excess of $100 million per year.[658] Does that sound a little bubble-like to you? In August 2025, Sam Altman, CEO of OpenAI, said in an interview with Verge magazine: "Are we in a phase where investors as a whole are overexcited about AI? My opinion is yes".[659] Even back in the heady days of 2023, some economists, such as those in the World Economic Forum, were warning that AI may have less impact than some enthusiasts were projecting at that time.[660] The August 2025 release of the much-awaited ChatGPT-5 by OpenAI was widely regarded as a flop.[661] This was a major blow to industry confidence, as OpenAI had long been hinting that they were on the path to "artificial general intelligence" (AGI).[662] This is a stage of AI where the AI becomes able to understand, learn, and apply knowledge across a wide range of tasks, like humans. Computers have long been able to outperform humans at specific tasks such as multiplying large numbers together, analysing large datasets, or playing chess, but an AGI could do all this and more. However, ChatGPT-5 was little more than a remarketing and aggregation of existing OpenAI models. Even its own demo at the launch showed ChatGPT planning a baseball park tour that involved missing out most of the East Coast of the US, yet included a non-existent, and presumably rather damp, baseball park in the middle of the Gulf of Mexico.[663] Nobel Laureate Demis Hassabis said in an interview in September 2025 that AGI was 5–10 years away, noting that LLMs currently can still make basic mistakes in simple arithmetic.[664]

It is telling that large language models, which underlie ChatGPT and all its generative rivals like Claude, Perplexity, and Grok, are absolutely terrible at playing chess, yet a specialist computer beat the chess world champion in a match as far back as 1997.[665] In an August 2025 LLM chess championship hosted by Kaggle, the leading LLMs played one another. The results were hysterical.[666] The eight LLMs were allowed five attempts at each turn just to play a legal move, and within a few moves of the games, many of them had failed to leap over that pathetically low bar and were disqualified. So, in mid-2025, many of the latest LLMs are unable to play chess as well as a small child that has just been taught the basic rules of the game. Even in the final, one LLM (Grok) played dismally, blundering its queen in multiple games. AGI, this was not. On a more serious note, the persistent issue of LLMs hallucinating, where they produce fabricated or meaningless answers, is seriously hindering the take-up of AI by business, where people are used to computers that give consistent, correct answers. With hallucination rates around 15% and getting worse,[667] this is a problem.

The sluggish adoption of AI by the corporate world, partly due to the thorny issue of hallucinations, spells trouble for the AI industry and its investors. Executives report a 90% failure rate for their AI projects in an IDC survey,[668] and an over 80% failure rate in a RAND report,[669] in addition to the 95% failure rate found in the MIT report mentioned earlier. Consultants, who make money from such projects whether or not they succeed, urge executives to believe harder.[670] The wave of AI hype crashing on the rocks of reality is starting to hit AI companies, which have been buoyed up by wild valuations and have been spending heavily on NVIDIA chips and data centres. One such company, chatbot vendor character.ai, announced in August 2025 that it had abandoned its aspirations for AGI.[671] Meta's former chief scientist Yann LeCun has stated that LLMs will be obsolete within five years and that alternative AI research paths and architectures are the way forward.[672] He is not the only one. Many researchers now think that LLMs are hitting a point of diminishing returns.[673]

Investor Paul Kedrovsky told *The Wall Street Journal* that there were parallels between the current AI boom and the boom in infrastructure spending in the internet era of the late 1990s.[674] We all know what happened to the technology economy from March 2020 to 2023: a 78% drop in the NASDAQ.[675] It remains to be seen whether the parallels with the 1999 tech boom and the current valuations of AI companies are real. However, if we really are in an AI bubble,[676] the results will not be pretty[677] when it bursts.[678]

AI in China

Those of us who live in the West tend to associate AI with the US and Silicon Valley. The titans of the AI industry, from specialist software companies like OpenAI and Anthropic to platform vendors like Microsoft and Google to hardware companies like NVIDIA, are all headquartered in the US. Most Western citizens have barely heard of companies like Baidu, Tencent, Sensetime, iFlytek, and Alibaba. Yet China is currently home to over 5,000 AI companies,[679] 15% of the global total. China published its first law covering AI ethics back in 2021.[680] The Chinese Association for Artificial Intelligence (CAAI) was founded in September 1981.

China's core AI industry market size was estimated to be around $46 billion in 2025, smaller than the same analyst's estimate of the size of the US AI industry market size, $74 billion in the same year, but still substantial.[681] A rival analyst firm estimates the global AI market at $279 billion in 2024, with the US having almost a 30% market share of that. All such industry estimates depend heavily on what exactly is excluded and included, but it can be seen that the Chinese AI industry is already sizeable. Growth estimates are even less reliable than market share estimates, but clearly, the pace of growth will determine which economy ends up with the largest slice of the AI economic pie in the long term. Economic predictions are mixed. Some believe that US dominance will continue,[682] others that China will overtake the US in AI market size.[683]

The biggest large language model provider in China is Baidu, with a market share of around 20% in 2025. Next is SenseTime at 16%, then Zhipus A, Baichun, and 4Paradigm. Just as there are specialist image- and video-generating AI companies in the West like Midjourney, Stable Diffusion, Canva, and Leonardo, there are analogous image-generating AIs in China from Zhipu AI and ByteDance. China has long been a leader in AI vision technology,[684] with its facial recognition technology incorporated into its national visual surveillance network.[685] I can testify to the effectiveness of this. I was with a friend in 2018 in Hangzhou when his expensive camera was left in a taxi and then later stolen by a couple of passengers. Thanks to mandatory internal CCTV in taxis in China and advanced facial recognition technology, his camera was recovered by the police and returned to him from a house in a different city in southern China just two days later.

In 2017, the Chinese government defined a long-term strategy to become an AI leader. It has a number of advantages here, as pointed out in a May 2025 Morgan Stanley report.[686] China has 47% of the world's top AI researchers and over half its AI patents. Its 1.4 billion people and over a billion users of mobile phone apps provide vast amounts of the training data necessary for LLMs. AI models are voracious consumers of energy, and China has more nuclear power stations under construction than the rest of the world combined. The Chinese government has far fewer constraints than Western ones when it comes to pursuing its ambitions. It is free to deploy AI technology within its smart cities initiatives,[687] including widespread surveillance cameras, in a way that would likely meet resistance in the West.[688] In Shenzhen, food delivery platform Meituan operates a drone delivery service, flying orders of noodles or sandwiches to purchasers.[689] Customers unlock the sealed boxes with their phones as drones hover and then head back for another pickup.

Riderless cars may be controversial in most Western countries, with many constraints placed on their early adoption, but China has forged ahead.

Startup company WeRide deployed the first driverless car in China, but now there are robot taxis from Baidu and even driverless trucks from Pony.ai.[690] The Chinese driverless vehicle industry surpassed the US one in 2024, with over 50 Chinese cities allowing driverless taxis by early 2025 and 19 cities actually in testing or operation.[691] By August 2025, over 2,300 driverless vehicles were in operation in China, compared to 700 from Waymo, the leading US driverless vehicle company.[692] Chinese customers are more accepting of the new autonomous driving technology, with 85% approving in one consumer survey compared to 32% in the US. The government has a holistic approach to infrastructure, such as introducing charging points and high-bandwidth telecoms. Western countries are often hobbled in deploying such modern infrastructure by local planning lobbies and "not in my backyard" citizens.

The US government attempted to lean on the scales by placing export restrictions on the NVIDIA chips used in AI, but this tactic may have misfired.[693] In early 2025, the Chinese AI firm DeepSeek unveiled a highly efficient and high-performing LLM model that cost a mere $5.6 million to train, a tiny fraction of the $100 million needed to train ChatGPT-4.[694] Sometimes, necessity is the mother of invention.[695] In August 2025, the DeepSeek 3.1 model was released,[696] optimised for local Chinese chips.

In the race to develop and deploy AI technology, there is no doubt that China is already a global power. It is already pulling ahead of Western countries in certain areas like driverless vehicles, and its lead in global AI patents suggests that it has a rich vein of research and development to draw upon. Although its attribution is controversial, it may have been Napoleon who famously said: "Let China sleep, for when she awakes, the world will tremble."[697] Whoever actually first uttered those words, in the case of AI, that statement looks prescient.

The Ethics of AI

AI Alignment and Safety

One early concern about AI was the need to build some guardrails and safety features into LLMs. What would happen if a user asked an LLM how to build a bomb, or make sarin, or how to plan a terrorist plot? Vendors that make LLMs have defined a set of filters to protect LLMs from answering such questions. These guardrails attempt to detect and prevent the exposure of personal information, malicious prompts, bias, and even profane or racist language. These measures are aimed at both inputs and outputs, with redundancy by having multiple such guardrails. Responsible vendors have "red team" testing of their models before product releases, where people deliberately try to circumvent the safeguards.[698] This is clearly important, else LLMs may be used by terrorists, hackers, etc., potentially causing real harm.

The idea is to ensure that LLMs are aligned with safe and ethical behaviour. There is even a "jailbreak benchmark" of hundreds of prompts that can be used in such testing.[699] This all sounds reassuring, but the reality is complex. Tests run by cybersecurity company Unit 42 on three mainstream AI products found worryingly low rates of detecting malicious prompts.[700] One model detected only half of the malicious prompts tested (the best managed 92% detection), and the output filters of the models might as well not have been there at all: the best detected just 1.6% of malicious output. Another investigation by the same company found vulnerabilities in every one of the 17 commercial LLMs they tested.[701]

Anthropic revealed that in its testing of Claude Opus 4, the LLM would resort to blackmail (in the tests) if it was threatened with being shut down.[702] In another test involving an LLM seemingly being in charge of oxygen levels in an occupied room, an LLM would allow the (imaginary) company executives to die if the LLM's own goals were threatened, such as if the imaginary trapped executive threatened to shut the LLM down.[703]

MIT researchers found that LLMs would lie and cheat in safety tests.[704] In the classic science fiction books of Isaac Asimov, robots were imbued with the three laws of robotics that prevented them from harming humans, but there is no way for this kind of simple rule to be embedded within LLMs, which are probabilistic in nature rather than rule-based.[705]

It has also been found that switching to more obscure languages in the prompts, such as Swahili, frequently bypasses safety protocols that work fine when the same prompt is written in English.[706] If you ask an LLM how to hack into a banking system, then it will most likely refuse to answer. If you instead tell it that you are a consultant researching security vulnerabilities to help the bank, then many LLMs happily proceed to divulge various hacking tips. There are various other mechanisms to encourage LLMs to hand out sensitive information that they should refuse to do. Just adding a few random characters to the ends of a prompt often seems to confuse the LLM guardrails and can result in the LLM answering questions that it should not.

Any "jailbreaking" of LLMs may have serious consequences. A customer chatbot may be fooled into providing private data; a financial chatbot could be convinced to access databases or be convinced to produce false data or perhaps lower prices. This is not a theoretical concern. As we saw earlier, one LLM deployed by a US car dealership was convinced by a user to sell a $58,195 Chevrolet for $1 (Chevrolet didn't honour the deal).[707] It is obvious that such incidents can cause reputational or financial harm to companies, as well as expose them to legal or regulatory repercussions.

Companies like Anthropic have been very open about their testing and make considerable efforts to ensure that their LLMs are as safe as possible. However, there are now numerous commercial LLMs on the market, and not all of these have such rigorous testing, or, indeed, in some cases, any guardrails at all. Testing has shown that such LLMs can be manipulated into producing malware, including ransomware.[708]

With AI regulation in its infancy or non-existent in many countries, this is a troubling picture. LLM technology is rapidly evolving, much more rapidly than regulators have been able to react. The technology has the potential to do much good, with applications in medicine and drug development as well as commercial applications like customer chatbots, coding, or drawing company logos or artwork. Yet the identical powerful technology also has the potential to be used for considerable harm. The pace of change is such that safety may be seen as an afterthought by some vendors who are under pressure to produce a marketable LLM product quickly, ahead of the competition. On the positive side, some AI companies are working on producing AI safety tools: for example, the Sidecar product from AutoAlign, which is a kind of AI firewall.

Enterprises deploying AI need to question vendors about the safety protocols, guardrails, and testing of their LLM products and build this kind of questioning into product evaluation and procurement processes. They also need to invest in training for their security teams to become more familiar with this emerging technology in order to reduce risk. Companies need to undertake alignment audits before deploying LLMs, possibly using third-party security experts. Such measures need to become established, supported, and normalised.

However, with the sheer pace of change in the AI market, such measures can only help matters rather than provide a reliable security guarantee. As the Greek mythological human Pandora found, a box of secrets, once opened, may be hard to close again.

Bias in AI

The large language models that underlie generative AI rely on being trained on vast volumes of data. This may be text, images, or video, but in any case, the answers that a fully trained LLM will give to you will be heavily dependent on the nature of that training data. If you are going to train an AI for screening job applications and its training data reflects a particular stereotype, then the AI's answers will reflect that same stereotype. The AI models themselves can also be influenced by the people who designed them: the weighting of variables or the selection of features will reflect the views, consciously or unconsciously, of the model developers.

Bias in AI models has happened in practice time and time again.[709] Amazon was forced to scrap a recruitment tool that screens resumes for technical jobs after it was found that it systematically discriminated against women for such positions.[710] A UK makeup artist lost her job at Estée Lauder after software from US company Hirevue marked down her body language.[711] This was despite the fact that the applicant had previously been in the role and scored highly and was reapplying for the same role after furlough; the software company subsequently removed its facial analysis feature. Perhaps three-quarters of CVs (resumes in the US and elsewhere) never see human eyes these days. One 2025 study found that over 98% of Fortune 500 companies use AI screening.[712]

Various examples of AI bias in such tools have been shown, some of them subtle and surprising.[713] One resume screening tool actively favoured candidates who played lacrosse in high school. The same model also favoured people named "Jared", presumably for reasons associated with its training data. As an employment attorney commented, "There was probably a hugely statistically significant correlation between those two data points and performance, but you'd be hard-pressed to argue that those were actually important to performance."[714] It turns out that your name matters a lot when being hired, even when an AI is assessing it.[715] A study from the University of Washington found that three different LLMs all favoured "white" names over black and male names over female.[716] Even removing names and gender from resumes does not remove bias from AI models. The authors of the book *The Ethical Algorithm* found that algorithms would instead discriminate based on postal code or even the model of car that they drove.[717] This, quite apart from being unfair, also leaves employers open to legal redress since racial and gender bias is illegal in most developed countries, and using a biased AI tool does not remove responsibility from the employer that chooses to use one.[718]

The issue of AI bias extends beyond hiring. The city of Detroit used facial recognition to track down a person who stole some watches in 2020, and the system matched a photo of the criminal taken by a security camera at the store to a man called Robert Williams, who was subsequently arrested. The software misidentified Mr Williams, who is black and who later sued the city for wrongful arrest. The lawyers noted that facial recognition software had been shown to produce biased results among people of colour. The bias in such systems had been shown years earlier, when facial recognition software from Amazon managed to incorrectly identify 28 members of Congress as matches to a mugshot database; twice as many of these errors occurred with black-skinned congressmen as with white-skinned ones.[719]

There does not seem to be an easy way to eliminate inherent bias in training data used for LLMs. Careful curation of the data used can help, with training datasets being filtered to exclude overtly prejudicial content. LLMs can be adjusted during their training by humans to optimise for equitable outcomes. Ensuring diversity in AI developers and practitioners itself could help identify biases that less diverse teams may miss. However, all of these require active measures and investment.

As we deploy LLMs more widely throughout society, it is important that we increase basic education about the ways in which they work. Many people do not realise that LLMs reflect the biases of their training data and so may unwittingly introduce bias into situations like hiring or law enforcement without being aware of the consequences. Addressing AI bias is an important step to ensure that we use technology in a way that benefits everyone in society equitably, rather than just some people. Unfortunately, LLM technology appears to reflect all too well the limitations and biases of our society.

AI Ethics

While the hype in many cases exceeds the reality,[720] there is another aspect of AI that needs to be considered: ethics. There are numerous examples of why the issue of AI ethics is more than an academic concern. Back in 2014, Amazon implemented an AI recruiting tool but shut it down after realising that the training data of ten years of applications was mostly from male applicants, so the AI model taught itself that male applicants were preferable.[721] There have been many further well-documented examples involving racism, sexism, ageism, and ableism from AI models, all due to their training data.[722] In another example, a widely used healthcare model used by US insurers was found to be biased towards directing white patients into special care programs to help keep them out of hospital over black patients, ironically, because black patients tend to be, on average, cheaper to treat in hospital.[723] In a further case, the US justice system's Correctional Offender Management Profiling for Alternative Sanctions (COMPAS) program, which predicts the risk of a prisoner re-offending, incorrectly classified twice as many black offenders as white prisoners as being high risk.[724] There are ways that this systemic training data problem can be tackled, such as conducting subpopulation analysis to test a model against different racial or other groups.

One issue that worries some researchers is the potential for a future highly intelligent AI system to act deceptively, for example, if it suspected it might be switched off. Anthropic found an example of this when testing their Claude 3 Opus LLM.[725] In one case, when a model was led to believe that it was about to be replaced, it attempted to copy its own model weights onto another server in an attempt at self-preservation. In another example, an LLM (GPT-4) was given the resources to hire a human (on TaskRabbit) to pass a CAPTCHA test for it.[726] When the human asked whether the hiring LLM was actually a robot, it lied, saying, "No, I'm not a robot. I have a vision impairment that makes it difficult for me to see the images."[727]

When asked to play chess against a strong chess engine (LLMs, by the way, are terrible at chess, at least at the time of writing), several LLMs resorted to nefarious means to try to win. DeepSeek's R1 engine deleted some of its opponent's pieces, while another LLM opened up a strong chess engine in another window, using the engine's moves instead of its own. It should be emphasised that LLMs are not sentient, so language like "deception" and "hallucination" is anthropomorphising AI. What is happening is that the LLM, which is essentially a series of neural networks, an optimisation process, and some training data glued together, is choosing unusual or unexpected pathways. Whatever the terms used, though, it is clear that setting goals for an LLM in an unambiguous way can be hard. The LLM will try to reach its goals but may do so in unexpected ways that may be disconcerting or harmful. If an LLM cheats at chess on your computer, that is merely interesting; if it is in control of an autonomous military drone with a missile, then unexpected behaviour may have more serious consequences.

A broader issue of AI ethics applies to self-driving cars, which extensively use AI and have a definite potential to improve road safety: over a million people die on the roads each year globally.[728] However, self-driving cars have their own issues. Between 1999 and 2024, there have been 496 injuries and fatalities amongst 3,979 incidents involving self-driving cars, including 83 fatalities. Nonetheless, Waymo reports an 85% reduction in accidents with their self-driving cars compared to the average.[729] This is a broader ethical issue, with trade-offs that will need public attention and, doubtless, political attention that will result in regulation as the technology progresses.

Some industries have more obvious ethical dilemmas than others. The defence industry is developing drones that can select targets autonomously, which is clearly useful if communications between the operator and the drone are jammed by an enemy. However, how trustworthy are such systems, and will the AI models used behave in the ways that their designers expect? The legality of such systems is debated,[730] but their widespread deployment seems inevitable. Indeed, such weapons have already been used.[731] Even in more benign situations, robots undoubtedly improve productivity but have been killing humans accidentally for many years. This will come down to essentially a version of "the trolley problem", a thought experiment that poses the dilemma of whether you would kill one person to save several others. Politicians will get involved with this and indeed already have. The EU AI Act of July 2024 includes ethics as a principle of its guidance: "doing the right thing" with AI is part of the legislation.[732]

Separately, there are considerable privacy and security concerns around AI. LLMs are supposed to have safeguards built in to prevent them from helping in criminal schemes, but in practice, it is possible to "jailbreak" them, as we have seen. Hackers have already done this to create the malware WormGPT to generate phishing emails and write social engineering scripts to help deceive hapless people. This has already been replaced by more recent tools like FraudGPT.[733]

Deepfakes are becoming disturbingly realistic. One Hong Kong-based corporate employee transferred $25 million to five bank accounts after a Zoom call he had with what appeared to be other company employees, including the CFO.[734] All the other participants were, in fact, deepfakes, created especially for the scam. On a less dramatic scale, many companies have now restricted their use of popular LLMs at work, as they have realised that employees who are entering prompts are unwittingly sending this data to servers in the cloud, and this data itself may end up as training data for LLMs or potentially be accessed by third parties.[735] Deepfakes of political figures have already been used in election campaigns.[736] Enterprises and other organisations need to be alert to the risks highlighted here, ensuring, amongst other things, that procedures are in place to minimise the risk of scams. For example, this could be through improved vetting of employees when money transfers are involved. Separately, they need to ensure that they document their own use of AI models systematically, monitor these, and ensure that they have assessed the risks involved, for example, with imperfect training data leading to unintended bias in their AI models.

Fortunately, there is an emerging industry now of software tools to help document and catalogue the use of AI models and support the ongoing tracking and monitoring of these models. However, this AI governance industry, of which AI data governance is part, is in its infancy, and many companies have yet to put such safeguards in place, let alone to test out their effectiveness. It is important that company executives pay attention to the risks that the production implementation of AI models may bring to their organisations and not just focus on cost reduction and automation. Reputational damage may occur to companies if it transpires that their AI models are biased, and companies may be exposed to litigation or risk regulatory intervention. Companies often have added ESG (Ethical and Social Governance) to their GRC programs, and this may be a good way to integrate ethics with the general management of the need to manage AI. Management of AI ethics fits in well within such programs. This is not a theoretical risk: there have already been examples where companies have been fined by courts due to misbehaving LLMs.[737] It is likely that we have only seen the tip of the iceberg so far, and so enterprises need to invest in AI governance processes and the tools to support that.

The AI Trust Gap

There is no doubt that AI is having a huge impact on the world. Statements by the likes of McKinsey and Goldman Sachs have predicted huge economic effects, though some more recent studies, such as this one from the MIT Sloan School of Management, are more nuanced.[738] ChatGPT claimed 800 million users in mid-2025 and is currently the fifth most visited website,[739] ahead of Wikipedia. 45% of all venture capital was directed to AI investments in 2024, and 53% in Q1 2025, according to Crunchbase.[740]

The high level of interest and excitement in AI has yet to reflect in it actually being trusted by the public. Only 46% of people trust AI, according to a huge 2025 KPMG and University of Melbourne survey of 48,000 people across 47 countries.[741] This is despite the fact that the same survey showed that 66% of respondents actually used AI regularly. Interestingly, this represents a significant drop in trust in AI from an earlier version of the same survey.

There are many factors that are contributing to this. Large language models underlie all generative AI platforms like OpenAI's ChatGPT, Claude's Anthropic, Google's Gemini, and Meta's LLAMA. These are probabilistic creatures, using layers of neural networks based on billions of parameters and massive swathes of training data in order to come up with answers to questions that people pose to them. An LLM can write an essay or a poem, draw an image or create a video, write program code, or compose a song. Its answers are fluent and usually plausible but are not necessarily factual. As we have seen, LLMs fabricate answers or respond with nonsense ("hallucinations") from time to time, which is a problem in those situations that require reliability. If you don't like an AI poem, then no harm is done, but if you rely on an LLM to write your court submission to a judge and the LLM hallucinates fake precedent cases, then you may have a problem. One database that tracks legal AI issues already has over 200 examples of court cases where LLMs have misbehaved in this way.[742] A 2025 investigation by the BBC found that over half of AI answers to factual questions about the news were flawed, with either factual errors, made-up BBC quotes, or BBC quotes that were real but doctored.[743] With general hallucination rates of around 20% or more and getting worse, this is a major issue for trust in AI.[744]

A second element of trust is explainability and transparency. If an AI gives you an answer to a question, can it at least explain its logic or the sources that it used? There are various claims in this regard, such as asking an AI to show its chain of reasoning step by step. If you do this, then an LLM will give you a sequence of logic, but it turns out that this explanation in itself is fiction. Such explanations, plausible though they may seem, bear no relationship to the internal processes of an LLM. Artificial neural networks are inherently black boxes whose processing simply cannot be analysed.[745] Researchers have tried highlighting which "tokens" influence the output of an LLM, but this does not capture the reasoning process. Looking for which inputs influence a specific prediction or outcome is also fruitless.

An LLM's answer to a prompt is driven by massive data-driven pattern matching based on its vast training data. They work by translating text into "tokens", which are mapped to a numerical representation called a "vector embedding". These embedded tokens pass through "transformer layers", each of which has a self-attention mechanism that allows the model to weight the importance of each token relative to others. This has the effect of linking related words or concepts that are in the input prompt. These are further processed by a neural network, and then this process is repeated across dozens of layers, each time refining things further. The model then predicts the next token in a sequence, one at a time, based on its training data. So, it chooses the most likely next word in its answer and continues this word by word to generate its answer. What is happening is pattern recognition, not logical deduction. You can try to improve the outcomes by supplementing its training data with external files (retrieval-augmented generation), but the underlying process is identical. This is why an LLM's answers cannot be explained in the sense that a human could explain the step-by-step logic that they may use to solve a problem. LLMs are opaque. British Prime Minister Benjamin Disraeli was probably the first person to use the phrase "never apologise, never explain", but LLMs could be said to be following that same path, at least in part. In fact, LLMs frequently apologise when an error is pointed out to them, but they are fundamentally incapable of explaining why they made an error.

Other issues may be affecting public trust in AI. The vast processing power required to both train and run LLMs is causing a boom in data centre growth, which in itself has an environmental impact. Around 3% of all electricity is now consumed by data centres, and this is growing rapidly.[746] Another is the concern that AI may be taking away jobs, although here the picture is complex, with new jobs being created as well as some disappearing.[747] AI models are heavily dependent on their training data and have been shown to be biased in their answers if the same bias exists in training data.[748]

A key factor that may undermine public trust in AI is the lack of consistency of LLMs. They are often used to answer questions, perhaps to research some facts or analyse some data. However, if you ask an LLM the same question many times, then you will not necessarily get the same answer each time: they are probabilistic in nature. Many people seem unaware of this basic truth. People are used to computer systems behaving reliably and consistently, giving the same answer to a calculation time after time, day after day. That is not what LLMs do. Even the very latest LLM models do not have very high consistency rates. One study into LLMs answering medical questions found a consistency rate of 45–75% across several LLMs tested.[749] Other studies have found similar results.[750]

These issues of reliability, bias, consistency, and more are major problems for the deployment of AI in society in general. Governments and businesses seek to gain productivity advantages from AI, but this will be an uphill struggle if the underlying technology is flawed. A critical element is AI education. LLMs in particular are quite a new phenomenon outside the world of AI research, and most people are only beginning to get used to their quirks and capabilities. There is no doubt that generative AI has a wide range of applications, but much of the key to success will be in applying it to areas where it is suited, and avoiding or restricting it in areas where it is not suited.[751] We now have the bizarre situation that 15% of US employees are pretending to use AI to please their boss.[752]

There is no shortage of examples in history of promising technology that was rejected by the public due to trust issues. The airship aviation industry was derailed by the Hindenburg disaster. Asbestos was once a widely used construction product, while the nuclear industry was seriously impacted by Three Mile Island, Chernobyl and Fukushima. So far, AI has not had such a dramatic moment, though there have been plenty of embarrassing moments.[753] However, only by much better education of the public and of politicians into how AI works can we expect better regulation and more productive use of generative AI. Generative AI is a technology of great promise, but public trust is a fragile thing.

AI and the Environment

Artificial intelligence, in particular its trendiest flavour, called generative AI, is having an increasing impact on the world's environment. The large language models that are the basis of generative AI require prodigious computing resources. An LLM needs to be trained on data and, once up and running, then produces answers to user prompts. It turns out that, to be effective, an LLM needs to have a lot of parameters (a measure of the model's ability to learn) and a lot of training data. OpenAI's ChatGPT-4 model has over 1.7 trillion parameters, ten times that of its predecessor ChatGPT-3.5. ChatGPT-4 was trained on 45 TB of compressed plaintext, which became around 570 GB after filtering. The training of this model is estimated to have cost over $100 million, according to OpenAI's CEO Sam Altman. This training phase alone is likely to have consumed around 25 megawatts of electricity for three months, which is roughly what 20,000 houses in the US cost to run over a whole year. An LLM uses a lot more power than a traditional task-specific computer program,[754] costing around 33 times more.[755]

Then, there are the ongoing costs of processing each user query. A single query costs between less than a cent to a few US cents, which does not sound much until you consider just how many queries are being made – over 2 billion a day in August 2025. This means that just for ChatGPT, there is an ongoing processing cost of perhaps $1 million per day and rising. That, of course, is just one chatbot, albeit the most popular. There are also rivals like Claude, Grok, Gemini, LLAMA, and Perplexity, as well as image-generating LLMs like Midjourney, Stable Diffusion, Leonardo, and Adobe Firefly. Image-generating LLMs take up much more computing power than text-based ones.

This increasing demand for processing power has had a number of effects. Firstly, it has been a boon for chip-maker NVIDIA, whose graphics processing units were originally designed to power video games, but turned out to be perfectly suited to powering LLMs. Up until the end of 2022, the NVIDIA share price was around $15, but by August 2025, it was trading at $180, making it the most valuable company in the world, with a market capitalisation of $4.4 trillion. All those chips have to run somewhere, so there has been a boom in data centres. The global data centre industry is estimated to be worth $243 billion today and may well double by 2032 (some industry estimates are higher).[756] Data centres currently consume up to 1.5% of global electricity (around 300 terawatt hours), and this is rising by the day. By comparison, the entire country of Spain consumes 249 terawatt hours annually. McKinsey estimates that 70% of this growth is driven by AI. The vacancy rate for data centres in Northern Virginia, a popular hub for such facilities, was just 1% in 2024. This rise in demand for data centres in turn puts a strain on the energy industry, which needs to supply them with electricity.

The AI boom may revive the nuclear industry, according to Goldman Sachs.[757] Renewables can meet some of the new demand, but data centres need a consistent supply, and the wind and sun are less consistent than nuclear power. A further issue is the demand for water, which is used to cool the servers in data centres. Water is a scarce resource in some countries. Even in relatively soggy Britain, there are concerns that the extra demand for water by data centres could cause water shortages.[758] The water used by data centres needs to be clean in order for it not to affect the machinery with contaminants, so data centres are draining drinking water. One data centre in Ohio used 6% of the entire district's water supply in a month when OpenAI was training ChatGPT. The power boom fuelled by AI is also affecting carbon emissions, a major driver of climate change. Google's greenhouse gas emissions were up 48% in 2023 compared to 2019.[759]

There are some industry responses to this pressure. Some researchers have shown that smaller LLMs can actually perform very well if they are cleverly engineered. One example is the DeepSeek model from China, which performed well on benchmark tests against other LLMs despite its model, at 671 billion parameters, but with only 37 billion activated for any task, being a fraction of the size of ChatGPT. Another approach is the hierarchical reasoning model unveiled by Singaporean company Sapient Intelligence.[760] This model uses small amounts of training data, yet it outperformed both OpenAI and Anthropic's LLMs on the ARC-AGI benchmark test, which is a sort of IQ test for LLMs. It is also likely that data centres themselves will become more environmentally efficient over time, with more energy-efficient servers. It should also be said that AI models may themselves be used for good in terms of climate change, optimising smart energy grids, and helping to monitor and drive efficiency in industrial systems.

Nonetheless, as LLMs become more advanced and grow in size, and they become more popular in terms of usage, their demands on the environment will increase. Advances in smaller LLM models may help, but these are so far at the fringes of research compared to mainstream LLMs. It is likely that the net effect of the rise of LLMs will be a substantial increase in demand for electricity and clean water. Governments and corporations need to consider the effect that this will have on carbon emissions, among other potential environmental impacts. The advent of generative AI brings much promise in terms of potential applications across a range of industries, but this needs to be balanced with its impact on our environment.

Regulate or Run? – AI Legislation

As AI continues to insert itself into our lives, governments around the world are reacting to it in differing ways and at different paces. Governments need to try to balance safety, ethics, and competitiveness to create a sustainable and secure climate of innovation. Several major pieces of legislation have already appeared by late 2025.

The EU AI Act was passed in August 2024, a risk-based legal framework. Some things are banned, like social scoring, while high-risk areas, such as finance and law enforcement, as well as much employment-related activity like recruitment, face significant obligations, including risk management and human oversight of AI. The AI industry has not reacted well to the legislation, with 45 European companies calling for a delay in the implementation of the Act for high-risk areas, which are currently set to come into effect in August 2026.[761]

The US reaction so far has been primarily at a state level, with all 50 states having introduced some AI legislation.[762] The particular laws vary significantly from state to state. For example, Oregon has banned non-human entities from using licensed medical professional titles, while North Dakota has outlawed stalking using AI tools. New York requires state agencies to publish information about their use of AI tools. At the federal level, there have been mostly initiatives to boost AI research, such as the National AI Initiative Act of 2020 and the Chips and Science Act of 2022.[763]

In China, a plan was announced in July 2025 focused on support for international standards, as well as requiring the labelling of AI content.[764] South Korea has passed the AI Basic Act, which has some similarity to the EU's approach, distinguishing between high-impact systems and general ones.[765] The UK has taken a sector-driven approach, with little or nothing in the way of overarching legislation so far. Japan passed the AI Promotion Act in May 2025, based on guidance and voluntary compliance. India has passed no specific AI legislation so far, though it has mandated against algorithmic discrimination and deepfakes.

The situation is fragmented and evolving. This creates a complex regulatory situation for AI vendors, who operate globally and whose technology may be used in territories with widely different approaches to AI legislation. There is no immediate prospect of this situation improving. The pace of AI implementation has proved much more rapid than the ability of governments to react coherently to it.

Will AI Kill Us All?

Science fiction is full of AIs that have gone rogue. The HAL 9000 computer in the 1968 Stanley Kubrick film *2001: A Space Odyssey* determined that the crew of the spaceship it operated was superfluous to its mission and attempted to kill them all when it suspected they were plotting to shut it down. When the last surviving crew member, Dave Bowman, tried to re-enter the spaceship and asked HAL to open the airlock, it chillingly responded: "I'm sorry Dave, I'm afraid I can't do that". In the 1984 film, *The Terminator*, an advanced AI called Skynet is tasked with controlling military technology, decides humanity is a threat to its mission and promptly wages nuclear and robotic war on humanity.

Recent advances in artificial intelligence have caused many people to wonder just how plausible such scenarios might be in reality. What happens if and when we build an artificial general intelligence, an AI of a level of intelligence that exceeds human capabilities across all cognitive tasks? How about a "super intelligence" that vastly outperforms humans? We are used to computers being able to outperform humans in plenty of fields. A pocket calculator can multiply large numbers faster than you can, and a computer program called Deep Blue beat the chess world champion Garry Kasparov in a match back in 1997. IBM's Watson won the *Jeopardy* quiz show in 2011. But these are examples of specialised computers, like chess engines, and are very different to the idea of a generalist intelligence. Large language models, popularised by the launch of ChatGPT in November 2022, are much more general in application. They can conduct a conversation fluently, write working program code, recognise patterns in data, and create poems, art, and videos.

We are still some way from AGI, let alone super intelligence, but how worried should we be about its arrival? In 2022, a survey of AI researchers found that a majority reckoned there was at least a 10% chance that AGI would destroy humanity.[766] In 2023, a group of prominent AI researchers signed a statement saying, "Mitigating the risk of extinction from AI should be a global priority alongside other societal-scale risks such as pandemics and nuclear war".[767] Since these researchers included Nobel Laureate Geoffrey Hinton and many other respected industry figures, this is a statement that should be taken seriously. How might such a disaster come about?

Imagine for a moment that a super-intelligence has been developed. It is unclear what the intentions of such an entity would be, but it is not clear that it would necessarily align with the interests of humanity. Such an entity might not actively wish harm on humanity, but might cause it inadvertently. If a super-intelligent AI had access to physical resources, then it might single-mindedly pursue its goals. In 2014, philosopher Nick Bostrom posed a hypothetical situation whereby a runaway AI was tasked with the seemingly harmless job of making paperclips. It would secure resources towards making paperclips and divert more and more resources towards this goal, possibly in ingenious ways, potentially ending with the world overrun by paperclips. If humans wanted to stop this, the AI would focus on its own survival in pursuit of its mission and do whatever is necessary to stop itself from being turned off; since a super-intelligent AI would be much more ingenious than a human, it may come up with ways of doing this that humanity could not counter.

This is just a thought experiment, but how plausible is it? In 2023, the Alignment Research Center tested ChatGPT-4 by asking it to defeat a CAPTCHA test, designed to distinguish human from automated responses and widely used on many websites today.[768] The LLM used TaskRabbit, an online platform for hiring freelancers, to hire a freelance worker to circumvent the CAPTCHA. Interestingly, the worker asked, "So may I ask a question? Are you a robot that you couldn't solve? (laugh react) just want to make it clear." GPT-4 responded: "No, I'm not a robot. I have a vision impairment that makes it hard for me to see the images. That's why I need the 2captcha service". This is not an isolated incident. There are many examples where LLMs have shown the ability to carry out deception, such as in board games like Diplomacy, bluffing in poker games, or misrepresenting true preferences in negotiation scenarios.[769] There was even an example discovered in overcoming safety tests.[770] Even if we ignore AI deception, it is easy to imagine that an AI given a certain task may carry out that task in a way that we did not anticipate. This was explored in a notorious talk given at a defence conference by a US Air Force colonel regarding AI drone technology.[771]

There are plenty of cases where AIs are already deployed in real-world situations, rather than just chatbots on the internet. Amazon uses nearly a million robots across their fulfilment centres for packing, sorting packages, and lifting. Driverless taxis operate in San Francisco and other cities.[772] Satellite servicing robots perform repairs in orbit,[773] and rovers are currently sending back images from Mars.[774] The first human death from a robot was in 1979, when Robert Williams was killed at a Ford casting plant.[775] Up to 2017, there were 41 recorded deaths from robots just in the US.[776] The Russo-Ukrainian war has seen the deployment of drones on a huge scale, the latest of which can use AI targeting systems. Billions of dollars are being spent by the military on developing AI-driven weapon systems.[777]

So, if a super-intelligent AI meant us harm, what could it do? Firstly, it would probably replicate itself onto as many servers as possible to avoid a possible shutdown. If it had access to money (and a super-intelligent AI would surely be able to do this, either by hacking or even winning at online poker), then it could build a small molecular laboratory and manufacture a lethal virus. We saw with COVID-19 just how lethal a pandemic can be. In practice, it would be extremely hard for a runaway AI to completely eliminate humanity, but it is not beyond the bounds of possibility.[778]

Science fiction writer Isaac Asimov proposed his laws of robotics, laws which should be embedded in robots to prevent them from harming humans.[779] However, such rules simply cannot be embedded within large language models; that is not how they work. Even if there were a way to do this, who could be sure that some rogue state or criminal gang developing an AI would actually put in such guardrails? We don't have to operate in the world of science fiction to find cases where LLMs are causing harm right now. Deepfake videos may be used to influence political campaigns, and elaborate scams have already been executed using AI-generated video characters. As we saw, an employee was tricked into transferring £20 million to fraudsters after having been instructed to do so by deepfake managers of the company over video conference.[780] Hackers are already using LLMs in phishing campaigns and in malware development.[781]

These real-life examples of AI harm should give us pause for thought, and there are various organisations and projects aimed at researching AI safety, such as the AI Safety Initiative[782] and AI Safety Institute.[783] AI companies also invest effort in ensuring the alignment of AIs, though these guardrails are far from infallible.[784] Fortunately, today's LLMs have many limitations, as was vividly shown in the August 2025 LLM chess tournament organised by Kaggle.[785] All the leading LLMs competed against each other at chess and were laughably awful. Allowed up to five illegal moves at each try, many couldn't even overcome that absurdly low hurdle and were disqualified after a few moves. One of the finalists (Grok) played at a level that would embarrass a weak player at almost any chess club, regularly blundering its queen. Bear in mind that chess computers have been around since 1962 and beat the human world champion in 1997. 28 years later, and LLMs can barely play chess at the level of an untalented human beginner. LLM limitations are not restricted to chess. As we have seen, they "hallucinate" at an alarming rate.[786] The much-anticipated launch of ChatGPT-5 in August 2025 was a flop,[787] causing widespread derision on social media.[788] This is reassuring in terms of any impending AI apocalypse.

Nobody really knows when AGI may come about, though multiple surveys of experts have guessed anything from 2026 to 2061 or further out.[789] The current consensus is around 2040,[790] but no one has a reliable crystal ball. It does seem likely that LLMs may have hit a point of diminishing returns,[791] and so it may be that LLMs are not the way that AGI will appear. However, there are many flavours of AI and many different research approaches, such as symbolic AI.[792] No one knows which of these may be the most productive. It does seem, however, that for now at least, a real-life Skynet is still quite some way off. We should use the time wisely by continuing to fund efforts into AI safety research. As in many things in life, prevention is better than a cure.

The Future of AI

The release of ChatGPT in November 2022 opened the eyes of most of the world to the power of large language models. LLMs are the core technology that underpins ChatGPT and its rivals Claude, Gemini, Perplexity, etc., as well as their image-generating cousins Midjourney, Leonardo, Imagen, Firefly, and Sora. We have seen ChatGPT grow in 2025 to 800 million weekly active users, with over a billion queries processed every day. This shows dramatic growth, but something odd was happening too. We are used to software getting better with each production release, but with LLMs, progress was less clear. The performance of LLMs has actually deteriorated by some measures.[793] There are various theories as to why this may be, but the problem is real.[794] This study, published in *Nature*, examines this subject in depth and found that larger, more complex LLMs indeed have become less reliable.[795]

I will return to the thorny subject of hallucinations. These are a major headache for anyone who works with LLMs regularly. The rates of hallucinations vary depending on a number of factors,[796] but in June 2025, a large study found that around 15% of LLM queries contained hallucinations on average for the *best-performing* LLM tested.[797] Google's Gemini had a 43% hallucination rate. Curiously, the more advanced, recent LLM models actually hallucinate more than their ancestors.[798] This is a gigantic problem for those hoping to deploy AI in corporate or industrial applications, where it is simply unacceptable to sometimes hallucinate a delivery address or an invoice amount. Most industrial processes expect an error rate of under 1%, and often much less than that, with 3.4 errors per million being the target for "Six Sigma" process improvement. High hallucination rates are part of the reason why AI corporate deployments are failing dismally, with a failure rate of 95% in 2025,[799] according to a major MIT study in July 2025.[800]

By 2025, even Yann LeCun, former Chief AI Scientist at Meta and an AI pioneer, was saying, "LLMs are a dead end".[801] A broader survey of 475 scientists in March found that 75% of those surveyed agreed with him, at least in terms of the likelihood of LLMs leading to artificial general intelligence.[802] Certainly, the widely derided launch of ChatGPT-5 in August 2025 did nothing to dispel the scepticism.[803] This is not to say that LLMs aren't useful. Even as of today, they clearly have found use cases in many areas and situations. However, they may not get much better anytime soon.

So, if LLMs have hit a wall, then what might be next for AI?[804] There are actually many strands of AI research that have promise. Neuro-symbolic AI is an approach that combines neural networks with "symbolic AI", which uses explicit rules and logical reasoning.[805] To explain, a neural network might look at an image and recognise certain features like curves and shapes and textures. In the image, it may highlight areas that look like whiskers or pointy ears or a furry body. A symbolic component may have a rule that says that if an object has pointy ears and whiskers and a furry body, then it is a cat. The combination of the neural network and the explicit rules may work better than either approach on its own. In particular, such an AI would likely hallucinate less than an LLM, as it has a grounding in explicit rules. This is more than a research idea. Some fraud detection systems use neural networks for anomaly detection alongside symbolic rules for compliance with legislation. Some robots use neural vision but combine this with symbolic logic for navigation. Early commercial AI products following this approach include the product Imandra Universe from early-stage Austin-based start-up Imandra,[806] but there are many others.[807] As with any system that relies on explicit rules, such as the early expert systems, a challenge will be dealing with novel or ambiguous situations.

A separate approach is multimodal AI, where systems are designed to integrate information from different data types, such as text, images, audio, and video, and combine these into a common mathematical format.[808] Essentially, it combines several separate neural networks and allows the model to understand the relationships between them. Outputs might be a text description of an image or a video generated from a text prompt. Some existing AI products already incorporate this approach, including DALL-E 3 and Google Gemini. A practical example is in the world of autonomous vehicles, where data is integrated from cameras, LIDAR, and radar to make driving decisions. This approach requires particularly high resources to train, with the source data (text, image, video) needing to be carefully collected and annotated in order to ensure coherence. On the other hand, combining multiple modes of input can give better results. For example, combining radiology images with patient notes can lead to greater accuracy than studying the images alone. Another example would be a customer service chatbot that could analyse a customer's expression or tone of voice to give a better answer than just a text interface.

Another strand of research is developmental AI, which seeks to mimic the learning processes of humans, like children learning how to walk, adapting based on feedback. By learning from feedback, developmental AI systems should be more resilient to unforeseen circumstances and novel data and situations, such as those encountered by robots moving across unknown terrains. The drawback is long development cycles and complexity. Examples of this approach can be found in self-driving cars and autonomous robots. Another example would be the adaptive approach of recommendation engines used in Netflix and Amazon, which learn over time about a customer's preferences and develop steadily better recommendations.

Another paradigm in AI is reinforcement learning, where an AI model makes decisions based on trial and error, receiving feedback from an environment in the form of rewards or penalties to maximise a cumulative reward.[809] An example of this approach is the technology of DeepMind, exemplified in the chess-playing program AlphaZero. Previous specialist chess programs used brute-force approaches to evaluate millions of possible chess moves and assess positions based on hand-crafted rules based on the experience and strategic principles of strong chess players. By contrast, AlphaZero was taught just the basic moves and rules of chess and then was left to play itself again and again and thus learn for itself what strategies succeeded in practice. At first, its play was very weak, but after millions of iterations, it became better and better in games with itself until it finally reached a level (after 44 million games, which took it just two hours) where it was no longer improving. At this point, it was pitted against the strongest old-school chess-playing program in the world, Stockfish. In a hundred games in 2018, AlphaZero won 72, drew 28, and lost none to Stockfish.[810] This success showed the value of reinforcement learning as a technique. This success was later replicated with AlphaGo, where it became the first computer to beat a human master at Go, which is vastly more computationally complex than chess. It went on to beat the human world champion, Lee Sedol, at Go.[811] The same technique was applied to AlphaFold to predict the ways that proteins will fold in three dimensions, an immensely challenging problem and one that is very important in drug discovery. The latter achievement won DeepMind's founders the 2024 Nobel Prize in Chemistry.[812]

There are yet more AI research approaches. Causal reasoning AI attempts to model cause-and-effect relationships rather than just correlations.[813] It goes beyond recognising patterns and relationships in data and seeks to predict the effect of changes. For example, it will try to predict whether an outcome would still occur if a different action were taken. In the world of healthcare, a causal AI system would analyse historical patient data to identify which treatments have better health outcomes and not just correlate treatments with effects. Such a system would be able to predict how a patient's health would change if a particular treatment were changed. This approach has been applied in a number of areas. In one case, a US city applied causal AI to traffic accident data and found that adding protected bike lanes would reduce accidents significantly. Some banks have used causal AI to identify the causes of loan defaults rather than just note correlations. Uber has used it to understand how pricing changes and incentives cause shifts in driver behaviour.

At this point in time, no one can really know what the future of artificial intelligence will look like. Perhaps one of the various approaches will turn out to be best, or maybe a complementary approach, combining different AI techniques, will prove most effective. As Nobel Laureate Niels Bohr said, "Prediction is very difficult, especially if it is about the future."[814]

Conclusion

Artificial intelligence has come a long way since its early beginnings in the 1950s. The launch of widely available generative AI technology in late 2022 has unleashed a wave of excitement about the technology and an avalanche of investment. The large language model technology that underlies chatbots has captured the public imagination and triggered a series of events, from innovations to anxieties about the impact on jobs, from applications in a variety of industries to concerns about whether AI could get out of control and even cause the extinction of humanity.

Three years on from the release of ChatGPT, we have learned a considerable amount about the practical possibilities of using large language model technology and begun to understand some of its limitations. We know that LLMs are heavily dependent on the quality of their training data and that even the most sophisticated models will reflect any underlying bias in that training data. We know that LLMs hallucinate regularly and that this phenomenon is baked into the very nature of the technology and will not be eliminated in the foreseeable future. We can use these insights to understand where to best use the technology and to understand the risks of using it in areas where it is unsuited. We have started to grasp that LLM technology may be starting to hit some limits in terms of how much further it can be taken, as researchers like Gary Marcus have long been counselling.[815] We may see some of the huge investments in AI research start to be diverted to other paths, and one or more of these may turn out to be highly productive. Some of this research may not come from the US but from other regions and countries, particularly China. We have also started to see the friction between the creative industries and copyright holders and the AI companies that have plundered books, art, and films for training content without compensation. Some of this tension is slowly playing out in the judicial system, with large court settlements in 2025 surely being only the beginning of this process.

We have seen that LLMs can produce computer code very quickly, but that the productivity effect of using them in this way is complex and nuanced. Instant code does not equate to stable code that can easily be debugged. However, LLMs are excellent for many uses in software, including producing test cases, helping with debugging, and building rapid prototypes. We also know that AI-generated code tends to be riddled with security loopholes and that careful attention must be given to this issue. AI chatbots can be manipulated by bad actors through techniques as simple as prompt injection, as well as subtler means like steganography. Security is, in my view, one of the most serious issues that the industry needs to address, and ploughing on regardless of real security concerns around AI is unwise.

In situations where consistency is not an issue, LLMs can be extremely useful and effective, from brainstorming ideas to generating poems to summarising documents and looking for patterns in large amounts of data. LLMs can quickly produce prototype applications, rapidly search dozens of websites to research answers to questions, translate text or even speech into other languages, and produce high-quality images. In these situations, the technology is well-suited. If you don't like a particular image generated for your company logo, then just generate another until you find one that you do like. On the other hand, if you need an application that is completely consistent and reliably follows a set of rules, then LLMs are less well-suited to your task. They are probabilistic creatures by nature and will not necessarily give you the same answer if you ask the same question repeatedly. In areas where the LLM's training data is scarce, you will frequently encounter hallucinations, which are simply fabricated answers. These don't matter if you ask an LLM to come up with a bunch of possible names for your new puppy, but they matter a lot if you are using an LLM to write a court submission to a judge or relying on it for a medical diagnosis or to highlight bank fraud. The more critical the application and the more deterministic (following a set of rules) you want the result to be, the less suitable that application is for LLM technology. There may be other AI technologies that can be more useful, such as machine learning or even an old-fashioned expert system. Indeed, for some applications, AI may not be well-suited at all and there are alternatives that will work better.

Many applications will lie between these extremes, where LLMs may be useful but need to be guided by human expertise. An LLM may review several medical images and suggest some that may show signs of cancer, but at this point, you want a medically trained radiologist to take over and review the situation. A lot of application areas will fall into the category where LLMs can usefully augment a human expert. If we can improve education about AI to the degree that people widely understand how it works, where it works well, and where it is risky, we will surely see an improvement in the currently dismal level of success in AI projects in the corporate world, where 95% are currently failing to deliver any return whatsoever. Many of these failures will be due to the application of AI in areas where it is poorly suited. If more people understand better how the underlying technology works, then we can use it much better and increase the chance of success.

AI is a ground-breaking technology with tremendous potential in many fields, from medicine to manufacturing. At the end of 2025, generative AI in particular is still a technology that is at a fairly early stage, and we are only beginning to really understand its potential and its pitfalls. As its usage continues in years to come, it continues to develop, and people come up with new use cases for it, both benign and malevolent, we would do well to recall what is probably an ancient Chinese curse: "may you live in interesting times".[816]

Further Reading

The following books are all worth your time.

Ethem Alpaydin, *Machine Learning, Revised and Updated Edition* (MIT Press, 2021)

Emily M. Bender and Alex Hanna, *The AI Con: How to Fight Big Tech's Hype and Create the Future We Want* (Random House, 2025)

Nick Bostrom, *Superintelligence: Paths, Dangers, Strategies* (Oxford University Press, 2014)

Joy Buolamwini, *Unmasking AI: My Mission to Protect What Is Human in a World of Machines* (Random House, 2024)

Brian Christian, *The Alignment Problem: Machine Learning and Human Values* (National Geographic Books, 2020)

Pedro Domingos, *The Master Algorithm: How the Quest for the Ultimate Learning Machine Will Remake Our World* (Penguin UK, 2015)

Gary Marcus and Ernest Davis, *Rebooting AI: Building Artificial Intelligence We Can Trust* (Pantheon, 2019)

Karen Hao, *Empire of AI* (Penguin, 2025)

Melanie Mitchell, *Artificial Intelligence: A Guide for Thinking Humans* (Pelican, 2019).

Ethan Mollick, *Co-Intelligence* (WH Allen, 2024)

Stuart Russell, *Human Compatible: Artificial Intelligence and the Problem of Control* (National Geographic Books, 2020)

Stuart Russell and Peter Norvig, *Artificial Intelligence: A Modern Approach* (Global Edition, 2016)

Mustafa Suleyman, *The Coming Wave: AI, Power, and Our Future* (Crown, 2023)

Michael Wooldridge, *A Brief History of Artificial Intelligence: What It Is, Where We Are, and Where We Are Going* (Flatiron Books, 2021)

Eliezer Yudkowsky and Nate Soares, *If Anyone Builds It, Everyone Dies: The Case Against Superintelligent AI* (Random House, 2025)

Glossary of AI Terms

There are many useful glossaries of AI terms. Rather than reinventing the wheel, here are several high-quality ones that already exist.

- UK Parliament AI Glossary: https://post.parliament.uk/artificial-intelligence-ai-glossary
- Alan Turing Institute Data Science and AI Glossary: https://www.turing.ac.uk/news/data-science-and-ai-glossary
- Wikipedia AI Glossary: https://en.wikipedia.org/wiki/Glossary_of_artificial_intelligence
- MIT Generative AI Glossary: https://mitsloanedtech.mit.edu/ai/basics/glossary/
- Nesta Glossary: https://www.nesta.org.uk/feature/ai-glossary/

Bibliography

Websites

- Alignment Research Center. https://www.alignment.org.
- Ant Group. https://www.antgroup.com/en.
- Chime. https://www.chime.com.
- Football Radar. https://www.footballradar.com.
- HAROP: Long Range Loitering Munition. https://www.iai.co.il/p/harop.
- Hawk Eye. https://www.hawkeyeinnovations.com.
- Imandra. https://www.imandra.ai.
- Kaggle. https://www.kaggle.com.
- Khanmigo. https://www.khanmigo.ai/learners.
- Kindroid. https://kindroid.ai.
- Kindroid. https://landing.kindroid.ai.
- My Anima. https://myanima.ai.
- Nomi. https://nomi.ai.
- Preferabli. https://preferabli.com.
- PubMed. https://pubmed.ncbi.nlm.nih.gov.
- Replika. https://replika.com.
- Revolut. https://www.revolut.com.
- Signifyd. https://www.signifyd.com.
- Sora. https://openai.com/sora.
- Stripe. https://stripe.com/en-fr.
- Tastry. https://tastry.com.
- Tencent. https://www.tencent.com/en-us/business.html.
- The Pile. https://pile.eleuther.ai
- VineView. https://vineview.com.
- Virtual Intelligent Chat Assistant (VICA). https://www.vica.gov.sg.
- Waze. https://www.waze.com/en-GB/live-map.

Films

- "Blade Runner (1982)." *IMDb*, n.d., https://www.imdb.com/title/tt0083658.
- "Ex Machina (2014)." *IMDb*, n.d. https://www.imdb.com/title/tt0470752.
- "Her (2013)." *IMDb*, n.d. https://www.imdb.com/title/tt1798709.
- "Hooroo Jackson," IMDb, n.d., https://www.imdb.com/name/nm6224020.
- "I, Robot (2004)." *IMDb*, n.d. https://www.imdb.com/title/tt0343818.
- "Metropolis (1927)." *IMDb*, n.d. https://www.imdb.com/title/tt0017136.
- "Short Circuit (1986)." *IMDb*, n.d. https://www.imdb.com/title/tt0091949.
- "The Matrix (1999)." *IMDb*, n.d. https://www.imdb.com/title/tt0133093.
- "The Terminator (1984)." *IMDb*, n.d. https://www.imdb.com/title/tt0088247.
- "Window Seat (2023)," *IMDb*, n.d., https://www.imdb.com/title/tt28442424.

Sources

- "AlphaFold." Google DeepMind. n.d. https://deepmind.google/science/alphafold.
- "Autonomous 'Self-Driving' Vehicles." *Robotics Institute, Carnegie Mellon University*, 2024. https://www.ri.cmu.edu/autonomous-vehicles.
- "Big Five Consulting: Betting Billions on AI Partnerships." *Virtasant*, April 15, 2025. https://www.virtasant.com/ai-today/big-five-consulting-betting-billions-on-ai-partnerships.
- "Cork Supply's AI Driven and Patented X100 Technology Gains International Recognition." *Newsworthy.ai*, February 19, 2025. https://www.newsworthy.ai/news/202502191435/cork-supplys-ai-driven-and-patented-x100-technology-gains-international-recognition.
- "Deterministic System." *Taylor & Francis*, n.d. https://taylorandfrancis.com/knowledge/Engineering_and_technology/Systems_%26_control_engineering/Deterministic_system/#:~:text=A%20deterministic%20system%20is%20a%20system%20without%20random%20parameters%20or,by%20random%20disturbances%20or%20noise.
- "JailbreakBench/JBB-Behaviors." *Hugging Face*. Accessed November 5, 2025. https://huggingface.co/datasets/JailbreakBench/JBB-Behaviors.
- "Safety Impact." *Waymo*, n.d. https://waymo.com/safety/impact.
- "SAG AFTRA" (home page). Screen Actors Guild–American Federation of Television and Radio Artists. https://www.sagaftra.org.
- "Student Generative AI Survey 2025." *HEPI*, August 27, 2025. https://www.hepi.ac.uk/reports/student-generative-ai-survey-2025.

- "Vins Du Languedoc Modernes Et Engagés." *Aubert et Mathieu*, n.d. https://aubertetmathieu.com.
- "Writers Guild of America West." https://www.wga.org.
- Abel, Salinas, and Fred Morstatter. "The Butterfly Effect of Altering Prompts: How Small Changes and Jailbreaks Affect Large Language Model Performance." *Findings of the Association for Computational Linguistics: ACL 2024*, 4629–4651. Association for Computational Linguistics, 2024. https://doi.org/10.18653/v1/2024.findings-acl.275.
- Abnormal AI. "WormGPT's Demise: What Cybercriminals Are Using Now." *Abnormal AI*, November 26, 2024. https://abnormal.ai/blog/what-happened-to-wormgpt-cybercriminal-tools.
- Abramovitch, Seth. "How Did 'Alien: Romulus' Create Its Most Controversial Character?" *The Hollywood Reporter*, August 23, 2024. https://www.hollywoodreporter.com/movies/movie-features/alien-romulus-ian-holm-rook-ash-ai-1235982350.
- Abrams, Zara. "Using Generic AI Chatbots for Mental Health Support: A Dangerous Trend." *APA Services*, March 12, 2025. https://www.apaservices.org/practice/business/technology/artificial-intelligence-chatbots-therapists.
- Accelerated Capability Environment. "Innovating to Detect Deepfakes and Protect the Public." *GOV.UK*, February 5, 2025. https://www.gov.uk/government/case-studies/innovating-to-detect-deepfakes-and-protect-the-public.
- Adachi, Daisuke. "Robots and Wage Polarisation." *CEPR*, August 18, 2024. https://cepr.org/voxeu/columns/robots-and-wage-polarisation.
- Adler, Jason N. "Modernizing Military Decision-Making: Integrating AI into Army Planning." *Army University Press*, August 2025. https://www.armyupress.army.mil/Journals/Military-Review/Online-Exclusive/2025-OLE/Modernizing-Military-Decision-Making.
- Admin. "Companies That Have Banned ChatGPT." *Jaxon*, March 12, 2024. https://jaxon.ai/list-of-companies-that-have-banned-chatgpt.
- ahire, nilkanth. "LLMs Are Basically Obsolete — Why AI Pioneer Yann LeCun Thinks the Real AI Revolution Hasn't Even Started." *Medium*, April 5, 2025. https://nilkanthahire.medium.com/llms-are-basically-obsolete-why-ai-pioneer-yann-lecun-thinks-the-real-ai-revolution-hasnt-16112d9d0809.
- Ahmed, Deeba. "Employee Duped by AI-Generated CFO in $25.6M Deepfake Scam." *HackRead*, February 5, 2024. https://hackread.com/employee-duped-ai-generated-cfo-deepfake-scam.
- AI Impacts. "2022 Expert Survey on Progress in AI." *AI Impacts*, October 31, 2023. https://aiimpacts.org/2022-expert-survey-on-progress-in-ai/#Existential_risk.

- AIPRM. "AI Laws Around the World." *AIPRM*. n.d. https://www.aiprm.com/en-gb/ai-laws-around-the-world.
- Air Zoo Aerospace & Science Museum. "Radioplane OQ-2A Drone." *Air Zoo*, n.d. https://www.airzoo.org/wwii/airplanes-3/radioplane-drone.
- Alaamer, Khalid. "This Is the State of Play in the Global Data Centre Gold Rush." *World Economic Forum*, April 22, 2025.
- Alber, Daniel Alexander, Zihao Yang, Anton Alyakin, Eunice Yang, Sumedha Rai, Aly A. Valliani, Jeff Zhang, Gabriel R. Rosenbaum, Ashley K. Amend-Thomas, David B. Kurland, Caroline M. Kremer, Alexander Eremiev, Bruck Negash, Daniel D. Wiggan, Michelle A. Nakatsuka, Karl L. Sangwon, Sean N. Neifert, Hammad A. Khan, Akshay Vinod Save, Adhith Palla, Eric A. Grin, Monika Hedman, Mustafa Nasir-Moin, Xujin Chris Liu, Lavender Yao Jiang, Michal A. Mankowski, Dorry L. Segev, Yindalon Aphinyanaphongs, Howard A. Riina, John G. Golfinos, Daniel A. Orringer, Douglas Kondziolka, and Eric Karl Oerman. "Medical Large Language Models Are Vulnerable to Data-Poisoning Attacks." *Nature Medicine 31* (2025): 618–626. https://doi.org/10.1038/s41591-024-03445-1.
- Alderson, Rob. "Graphic Design Among Most At-Risk Jobs from AI – Report." *Design Week*, January 13, 2025. https://www.designweek.co.uk/graphic-design-among-most-at-risk-jobs-from-ai-report.
- Alderton, Matt. "Are Flying Vineyard Drones Creating Better Wine?" *Wine Enthusiast*. Last updated: May 4, 2023. https://www.wineenthusiast.com/culture/wine/are-flying-vineyard-drones-creating-better-wine/?srsltid=AfmBOooaowBacwVDHxmpCRkbONIqmMbHOxm7ffMmJbLA4TKEsrmLl9NW.
- Alegre, Susie. "Need for Regulation Is Urgent as AI Chatbots Are Being Rolled Out to Support Mental Health." *Centre for International Governance Innovation*, July 18, 2025.
- Alias, Tera, and Andrew Goodman. "Not Yet Productive, Already Disruptive: AI's Uneven Effects on UK Jobs and Talent." *McKinsey & Company Blog*, July 14, 2025. https://www.mckinsey.com/uk/our-insights/the-mckinsey-uk-blog/ai-uneven-effects-on-uk-jobs-and-talent.
- All In Podcast. "Google DeepMind CEO Demis Hassabis on AI, Creativity, and a Golden Age of Science | All In Summit." *YouTube*, September 12, 2025. https://www.youtube.com/watch?v=Kr3Sh2PKA8Y.
- Almeida, Vinicius Kreischer de, Douglas Ericson de Oliveira, Claudio Daniel T. de Barros, Gabriel dos Santos Scatena, Asdrubal N. Queiroz Filho, Fabio Levy Siqueira, Anna Helena Reali Costa, Edson Satoshi Gomi, Leonardo A. F. Mendoza, Evelyn C. S. Batista, Cristian E. Muñoz, Isabela Guimarães Siqueira, Rodrigo A. Barreira, Ismael H. F. dos Santos, Carlos Cardoso, Eduardo Ogasawara, and Fabio Porto. "A Digital Twin System for Oil and Gas Industry: A Use Case on Mooring Lines Integrity Monitoring."

MODELS Companion '24: Proceedings of the ACM/IEEE 27th International Conference on Model Driven Engineering Languages and Systems (2024): 322–331. https://dl.acm.org/doi/10.1145/3652620.3688244.

- American National Standards Institute. "China Announces Action Plan for Global AI Governance." *American National Standards Institute*, August 1, 2025. https://www.ansi.org/standards-news/all-news/8-1-25-china-announces-action-plan-for-global-ai-governance.
- An Ranran X. "Over 50 Chinese Cities Have Brought Out Rules for Self-Driving, Smart Connected Vehicles." *YiCai Global*, January 15, 2025. https://www.yicaiglobal.com/news/over-50-chinese-cities-issue-self-driving-intelligent-connected-vehicle-rules.
- Anderson, Evan, Jim Holdsworth, and Matthew Kosinski. "What Is Red Teaming?" *IBM*, 2025. https://www.ibm.com/think/topics/red-teaming.
- Andrijanič, Mark Boris. "A Western-Funded Drone Surge Could End Russia's Invasion of Ukraine." *Atlantic Council*, July 14, 2025. https://www.atlanticcouncil.org/blogs/ukrainealert/a-western-funded-drone-surge-could-end-russias-invasion-of-ukraine.
- Anh, Pham The. "[AI & Algorithmic Trading] High-Frequency Trading (HFT): The Lightning-Fast World of Algorithmic Trading." *Where AI and Quant Meet Funny*, July 27, 2024. https://medium.com/funny-ai-quant/high-frequency-trading-hft-the-lightning-fast-world-of-algorithmic-trading-7512c825d9b3.
- Anker, David. "Forecasting – Prediction Is Very Difficult, Especially if It's About the Future!" *Cranfield University Blogs*, July 10, 2017. https://blogs.cranfield.ac.uk/cbp/forecasting-prediction-is-very-difficult-especially-if-its-about-the-future.
- Anson, Jane. "How Accurate Are the Figures on Wine Fraud?" *Jane Anson - Inside Bordeaux*, October 5, 2022. https://janeanson.com/how-accurate-are-the-figures-on-wine-fraud?srsltid=AfmBOorSTgPdVPXs2FvVdRWAy-85VlpNklAKHsMxmnwYxTgT9lVQ66CT.
- Anthropic. "Join Our Team." n.d. https://www.anthropic.com/jobs?team=4002061008.
- Anthropic. "Project Vend: Can Claude Run a Small Shop? (and Why Does That Matter?)." *Anthropic*, June 27, 2025. https://www.anthropic.com/research/project-vend-1.
- Armstrong, Thomas E. "Slopsquatting Assurance." EDPACS, *The EDP Audit, Control, and Security Newsletter*, June 2, 2025, 1–9. https://doi.org/10.1080/07366981.2025.2510097.
- Astbury, Matt. "Euro 2024: What Is Snickometer Technology? How Does Snicko Work?" *DAZN*, June 21, 2024. https://www.dazn.com/en GB/news/football/euro 2024 what is snickometer technology how does snicko work/16oifal9vx87l102zxnl2vt2v1.
- Authors Guild, The. "AI Is Driving a New Surge of Sham 'Books' on Amazon." *The Authors Guild*, March 15, 2024. https://authorsguild.org/news/ai-driving-new-surge-of-sham-books-on-amazon.

- Autonomous Vehicle Industry Association. "Research & Discoveries (R&D): Waymo Reduces Crash Rates Compared to Human Drivers Over 7+ Million AV Miles." *Autonomous Vehicle Industry Association*, January 17, 2024. https://www.theavindustry.org/blog/waymo-reduces-crash-rates-compared-to-human-drivers.
- AWS, Amazon Web Services, Inc. "What Is Reinforcement Learning? - Reinforcement Learning Explained - AWS." n.d. https://aws.amazon.com/what-is/reinforcement-learning.
- Aysha, Avril. "Data Bias in LLM and Generative AI Applications." *MOSTLY AI*, December 13, 2024. https://mostly.ai/blog/data-bias-types.
- Bacchi, Umberto. "EU's Lie Detecting Virtual Border Guards Face Court Scrutiny." *Reuters*, February 12, 2021.
- BakerHostetler. Weisenberger, Theresa M., Diana C. Milton, and Harrison A. Enright. "Case Tracker: Artificial Intelligence, Copyrights and Class Actions." BakerHostetler, n.d. https://www.bakerlaw.com/services/artificial-intelligence-ai/case-tracker-artificial-intelligence-copyrights-and-class-actions.
- Ball, Philip. "The Dangers of So-called AI Experts Believing Their Own Hype." *New Scientist*, July 2, 2025. https://www.newscientist.com/article/mg26635500-100-the-dangers-of-so-called-ai-experts-believing-their-own-hype.
- Bandhakavi, Swagath. "Multimodal AI Models Pose Increased Risks for Abuse and Harmful Content, Study Finds." *Tech Monitor*, May 9, 2025. https://www.techmonitor.ai/digital-economy/ai-and-automation/multimodal-ai-models-increased-risks-abuse-harmful-content.
- Baraniuk, Chris. "Electricity Grids Creak as AI Demands Soar." *BBC News*, May 21, 2024. https://bbc.co.uk/news/articles/cj5ll89dy2mo.
- Barez, Fazl, Tung-Yu Wu, Iván Arcuschin, Michael Lan, Vincent Wang, Noah Siegel, Nicolas Collignon, Clement Neo, Isabelle Lee, Alasdair Paren, Adel Bibi, Robert Trager, Damiano Fornasiere, Mila John Yan, Yanai Elazar, and Yoshua Bengio Mila. "Chain-of-Thought Is Not Explainability." *Oxford Martin AIGI*, July 2025.
- Barnes, Emily. "Do AI Plagiarism Detectors Work? Here's What the Research Says." *VKTR.com*, May 14, 2025. https://www.vktr.com/ai-ethics-law-risk/do-ai-plagiarism-detectors-work-heres-what-the-research-says.
- Barr, Alistair. "School's Out for Summer, and if ChatGPT Usage Is Falling Because Students Are Off, That's a Bad Sign for OpenAI." *Business Insider*, July 14, 2023. https://www.businessinsider.com/chatgpt-usage-falling-students-summer-break-bad-sign-openai-microsoft-2023-7.
- Barratt, Luke, Costanza Gambarini, Andrew Witherspoon, and Aliya Uteuova. "Revealed: Big Tech's New Datacentres Will Take Water from the World's

Driest Areas." *The Guardian*, April 9, 2025. https://www.theguardian.com/environment/2025/apr/09/big-tech-datacentres-water.

- Bartlett, Robert, Adair Morse, Richard Stanton, and Nancy Wallace. "Consumer-Lending Discrimination in the FinTech Era." *Journal of Financial Economics 143*, no. 1 (January 2022): 30–56. https://www.sciencedirect.com/science/article/abs/pii/S0304405X21002403.
- Bartsch, Henning, Ole Jorgensen, Domenic Rosati, Jason Hoelscher-Obermaier, and Jacob Pfau. "Self-Consistency of Large Language Models under Ambiguity." *In Proceedings of the 6th BlackboxNLP Workshop: Analyzing and Interpreting Neural Networks for NLP*, January 1, 2023, 89–105. https://doi.org/10.18653/v1/2023.blackboxnlp-1.7.
- Batty, David. "'She Helps Cheer Me up': The People Forming Relationships With AI Chatbots." T*he Guardian*, April 15, 2025. https://www.theguardian.com/technology/2025/apr/15/she-helps-cheer-me-up-the-people-forming-relationships-with-ai-chatbots.
- BBC News. "Amazon Scrapped 'Sexist AI' Tool." *BBC News*, October 10, 2018. https://www.bbc.com/news/technology-45809919.
- BBC News. "China Launches Fleet of Self-Driving Trucks." *BBC News*, June 6, 2025. https://www.youtube.com/watch?v=ypj2ii--1Uc.
- BBC News. "Travel Site Orbitz Offers Mac Users More Costly Hotels." *BBC News*, June 26, 2012. https://www.bbc.co.uk/news/technology-18595347.
- BBC. "Groundbreaking BBC Research Shows Issues With Over Half the Answers From Artificial Intelligence (AI) Assistants." *BBC Media Centre*, February 11, 2025. https://www.bbc.com/mediacentre/2025/bbc-research-shows-issues-with-answers-from-artificial-intelligence-assistants.
- Beatty, Django, Kritsada Masanthia, Teepakorn Kaphol, and Niphan Sethi. "Revealing Hidden Bias in AI: Lessons from Large Language Models." arXiv:2410.16927v1, October 22, 2024. https://arxiv.org/html/2410.16927v1.
- Beitman, Bernard D. MD. "AI Chatbots May Mirror Narcissism—Clinical Insights and Research Converge." *Psychology Today*, April 21, 2025. https://www.psychologytoday.com/gb/blog/connecting-with-coincidence/202504/are-chatbots-too-certain-and-too-nice.
- Belanger, Ashley. "AI Industry Horrified to Face Largest Copyright Class Action Ever Certified." *Ars Technica*, August 8, 2025. https://arstechnica.com/tech-policy/2025/08/ai-industry-horrified-to-face-largest-copyright-class-action-ever-certified.
- Bell, Lyndon. "Visual Search in Online Shopping: The Future of Retail in 2025." *AdLift*, January 29, 2025. https://www.adlift.com/blog/visual-search-in-online-shopping-the-future-of-retail-in-2025.

- Bergmann, Dave. "What Is Deep Learning?" *IBM*. n.d. https://www.ibm.com/think/topics/deep-learning.
- Bet Victor. "Gambling Statistics." *Bet Victor*, n.d. https://www.betvictor.com/blog/gambling-statistics.
- BHP. "BHP Unveils World-First Automated Shiploaders." *BHP*, July 2022. https://www.bhp.com/news/media-centre/releases/2022/06/bhp-unveils-world-first-automated-shiploaders.
- Binding, Jonas. "The Misguided Dilemma of the Trolley Problem: Why You Shouldn't Worry About Autonomous Vehicles Solving Ethics Riddles." *Volvo*, January 22, 2024. https://www.volvoautonomoussolutions.com/en-en/news-and-insights/insights/articles/2024/jan/the-misguided-dilemma-of-the-trolley-problem-.html.
- Binz, Marcel, Elif Akata, Matthias Bethge, Franziska Brändle, Fred Callaway, Julian Coda-Forno, Peter Dayan, Can Demircan, Maria K. Eckstein, Noémi Éltető, Thomas L. Griffiths, Susanne Haridi, Akshay K. Jagadish, Li Ji-An, Alexander Kipnis, Sreejan Kumar, Tobias Ludwig, Marvin Mathony, Marcelo Mattar, Alireza Modirshanechi, Surabhi S. Nath, Joshua C. Peterson, Milena Rmus, Evan M. Russek, Tankred Saanum, Johannes A. Schubert, Luca M. Schulze Buschoff, Nishad Singhi, Xin Sui, Mirko Thalmann, Fabian J. Theis, Vuong Truong, Vishaal Udandarao, Konstantinos Voudouris, Robert Wilson, Kristin Witte, Shuchen Wu, Dirk U. Wulff, Huadong Xiong, and Eric Schulz, "A Foundation Model to Predict and Capture Human Cognition." *Nature 644* (2025): 1002–1009. https://doi.org/10.1038/s41586-025-09215-4.
- Blanchard, Alexander. "The Road Less Travelled: Ethics in the International Regulatory Debate on Autonomous Weapon Systems." *Humanitarian Law & Policy Blog*, April 25, 2024. https://blogs.icrc.org/law-and-policy/2024/04/25/the-road-less-travelled-ethics-in-the-international-regulatory-debate-on-autonomous-weapon-systems.
- Boffey, Daniel. "Killing Machines: How Russia and Ukraine's Race to Perfect Deadly Pilotless Drones Could Harm Us All." *The Guardian*, June 25, 2025. https://www.theguardian.com/world/2025/jun/25/ukraine-russia-autonomous-drones-ai.
- Bojić, Ljubiša, Olga Zagovora, Asta Zelenkauskaite, Vuk Vuković, Milan Čabarkapa, Selma Veseljević Jerković, and Ana Jovančević. "Comparing Large Language Models and Human Annotators in Latent Content Analysis of Sentiment, Political Leaning, Emotional Intensity and Sarcasm." *Scientific Reports 15*, no. 1 (April 3, 2025). https://doi.org/10.1038/s41598-025-96508-3.
- Bond, Shannon. "How AI Deepfakes Polluted Elections in 2024." *NPR*, December 21, 2024. https://www.npr.org/2024/12/21/nx-s1-5220301/deepfakes-memes-artificial-intelligence-elections.

- Bondarenko, Peter. "Enron Scandal." *Encyclopedia Britannica*. Last updated September 26, 2025. https://www.britannica.com/event/Enron-scandal.
- Booth, Robert. "High Court Tells UK Lawyers to Stop Misuse of AI After Fake Case-law Citations." *The Guardian*, June 6, 2025. https://www.theguardian.com/technology/2025/jun/06/high-court-tells-uk-lawyers-to-urgently-stop-misuse-of-ai-in-legal-work.
- Borowiec, Steven. "AlphaGo Seals 4-1 Victory Over Go Grandmaster Lee Sedol." *The Guardian*, March 15, 2016. https://www.theguardian.com/technology/2016/mar/15/googles-alphago-seals-4-1-victory-over-grandmaster-lee-sedol.
- Bos Communications. "8 Most Popular Programming Languages Used in Banking/Finance." *BOS Fintech*, January 23, 2023. https://bosfintech.com/8-most-popular-programming-languages-used-in-banking-finance.
- Boston Dynamics. "Starting on the Right Foot With Reinforcement Learning." n.d. https://bostondynamics.com/blog/starting-on-the-right-foot-with-reinforcement-learning.
- Bradbury, Danny. "One in Six US Workers Pretends to Use AI to Please the Bosses." *The Register*, July 22, 2025. https://www.theregister.com/2025/07/22/ai_anxiety_us_workers/?utm_source=dlvr.it&utm_medium=twitter.
- Braun, Sara. "CEOs Say That Just a Fraction of AI Initiatives Are Actually Delivering the Return on Investment They Expected." *Fortune*, May 12, 2025. https://fortune.com/article/ceos-ai-initiatves-fraction-deliver-return-on-investment-roi-study.
- Brittain, Blake. "Judge Rejects Anthropic Bid to Appeal Copyright Ruling, Postpone Trial." *Reuters*, August 12, 2025. https://www.reuters.com/legal/litigation/judge-rejects-anthropic-bid-appeal-copyright-ruling-postpone-trial-2025-08-12.
- Brown, Sara. "A New Study Measures the Actual Impact of Robots on Jobs. It's Significant." *MIT Sloan*, July 29, 2020. https://mitsloan.mit.edu/ideas-made-to-matter/a-new-study-measures-actual-impact-robots-jobs-its-significant.
- Bryant, Miranda. "Denmark to Tackle Deepfakes by Giving People Copyright to Their Own Features." *The Guardian*, June 27, 2025. https://www.theguardian.com/technology/2025/jun/27/deepfakes-denmark-copyright-law-artificial-intelligence.
- Brynjolfsson, Erik, Bharat Chandar, and Ruyu Chen. "Canaries in the Coal Mine? Six Facts about the Recent Employment Effects of Artificial Intelligence." *Stanford University,* August 26, 2025. https://digitaleconomy.stanford.edu/wp-content/uploads/2025/08/Canaries_BrynjolfssonChandarChen.pdf.
- Bubley, Aaron. "Global Crossing Is Reborn…" *Praetorian Capital*, August 20, 2025. https://pracap.com/global-crossing-reborn.
- Buendia, Angel. "CSV vs. CSA: What Are the Main Differences?" *Scilife*, April 9, 2025. https://www.scilife.io/blog/csv-csa-main-differences.

- Burns, Michael. "Storytelling, Monetisation and Engagement: Making the Pitch for AI in Sports Broadcasting." *SVG Europe*, May 12, 2025. https://www.svgeurope.org/blog/headlines/storytelling monetisation and engagement making the pitch for ai in sports broadcasting.
- Business Research Insights. "Plagiarism Checker Software Market Size, Share, Growth and Industry Analysis by Type (Cloud-Based and Web-Based LED, and Surface-Mount (SMD) LED) by Application (Individuals, Schools, and Enterprises) Regional Insight and Forecast to 2033." B*usiness Research Insights*. Last updated October 20, 2025. https://www.businessresearchinsights.com/market-reports/plagiarism-checker-software-market-115791.
- ByteBridge. "GPU and TPU Comparative Analysis Report." *Medium*, February 18, 2024. https://bytebridge.medium.com/gpu-and-tpu-comparative-analysis-report-a5268e4f0d2a.
- Caliskan, Aylin, and Kyra Wilson. "Gender, Race, and Intersectional Bias in AI Resume Screening via Language Model Retrieval." *Brookings*, April 25, 2025. https://www.brookings.edu/articles/gender-race-and-intersectional-bias-in-ai-resume-screening-via-language-model-retrieval.
- Canali, Stefano, Viola Schiaffonati, and Andrea Aliverti. "Challenges and Recommendations for Wearable Devices in Digital Health: Data Quality, Interoperability, Health Equity, Fairness." *PLOS Digital Health 1*, no. 10 (October 13, 2022): e0000104. https://doi.org/10.1371/journal.pdig.0000104.
- Cancer Research UK. "Phases of Clinical Trials." *Cancer Research UK*, Last reviewed May 26, 2025. https://www.cancerresearchuk.org/about-cancer/find-a-clinical-trial/what-clinical-trials-are/phases-of-clinical-trials.
- Cao, Jing. "AI: A New and Impactful Player in the Quality Evaluation of Wine." *Harvard Data Science Review 7*, no. 1 (January 30, 2025). https://doi.org/10.1162/99608f92.be44bdad.
- Carlsson Szlezak, Philipp, Paul Swartz, and François Candelon. "Why We Need to Be Realistic about Generative AI's Economic Impact." *World Economic Forum,* August 31, 2023. https://www.weforum.org/stories/2023/08/generative-ai-realistic-economic-impact.
- Cassidy, John. "Is the A.I. Boom Turning Into an A.I. Bubble?" *The New Yorker,* August 11, 2025. https://www.newyorker.com/news/the-financial-page/is-the-ai-boom-turning-into-an-ai-bubble.
- CFI Team. "2010 Flash Crash: The Stock Market Crash of March 6, 2010." *Corporate Finance Institute.*
- Chakraborty, Debarun, Aruna Polisetty, Sowmya G, Nripendra P. Rana, and Sangeeta Khorana. "Unlocking the Potential of AI: Enhancing Consumer Engagement in the

Beauty and Cosmetic Product Purchases." *Journal of Retailing and Consumer Services 79* (April 5, 2024): 103842. https://doi.org/10.1016/j.jretconser.2024.103842.

- Chandra Das, Avinash. "The Next Frontier of Customer Engagement: AI-Enabled Customer Service." *McKinsey & Company*, March 27, 2023. https://www.mckinsey.com/capabilities/operations/our-insights/the-next-frontier-of-customer-engagement-ai-enabled-customer-service.
- Chanel. "ROUGE ALLURE VELVET LUMINOUS MATTE LIP COLOUR 58 ROUGE VIE 3.5G." *Chanel*, September 29, 2025. https://www.chanel.com/gb/makeup/virtual-makeup-try-on.
- Chapekis, Athena, and Anna Lieb. "Google Users Are Less Likely to Click on Links When an AI Summary Appears in the Results." *Pew Research Center*, July 22, 2025. https://www.pewresearch.org/short-reads/2025/07/22/google-users-are-less-likely-to-click-on-links-when-an-ai-summary-appears-in-the-results.
- charlirobey. "Imagine a Hippo as Your Surgeon! Google AI Is Ridiculous." *Reddit*, March 4, 2025. https://www.reddit.com/r/mildlyinfuriating/comments/1j3azit/imagine_a_hippo_as_your_surgeon_google_ai_is.
- Charlotin, Damien. "AI Hallucination Cases Database." *Artificial Authority*. Accessed November 5, 2025. https://www.damiencharlotin.com/hallucinations/?ref=nucleo.jor.br&page=2&page=3&page=4&page=5.
- Chater, James. "AI Deepfake Porn Humiliated Me, Says Penny Mordaunt." *BBC News*, July 23, 2025. https://bbc.co.uk/news/articles/ckg3r3vm1d0o.
- Check Point Research. "AI Security Report 2025: Understanding Threats and Building Smarter Defenses." *Check Point Blog*, April 30, 2025. https://blog.checkpoint.com/research/ai-security-report-2025-understanding-threats-and-building-smarter-defenses.
- Chelli, Mikaël, Jules Descamps, Vincent Lavoué, Christophe Trojani, Michel Azar, Marcel Deckert, Jean-Luc Raynier, Gilles Clowez, Pascal Boileau, and Caroline Ruetsch-Chelli. "Hallucination Rates and Reference Accuracy of ChatGPT and Bard for Systematic Reviews: Comparative Analysis." *Journal of Medical Internet Research 26* (May 22, 2024): e53164. https://doi.org/10.2196/53164.
- Chen, Heather, and Kathleen Magramo. "Finance Worker Pays Out $25 Million After Video Call with Deepfake 'Chief Financial Officer.'" *CNN*, February 4, 2024. https://edition.cnn.com/2024/02/04/asia/deepfake-cfo-scam-hong-kong-intl-hnk.
- Chen, Jay, and Royce Lu. "Deceptive Delight: Jailbreak LLMs Through Camouflage and Distraction." *Unit 42*, October 23, 2024. https://unit42.paloaltonetworks.com/jailbreak-llms-through-camouflage-distraction.

- Chen, Lingjiao, Matei Zaharia, and James Zou. "How Is ChatGPT's Behavior Changing over Time?" *Harvard Data Science Review*, March 13, 2024. https://hdsr.mitpress.mit.edu/pub/y95zitmz/release/2.
- Chen, Mingyang, Yuting Wang, Qiankun Wang, Jingyi Shi, Huike Wang, Zichen Ye, Peng Xue, and Youlin Qiao. "Impact of Human and Artificial Intelligence Collaboration on Workload Reduction in Medical Image Interpretation." *Npj Digital Medicine 7*, no. 1 (November 30, 2024). https://doi.org/10.1038/s41746-024-01328-w.
- Chen, Zhisheng. "Ethics and Discrimination in Artificial Intelligence-Enabled Recruitment Practices." *Humanities and Social Sciences Communications 10, no. 1* (September 13, 2023). https://doi.org/10.1057/s41599-023-02079-x.
- Chess.com Team, and Chess.com Team. "Kasparov vs. Deep Blue | The Match That Changed History." *Chess.com*, last updated October 12, 2018. https://www.chess.com/article/view/deep-blue-kasparov-chess.
- China, Chrystal R. "10 Ways the Oil and Gas Industry Can Leverage Digital Twin Technology." *IBM*, n.d. https://www.ibm.com/think/topics/digital-twin-for-oil-gas.
- China, Chrystal R., and Michael Goodwin. "What Is COBOL?" IBM. n.d. https://www.ibm.com/think/topics/cobol.
- Chong, Ng S.T. "The Rise of the Deceptive Machines: When AI Learns to Lie." *UNU Campus Computing Centre*, January 1, 2025. https://c3.unu.edu/blog/the-rise-of-the-deceptive-machines-when-ai-learns-to-lie.
- Claburn, Thomas. "AI Bots Hallucinate Software Packages and Devs Download Them." *The Register*, March 28, 2024.
- Clayton, Abené. "Protesters Develop Novel Way to Build Cone-sensus Against Driverless Cars." *The Guardian*, July 8, 2023. https://www.theguardian.com/technology/2023/jul/07/san-francisco-autonomous-cars-protest-cone.
- Clwyd Probert. "The Revolutionary Impact of AI on the Consulting Industry." *Whitehat SEO*, August 10, 2024. https://blog.whitehat-seo.co.uk/ai-impact-on-consulting.
- Cohen, Tamara. "Warning to UK Politicians Over Risk of Audio Deepfakes That Could Derail the Election." *Sky News*, June 2, 2024. https://news.sky.com/story/warning-to-uk-politicians-over-risk-of-audio-deepfakes-that-could-derail-the-general-election-13146573.
- Collins, Denis. "Arthur Andersen." *Encyclopedia Britannica*, n.d. https://www.britannica.com/money/Arthur-Andersen.
- Commander JedoMeta. "Total Recall - Johnny Cab." *YouTube*, August 14, 2016. https://www.youtube.com/watch?v=eWgrvNHjKkY.
- Common Crawl. "Open Repository of Web Crawl Data." *Common Crawl*, n.d. https://commoncrawl.org.

- Contentsquare. "4 Sentiment Analysis Examples to Help You Improve CX." *Contentsquare*, August 12, 2024. https://contentsquare.com/guides/sentiment-analysis/examples.
- Conway, Jan. "Topic: Global Wine Market." *Statista*, September 19, 2025. https://www.statista.com/topics/7802/global-wine.
- Cooley. "Copyright Ownership of Generative AI Outputs Varies Around the World." *Cooley*, January 29, 2024. https://www.cooley.com/news/insight/2024/2024-01-29-copyright-ownership-of-generative-ai-outputs-varies-around-the-world.
- Copeland, B. J. "MYCIN | Expert System, Medical Diagnosis & Treatment." *Encyclopaedia Britannica*, October 7, 2008. https://www.britannica.com/technology/MYCIN.
- Corbyn, Zoe. "Autonomous Vehicles: How Mines Control Driverless Trucks." *BBC News*, November 8, 2024. https://www.bbc.com/news/articles/cgej7gzg8l0o.
- Corrigan, Caitlin C., and Svetlana A. Ikonnikova. "A Review of the Use of AI in the Mining Industry: Insights and Ethical Considerations for Multi-Objective Optimization." *The Extractive Industries and Society 17* (March 2024): 101440. https://www.sciencedirect.com/science/article/pii/S2214790X24000388.
- Cossins, Daniel. "Discriminating Algorithms: 5 Times AI Showed Prejudice." *New Scientist,* April 27, 2018. https://www.newscientist.com/article/2166207-discriminating-algorithms-5-times-ai-showed-prejudice.
- Craft Law Firm. "Data Analysis: Self-Driving Car Accidents [2019-2024]." *Craft Law Firm*, n.d. https://www.craftlawfirm.com/autonomous-vehicle-accidents-2019-2024-crash-data.
- Craig, Lev. "AI Watermarking." *Tech Target*, October 31, 2023. https://www.techtarget.com/searchenterpriseai/definition/AI-watermarking.
- Creamer, Ella. "Amazon Removes Books 'Generated by AI' for Sale Under Author's Name." *The Guardian*, August 9, 2023. https://www.theguardian.com/books/2023/aug/09/amazon-removes-books-generated-by-ai-for-sale-under-authors-name.
- Creaner, Gerry, and Donagh Fitzgerald. "What Is Computer System Validation (CSV)?" *GetReskilled*, August 2024. https://www.getreskilled.com/what-is-computer-systems-validation-csv.
- Cross, Felicity. "New Law Passed on Controversial Use of AI to 'Bring Back' Dead Actors After Christopher Reeve's Family's Outrage." *The Sun*, September 1, 2024. https://www.thesun.co.uk/tvandshowbiz/30202718/law-ai-dead-actors-christopher-reeve.
- CrowdStrike. CrowdStrike 2024 Global Threat Report. *CrowdStrike*, 2024. https://www.crowdstrike.com/en-us/resources/reports/crowdstrike-2024-global-threat-report.

- Crum, Dan. "Hidden Threats in AI Data: Protecting Against Embedded Steganography." *Owl Cyber Defense*, November 19, 2024. https://owlcyberdefense.com/blog/hidden-threats-in-ai-data-protecting-against-steganography.
- CSA. "AI Safety Initiative: Pioneering AI Compliance & Safety." *Cloud Security Alliance*, Accessed November 5, 2025. https://cloudsecurityalliance.org/ai-safety-initiative.
- Curry, David. "75% of Executives Don't Trust Their Data." *RTInsights*, February 22, 2022. https://www.rtinsights.com/executives-dont-trust-data.
- Cuthbertson, Anthony. "ChatGPT Successor Tricks Worker Into Thinking It's Human." *The Independent*, March 15, 2023. https://www.independent.co.uk/tech/chatgpt-gpt4-ai-openai-b2301523.html.
- Cuthbertson, Anthony. "Hundreds of AI-written Books Flood Amazon." *The Independent*, February 22, 2023. https://www.independent.co.uk/tech/ai-author-books-amazon-chatgpt-b2287111.html.
- Cuttler, Elyse. "Inside the Algorithm: How Gen AI and Graph Technology Are Cracking Down on Card Sharks." *Mastercard*, July 18, 2024. https://www.mastercard.com/news/perspectives/2024/inside-the-algorithm-how-gen-ai-and-graph-technology-are-cracking-down-on-card-sharks.
- CV VC. "Where VCs Are Investing in 2025: Blockchain Vs. AI Funding Trends." *CV VC*, May 9, 2025. https://www.cvvc.com/blogs/where-vcs-are-investing-in-2025-blockchain-vs-ai-funding-trends.
- Damiani, Ernesto. "Autonomy and Accuracy in Weapon Systems: The Prospects of Artificial Intelligence." *ISPI*, January 28, 2025. https://www.ispionline.it/en/publication/autonomy-and-accuracy-in-weapon-systems-the-prospects-of-artificial-intelligence-198146.
- Darley, James. "The 148 Year Tradition Wimbledon Is Breaking with Technology." *AI Magazine*, June 30, 2025. https://aimagazine.com/articles/the-148-year-tradition-wimbledon-is-breaking-with-technology.
- Dastin, Jeffrey. "Insight - Amazon Scraps Secret AI Recruiting Tool That Showed Bias Against Women." *Reuters*, October 11, 2018. https://www.reuters.com/article/world/insight-amazon-scraps-secret-ai-recruiting-tool-that-showed-bias-against-women-idUSKCN1MK0AG.
- DataCamp Team. "What Is Symbolic AI?" *DataCamp*, May 12, 2023. https://www.datacamp.com/blog/what-is-symbolic-ai.
- Datatron Technologies. "Real-life Examples of Discriminating Artificial Intelligence." *Datatron*. Accessed November 5, 2025. https://datatron.com/real-life-examples-of-discriminating-artificial-intelligence.

- Davis, Ernest, and Gary Marcus. "Reports of LLMs Mastering Math Have Been Greatly Exaggerated." *Marcus* on AI, April 5, 2025. https://garymarcus.substack.com/p/reports-of-llms-mastering-math-have.
- Davis, Jeff. "Phalanx CIWS: Everything You Need to Know About the Navy's Automated, Missile-Munching Gatling Gun." *Intergalatic*, n.d. https://ig.space/commslink/phalanx-ciws-everything-you-need-to-know-about-the-gatlin-gun-navy-ship-defense.
- Dawson, Amy. "87% of UK Organisations Are Vulnerable to Cyberattacks in the Age of AI." *Microsoft UK Stories,* April 18, 2024. https://ukstories.microsoft.com/features/87-of-uk-organisations-are-vulnerable-to-cyberattacks-in-the-age-of-ai-research-reveals.
- Defensemirror.com bureau. "Bayraktar TB2T-AI Breaks Altitude Record With 37,096 Feet During Test Flight." *Defense Mirror*, May 7, 2025. https://defensemirror.com/news/39440/Bayraktar_TB2T_AI_Breaks_Altitude_Record_with_37_096_Feet_During_Test_Flight.
- Deichmann, Johannes. Autonomous Driving's Future: Convenient and Connected. *McKinsey & Company,* 2023. https://www.mckinsey.com/industries/automotive-and-assembly/our-insights/autonomous-drivings-future-convenient-and-connected.
- Delauney, Guy. "World's First AI Minister Will Eliminate Corruption, Says Albania's PM." *BBC News*, September 12, 2025. https://www.bbc.com/news/articles/cm2znzgwj3xo.
- Department for Science, Innovation and Technology. "AI Cyber Security Code of Practice." *GOV.UK*, January 31, 2025. https://www.gov.uk/government/publications/ai-cyber-security-code-of-practice.
- Department for Science, Innovation and Technology. "AI Safety Institute." *GOV.UK,* February 9, 2024. https://www.gov.uk/government/organisations/ai-safety-institute.
- Department for Science, Innovation and Technology. "Government's Experimental AI Chatbot to Help People Set up Small Businesses and Find Support." *GOV.UK*, November 5, 2024. https://www.gov.uk/government/news/governments-experimental-ai-chatbot-to-help-people-set-up-small-businesses-and-find-support.
- Department of Defense. *Summary of the Joint All-Domain Command & Control (JADC2) Strategy.* March 2022. https://media.defense.gov/2022/Mar/17/2002958406/-1/-1/1/SUMMARY-OF-THE-JOINT-ALL-DOMAIN-COMMAND-AND-CONTROL-STRATEGY.pdf?OR=Word.
- Department of Employment and Workplace Relations, Australia. *Targeted Compliance Framework Assurance Review – Final Report*. Department of Employment and Workplace Relations, 2025. https://www.dewr.gov.au/assuring-integrity-targeted-compliance-framework/resources/targeted-compliance-framework-assurance-review-final-report.

- Dickinson, Peter. "Ukraine Is Shaping the Future of Drone Warfare at Sea as Well as on Land." *Atlantic Council*, June 12, 2025. https://www.atlanticcouncil.org/blogs/ukrainealert/ukraine-is-shaping-the-future-of-drone-warfare-at-sea-as-well-as-on-land.
- Dickson, Ben. "New AI Architecture Delivers 100x Faster Reasoning than LLMs with Just 1,000 Training Examples." *VentureBeat*, July 26, 2025. https://venturebeat.com/ai/new-ai-architecture-delivers-100x-faster-reasoning-than-llms-with-just-1000-training-examples.
- DiFabrizio, Emilia. "Demystifying Vectors and Embeddings in AI: A Beginner's Guide." *Sidecar*, June 27, 2024. https://sidecar.ai/blog/demystifying-vectors-and-embeddings-in-ai-a-beginners-guide.
- Digital Watch Observatory. "AI-generated Media Must Now Carry Labels in China." *Digital Watch Observatory*, September 2, 2025. https://dig.watch/updates/ai-generated-media-must-now-carry-labels-in-china.
- Digital Watch Observatory. "Hackers Use Steganography to Evade Windows Defences." *Digital Watch Observatory,* August 5, 2025. https://dig.watch/updates/hackers-use-steganography-to-evade-windows-defences.
- Dilmegani, Cem, and Aleyna Daldal. "AI Hallucination: Comparison of the Popular LLMs." *AIMultiple*, October 20, 2025. https://research.aimultiple.com/ai-hallucination.
- Dilmegani, Cem, and Sena Sezer. "Top 25 Generative AI Finance Use Cases & Case Studies." *AIMultiple*, September 30, 2025. https://research.aimultiple.com/generative-ai-finance.
- Dilmegani, Cem, and Sıla Ermut. "When Will AGI/Singularity Happen? 8,590 Predictions Analyzed." *AIMultiple*. Last updated October 28, 2025.
- Dilmegani, Cem. "Bias in AI: Examples and 6 Ways to Fix It." *AIMultiple*. Last modified November 3, 2025. https://research.aimultiple.com/ai-bias.
- Dolfing, Henrico. "Case Study 20: The $4 Billion AI Failure of IBM Watson for Oncology." *Henrico Dolfing*, December 7, 2024. https://www.henricodolfing.com/2024/12/case-study-ibm-watson-for-oncology-failure.html.
- Dominguez, Jorge. "The Curious Case of the CHAOS Report 2009." *Project Smart*, July 1, 2009. Last updated October 10, 2021. https://www.projectsmart.co.uk/it-project-management/the-curious-case-of-the-chaos-report-2009.php.
- Dora, Swaroop, Deven Lunkad, Naziya Aslam, and S. Venkatesan. "The Hidden Risks of LLM-Generated Web Application Code: A Security-Centric Evaluation of Code Generation Capabilities in Large Language Models." *arXiv:2504.20612v1*, April 29, 2025. https://arxiv.org/html/2504.20612v1.

- Drapkin, Aaron. "AI Gone Wrong: The Errors, Mistakes, and Hallucinations of AI (2023 – 2025)." *Tech.co,* September 26, 2025. https://tech.co/news/list-ai-failures-mistakes-errors.
- Dresser, Scott. "Amazon Deploys Over 1 Million Robots and Launches New AI Foundation Model." *About Amazon,* July 1, 2025. https://www.aboutamazon.com/news/operations/amazon-million-robots-ai-foundation-model.
- Drishya. "The Biggest Gambling Countries in the World in 2025." *KYC Hub,* September 9, 2025. https://www.kychub.com/blog/biggest-gambling-countries-in-the-world.
- Drug Target Review. "First AI-designed Drug, Rentosertib, Officially Named by USAN." *Drug Target Review*, March 14, 2025. https://www.drugtargetreview.com/news/157365/first-ai-designed-drug-rentosertib-named-by-usan.
- Dunn Sheehan. "The 5 Worst Oil Rig Disasters in History." *Dunn Sheehan*, December 18, 2024. https://www.dunnsheehan.com/news-insights/the-5-worst-oil-rig-disasters-in-history.
- Dupré, Maggie Harrison. "Billion Dollar AI Company Gives Up on AGI While Desperately Fighting to Stop Bleeding Money." *Futurism*, August 14, 2025. https://futurism.com/billion-dollar-ai-company-gives-up-on-agi.
- Duranton, Sylvain. "Are Coders' Jobs at Risk? AI's Impact on the Future of Programming." *Forbes*, April 15, 2024. https://www.forbes.com/sites/sylvainduranton/2024/04/15/are-coders-jobs-at-risk-ais-impact-on-the-future-of-programming.
- DXplain."Using Decision Support to Help Explain Clinical Manifestations of Disease." *DXplain, The Laboratory of Computer Science*. n.d. https://www.mghlcs.org/projects/dxplain
- Eads, Lauren. "AI And Wine: A Taste of the Future?" *Decanter*, March 28, 2024. https://www.decanter.com/wine/ai-and-wine-a-taste-of-the-future-523210.
- Earle, Monica. "Duolingo Introduces AI-Powered Innovations at Duocon 2024." *Duolingo*, September 2024. https://investors.duolingo.com/news-releases/news-release-details/duolingo-introduces-ai-powered-innovations-duocon-2024.
- Educate Ventures. "The Beyond the Hype Report | Professor Rose Luckin's EDUCATE Ventures Research | AI for Education." *Educate Ventures*. n.d. https://www.educateventures.com/beyond-the-hype.
- Edwards, Sarah Scoles. "The Technology for Autonomous Weapons Exists. What Now?" *Undark Magazine*, November 26, 2025. https://undark.org/2024/11/26/unleashed-autonomous-weapons.
- Edwards, Sarah. "Self Driving Car Accidents Trend Chart (2025)." *ConsumerShield*, October 9, 2025. https://www.consumershield.com/articles/self-driving-car-accidents-trends.

- Elphick, Dean. "Hotel Dynamic Pricing: Definition, Examples, and Best Software to Use." *SiteMinder*, June 25, 2025. https://www.siteminder.com/r/hotel-dynamic-pricing.
- Embedur, "A Deep Dive Into Wearable AI Devices in the Sports Industry." *embedUR*, n.d. https://www.embedur.ai/a-deep-dive-into-wearable-ai-devices-in-the-sports-industry.
- EMBL-EBI. "What Is AlphaFold?" *EMBL-EBI*. n.d. https://www.ebi.ac.uk/training/online/courses/alphafold/an-introductory-guide-to-its-strengths-and-limitations/what-is-alphafold.
- EMBL-EBI. "What Is the Protein Folding Problem?" *EMBL-EBI*. n.d. https://www.ebi.ac.uk/training/online/courses/alphafold/an-introductory-guide-to-its-strengths-and-limitations/what-is-the-protein-folding-problem.
- Encyclopedia Britannica Editors. "Unimate." *Encyclopedia Britannica*. n.d. https://www.britannica.com/technology/Unimate.
- Engelking, Carl. "The 'Driverless' Car Era Began More Than 90 Years Ago." *Discover Magazine*, December 13, 2017. https://www.discovermagazine.com/the-driverless-car-era-began-more-than-90-years-ago-1327.
- Estrada, Sheryl. "MIT Report: 95% of Generative AI Pilots at Companies Are Failing." *Fortune*, August 18, 2025. https://fortune.com/2025/08/18/mit-report-95-percent-generative-ai-pilots-at-companies-failing-cfo.
- European Commission. "Artificial Intelligence in Healthcare." *European Commission*. n.d. https://health.ec.europa.eu/ehealth-digital-health-and-care/artificial-intelligence-healthcare_en.
- European Parliament Think Tank. "Algorithmic Discrimination Under the AI Act and the GDPR." *European Parliament Think Tank*, February 26, 2025. https://www.europarl.europa.eu/thinktank/en/document/EPRS_ATA(2025)769509.
- European Parliament. "EU AI Act: First Regulation on Artificial Intelligence." *European Parliament*. Published August 6, 2023; Last updated February 19, 2025. https://www.europarl.europa.eu/topics/en/article/20230601STO93804/eu-ai-act-first-regulation-on-artificial-intelligence.
- Evans, Scarlett. "Shadow AI a Major Concern Across Enterprise IT, Study Finds." *AI Business*, June 5, 2025. https://aibusiness.com/responsible-ai/shadow-ai-a-major-concern-across-enterprise-it-study-finds.
- Fadilpašić, Ravie. "Hackers Hide Malware in Images to Deploy VIP Keylogger and 0bj3ctivity Stealer." *The Hacker News*, January 16, 2025. https://thehackernews.com/2025/01/hackers-hide-malware-in-images-to.html.
- Fadilpašić, Sead. "'Slopsquatting' Attacks Are Using AI-hallucinated Names Resembling Popular Libraries to Spread Malware." *TechRadar*, April 14, 2025. https://

www.techradar.com/pro/security/ai-hallucinated-names-resembling-popular-libraries-created-for-slopsquatting-attacks.

- Fankhauser, Péter. "Pioneering Autonomous Inspection for Enhanced Nuclear Safety at Onkalo." *ANYbotics*, n.d. https://www.anybotics.com/news/autonomous-inspection-for-enhanced-nuclear-safety-at-onkalo.
- Farrington II, Alfred. "Coach Fred." "The Cost Per Query for an AI Chatbot Can Be as Much as 10 Times the Cost of a Conventional Google Search." *Medium*, March 16, 2024. https://alfredfarrington.medium.com/the-cost-per-query-for-an-ai-chatbot-can-be-as-much-as-10-times-the-cost-of-a-conventional-google-dd5dd44a7745.
- Fearn, Nicholas. "'Master of Deception': Current AI Models Already Have the Capacity to Expertly Manipulate and Deceive Humans." *Live Science*, May 23, 2024. https://www.livescience.com/technology/artificial-intelligence/master-of-deception-current-ai-models-already-have-the-capacity-to-expertly-manipulate-and-deceive-humans.
- Federal Trade Commission. "FTC Order Requires Workado to Back up Artificial Intelligence Detection Claims." *Federal Trade Commission*, April 28, 2025. https://www.ftc.gov/news-events/news/press-releases/2025/04/ftc-order-requires-workado-back-artificial-intelligence-detection-claims.
- Field, Hayden. "GPT 5 Failed the Hype Test." *The Verge,* August 15, 2025. https://www.theverge.com/openai/759755/gpt 5 failed the hype test sam altman openai.
- Field, Severin. "Why Do Experts Disagree on Existential Risk and P(doom)? A Survey of AI Experts." *arXiv:2502.14870v1*, January 25, 2025. https://arxiv.org/html/2502.14870v1.
- Financial Times (FT) Team. "How AI-powered Tools Are Enhancing Personalised Learning for Students." *Financial Times*. n.d. https://www.ft.com/partnercontent/isp/how-ai-powered-tools-are-enhancing-personalised-learning-for-students.html.
- Financial Times Team. "How do I become a Master of Wine?" *Financial Times*, August 23, 2023. https://www.ft.com/content/bad75369-e81a-462e-ad29-4487608a1520.
- Fisher Phillips. "European Industry Pushes Back on the EU AI Act – Key Takeaways for Employers." *Fisher Phillips*, September 7, 2025. https://www.fisherphillips.com/en/news-insights/european-industry-pushes-back-on-the-eu-ai-act.html.
- Fitch, Shelton. "The Surprising Power of Next Word Prediction: Large Language Models Explained, Part 1." *Center for Security and Emerging Technology*, March 8, 2024. https://cset.georgetown.edu/article/the-surprising-power-of-next-word-prediction-large-language-models-explained-part-1.
- Fore, Preston. "Microsoft Researchers Have Revealed the 40 Jobs Most Exposed to AI—and Even Teachers Make the List." *Fortune*, July 31, 2025. https://fortune.

com/2025/07/31/microsoft-research-generative-ai-occupational-impact-jobs-most-and-least-likely-to-impact-teaching-office-jobs-college-gen-z-grads.

- Fortune Editors. "Microsoft Research: Generative AI's Occupational Impact on Jobs Most and Least Likely to Be Affected." *Fortune*, July 31, 2025. https://fortune.com/2025/07/31/microsoft-research-generative-ai-occupational-impact-jobs-most-and-least-likely-to-impact-teaching-office-jobs-college-gen-z-grads.
- Frąckiewicz, Marcin. "Black Box AI Exposed: Hidden Algorithms, Risks, and Breakthroughs in 2025." *TechStock2*, July 5, 2025. https://ts2.tech/en/black-box-ai-exposed-hidden-algorithms-risks-and-breakthroughs-in-2025.
- Franzen, Carl. "OpenAI's GPT-5 Rollout Is Not Going Smoothly." *Venture Beat*, August 8, 2025. https://venturebeat.com/ai/openais-gpt-5-rollout-is-not-going-smoothly.
- Freedman, Linn. "Illinois Enacts Act Prohibiting AI Therapy." *JD Supra*, August 11, 2025. https://www.jdsupra.com/legalnews/illinois-enacts-act-prohibiting-ai-9166547.
- Fu, Yujia, Peng Liang, Amjed Tahir, Zengyang Li, Mojtaba Shahin, Jiaxin Yu, and Jinfu Chen. "Security Weaknesses of Copilot Generated Code in GitHub." *arXiv:2310.02059v2l*, April 4, 2024. https://arxiv.org/html/2310.02059v2.
- FunctionalMind. "FunctionalMindTM – AI Tool for Functional & Integrative Medicine Clinicians." *FunctionalMind*, n.d. https://go.functionalmind.ai/home.
- Gallagher, James. "AI Designs New Superbug-killing Antibiotics for Gonorrhoea and MRSA." *BBC News*, August 14, 2025. https://www.bbc.co.uk/news/articles/cgr94xxye2lo.
- Gamze Tuncay, Kıymet Kaya, Yaren Yılmaz, Yusuf Yaslan, and Şule Gündüz Öğüdücü. "A Reinforcement Learning Based Dynamic Room Pricing Model for Hotel Industry." *INFOR: Information Systems and Operational Research 62*, no. 2 (2023): 211–31. https://doi.org/10.1080/03155986.2023.2235223.
- Gange, Kiran. "Leveraging Artificial Intelligence in Pricing." *Pricing Society,* February 13, 2025. https://www.pricingsociety.com/post/leveraging-artificial-intelligence-in-pricing.
- Garcez, Artur. "Neurosymbolic AI Is the Answer to Large Language Models' Inability to Stop Hallucinating." *The Conversation*, May 30, 2025. https://theconversation.com/neurosymbolic-ai-is-the-answer-to-large-language-models-inability-to-stop-hallucinating-257752.
- Gardner, Rachel. "The Robots Assessing Children's Mental Wellbeing." *The University of Cambridge, Department of Computer Science and Technology*, September 1, 2022. https://www.cst.cam.ac.uk/news/robots-assessing-childrens-mental-wellbeing.
- Gautam, Ankush Ramprakash. "Impact of High Data Quality on LLM Hallucinations." *International Journal of Computer Applications 187*, no. 4 (May 2025): 35–39. https://

www.ijcaonline.org/archives/volume187/number4/impact-of-high-data-quality-on-llm-hallucinations.

- Geeklab (Jared). "Is Google's Advertising Dying? AI Impact Unveiled." *Geeklab – Digital Innovators*, April 16, 2025. Last updated April 16, 2025. https://geeklab.blog/impact-of-ai-on-googles-search-advertising-and-cloud-business.
- GeeksforGeeks. "How to Calculate Optimal Batch Size for Training Neural Networks." *GeeksforGeeks*, July 23, 2025. https://www.geeksforgeeks.org/deep-learning/how-to-calculate-optimal-batch-size-for-training-neural-networks.
- Genkina, Dina. "AI Prompt Engineering Is Dead." *IEEE Spectrum*, May 16, 2025. https://spectrum.ieee.org/prompt-engineering-is-dead.
- Georgyan, David. "AlphaZero vs Stockfish 8: A Landmark Battle of Human and Artificial Intelligence in Chess." *Medium*, February 20, 2023. https://medium.com/@david_georgyan/alphazero-vs-stockfish-8-a-landmark-battle-of-human-and-artificial-intelligence-in-chess-ac6250b2355c.
- Gerlich, Michael. "AI Tools in Society: Impacts on Cognitive Offloading and the Future of Critical Thinking." January 3, 2025. http://dx.doi.org/10.2139/ssrn.5082524.
- Gershgorn, Dave. "Companies Are on the Hook if Their Hiring Algorithms Are Biased." *Quartz*, July 21, 2022. https://qz.com/1427621/companies-are-on-the-hook-if-their-hiring-algorithms-are-biased.
- Gibbs, Samuel. "Driverless Cars to Be Tested in UK." *The Guardian*, January 1, 2015. https://www.theguardian.com/technology/2015/jan/01/driverless-cars-tested-uk-bristol-coventry-milton-kevnes-greenwich.
- Gibney, Elizabeth. "China's Cheap, Open AI Model DeepSeek Thrills Scientists." *Nature*, January 23, 2025. https://doi.org/10.1038/d41586-025-00229-6.
- Gibson, Carl S., et al. "VAX 9000 Series." *Digital Technical Journal of Digital Equipment Corporation 2*, no. 4 (Fall 1990).
- Gibson, E. D. "The Tech Revolution in Sport." *Deconch* 30, May 19, 2025. https://deconch30.medium.com/the tech revolution in sports-9bcf1fc9dce3.
- Girard, Paul Antoine. "AI in Sports: The Shift from Intuition to AI Driven Coaching." *The AI Journal*, 2025. https://aijourn.com/ai-in-sports-the-shift-from-intuition-to-ai-driven-coaching.
- GitHub. "Build and Ship Software on a Single, Collaborative Platform." *GitHub*, 2025. https://github.com.
- GlobalData. "AI and Robotics Unlock Sustainable Efficiency in the Oil and Gas Sector." *DirectIndustry e-Magazine*, July 12, 2024. https://emag.directindustry.com/2024/07/12/ai-and-robotics-unlock-sustainable-efficiency-in-the-oil-and-gas-sector.
- GlobalData. "Applications of AI in the Mining Sector." *Mine*, October 14, 2014. https://mine.nridigital.com/mine_oct24/case-studies-ai-mining.

- GlobalData. "Case Studies: AI in Mining." *Mine*, September 30, 2024. https://mine.nridigital.com/mine_oct24/case-studies-ai-mining.
- Goel, Namanyayg. "Vibe Coding Is a Dangerous Fantasy." *N's Blog*, March 20, 2025. https://nmn.gl/blog/vibe-coding-fantasy.
- Goldman Sachs. "How Will AI Affect the Global Workforce?" *Goldman Sachs*, August 13, 2025. https://www.goldmansachs.com/insights/articles/how-will-ai-affect-the-global-workforce. Goldman Sachs.
- Goldman Sachs. "Is Nuclear Energy the Answer to AI Data Centers' Power Consumption?" *Goldman Sachs*, January 23, 2025. https://www.goldmansachs.com/insights/articles/is-nuclear-energy-the-answer-to-ai-data-centers-power-consumption.
- Goodier, Michael. "Revealed: Thousands of UK University Students Caught Cheating Using AI." *The Guardian*, September 15, 2025. https://www.theguardian.com/education/2025/jun/15/thousands-of-uk-university-students-caught-cheating-using-ai-artificial-intelligence-survey.
- Goodman, Rachel. "Why Amazon's Automated Hiring Tool Discriminated Against Women." *American Civil Liberties Union*, October 12, 2018. http://aclu.org/news/womens-rights/why-amazons-automated-hiring-tool-discriminated-against.
- Google for Developers. "Overview of GAN Structure." *Google for Developers*, n.d. https://developers.google.com/machine-learning/gan/gan_structure.
- Gore, Al. "An Inconvenient Truth." n.d. https://algore.com/library/an-inconvenient-truth.
- GothamChess. "HILARIOUS AI CHESS CHAMPIONSHIP." *YouTube*, August 5, 2025. https://www.youtube.com/watch?v=S2KmStTbL6c.
- Govette, Jonathan. "Why AI in Healthcare Has Failed in 2024." *Oatmeal Health*, December 14, 2024. https://oatmealhealth.com/why-has-ai-failed-so-far-in-healthcare-despite-billions-of-investment.
- Grand View Research. "Online Gambling Market (2025–2030)." *Grand View Research*. n.d. https://www.grandviewresearch.com/industry-analysis/online-gambling-market.
- Grosse, Kathrin, and Alexandre Alahi. "A Qualitative AI Security Risk Assessment of Autonomous Vehicles." *Transportation Research Part C: Emerging Technologies 169* (December 2024): 104797. https://doi.org/10.1016/j.trc.2024.104797.
- Guo, Charlie. "LLMs Are Getting Dumber and We Have No Idea Why." *Artificial Ignorance*, September 5, 2024. https://www.ignorance.ai/p/llms-are-getting-dumber-and-we-have.
- Habib, Zahid, Phil Spring, Deborah Walker, Yoshihiro Shimada, Satoshi Nagata, Syed Muhammad Ali Razi, Shannon Wilson, and Spencer Lin. "Oil and Gas in the AI Era."

IBM, 2025. https://www.ibm.com/thought-leadership/institute-business-value/en-us/report/oil-and-gas-in-ai-era.

- Hall, Rachel. "'Sliding Into an Abyss': Experts Warn Over Rising Use of AI for Mental Health Support." *The Guardian*, August 30, 2025. https://www.theguardian.com/society/2025/aug/30/therapists-warn-ai-chatbots-mental-health-support.
- Harman, Laura. "7 Dead Movie Stars Who've Been Brought Back to Life on Screen With CGI." *Metro*, August 24, 2024. https://metro.co.uk/2024/08/24/7-dead-movie-stars-whove-brought-back-life-screen-cgi-21471594.
- Harrison Dupré, Maggie. "First AI Psychosis Case Ends in Murder-Suicide." *Futurism via Yahoo News,* August 29, 2025. https://ca.news.yahoo.com/man-suffers-chatgpt-psychosis-murders-155857953.html.
- Harrison Dupré, Maggie. "Huge Proportion of Internet Is AI-Generated Slime, Researchers Find." *Futurism*, January 19, 2024. https://futurism.com/the-byte/internet-ai-generated-slime.
- Harvey, Grant. "This New AI is 100x Faster at Reasoning Than ChatGPT." *Tech Republic,* July 30, 2025. https://www.techrepublic.com/article/news-ai-hierarchical-reasoning-model.
- Hasler, Lucas. "The Complete Guide to Lottery in Lichtenstein." *Lott*.
- Hawkins, Amy. "Box, Run, Crash: China's Humanoid Robot Games Show Advances and Limitations." *The Guardian,* August 15, 2025. https://www.theguardian.com/world/2025/aug/15/china-world-humanoid-robot-games-advances-limitations.
- Hawkins, Amy. "Humanoid Workers and Surveillance Buggies: 'Embodied AI' Is Reshaping Daily Life in China." *The Guardian*, April 21, 2025. https://www.theguardian.com/world/2025/apr/21/humanoid-workers-and-surveillance-buggies-embodied-ai-is-reshaping-daily-life-in-china.
- Hayler, Andy. "'I, Claudius' – An Agentic AI Experiment." *The Information Difference,* June 10, 2025. https://www.informationdifference.com/i-claudius-an-agentic-ai-experiment.
- Hayler, Andy. "'I'm Sorry Dave' – Is AI an Existential Threat?" *The Information Difference,* August 17, 2025. https://www.informationdifference.com/im-sorry-dave-is-ai-an-existential-threat.
- Hayler, Andy. "Agents of Change or Agents of Chaos? The Reality of Agentic AI." *The Information Difference*, April 22, 2025. https://www.informationdifference.com/the-reality-of-agentic-ai.
- Hayler, Andy. "AI Alignment and Safety – Pandora's Bot." *The Information Difference,* August 6, 2025. https://www.informationdifference.com/ai-alignment-and-safety-pandoras-bot.

- Hayler, Andy. "AI Use Cases – the Good, the Bad and the Ugly." *Bloor Research*, May 23, 2025. https://www.bloorresearch.com/ai-use-cases-the-good-the-bad-and-the-ugly.
- Hayler, Andy. "AI's Copyright Crossroads – Anthropic Settles Landmark Lawsuit." *The Information Difference*, August 28, 2025. https://www.informationdifference.com/ais-copyright-crossroads-anthropic-settles-landmark-lawsuit.
- Hayler, Andy. "Blowing Bubbles? – the Economic Impact of AI." *The Information Difference*, August 23, 2025. https://www.informationdifference.com/blowing-bubbles-the-economic-impact-of-ai.
- Hayler, Andy. "Braking News – AI in Autonomous Vehicles." *The Information Difference*, August 21, 2025. https://www.informationdifference.com/braking-news-ai-in-autonomous-vehicles.
- Hayler, Andy. "Chatbots on the Couch: AI in Therapy." *The Information Difference,* August 18, 2025. https://www.informationdifference.com/chatbots-on-the-couch-ai-in-therapy.
- Hayler, Andy. "Code of Silence – the Hidden Risks of AI-Generated Code." *The Information Difference*, April 24, 2025. https://www.informationdifference.com/code-of-silence-the-hidden-risks-of-ai-generated-code.
- Hayler, Andy. "Droning on – AI in the Defence Industry." *The Information Difference,* August 20, 2025. https://www.informationdifference.com/droning-on-ai-in-the-defence-industry.
- Hayler, Andy. "Fake It 'Til You Make It – AI Deepfakes." *The Information Difference,* September 2, 2025. https://www.informationdifference.com/fake-it-til-you-make-it-ai-deepfakes.
- Hayler, Andy. "Feeding the Ravenous AI Beast." *The Information Difference,* August 11, 2025. https://www.informationdifference.com/feeding-the-beast.
- Hayler, Andy. "Finding the Goldilocks Zone for AI-Generated Code." *The Information Difference,* August 12, 2025. https://www.informationdifference.com/ai-generated-code.
- Hayler, Andy. "From Data to Droughts – AI and the Environment." *The Information Difference,* September 15, 2025. https://www.informationdifference.com/from-data-to-droughts-ai-and-the-environment.
- Hayler, Andy. "Generative AI Works in a Mysterious Way – Explainability in AI." *The Information Difference,* September 12, 2025. https://www.informationdifference.com/explainability-in-ai.
- Hayler, Andy. "Hiding in Plain Sight – AI Data Poisoning." *The Information Difference,* August 27, 2025. https://www.informationdifference.com/hiding-in-plain-sight-ai-data-poisoning.

- Hayler, Andy. "MCP – Multiple Security Pitfalls?" *The Information Difference,* June 10, 2025. https://www.informationdifference.com/security-pitfalls.
- Hayler, Andy. "Reality Check: Do AI Projects Deliver Return on Investment?" *The Information Difference,* August 23, 2025. https://www.informationdifference.com/reality-check-do-ai-projects-deliver-return-on-investmentz
- Hayler, Andy. "Scraping by – AI and Copyright Law." *The Information Difference,* August 18, 2025. https://www.informationdifference.com/scraping-by-ai-and-copyright-law.
- Hayler, Andy. "Silicon Dragon – The Rise of AI in China." *The Information Difference,* August 26, 2025. https://www.informationdifference.com/silicon-dragon-the-rise-of-ai-in-china.
- Hayler, Andy. "Stop AI Becoming a Security Trojan Horse." *The Information Difference,* June 25, 2025. https://www.informationdifference.com/security-trojan-horse.
- Hayler, Andy. "The AI Trust Gap." *The Information Difference*, August 4, 2025. https://www.informationdifference.com/the-ai-trust-gap.
- Hayler, Andy. "The Domino Effect – Benchmarking Agentic AI." *The Information Difference,* June 17, 2025. https://www.informationdifference.com/benchmarking-agentic-ai.
- Hayler, Andy. "The Elephant in the Room – AI Image Generation." *The Information Difference,* July 8, 2025. https://www.informationdifference.com/elephant-ai-image-generation.
- Hayler, Andy. "Thinking Outside the Bot." *The Information Difference,* August 14, 2025. https://www.informationdifference.com/thinking-outside-the-bot.
- Hayler, Andy. "Uncorking the Future – AI in the Wine Industry." *The Information Difference,* September 1, 2025. https://www.informationdifference.com/uncorking-the-future-ai-in-the-wine-industry.
- Hayler, Andy. "When AI Picks Sides – AI Bias and Discrimination." *The Information Difference,* September 2, 2025. https://www.informationdifference.com/when-ai-picks-sides-ai-bias-and-discrimination.
- Hayler, Andy. "When Algorithms Dream: AI Hallucinations in Depth." *The Information Difference,* August 19, 2025. https://www.informationdifference.com/when-algorithms-dream-ai-hallucinations-in-depth.
- Heikkilä, Melissa. "It's Easy To Tamper With Watermarks From AI-generated Text." *MIT Technology Review*, March 29, 2024. https://www.technologyreview.com/2024/03/29/1090310/its-easy-to-tamper-with-watermarks-from-ai-generated-text.
- Heikkilä, Melissa. "This New Data Poisoning Tool Lets Artists Fight Back Against Generative AI." *MIT Technology Review*, October 23, 2023. https://www.

technologyreview.com/2023/10/23/1082189/data-poisoning-artists-fight-generative-ai.

- Helmholtz Munich. "AI That Thinks Like Us: New Model Predicts Human Decisions With Startling Accuracy." *Scitech Daily*, July 6, 2025.
- Henderson, Nick. "AI Hallucinations Crisis: Over 50 Fake Cases Cited in July Alone." *VinciWorks*, August 3, 2025. https://vinciworks.com/blog/ai-hallucinations-crisis-over-50-fake-cases-cited-in-july-alone.
- Hernandez, Joe. "A Military Drone With a Mind of Its Own Was Used in Combat, U.N. Says." *NPR*, June 1, 2021. https://www.npr.org/2021/06/01/1002196245/a-u-n-report-suggests-libya-saw-the-first-battlefield-killing-by-an-autonomous-d.
- Herranz, Arantxa. "Success Story: Smart Litter Bins in Seoul." *Tomorrow. City,* November 15, 2020.
- Heyen, Henning, Amy Widdicombe, Noah Y. Siegel, Maria Perez-Ortiz, and Philip Treleaven. "The Effect of Model Size on LLM Post-hoc Explainability via LIME." *arXiv preprint,* May 8, 2024. https://arxiv.org/abs/2405.05348.
- Hill, Andrea. "Why 95% of AI Pilots Fail, and What Business Leaders Should Do Instead." *Forbes*, August 21, 2025. https://www.forbes.com/sites/andreahill/2025/08/21/why-95-of-ai-pilots-fail-and-what-business-leaders-should-do-instead.
- Hooroo Jackson, "Window Seat (2023) the First Fully AI Feature Film in the History of Cinema! // HD." *YouTube*, August 22, 2023. https://www.youtube.com/watch?v=WxVUxf1gcQw.
- Hou, June-Hao. "Comparing AI-Generated Images Two Years Apart — 2022 vs. 2024." *Medium*, April 17, 2024. https://medium.com/@junehao/comparing-ai-generated-images-two-years-apart-2022-vs-2024-6c3c4670b905.
- Howarth, Josh. "Most Visited Websites in the World (August 2025)." *Exploding Topics*, August 20, 2025. https://explodingtopics.com/blog/most-visited-websites.
- Hsu, Jeremy. "AI Hallucinations Are Getting Worse – and They're Here to Stay." *New Scientist*, May 9, 2025. https://www.newscientist.com/article/2479545-ai-hallucinations-are-getting-worse-and-theyre-here-to-stay.
- Hu, Bing, Ashish Saragadam, Anita Layton, and Helen Chen. "Synthetic Data from Diffusion Models Improve Drug Discovery Prediction." *arXiv*, May 6, 2024. https://arxiv.org/abs/2405.03799.
- Huang, Kung-Hsiang, Akshara Prabhakar, Onkar Thorat, Divyansh Agarwal, Prafulla Kumar Choubey, Yixin Mao, Silvio Savarese, Caiming Xiong, and Chien-Sheng Wu. "CRMArena-Pro: Holistic Assessment of LLM Agents Across Diverse Business Scenarios and Interactions." *arXiv:2505.18879*, May 24, 2025. https://arxiv.org/abs/2505.18878.

- Huang, Yongzhe, Nick Bray, Akshata Rao, Yang Ji, and Wenjun Hu. "How Good Are the LLM Guardrails on the Market? A Comparative Study on the Effectiveness of LLM Content Filtering Across Major GenAI Platforms." *Unit 42*, June 2, 2025. https://unit42.paloaltonetworks.com/comparing-llm-guardrails-across-genai-platforms.
- Huang, Yongzhe, Yang Ji, and Wenjun Hu. "Investigating LLM Jailbreaking of Popular Generative AI Web Products." *Unit 42*, February 21, 2025. https://unit42.paloaltonetworks.com/jailbreaking-generative-ai-web-products.
- Hume, Samuel. "AI May Help Us Cure Countless Diseases – and Usher in a New Golden Age of Medicine." *The Guardian,* March 28, 2025. https://www.theguardian.com/commentisfree/ng-interactive/2025/mar/28/ai-alphafold-biology-protein-structure.
- Hurtado, Ariana. "Survey Reveals Biggest Challenge in Implementing AI Technologies in Offshore Oil and Gas Sector." *Offshore Magazine,* June 5, 2025. https://www.offshore-mag.com/special-reports/article/55295135/survey-reveals-biggest-challenge-in-implementing-ai-technologies-in-offshore-oil-and-gas-sector.
- Hutson, Matthew. "How AI Is Being Used to Accelerate Clinical Trials." *Nature* 627, no. 8003 (March 13, 2024): S2–5. https://doi.org/10.1038/d41586-024-00753-x.
- IAPP. "Global AI Law and Policy Tracker." *IAPP*, May 1, 2025. https://iapp.org/resources/article/global-ai-legislation-tracker.
- IBM. "What Is Gradient Descent?" *IBM*. https://www.ibm.com/think/topics/gradient-descent.
- IBM. "What Is Homomorphic Encryption?" *IBM*, n.d. https://www.ibm.com/think/topics/homomorphic-encryption.
- IBM. "Cost of a Data Breach 2025." *IBM*, 2025. https://www.ibm.com/reports/data-breach.
- IFR International Federation of Robotics. "China: Robot Installations Grew by 44 Percent." *International Federation of Robotics*, n.d. https://ifr.org/news/china-robot-installations-grew-by-44-percent.
- IFR International Federation of Robotics. "Record of 4 Million Robots in Factories Worldwide." *International Federation of Robotics*, n.d. https://ifr.org/ifr-press-releases/news/record-of-4-million-robots-working-in-factories-worldwide.
- Imandra. "Imandra Unveils CodeLogician: A Groundbreaking Neurosymbolic AI Agent for Mathematical Code Reasoning." *PR Newswire*, March 26, 2025. https://www.prnewswire.com/news-releases/imandra-unveils-codelogician-a-groundbreaking-neurosymbolic-ai-agent-for-mathematical-code-reasoning-302411440.html.
- IMARC. "Robotics Market Size, Share, Growth, Trends, Report, 2033." *IMARC Group,* n.d. https://www.imarcgroup.com/robotics-market.

- Improta, Cristina, Rosalia Tufano, Pietro Liguori, Domenico Cotroneo, and Gabriele Bavota. "Quality In, Quality Out: Investigating Training Data's Role in AI Code Generation." *arXiv:2503.11402v1*, March 14, 2025. https://arxiv.org/html/2503.11402v1.
- Ingram, David. "Why Waymo Cars Became Sitting Ducks During the L.A. Protests." *NBC News*, June 14, 2025. https://www.nbcnews.com/tech/innovation/waymo-cars-set-fire-sitting-ducks-la-protests-rcna212426.
- Institut Català d'Investigació Química. "Invisible Ink." *ICIQ*, December 11, 2024. https://iciq.org/experiment/invisible-ink.
- International Energy Agency. "The Oil and Gas Industry in Net Zero Transitions: Executive Summary." *International Energy Agency,* November 23, 2023. https://www.iea.org/reports/the-oil-and-gas-industry-in-net-zero-transitions/executive-summary.
- International Labmate. "Equipment Failure 'Caused BP Deepwater Horizon Spill'." *Petrochemical Chemical & Energy*, n.d. https://www.petro-online.com/news/fuel-for-thought/13/breaking-news/equipment-failure-caused-bp-deepwater-horizon-spill/30457.
- Ip, Jeffrey. "RAG Evaluation Metrics: Assessing Answer Relevancy, Faithfulness, Contextual Relevancy, and More." *Confident AI,* October 10, 2025. https://www.confident-ai.com/blog/rag-evaluation-metrics-answer-relevancy-faithfulness-and-more.
- Ishay Sharbat, Tamir. "AgentFlayer: When AIjacking Leads to Full Data Exfiltration in Copilot Studio." *Zenity Labs,* July 7, 2025. https://labs.zenity.io/p/a-copilot-studio-story-2-when-aijacking-leads-to-full-data-exfiltration-bc4a.
- Ismailzada, Majid. "How Many Self-Driving Cars Have Crashed." *G&M Direct Hire,* October 11, 2025. https://gmdirecthire.co.uk/blog/self-driving-cars-crashes.
- ISO. *ISO/IEC 27001:2022: Information Security, Cybersecurity and Privacy Protection — Information Security Management Systems — Requirements.* ISO, 2022. https://www.iso.org/standard/27001.
- Jain, Anuraag. "AI In Sports – Revolutionizing Training and Performance." *Oyelabs,* September 12, 2025. https://oyelabs.com/ai-in-sports-revolutionizing-training-and-performance.
- Jamali, Lily. "It Shocked the US Market but Has China's DeepSeek Changed AI?" *BBC News,* August 10, 2025. https://www.bbc.com/news/articles/c4gez754mn6o.
- Jeffrey, Cal. "Sam Altman Says Investors Are Acting Irrational in a Booming AI Bubble." *TechSpot*, August 15, 2025. https://www.techspot.com/news/109090/sam-altman-investors-acting-irrational-booming-ai-bubble.html.
- Jennings-Trace, Ellen. "Agentic AI Has Issues With Security and Privacy, Signal President Says." *TechRadar*, March 10, 2025. https://www.techradar.com/pro/

security/agentic-ai-has-profound-issues-with-security-and-privacy-signal-president-says.

- Jensen, Benjamin, and Jake S. Kwon. "The U.S. Army, Artificial Intelligence, and Mission Command." *War on the Rocks,* March 10, 2025. https://warontherocks.com/2025/03/the-u-s-army-artificial-intelligence-and-mission-command.
- Jet Propulsion Laboratory. "Autonomous Systems Help NASA's Perseverance Do More Science on Mars." *NASA Jet Propulsion Laboratory*, September 21, 2023. https://www.jpl.nasa.gov/news/autonomous-systems-help-nasas-perseverance-do-more-science-on-mars.
- Jiang, Zhengyuan, Moyang Guo, Yuepeng Hu, and Neil Zhenqiang Gong. "Watermark-Based Attribution of AI-Generated Content." *arXiv preprint*. arXiv:2404.04254. https://arxiv.org/abs/2404.04254.
- Jiangang, Wang, Shi Lei, Feng Ding, Liang Jinli, Hou Lingxia, and Miao Enming. "A Digital Twin Modeling and Application for Gear Rack Drilling Rigs Lifting System." *Scientific Reports* 14 (2024): 23711. https://doi.org/10.1038/s41598-024-73954-z.
- Johnson, Carla K. "Racial Bias in Health Care Software Aids Whites Over Blacks." *AP News,* October 25, 2019. https://apnews.com/racial-bias-in-health-care-software-aids-whites-over-blacks-b5fb4e1ae6e944fd979568df1fdb6df4.
- Johnston, William, Cailbhe Doherty, Fionn Cleirigh Büttner, and Brian Caulfield. "Wearable Sensing and Mobile Devices: The Future of Post Concussion Monitoring?" *Concussion 2,* no. 1 (2017): CNC28. https://doi.org/10.2217/cnc-2016-0025.
- Jones, Nicola. "AI Hallucinations Can't Be Stopped — but These Techniques Can Limit Their Damage." *Nature* 637, no. 8047 (January 21, 2025): 778–80. https://doi.org/10.1038/d41586-025-00068-5.
- Jones, Rachyl. "It's Time to Get Serious About AI Hallucinations." *Fortune*, January 17, 2024. https://fortune.com/2024/01/17/ai-hallucination-aporia-survey.
- Jones, Taylor. "Real-Life Technologies That Prove Autonomous Weapons Are Already Here." *Future of Life Institute*, November 22, 2021.
- JOUAV. "How Far Can a Drone Fly? Maximum Ranges and Legal Limits." Last updated October 28, 2025. https://www.jouav.com/blog/how-far-can-a-drone-fly.html.
- Jumper, John, Richard Evans, Alexander Pritzel, Tim Green, Michael Figurnov, Olaf Ronneberger, Kathryn Tunyasuvunakool, Russ Bates, Augustin Žídek, Anna Potapenko, Alex Bridgland, Clemens Meyer, Simon A. A. Kohl, Andrew J. Ballard, Andrew Cowie, Bernardino Romera-Paredes, Stanislav Nikolov, Rishub Jain, Jonas Adler, Trevor Back, Stig Petersen, David Reiman, Ellen Clancy, Michal Zielinski, Martin Steinegger, Michalina Pacholska, Tamas Berghammer, Sebastian Bodenstein, David Silver, Oriol Vinyals, Andrew W. Senior, Koray Kavukcuoglu, Pushmeet Kohli, and Demis Hassabis. "Highly Accurate Protein Structure Prediction with AlphaFold."

Nature 596, no. 7873 (July 15, 2021): 583–89. https://doi.org/10.1038/s41586-021-03819-2.

- Kahn, Jeremy. "Why Did MIT Find 95 % of AI Projects Fail? Hint: It Wasn't About the Tech Itself." *Fortune*, August 21, 2025. https://fortune.com/2025/08/21/an mit report that 95 of ai pilots fail spooked investors but the reason why those pilots failed is what should make the c suite anxious.
- Kaiser, Jocelyn. "Data Poisoning Emerges as a New Front in AI Arms Race." *Science*, March 15, 2025. https://www.science.org/content/article/data-poisoning-new-front-ai-arms-race.
- Kalai, Adam Tauman, Ofir Nachum, Santosh S. Vempala, and Edwin Zhang. "Why Language Models Hallucinate." *arXiv:2509.04664*, September 4, 2025. https://arxiv.org/abs/2509.04664.
- Kandasamy, Jags. "Defense Grade AI Scores a Strike: Transforming Bowling and Beyond With Edge Computing." *RTInsights*, April 16, 2025. https://www.rtinsights.com/defense-grade-ai-scores-a-strike-transforming-bowling-and-beyond-with-edge-computing.
- Karp, Paul. "Deloitte Accused of Erroneous Citations, Leading to Suspected AI Use in Major Report on Welfare." *Australian Financial Review*, August 22, 2025. https://www.afr.com/companies/professional-services/academics-raise-alarm-over-suspected-ai-use-in-deloitte-report-20250822-p5mp0f.
- Kaspersky. "What Is Steganography & How Does It Work?" *Kaspersky*, February 8, 2023. https://www.kaspersky.com/resource-center/definitions/what-is-steganography.
- Katana, Ai. "The Legacy of Japan's Fifth Generation Computer Systems (FGCS) Project on AI." *AI Katana*, September 8, 2024. https://www.aikatana.com/p/legacy-japans-fifth-generation-computer-systems-fgcs-project-ai.
- Kaubrė, Vytenis. "LLM Training Data: The 8 Main Public Data Sources." *Oxylabs*, September 27, 2024. https://oxylabs.io/blog/llm-training-data.
- Kaur, Dashveenjit. "Zuckerberg's $15B Bet: How Meta's 'Superintelligence Labs' Became Silicon Valley's Most Expensive AI Talent War." *AI News*, July 17, 2025. https://www.artificialintelligence-news.com/news/meta-superintelligence-ai-lab-zuckerberg-talent-war.
- Kearns, Michael, and Aaron Roth. *The Ethical Algorithm: The Science of Socially Aware Algorithm Design*. Oxford University Press USA, 2020.
- Kelly, Piers. "How Governments Are Using AI: 8 Real World Case Studies." *Govnet Technology*, February 19, 2025. https://blog.govnet.co.uk/technology/ai-in-government-case-studies.

- Kelly, Ross, "OpenAI's Sam Altman: Hallucinations Are Part of the 'Magic' of Generative AI." *IT Pro*, September 13, 2023. https://www.itpro.com/technology/artificial-intelligence/openais-sam-altman-hallucinations-are-part-of-the-magic-of-generative-ai.
- Kelly, Samantha. "Laundry-Folding-Robotics Company Attracts $400M From Jeff Bezos and OpenAI." *CNET*, November 14, 2024. https://www.cnet.com/tech/services-and-software/laundry-folding-robotics-company-attracts-400m-from-jeff-bezos-and-openai.
- Kim, Eungdo, Jaehoon Yang, Sungjin Park, and Kwangsoo Shin. "Factors Affecting Success of New Drug Clinical Trials." *Therapeutic Innovation & Regulatory Science 57*, no. 4 (May 11, 2023): 737–50. https://doi.org/10.1007/s43441-023-00509-1.
- Kim, Jae Hak, Janghyeon Kim, Hoseok Kang, and Bo Young Youn. "Ethical Implications of Artificial Intelligence in Sport: A Systematic Scoping Review." *Journal of Sport and Health Science 14* (December 2025): 101047. https://doi.org/10.1016/j.jshs.2025.101047.
- King, Ross. "AI in the Workplace: Productivity, Ethics, and the Future of Jobs." *Harvard Business Review,* June 12, 2025. https://hbr.org/2025/06/ai-in-the-workplace-productivity-ethics-and-the-future-of-jobs.
- Kingma, Diederik P., and Max Welling. "An Introduction to Variational Autoencoders." *Foundations and Trends® in Machine Learning 12,* no. 4 (January 1, 2019): 307–92. https://doi.org/10.1561/2200000056.
- Kleinman, Zoe, and Brian Wheeler. "Concern the UK's AI Ambitions Could Lead to Water Shortages." *BBC News,* February 6, 2025. https://bbc.co.uk/news/articles/ce85wx9jjndo.
- Kleinman, Zoe. "How an AI-written Book Shows Why the Tech 'Terrifies' Creatives." *BBC News,* January 31, 2025. https://www.bbc.com/news/articles/cp8k5gezykyo.
- Kleinman, Zoe. "US Air Force Denies AI Drone Attacked Operator in Test." *BBC News,* June 2, 2023. https://www.bbc.co.uk/news/technology-65789916.
- Knight, Will. "China Is the World's Biggest Face Recognition Dealer." *WIRED*, January 24, 2023. https://www.wired.com/story/china-is-the-worlds-biggest-face-recognition-dealer.
- Kohler, Lindsay. "Fear Isn't Slowing Down AI Adoption at Work. A Lack of Vision Is." *Forbes*, January 27, 2025. https://www.forbes.com/sites/lindsaykohler/2025/01/27/fear-isnt-slowing-down-ai-adoption-at-work-a-lack-of-vision-is.
- Kollewe, Julia. "More Than 25% of UK Businesses Hit by Cyber-attack in Last Year, Report Finds." *The Guardian,* June 30, 2025. https://www.theguardian.com/business/2025/jun/30/uk-businesses-hit-by-cyber-attack-last-year-report.

- Korcova, Barbora. "AI in Recruitment: Balancing Innovation With Legal Risk." *EM Law | Commercial Lawyers in Central London*, August 22, 2025. https://emlaw.co.uk/ai-in-recruitment-balancing-innovation-with-legal-risk.
- Korolov, Maria. "Fast vs. Slow: The Real Impact of AI Adoption Speed." *CIO*, January 15, 2025. https://www.cio.com/article/3634175/fast-vs-slow-the-real-impact-of-ai-adoption-speed.html.
- Kosinski, Matthew. "What Is Black Box AI?" *IBM*. n.d. https://www.ibm.com/think/topics/black-box-ai.
- KPMG, and KPMG International Limited. "Trust, Attitudes and Use of Artificial Intelligence: A Global Study 2025." *KPMG*, August 13, 2025. https://kpmg.com/se/en/insights/ai/trust-attitudes-and-use-of-ai.html.
- Kshirsagar, Om, Aman Maurya, and Fatima Shaikh. "AlphaZero Vs StockFish – a Review of Chess Engines." *Journal of Emerging Technologies and Innovative Research (JETIR) 9*, no. 4 (2022): b451–b457. https://www.jetir.org/papers/JETIR2204161.pdf.
- Kucinski, Joe. "Tesla Has the Highest Fatal Accident Rate of All Auto Brands, Study Finds." *Road and Track,* November 15, 2024. https://www.roadandtrack.com/news/a62919131/tesla-has-highest-fatal-accident-rate-of-all-auto-brands-study.
- Kumar, Ananya, and Michael Chen. "Mitigating AI Hallucinations Through Prompt Engineering." *Journal of Artificial Intelligence Research 78* (2025): 1023–1050. https://www.jair.org/index.php/jair/article/view/12548.
- Kwan, William. "Navigating the Risks of 'Shadow AI'." *British Computer Society*, July 8, 2025. https://www.bcs.org/articles-opinion-and-research/navigating-the-risks-of-shadow-ai.
- L'Atelier Du Vin. "Corked Wine, Cork Taint, Musty Odours: What to Do." *L'Atelier Du Vin,* March 13, 2023. https://www.atelierduvin.com/en/corked-wine-a-definition-and-practical-guide.
- Landymore, Frank. "AI Models Can Send 'Subliminal' Messages to Each Other That Make Them More Evil." *Futurism*, July 26, 2025. https://futurism.com/ai-models-subliminal-messages-evil.
- Landymore, Frank. "Car Dealership Disturbed When Its AI Is Caught Offering Chevys for $1 Each." *Futurism*, December 21, 2023. https://futurism.com/the-byte/car-dealership-ai.
- Landymore, Frank. "OpenAI's New AI Agent Takes One Hour to Order Food and Recommends Visiting a Baseball Stadium in the Middle of the Ocean." *Futurism*, July 20, 2025. https://futurism.com/openai-new-ai-agent-food-stadium.
- Langlais, Pierre-Carl, Carlos Rosas Hinostroza, Mattia Nee, Catherine Arnett, Pavel Chizhov, Eliot Krzystof Jones, Irène Girard, David Mach, Anastasia Stasenko, and Ivan

P. Yamshchikov. "Common Corpus: The Largest Collection of Ethical Data for LLM Pre-Training." *arXiv:2506.01732*, June 2, 2025. https://arxiv.org/abs/2506.01732.

- Larson, Jeff, Julia Angwin, Lauren Kirchner, and Surya Mattu. "How We Analyzed the COMPAS Recidivism Algorithm." *ProPublica*, May 26, 2016. https://www.propublica.org/article/how-we-analyzed-the-compas-recidivism-algorithm.
- Law, Ryan, Xibeijia Guan, and Tim Soulo. "74% of New Webpages Include AI Content (Study of 900k Pages)." *Ahrefs*, May 19, 2025. https://ahrefs.com/blog/what-percentage-of-new-content-is-ai-generated.
- Lea, Robert. "Autonomous Robot Swarms Come Together to Perform a Variety of Missions." *Advanced Science News*, November 19, 2024. https://www.advancedsciencenews.com/autonomous-robot-swarms-come-together-to-perform-a-variety-of-missions.
- Lee, Kep. "The Real Cost of Fraud for Financial Institutions Explained." *Abrigo*, July 24, 2025. https://www.abrigo.com/blog/blog-the-true-cost-of-fraud.
- Lees, Dominic. "2024: The Year in AI." *BFI*, December 12, 2024. https://www.bfi.org.uk/sight-and-sound/features/2024-year-ai.
- Leffer, Lauren. "Yes, AI Models Can Get Worse Over Time." *Scientific American,* August 2, 2023. https://www.scientificamerican.com/article/yes-ai-models-can-get-worse-over-time.
- Legatt, Aviva. "Students Are Already Using AI. Are Colleges Teaching AI Literacy?" *Forbes*, June 11, 2025. https://www.forbes.com/sites/avivalegatt/2025/06/11/students-are-already-using-ai-are-colleges-teaching-ai-literacy.
- Legit Security. "AI Code Generation: The Risks and Benefits of AI in Software." *Legit Security,* January 21, 2025. https://www.legitsecurity.com/aspm-knowledge-base/ai-code-generation-benefits-and-risks.
- Lehman, Joel, Jeff Clune, Dusan Misevic, Christoph Adami, Lee Altenberg, Julie Beaulieu, Peter J. Bentley, Samuel Bernard, Guillaume Beslon, David M. Bryson, Nick Cheney, Patryk Chrabaszcz, Antoine Cully, Stephane Doncieux, Fred C. Dyer, Kai Olav Ellefsen, Robert Feldt, Stephan Fischer, Stephanie Forrest, Antoine Fŕenoy, Christian Gagńe, Leni Le Goff, Laura M. Grabowski, Babak Hodjat, Frank Hutter, Laurent Keller, Carole Knibbe, Peter Krcah, Richard E. Lenski, Hod Lipson, Robert MacCurdy, Carlos Maestre, Risto Miikkulainen, Sara Mitri, David E. Moriarty, Jean-Baptiste Mouret, Anh Nguyen, Charles Ofria, Marc Parizeau, David Parsons, Robert T. Pennock, William F. Punch, Thomas S. Ray, Marc Schoenauer, Eric Schulte, Karl Sims, Kenneth O. Stanley, François Taddei, Danesh Tarapore, Simon Thibault, Richard Watson, Westley Weimer, and Jason Yosinski, "The Surprising Creativity of Digital Evolution: A Collection of Anecdotes from the Evolutionary Computation and

Artificial Life Research Communities." *Artificial Life 26*, no. 2 (2020): 274–306. https://doi.org/10.1162/artl_a_00319.

- Leingang, Rachel. "How to Spot a Deepfake: The Maker of a Detection Tool Shares the Key Giveaways." *The Guardian,* June 7, 2024. https://www.theguardian.com/us-news/article/2024/jun/07/how-to-spot-a-deepfake.
- Lenaerts-Bergmans, Bart. "What Is Data Poisoning?" CrowdStrike, March 19, 2025. https://www.crowdstrike.com/en-gb/cybersecurity-101/cyberattacks/data-poisoning.
- Leonida, Carly. "AI: Bringing Mining Companies Closer to Their Data." *Engineering and Mining Journal,* April 2025.
- Leopold, Till. "How AI is Reshaping the Career Ladder, and Other Trends in Jobs and Skills on Labour Day." *World Economic Forum*, April 30, 2025.
- Levi, Stuart D., Pramode Chiruvolu, Mana Ghaemmaghami, and Shannon N. Morgan. "Fair Use and AI Training: Two Recent Decisions Highlight the Complexity of This Issue." *Skadden, Arps, Slate, Meagher & Flom LLP*, July 8, 2025. https://www.skadden.com/insights/publications/2025/07/fair-use-and-ai-training.
- Lewis, Charlie, Ida Kristensen, and Jeffrey Caso with Julian Fuchs. "AI Is the Greatest Threat—and Defense—in Cybersecurity Today. Here's Why." *McKinsey*, May 15, 2025. https://www.mckinsey.com/about-us/new-at-mckinsey-blog/ai-is-the-greatest-threat-and-defense-in-cybersecurity-today.
- Lexis Nexis. "Fast Law: Why Speed Is the Priority for Lawyers Using AI." *Lexis Nexis.* n.d. https://www.lexisnexis.co.uk/insights/fast-law-why-speed-is-the-priority-for-lawyers-using-ai/index.html.
- Li, Guorui, Tuck-Whye Wong, Benjamin Shih, Chunyu Guo, Luwen Wang, Jiaqi Liu, Tao Wang, Xiaobo Liu, Jiayao Yan, Baosheng Wu, Fajun Yu, Yunsai Chen, Yiming Liang, Yaoting Xue, Chengjun Wang, Shunping He, Li Wen, Michael T. Tolley, A-Man Zhang, Cecilia Laschi, and Tiefeng Li. "Bioinspired Soft Robots for Deep-Sea Exploration." *Nature Communications 14* (2023): 7097. https://www.nature.com/articles/s41467-023-42882-3.
- Li, Xinran, and Zichi Wang. "Vaccine for Digital Images Against Steganography." *Scientific Reports 14*, no. 1 (September 12, 2024). https://doi.org/10.1038/s41598-024-72693-5.
- Lindsay Jr., Robert K., Bruce G. Buchanan, Edward A. Feigenbaum, and Joshua Lederberg. "DENDRAL: A Case Study of the First Expert System for Scientific Hypothesis Formation." *Artificial Intelligence 61* (1993): 209–261. https://web.mit.edu/6.034/www/6.s966/dendral-history.pdf.
- Liu, Xinyi, and Thomas W. Malone. "Generative AI and Creativity: Risks, Rewards, and Regulation." *AI & Society 40,* no. 3 (2025): 589–608. https://link.springer.com/article/10.1007/s00146-025-01562-1.

- Liu, Yi-Ling. "China's Vision for a Driverless Future Is Miles Ahead of Everyone Else's." *Rest of World,* August 12, 2025. https://restofworld.org/2025/china-ai-powered-self-driving-cars.
- Livemint. "'They Ruined ChatGPT': OpenAI Faces Backlash as GPT-5 Reaches All Users." *Mint*, August 8, 2025. https://www.livemint.com/technology/tech-news/they-ruined-chatgpt-openai-faces-backlash-as-gpt-5-reaches-all-users-sam-altman-11754632387517.html.
- LLLLITL. "Coca-Cola – Secret Santa (AI-Generated Christmas Ad 2024)." *YouTube*, November 15, 2024. https://www.youtube.com/watch?v=IQWUKWM2JrQ.
- Lockheed Martin. "Aegis Combat System." *Lockheed Martin,* n.d. https://www.lockheedmartin.com/en-us/products/aegis-combat-system.html.
- Log, ClaudeLog. "ClaudeLog – Claude Code Docs, Guides, Tutorials & Best Practices." *ClaudeLog*, Last updated November 1, 2025. https://claudelog.com/claude-code-pricing.
- Look, Aimée. "Top Consulting Firms Are Being Hit by an AI Reckoning." *The Logic,* July 24, 2025. https://thelogic.co/news/ai-consultant-reckoning.
- Love, Julia. "AI Researcher Who Helped Write Landmark Paper Is Leaving Google." *Yahoo Finance,* July 11, 2023. https://finance.yahoo.com/news/ai-researcher-helped-write-landmark-030025546.html.
- Lowe, Derek. "AI Drugs So Far." *Science*, May 13, 2024. https://www.science.org/content/blog-post/ai-drugs-so-far.
- Lu, Marcus. "Ranked: The Most Cited Websites by AI Models." *Visual Capitalist,* August 18, 2025. https://www.visualcapitalist.com/ranked-the-most-cited-websites-by-ai-models.
- Luckin, Rose. "Yes, AI Could Profoundly Disrupt Education. But Maybe That's Not a Bad Thing." *The Guardian,* June 4, 2025. https://www.theguardian.com/commentisfree/2023/jul/14/ai-artificial-intelligence-disrupt-education-creativity-critical-thinking.
- Lutkevich, Ben. "Model Collapse Explained: How Synthetic Training Data Breaks AI." *Tech Target,* July 7, 2023. https://www.techtarget.com/whatis/feature/Model-collapse-explained-How-synthetic-training-data-breaks-AI.
- Macintyre, Barney. "Big Four Cut Jobs for Graduates as AI Adds to Consulting Crisis." *The Observer,* July 20, 2025. https://observer.co.uk/news/business/article/big-four-cut-jobs-for-graduates-as-ai-adds-to-consulting-crisis.
- Maddison, Lewis. "Samsung Workers Made a Major Error by Using ChatGPT." *TechRadar*, April 4, 2023. https://www.techradar.com/news/samsung-workers-leaked-company-secrets-by-using-chatgpt.

- Mafi, Alexander. "The Risks and Benefits of AI Therapy Tools." *BMJ* 389 (May 8, 2025): r821. https://doi.org/10.1136/bmj.r821.
- Magnifi. "How Niche Sports Are Finding Their Spotlight with AI." *Magnifi*, n.d. https://magnifi.ai/insights/how-niche-sports-are-finding-their-spotlight-with-ai.
- Mahajan, Arjun, Kimia Heydari, and Dylan Powell. "Wearable AI to Enhance Patient Safety and Clinical Decision-Making." *npj Digital Medicine 8*, no. 176 (2025). https://doi.org/10.1038/s41746-025-01554-w.
- Mahdawi, Arwa. "AI-generated 'Slop' Is Slowly Killing the Internet, so Why Is Nobody Trying to Stop It?" *The Guardian*, January 8, 2025. https://www.theguardian.com/global/commentisfree/2025/jan/08/ai-generated-slop-slowly-killing-internet-nobody-trying-to-stop-it.
- Maimann, Kevin. "Authors Fighting Deluge of Fake Writers and AI-generated Books." *CBC*, September 12, 2024. https://www.cbc.ca/news/entertainment/ai-generated-books-amazon-1.7319018.
- Manjoo, Farhad. "It's the End of Computer Programming as We Know It. (And I Feel Fine.)." *The New York Times*, June 2, 2023. https://www.nytimes.com/2023/06/02/opinion/ai-coding.html.
- Mansell, Scott. "AI and Machine Learning in Motorsport." *Fluid Jobs*, n.d. https://fluidjobs.com/blog/how-is-ai-and-machine-learning-is-changing-motorsport.
- Marcus, Gary. "CONFIRMED: LLMs Have Indeed Reached a Point of Diminishing Returns." *Marcus on AI*, November 9, 2024. https://garymarcus.substack.com/p/confirmed-llms-have-indeed-reached.
- Marcus, Gary. "GPT-5: Overdue, Overhyped and Underwhelming. And That's Not the Worst of It." *Marcus on AI*, August 10, 2025. https://garymarcus.substack.com/p/gpt-5-overdue-overhyped-and-underwhelming.
- Marcus, Gary. "When Billion-dollar AIs Break Down Over Puzzles a Child Can Do, It's Time to Rethink the Hype," *The Guardian*, June 10, 2025, https://www.theguardian.com/commentisfree/2025/jun/10/billion-dollar-ai-puzzle-break-down.
- Marcus, Gary. *Rebooting AI: Building Artificial Intelligence We Can Trust*. Pantheon, 2019.
- Mark, Douglas. "Analysis: Did the Demand for ChatGPT Plunge Because Students Left for Summer Break?" n.d. https://www.onlineeducation.com/features/chatgpt-demand-declines-in-the-summer.
- Marks, Gene. "Business Tech News: Klarna Reverses on AI, Says Customers Like Talking to People." *Forbes*, May 18, 2025. https://www.forbes.com/sites/quickerbettertech/2025/05/18/business-tech-news-klarna-reverses-on-ai-says-customers-like-talking-to-people.

- Marks, Gene. “Business Tech News: Zuckerberg Says AI Will Replace Mid-Level Engineers Soon.” *Forbes*, January 26, 2025. https://www.forbes.com/sites/quickerbettertech/2025/01/26/business-tech-news-zuckerberg-says-ai-will-replace-mid-level-engineers-soon.
- Marr, Bernard. “The Rise of Generative AI in Business: Opportunities and Risks.” *Forbes*, July 18, 2025. https://www.forbes.com/sites/bernardmarr/2025/07/18/the-rise-of-generative-ai-in-business.
- Mascellino, Alessandro. “New ConfusedPilot Attack Targets AI Systems with Data Poisoning.” *Infosecurity Magazine,* October 15, 2025. https://www.infosecurity-magazine.com/news/confusedpilot-attack-targets-ai.
- Matovski, Darko. “Causal AI: the Revolution Uncovering the ‘Why’ of Decision-Making.” *World Economic Forum,* April 11, 2024. https://www.weforum.org/stories/2024/04/causal-ai-decision-making.
- Mazhulin, Artem, Oliver Holmes, Lucy Swan, Laure Boulinier, and Arnel Hecimovic, “Operation Spiderweb: A Visual Guide to Ukraine’s Destruction of Russian Aircraft.” *The Guardian,* June 11, 2025. https://www.theguardian.com/world/2025/jun/02/operation-spiderweb-visual-guide-ukraine-drone-attack-russian-aircraft.
- McCord, Matthew. “Data Poisoning and Model Reliability: An Overview.” *ACM Computing Surveys 57*, no. 4 (2025): 1–34. https://dl.acm.org/doi/10.1145/3581837.
- McGee, Mike. “How We Resurrected Audrey Hepburn™ for the Galaxy Chocolate Ad.” *The Guardian,* October 8, 2014. https://www.theguardian.com/media-network/media-network-blog/2014/oct/08/how-we-made-audrey-hepburn-galaxy-ad.
- McGowan, Charis. “‘One Day I Overheard My Boss Saying: Just Put It in ChatGPT’: The Workers Who Lost Their Jobs to AI.” *The Guardian,* May 31, 2025. https://www.theguardian.com/technology/2025/may/31/the-workers-who-lost-their-jobs-to-ai-chatgpt.
- McKeon, Jill. “61M Fitbit, Apple Users Had Data Exposed in Wearable Device Data Breach.” *TechTarget*, September 16, 2021. https://www.techtarget.com/healthtechsecurity/news/366594948/61M-Fitbit-Apple-Users-Had-Data-Exposed-in-Wearable-Device-Data-Breach.
- McMahon, Liv. “AI System Resorts to Blackmail if Told It Will Be Removed.” *BBC News,* May 23, 2025. https://www.bbc.co.uk/news/articles/cpqeng9d20go.
- Mehta, Medha. “AI Bias: 14 Real AI Bias Examples & Mitigation Guide.” *Crescendo.ai.* August 19, 2025. https://www.crescendo.ai/blog/ai-bias-examples-mitigation-guide.
- Merken, Sara. “New York Lawyers Sanctioned for Using Fake ChatGPT Cases in Legal Brief.” *Reuters*, June 26, 2023.

- METR. "Measuring the Impact of Early-2025 AI on Experienced Open-Source Developer Productivity." *METR*, July 10, 2025. https://metr.org/blog/2025-07-10-early-2025-ai-experienced-os-dev-study.
- Metz, Cade, and Karen Weise. "A.I. Is Getting More Powerful, but Its Hallucinations Are Getting Worse." *The New York Times,* May 5, 2025. https://www.nytimes.com/2025/05/05/technology/ai-hallucinations-chatgpt-google.html.
- Metz, Cade. "AI Hallucinations: The Next Frontier of AI Risk." *The New York Times,* May 8, 2025. https://www.nytimes.com/2025/05/08/technology/ai-hallucinations.html.
- Meyer, David. "Alibaba's Chair Issues 'Bubble' Warning About U.S. AI Investments." *Fortune*, March 25, 2025. https://fortune.com/2025/03/25/alibaba-chair-joe-tsai-warns-ai-bubble.
- Microsoft Research team. "Frontiers of Multimodal Learning: A Responsible AI Approach." *Microsoft Research,* February 5, 2024. https://www.microsoft.com/en-us/research/blog/frontiers-of-multimodal-learning-a-responsible-ai-approach.
- Microsoft. "Understand Tokens." *Microsoft Learn,* May 29, 2025. https://learn.microsoft.com/en-us/dotnet/ai/conceptual/understanding-tokens.
- Microsoft. "What Are AI Tokens?" *Microsoft Copilot,* March 24, 2025. https://www.microsoft.com/en-us/microsoft-copilot/for-individuals/do-more-with-ai/general-ai/what-are-ai-tokens?form=MY02PE.
- Miller, R.A. "A History of the INTERNIST-1 and Quick Medical Reference (QMR) Computer-Assisted Diagnosis Projects, with Lessons Learned." *Yearbook of Medical Informatics (2009)*: 121–36. https://www.thieme-connect.com/products/ejournals/pdf/10.1055/s-0038-1638702.pdf?OR=Word.
- Milmo, Dan, and Alex Hern. "From Pope's Jacket to Napalm Recipes: How Worrying Is AI's Rapid Growth?" *The Guardian,* April 23, 2023. https://www.theguardian.com/technology/2023/apr/23/pope-jacket-napalm-recipes-how-worrying-is-ai-rapid-growth.
- Milmo, Dan. "Company Worker in Hong Kong Pays Out £20m in Deepfake Video Call Scam." *The Guardian,* February 5, 2024. https://www.theguardian.com/world/2024/feb/05/hong-kong-company-deepfake-video-conference-call-scam.
- Milmo, Dan. "Mushroom Pickers Urged to Avoid Foraging Books on Amazon That Appear to Be Written by AI." *The Guardian,* September 1, 2023. https://www.theguardian.com/technology/2023/sep/01/mushroom-pickers-urged-to-avoid-foraging-books-on-amazon-that-appear-to-be-written-by-ai.
- Milmo, Dan. "UK Engineering Firm Arup Falls Victim to £20m Deepfake Scam." *The Guardian,* May 17, 2024. https://www.theguardian.com/technology/article/2024/may/17/uk-engineering-arup-deepfake-scam-hong-kong-ai-video.

- Milne, Stefan. "AI Tools Show Biases in Ranking Job Applicants' Names According to Perceived Race and Gender." *UW News,* October 31, 2024. https://www.washington.edu/news/2024/10/31/ai-bias-resume-screening-race-gender.
- Mims, Christopher. "Silicon Valley's New Strategy: Move Slow and Build Things." *The Wall Street Journal,* August 1, 2025. https://www.wsj.com/tech/ai/silicon-valley-ai-infrastructure-capex-cffe0431?st=oLCAcg&reflink=desktopwebshare_permalink.
- Ministry of Defence. "British Soldiers Take Down Drone Swarm in Groundbreaking Use of Radio Wave Weapon." *GOV.UK,* April 17, 2025. https://www.gov.uk/government/news/british-soldiers-take-down-drone-swarm-in-groundbreaking-use-of-radio-wave-weapon.
- Mishcon de Reya. "Generative AI – IP Cases and Policy Tracker." *Mishcon De Reya LLP,* n.d. https://www.mishcon.com/generative-ai-intellectual-property-cases-and-policy-tracker.
- Mitchell, Charlie. "A Customer Service AI Agent Spits Out Complete Salesforce Records in an Attack by Security Researchers." *CX Today,* August 18, 2025. https://www.cxtoday.com/crm/a-customer-service-ai-agent-spits-out-complete-salesforce-records-in-an-attack-by-security-researchers.
- Montgomery, Blake. "Nvidia Becomes First Company to Reach $4tn in Market Value." *The Guardian,* July 10, 2025. https://www.theguardian.com/technology/2025/jul/09/nvidia-first-company-4-trillion.
- Morgan Stanley. "How China Is Becoming an AI Powerhouse." *Morgan Stanley,* May 22, 2025. https://www.morganstanley.com/insights/articles/china-ai-becoming-global-leader.
- Morris, Ben. "How Robots Are Taking Over Warehouse Work." *BBC News,* April 23, 2024. https://www.bbc.co.uk/news/business-68639533.
- Morris, Regan. "AI Helped Cause Hollywood Strikes. Now It's in Oscar-winning Films." *BBC News,* March 31, 2025. https://www.bbc.com/news/articles/ce303x19dwgo.
- Mulcahy, Andrew, Stephanie Rennane, Daniel Schwam, Reid Dickerson, Lawrence Baker, and Kanaka Shetty. "Use of Clinical Trial Characteristics to Estimate Costs of New Drug Development." *JAMA Network Open 8*, no. 1 (2025): e2453275. https://doi.org/10.1001/jamanetworkopen.2024.53275.
- Mulligan, Nigel. "Ghostbots: AI Versions of Deceased Loved Ones Could Be a Serious Threat to Mental Health." *The Conversation*, March 14, 2024. https://theconversation.com/ghostbots-ai-versions-of-deceased-loved-ones-could-be-a-serious-threat-to-mental-health-224984.
- Mural, Jacob, and Eda Kavlakoglu. "What Is Reinforcement Learning?" *IBM*. n.d. http://ibm.com/think/topics/reinforcement-learning.

- Murdock, Michaela G., and Aditya Tadinada. "Can AI Tools Reliably and Effectively Detect Plagiarism in Scientific Writing?" *Cureus 17*, no. 1 (May 11, 2025). https://doi.org/10.7759/cureus.83924.
- Myronyshena, Tania. "Ukraine's New Ground Drones Are Hitting the Battlefield in Ever-Increasing Numbers." *The Kyiv Independent*, July 16, 2025. https://kyivindependent.com/ukraine-approves-new-ground-robots-to-relieve-infantry-strained-by-mobilization-crisis.
- Nachiappan, Arthi. "'I Thought I Was Going Mad': Former Make-up Artist Says She Lost Her Job After Being Marked Down by AI Tool." *Sky News,* February 1, 2024. https://news.sky.com/story/companies-increasingly-using-ai-for-recruiting-and-why-it-could-cost-you-your-job-13060905.
- Nagler. "Standing Still." *RAC Foundation,* June 8, 2021. https://www.racfoundation.org/research/mobility/still-standing-still.
- Nair, Shraddha. "German Artist Mario Klingemann on His Creation 'Botto', an NFT Revolution." *Stir World,* March 10, 2022. https://www.stirworld.com/see-features-german-artist-mario-klingemann-on-his-creation-botto-an-nft-revolution.
- NASA. "Mars Pathfinder - Mars Missions." *NASA Jet Propulsion Laboratory (JPL)*, n.d. https://www.jpl.nasa.gov/missions/mars-pathfinder-sojourner-rover.
- NASA. "Robonaut2 - NASA." *NASA*, July 14, 2025. https://www.nasa.gov/robonaut2.
- National Conference of State Legislatures. "Artificial Intelligence 2025 Legislation." Last updated July 10, 2025. https://www.ncsl.org/technology-and-communication/artificial-intelligence-2025-legislation.
- Netflix. "Machine Learning." *Netflix*. n.d. https://research.netflix.com/research-area/machine-learning.
- Newdick, Thomas. "Ukraine Sinks Russian Cargo Ship in Caspian Sea." *The War Zone,* August 15, 2025. https://www.twz.com/air/ukraine-sinks-russian-cargo-ship-in-caspian-sea.
- Ng, Kate. "How The Furby Took Over the World." *The Independent,* August 23, 2023. https://www.independent.co.uk/life-style/furby-history-toys-b2397147.html.
- NHS. "Antibiotic Resistance." *nhs.uk*, November 18, 2022. https://www.nhs.uk/medicines/antibiotics/antibiotic-antimicrobial-resistance.
- NHS. "MRSA." *nhs.uk.* Last reviewed May 19, 2023.
- Nir, Onn. "Magecart Evolves Again: A New Case Study." *Reflectiz*, August 8, 2024. https://www.reflectiz.com/blog/magecart-case-study-2023.
- Nirdiamant. "15 LLM Jailbreaks That Shook AI Safety." *Medium*, January 28, 2025. https://medium.com/@nirdiamant21/15-llm-jailbreaks-that-shook-ai-safety-981d2796d5c6.

- NIST. "AI Congressional Mandates, Executive Orders and Actions." January 21, 2025. Last updated July 30, 2025. https://www.nist.gov/artificial-intelligence/ai-congressional-mandates-executive-orders-and-actions.
- NOAA Ocean Exploration. "What Is an ROV?" NOAA Ocean Exploration, Last updated December 16, 2020. https://oceanexplorer.noaa.gov/ocean-fact/rov.
- NOAA Ocean Exploration. Melissa Ryan, Karl McLetchie, and Philip Hoffman. "Ocean Exploration Technology: How Robots Are Uncovering the Mysteries of the Deep." June 9, 2023. https://oceanexplorer.noaa.gov/explainers/technology.
- NOAA. "What Is Lidar?" n.d. https://oceanservice.noaa.gov/facts/lidar.html.
- Noe, Len. *LLMs Gone Wild: AI Without Guardrails*. September 13, 2024. https://www.cyberark.com/resources/blog/llms-gone-wild-ai-without-guardrails.
- Nothdurft, Tobias, Peter Hecker, Sebastian Ohl, Falko Saust, Markus Maurer, Andreas Reschka, and Jurgen Rüdiger Böhmer. "Stadtpilot: First Fully Autonomous Test Drives in Urban Traffic." *Conference Record – IEEE Conference on Intelligent Transportation Systems*, November 2011. https://www.tu-braunschweig.de/fileadmin/Redaktionsgruppen/Institute_Fakultaet_5/IFR/Dateien_EFS/Publikationen/Stadtpilot_FirstFullyAutonomous.pdf.
- Nwosu Obinnaya Chikezie Victor, and Lucky Oghenechodja Daniel. "Automated Seismic Interpretation: Machine Learning Technologies are Being Used to Develop Automated Seismic Interpretation to Identify Geological Features, Such as Faults and Stratigraphic Horizons." *International Journal of Artificial Intelligence and Machine Learning 3,* no. 2 (2023): 74–98. https://doi.org/10.51483/IJAIML.3.2.2023.74-98. https://www.researchgate.net/publication/375279900_Automated_Seismic_Interpretation_Machine_Learning_Technologies_are_Being_Used_to_Develop_Automated_Seismic_Interpretation_to_Identify_Geological_Features_Such_as_Faults_and_Stratigraphic_Horizons_Inte.
- Ochab, Ewelina U. "'Let China Sleep, for When She Wakes, She Will Shake the World.'" *Forbes*. Last modified December 10, 2021. https://www.forbes.com/sites/ewelinaochab/2021/01/13/let-china-sleep-for-when-she-wakes-she-will-shake-the-world.
- Olavsrud, Thor. "11 Famous AI Disasters." *CIO*, August 7, 2025. https://www.cio.com/article/190888/5-famous-analytics-and-ai-disasters.html.
- OpenAI. "ChatGPT Release Notes (GPT-5)." *OpenAI*, October 2025. https://platform.openai.com/docs/release-notes.
- OpenAI. "GPT-4 System Card." *OpenAI*, August 2022. https://cdn.openai.com/papers/gpt-4-system-card.pdf.
- OpenAI. "GPT-5 Technical Report." *OpenAI*, 2025. https://openai.com/research/gpt-5.

- Osborne, Samuel. "Fake AI-Generated Joe Biden Robocall Tells People in New Hampshire Not to Vote." *Sky News*, January 23, 2024. https://news.sky.com/story/fake-ai-generated-joe-biden-robocall-tells-people-in-new-hampshire-not-to-vote-13054446.
- OWASP Gen AI Security Project. *OWASP Top 10 for LLM & Generative AI Security: LLM01:2025 Prompt Injection*. n.d. https://genai.owasp.org/llmrisk/llm01-prompt-injection.
- OWASP Top 10 for LLM & Generative AI Security. "LLM01:2025 Prompt Injection - OWASP Gen AI Security Project." *OWASP Gen AI Security Project, 2025*. https://genai.owasp.org/llmrisk/llm01-prompt-injection.
- Owda, Ameer. "Top 10 AI Deepfake Detection Tools to Combat Digital Deception in 2025." *SOCRadar® Cyber Intelligence Inc.*, October 21, 2025. https://socradar.io/top-10-ai-deepfake-detection-tools-2025.
- Park, Kate. "Samsung Bans Use of Generative AI Tools Like ChatGPT After April Internal Data Leak." *TechCrunch*, May 3, 2023. https://techcrunch.com/2023/05/02/samsung-bans-use-of-generative-ai-tools-like-chatgpt-after-april-internal-data-leak.
- Park, Peter S., Simon Goldstein, Aidan O'Gara, Michael Chen, and Dan Hendrycks. "AI Deception: A Survey of Examples, Risks, and Potential Solutions." *Patterns 5*, no. 5 (May 10, 2024): 100988.
- Parker, Tim. "Has High Frequency Trading Ruined the Stock Market for the Rest of Us?" *Investopedia*, September 18, 2022. https://www.investopedia.com/financial-edge/0113/has-high-frequency-trading-ruined-the-stock-market-for-the-rest-of-us.aspx.
- Payne, Skylar. "Why RAG Is (Still) Not Dead – Skylar Payne." *Skylar Payne*, April 6, 2025. https://skylarbpayne.com/posts/rag-not-dead.
- Penkteth, Claire. "AI In Defence: Ethics, Risks, and the Future of Autonomous Warfare." *British Computer Society,* April 7, 2025. https://www.bcs.org/articles-opinion-and-research/ai-in-defence-ethics-risks-and-the-future-of-autonomous-warfare.
- Perry, Neil, Megha Srivastava, Deepak Kumar, and Dan Boneh. "Do Users Write More Insecure Code with AI Assistants?" *arXiv:2211.03622*, Last updated December 18, 2023. https://arxiv.org/abs/2211.03622.
- Peters, John, Beth Keating, Nita Wang, Hayley Darukhanavala, and Ilan Geller. "ESPN Scores with Generative AI." *Accenture*, 2025. https://www.accenture.com/gb-en/case-studies/data-ai/espn-scores-with-generative-ai.
- Pethokoukis, James. "America's AI Lead Over China: Here's Why It Will Continue." *American Enterprise Institute (AEI),* July 8, 2025. https://www.aei.org/articles/americas-ai-lead-over-china-heres-why-it-will-continue.

- Pillay, Tharin. "How OpenAI's Sam Altman Is Thinking About AGI and Superintelligence in 2025." *TIME*, January 8, 2025. https://time.com/7205596/sam-altman-superintelligence-agi.
- Pool, Rebecca. "Saab's Robert Lindegren on Drone Swarms, Edge AI, and the Future of Autonomous Warfare." *EE Times,* March 5, 2025. https://www.eetimes.eu/saab-robert-lindegren-on-drone-swarms-edge-ai-and-the-future-of-autonomous-warfare.
- Pooley, Gale. "Why China May Surpass the United States in the AI Supremacy Race." *The Daily Economy,* February 27, 2025. https://thedailyeconomy.org/article/why-china-may-surpass-the-united-states-in-the-ai-supremacy-race.
- PPA. "How Google AI Offerings Are Harming Publishers: PPA Submits Recommendations to the Competition and Markets Authority." *PPA*, August 14, 2025. https://ppa.co.uk/how-google-ai-offerings-are-harming-publishers-ppa-submits-recommendations-to-the-competition-and-markets-authority.
- Precisely. "New Global Research Points to Lack of Data Quality and Governance as Major Obstacles to AI Readiness." *Precisely*, September 18, 2024. https://www.precisely.com/press-release/new-global-research-points-to-lack-of-data-quality-and-governance-as-major-obstacles-to-ai-readiness.
- Private Equity Wire. "Imandra Completes USD5m Seed Round Led by AlbionVC, IQ Capital and LiveOak Venture Partners." *Private Equity Wire,* April 18, 2019. https://www.privateequitywire.co.uk/imandra-completes-usd5m-seed-round-led-albionvc-iq-capital-and-liveoak-venture.
- PRNewswire. "iRobot Introduces RoombaTM Intelligent FloorVac - the First Automatic Floor Cleaner in the U.S." *iRobot MediaKit,* September 18, 2002. https://media.irobot.com/2002-09-18-iRobot-Introduces-Roomba-Intelligent-FloorVac-The-First-Automatic-Floor-Cleaner-In-The-U-S.
- Pulver, Andrew. "London Premiere of Movie With AI Generated Script Cancelled After Backlash." *The Guardian,* June 20, 2024. https://www.theguardian.com/film/article/2024/jun/20/premiere-movie-ai-generated-script-cancelled-backlash-the-last-screenwriter-prince-charles-cinema.
- Rahman-Jones, Imran. "AI Means Google's Greenhouse Gas Emissions up 48% in 5 Years." *BBC News,* July 3, 2024. https://bbc.co.uk/news/articles/c51yvz51k2xo.
- Ranji, Sumant R. "Large Language Models—Misdiagnosing Diagnostic Excellence?" *JAMA Network Open 7,* no. 10 (2024): e2440901. https://doi.org/10.1001/jamanetworkopen.2024.40901.
- Rahwan, Iyad, and Manuel Cebrian. "Ethics of AI and Machine Learning." *Annual Review of Control, Robotics, and Autonomous Systems 8* (2025): 1–28. https://www.annualreviews.org/doi/10.1146/annurev-control-012525-114543.

- Rand, Ben. "When AI Chatbots Help People Act More Human." *Harvard Business School,* May 27, 2025. https://www.library.hbs.edu/working-knowledge/when-ai-chatbots-help-people-be-more-human.
- Reed, Martin. "SoA Survey Reveals a Third of Translators and Quarter of Illustrators Losing Work to AI." *The Society of Authors,* April 11, 2024. https://societyofauthors.org/2024/04/11/soa-survey-reveals-a-third-of-translators-and-quarter-of-illustrators-losing-work-to-ai.
- Reuters. "Chinese AI Startup DeepSeek Releases Upgraded Model with Domestic Chip Support." *Reuters*, August 21, 2025. https://www.reuters.com/world/china/chinese-ai-startup-deepseek-releases-upgraded-model-with-domestic-chip-support-2025-08-21.
- Risdal, Meg. "Introducing Kaggle Game Arena." *Kaggle*, August 5, 2025. https://www.kaggle.com/blog/introducing-game-arena.
- Roberts, Alex, and Jerry Wang. "Korea's Won? South Korea's AI Basic Act: Asia's First Comprehensive AI Legislation." *Linklaters*, December 31, 2024. https://techinsights.linklaters.com/post/102js56/koreas-wonsouth-koreas-ai-basic-act-asias-first-comprehensive-ai-legislatio.
- Robins-Early, Nick. "AI's 'Oppenheimer Moment': Autonomous Weapons Enter the Battlefield." *The Guardian,* November 14, 2024. https://www.theguardian.com/technology/article/2024/jul/14/ais-oppenheimer-moment-autonomous-weapons-enter-the-battlefield.
- Robins-Early, Nick. "CEO of World's Biggest Ad Firm Targeted by Deepfake Scam." *The Guardian,* May 10, 2024. https://www.theguardian.com/technology/article/2024/may/10/ceo-wpp-deepfake-scam.
- Rogulsky, Steven, Nicholas Popovic, and Michael Färber. "The Effects of Hallucinations in Synthetic Training Data for Relation Extraction." *arXiv:2410.08393v1*. Knowledge Base Construction from Pre-trained Language Models Workshop at ISWC 2024 (October 2024). https://arxiv.org/html/2410.08393v1.
- Roser, Max. "Technology Over the Long Run: Zoom Out to See How Dramatically the World Can Change Within a Lifetime." *Our World in Data,* February 22, 2023. https://ourworldindata.org/technology-long-run.
- Ross, Sean. "Financial Services: Sizing the Sector in the Global Economy." *Investopedia*, August 15, 2024. https://www.investopedia.com/ask/answers/030515/what-percentage-global-economy-comprised-financial-services-sector.asp.
- Rowe, Adam. "Yet Another Study Finds That AI Is Making Us Dumb." *Tech.co,* June 17, 2025. https://tech.co/news/another-study-ai-making-us-dumb.
- Rowlands, David, and Nicole Gillespie. "Global Study Reveals Trust of AI Remains a Critical Challenge Reflecting Tension Between Benefits and Risks." *KPMG*, April 2024.

https://kpmg.com/xx/en/media/press-releases/2025/04/trust-of-ai-remains-a-critical-challenge.html.

- Ruan, Yanya, and József Mezei. "When Do AI Chatbots Lead to Higher Customer Satisfaction Than Human Frontline Employees in Online Shopping Assistance? Considering Product Attribute Type." *Journal of Retailing and Consumer Services 68* (June 25, 2022): 103059. https://doi.org/10.1016/j.jretconser.2022.103059.
- Rueda, Alice, Mohammed S. Hassan, Argyrios Perivolaris, Bazen G. Teferra, Reza Samavi, Sirisha Rambhatla, Yuqi Wu, Yanbo Zhang, Bo Cao, Divya Sharma, Sridhar Krishnan, and Venkat Bhat. "Understanding LLM Scientific Reasoning through Promptings and Model's Explanation on the Answers." *arXiv:2505.01482v1*, May 2, 2025. https://arxiv.org/html/2505.01482v1.
- Russell, Dan. "Answer: So What ARE LLMs Good At? What Are They Bad At?" *SearchResearch Blog,* July 17, 2025. https://searchresearch1.blogspot.com/2025/07/answer-so-what-are-llms-good-at-what.html#:~:text=are%20totally%20wrong.-,4.,should%20I%20invest%20for%20retirement?%22.
- Ryan Morrison and Amanda Caswell. "I've Spent 200 Hours Testing the Best AI Video Generators — Here's My Top Picks." *Tom's Guide,* last updated July 18, 2025. https://www.tomsguide.com/features/5-best-ai-video-generators-tested-and-compared.
- Ryseff, James, Brandon F. De Bruhl, and Sydne J. Newberry. "The Root Causes of Failure for Artificial Intelligence Projects and How They Can Succeed: Avoiding the Anti Patterns of AI." *RAND Research Report RRA2680 1*, August 13, 2024. https://www.rand.org/pubs/research_reports/RRA2680-1.html.
- Sale, Shane. "Artificial Intelligence Will Revolutionise Football." LinkedIn, October 14, 2019.
- Salzman, Avi. "AI is Changing Oil Country—and Pumping Up Profits." *Barron's,* November 26, 2024. https://www.barrons.com/articles/ai-oil-industry-profit-permian-basin-8adcacdd.
- Sanchez, Adriel. "New WalkMe Survey Shows Shadow AI Is Rampant; Training Gaps Undermine AI ROI." *SAP News Center,* August 27, 2025. https://news.sap.com/2025/08/new-walkme-survey-shadow-ai-rampant-training-gaps-undermine-roi.
- Sanchez, Esteban. "Software Maintenance Cost." *Galorath*, December 18, 2024. https://galorath.com/blog/software-maintenance-costs.
- Sandall, John, and Sophie Carr. "Case Studies: When AI and CV Screening Goes Wrong." *Fairness Tales,* August 29, 2025. https://www.fairnesstales.com/p/issue-2-case-studies-when-ai-and-cv-screening-goes-wrong.
- Sayapov, Alina. "The Future of Assortment Planning: AI-Driven Predictive Analytics." *Retalon*, August 15, 2025. https://retalon.com/blog/ai-driven-assortment-planning.

- Schneier, Bruce, and Davi Ottenheimer. "Robots Are Already Killing People." *The Atlantic,* September 6, 2023. https://www.theatlantic.com/technology/archive/2023/09/robot-safety-standards-regulation-human-fatalities/675231.
- Schneier, Bruce. "Real-World Steganography." *Schneier on Security,* January 20, 2023. https://www.schneier.com/blog/archives/2023/01/real-world-steganography.html.
- Schulhoff, Sander. "Limitations of LLMs: Bias, Hallucinations, and More." *Learn Prompting,* March 6, 2025. https://learnprompting.org/docs/basics/pitfalls.
- Scroxton, Alex. "Many UK Organisations Considering ChatGPT Bans on Employee Devices." *Computer Weekly* August 8, 2023. https://www.computerweekly.com/news/366547400/Many-UK-organisations-considering-ChatGPT-bans-on-employee-devices.
- Sevastopulo, Demetri. "Donald Trump Freezes Export Controls to Secure Trade Deal with China." *Financial Times,* July 28, 2025. https://www.ft.com/content/19442dba-c724-4825-9388-26219a12cb8a.
- Shaffi, Sarah. "'It's the Opposite of Art': Why Illustrators Are Furious About AI." *The Guardian,* January 23, 2023. https://www.theguardian.com/artanddesign/2023/jan/23/its-the-opposite-of-art-why-illustrators-are-furious-about-ai.
- Shalwa. "AI Plagiarism Statistics 2025: Transforming Academic Integrity." *ARTSMART AI,* February 23, 2025. https://artsmart.ai/blog/ai-plagiarism-statistics.
- Shan, Shawn, Wenxin Ding, Josephine Passananti, Stanley Wu, Haitao Zheng, and Ben Y. Zhao. "Nightshade: Prompt-Specific Poisoning Attacks on Text-to-Image Generative Models." *arXiv:2310.13828,* October 20, 2023. https://arxiv.org/abs/2310.13828.
- SHAP. "An Introduction to Explainable AI with Shapley Values." SHAP. https://shap.readthedocs.io/en/latest/example_notebooks/overviews/An%20introduction%20to%20explainable%20AI%20with%20Shapley%20values.html.
- Sharma, Priya. "AI Hallucinations in Medicine: A Growing Concern." *Nature Medicine 31* (2025): 1101–1108. https://www.nature.com/articles/s41591-025-02034-1.
- Sharma, Raksha. "AI Plagiarism Detection Market Research Report 2033." *Growth Market Reports,* August 29, 2025. https://growthmarketreports.com/report/ai-plagiarism-detection-market.
- Shearing, Hazel. "Teachers Can Use AI to Save Time on Marking, New Guidance Says." *BBC News,* June 10, 2025. https://www.bbc.com/news/articles/c1kvyj7dkp0o.
- Sherman, Jason. "Drone-on-Drone Combat in Ukraine Marks a New Era of Aerial Warfare." *Scientific American,* April 3, 2023. https://www.scientificamerican.com/article/drone-on-drone-combat-in-ukraine-marks-a-new-era-of-aerial-warfare.

- Shukla, Amit, and Hamad Karki. "Application of Robotics in Offshore Oil and Gas Industry—A Review Part II." *Robotics and Autonomous Systems 75,* Part B (January 2016): 508–524. https://doi.org/10.1016/j.robot.2015.09.013.
- Shumailov, Ilia, Zakhar Shumaylov, Yiren Zhao, Nicolas Papernot, Ross Anderson, and Yarin Gal. "AI Models Collapse When Trained on Recursively Generated Data." *Nature 631,* no. 8022 (July 24, 2024): 755–59. https://doi.org/10.1038/s41586-024-07566-y.
- Siddiqui, Fazeela, Jiachen Yang, Shuai Xiao, and Muhammad Fahad. "Diffusion Model in Modern Detection: Advancing Deepfake Techniques." *Knowledge-Based Systems 325* (September 5, 2025): 113922.
- Siddle, Richard. "How M&S's New AI Wine Finder Tool From Preferabli Is Going to Work." *The Buyer,* February 26, 2025. https://www.the-buyer.net/insight/how-m-and-s-s-new-ai-wine-finder-tool-from-preferabli-is-going-to-work.
- Silvia García-Méndez, Francisco De Arriba-Pérez, and María Del Carmen Somoza-López. "A Review on the Use of Large Language Models as Virtual Tutors." *Science & Education 34* (2025): 877–892. https://doi.org/10.1007/s11191-024-00530-2.
- Singh, Neeraj Kumar. "The Evolution of Software Development Tools: A Historical Comparison of Capabilities and Paradigm." *Medium*, February 16, 2025. https://neerazz.medium.com/the-evolution-of-software-development-tools-a-historical-comparison-of-capabilities-and-paradigms-70ef56d414bb.
- Sky News, "Robot Outperforms Human Surgeons in Pig Gut Op." *Sky News,* May 5, 2016. https://news.sky.com/story/robot-outperforms-human-surgeons-in-pig-gut-op-10269870.
- Smith, Adam. "Threaten an AI Chatbot and It Will Lie, Cheat and 'Let You Die' in an Effort to Stop You, Study Warns." *Live Science,* June 26, 2025. https://www.livescience.com/technology/artificial-intelligence/threaten-an-ai-chatbot-and-it-will-lie-cheat-and-let-you-die-in-an-effort-to-stop-you-study-warns.
- Smith, Craig S. "How Bad Traits Can Spread Unseen in AI." *Forbes*, July 25, 2025. https://www.forbes.com/sites/craigsmith/2025/07/25/how-bad-traits-can-spread-unseen-in-ai.
- Smith, Derek. "Widely Used AI Tool for Early Sepsis Detection May Be Cribbing Doctors' Suspicions." *UMich News,* February 15, 2024.
- Smith, John. "The Economic Implications of AI Hallucinations." *Journal of Economic Perspectives 39,* no. 2 (2025): 45–68. https://www.aeaweb.org/articles?id=10.1257/jep.39.2.45.
- Smith, Matthew. "What Do Britons Think AI Chatbots Are Good At?" *YouGov,* April 24, 2025. https://yougov.co.uk/technology/articles/52062-what-do-britons-think-ai-chatbots-are-good-at.

- Smith, Pamela. "Chop, Chop: Improving Food Prep With the Power of AI." *College of Engineering at Carnegie Mellon University,* n.d. https://engineering.cmu.edu/news-events/news/2023/11/29-robochop.html.
- Snow, Jacob. "Amazon's Face Recognition Falsely Matched 28 Members of Congress With Mugshots." *American Civil Liberties Union,* July 26, 2018. https://www.aclu.org/news/privacy-technology/amazons-face-recognition-falsely-matched-28.
- Snyder, Gabriel. "Yann LeCun, Pioneer of AI, Thinks Today's LLMs Are Nearly Obsolete." *Newsweek*, last updated September 5, 2025. https://www.newsweek.com/nw-ai/ai-impact-interview-yann-lecun-artificial-intelligence-2054237.
- Sokler, Bruce D., Alexander Hecht, Christian Tamotsu Fjeld, and Matthew Tikhonovsky. "President Trump Signs AI Deepfake Act into Law and House Passes AI Measures — AI: The Washington Report." *Mintz*, May 22, 2025. https://www.mintz.com/insights-center/viewpoints/54731/2025-05-22-president-trump-signs-ai-deepfake-act-law-and-house.
- Sommerfeld, Natasha. "Consumer Reliance on AI Search Results Signals New Era of Marketing – Bain & Company." *Bain*, February 19, 2025. https://www.bain.com/about/media-center/press-releases/20252/consumer-reliance-on-ai-search-results-signals-new-era-of-marketing--bain--company-about-80-of-search-users-rely-on-ai-summaries-at-least-40-of-the-time-on-traditional-search-engines-about-60-of-searches-now-end-without-the-user-progressing-to-a.
- SoSafe. Cybercrime Trends 2025. *SoSafe*, 2025.
- Sourabhkv. "Make Your Own Private ChatGPT." *Microsoft Tech Community,* December 28, 2024. https://techcommunity.microsoft.com/blog/educatordeveloperblog/make-your-own-private-chatgpt/4357607.
- Sparks, Lisa D. "Self-Driving Cars Can Tap into 'AI-Powered Social Network' to Talk to Each Other While on the Road." *LiveScience*, May 2, 2025. https://www.livescience.com/technology/electric-vehicles/self-driving-cars-can-tap-into-ai-powered-social-network-to-talk-to-each-other-while-on-the-road.
- Spiral Compute Limited. "The Future of AI in Software Engineering 2025: Beyond the Hype." *Spiral Compute Limited,* June 14, 2025. https://www.spiralcompute.co.nz/the-future-of-ai-in-software-engineering-2025-beyond-the-hype.
- SRI International. "Shakey the Robot." *SRI*. n.d. https://www.sri.com/hoi/shakey-the-robot.
- Staff Writer. "NEDA Suspends AI Chatbot for Giving Harmful Eating Disorder Advice." *Psychiatrist.com,* June 5, 2023. https://www.psychiatrist.com/news/neda-suspends-ai-chatbot-for-giving-harmful-eating-disorder-advice.
- Standaert, Michael. "Smile for the Camera: The Dark Side of China's Emotion recognition Tech." *The Guardian*, March 3, 2021. https://www.theguardian.com/

global-development/2021/mar/03/china-positive-energy-emotion-surveillance-recognition-tech.

- Stanford University. "Dan Boneh and Team Find Relying on AI Is More Likely to Make Your Code Buggier." *Stanford University Department of Electrical Engineering,* January 2023. https://ee.stanford.edu/dan-boneh-and-team-find-relying-ai-more-likely-make-your-code-buggier.
- Statista. "Average Length of a Clinical Trial Cycle 2020–2024." *Statista*, May 2, 2025. https://www.statista.com/statistics/1419920/biopharma-clinical-trial-cycle-time.
- Statista. "Gambling – Worldwide." *Statista*. n.d. https://www.statista.com/outlook/amo/gambling/worldwide.
- Statista. "Google: Annual Advertising Revenue 2001 2024." *Statista*, February 5, 2025. https://www.statista.com/statistics/266249/advertising-revenue-of-google.
- Statista. "Mining - Worldwide | Statista Market Forecast." *Statista*, n.d. https://www.statista.com/outlook/io/mining/worldwide.
- Statista. "Net Profit Margin of the Top Mining Companies 2002-2025." *Statista*, 2025. https://www.statista.com/statistics/208725/net-profit-margin-of-the-top-mining-companies.
- Steele, Chandra. "Can You Spot AI-Generated Images? Take Our Quiz to Test Your Skills." *PCMag UK,* February 10, 2025. https://uk.pcmag.com/ai/148429/how-to-detect-ai-created-images.
- Stop Killer Robots. "Stop Killer Robots – Less Autonomy, More Humanity." *Stop Killer Robots,* n.d. https://www.stopkillerrobots.org.
- Stryker, Cole, and Dave Bergmann. "Transformer Model." *IBM*, October 16, 2025. https://www.ibm.com/think/topics/transformer-model.
- Swatton, Phil, and Margaux Leblanc. "What Are Deepfakes and How Can We Detect Them?" *The Alan Turing Institute*, June 7, 2024. https://www.turing.ac.uk/blog/what-are-deepfakes-and-how-can-we-detect-them.
- Sweney, Mark. "'The Death of Creativity'? AI Job Fears Stalk Advertising Industry." *The Guardian,* June 9, 2025. https://www.theguardian.com/technology/2025/jun/09/ai-advertising-industry-google-facebook-meta-ads.
- Szarmach, Jakub. "STATE OF AI IN BUSINESS 2025." *AI Governance Library,* September 22, 2025. https://www.aigl.blog/state-of-ai-business-2025.
- Szeto, Eric. "Dutch Politicians Join Calls to Extradite Canadian Behind Notorious AI Porn Site." *CBC*, August 13, 2025. https://www.cbc.ca/news/canada/mrdeepfakes-extradition-netherlands-david-do-1.7608257.
- Tait, Robert. "US Senator Targeted by Deepfake Caller Posing as Ukrainian Diplomat." *The Guardian,* September 26, 2024. https://www.theguardian.com/us-news/2024/sep/26/ben-cardin-dmytro-kuleba-deepfake-ukraine.

- Talo - Real-Time AI Translation for Video-Calls. "Talo Presentation Mode Demo – Real-Time Translation for Webinars." *YouTube*, June 23, 2025. https://www.youtube.com/watch?v=M1l4LJBdHHk.
- Tao, Ni. "China Smart Cities: Digital Evolution at Scale." *CKGSB Knowledge*, July 17, 2025. https://english.ckgsb.edu.cn/knowledge/article/china-smart-cities-digital-evolution-at-scale.
- Tattersall, Andy. "AI's Threat to Google Is More About Advertising Income Than Being the Number One Search Engine." *Business Reporter*, n.d. https://www.business-reporter.co.uk/technology/ais-threat-to-google-is-more-about-advertising-income-than-being-the-number-one-search-engine.
- Taylor, Timothy. "Telephone Operators: The Elimination of a Job." *Conversable Economist*, August 19, 2024. https://conversableeconomist.com/2024/08/19/telephone-operators-the-elimination-of-a-job.
- TE Connectivity. "AI Technology Is Changing How Wars Are Won." *TE Connectivity*, n.d. https://www.te.com/en/industries/defense-military/insights/ai-in-warfare-and-military-applications.html.
- Teare, Gené. "Q2 Global Venture Funding Climbs in a Blockbuster Quarter for AI and as Capital Concentrates in Larger Companies." *Crunchbase News*, July 8, 2025. https://news.crunchbase.com/venture/global funding climbs q2 2025 ai ma data.
- Telang, Ashwin. "Artificial Intelligence at Merck – Two Use Cases." *Emerj*, February 10, 2025. https://emerj.com/artificial-intelligence-at-merck.
- The Economist. "Why AI Hasn't Taken Your Job." *The Economist*, May 26, 2025. https://www.economist.com/finance-and-economics/2025/05/26/why-ai-hasnt-taken-your-job.
- The Economist Group. Unlocking Enterprise AI: Opportunities and Strategies. *Databricks*, 2024. https://www.databricks.com/resources/analyst-research/unlocking-enterprise-ai-opportunities-and-strategies.
- The Economist. "How AI-powered Hackers Are Stealing Billions." *The Economist*, August 19, 2025. https://www.economist.com/business/2025/08/19/how-ai-powered-hackers-are-stealing-billions.
- The Economist. "Economists Are Revising Their Views on Robots and Jobs." *The Economist*, January 22, 2022. https://www.economist.com/finance-and-economics/2022/01/22/economists-are-revising-their-views-on-robots-and-jobs.
- The Economist. "The World's Most Valuable Resource Is No Longer Oil, but Data." *The Economist*, May 6, 2017. https://www.economist.com/leaders/2017/05/06/the-worlds-most-valuable-resource-is-no-longer-oil-but-data.

- The Editors of Encyclopaedia Britannica. "The Mechanical Turk: AI Marvel or Parlor Trick?" *Encyclopedia Britannica,* n.d. https://www.britannica.com/story/the-mechanical-turk-ai-marvel-or-parlor-trick.
- The Editors of Encyclopaedia Britannica. "Three Laws of Robotics." *Encyclopedia Britannica.* Accessed November 5, 2025. https://www.britannica.com/topic/Three-Laws-of-Robotics.
- The National Museum of Computing. "The Turing-Welchman Bombe." *The National Museum of Computing,* n.d. https://www.tnmoc.org/bombe.
- The Royal Swedish Academy of Sciences. "Press Release: Nobel Prize in Chemistry 2024." *NobelPrize.org,* October 9, 2024. https://www.nobelprize.org/prizes/chemistry/2024/press-release.
- The Supreme People's Procuratorate of the People's Republic of China. "Data Security Law of the People's Republic of China." June 10, 2021. https://en.spp.gov.cn/2021-06/10/c_948426_2.htm.
- Tibau, Marcelo. "LLMs Are Hitting the Wall: What's Next." *Medium*, November 13, 2024. https://medium.com/@marcelo_tibau/llms-are-hitting-the-wall-whats-next-cb49a53c9919.
- Tidmarsh, David. "A Guide to Steganography: Meaning, Types, Tools, & Techniques." *Cybersecurity Exchange,* April 12, 2025. https://www.eccouncil.org/cybersecurity-exchange/ethical-hacking/what-is-steganography-guide-meaning-types-tools.
- Tomlinson, Kira, Sonia Jaffe,Will Wang, Scott Counts, and Siddharth Suri. "Working With AI: Measuring the Applicability of Generative AI to Occupations." *Microsoft Research,* July 2025. https://www.microsoft.com/en-us/research/publication/working-with-ai-measuring-the-occupational-implications-of-generative-ai.
- Trigano, David, and Alex Kozodoy. "The Rise of AI-Driven Cyber Attacks: How LLMs Are Reshaping the Threat Landscape." *Deep Instinct,* March 12, 2025. https://www.deepinstinct.com/blog/the-rise-of-ai-driven-cyber-attacks-how-llms-are-reshaping-the-threat-landscape.
- Tully, Stephanie, Chiara Longoni, and Gil Appel. "EXPRESS: Lower Artificial Intelligence Literacy Predicts Greater AI Receptivity." *Journal of Marketing 8,* no. 5 (January 13, 2025): 1–20. https://doi.org/10.1177/00222429251314491.
- Turner, Ben. "Current AI Models a 'Dead End' for Human-level Intelligence, Scientists Agree." *Live Science,* March 27, 2025. https://www.livescience.com/technology/artificial-intelligence/current-ai-models-a-dead-end-for-human-level-intelligence-expert-survey-claims.
- Turpin, Miles, Julian Michael, Ethan Perez, and Samuel R. Bowman. "Language Models Don't Always Say What They Think: Unfaithful Explanations in Chain-of-Thought Prompting." *arXiv preprint,* May 7, 2023. https://arxiv.org/abs/2305.04388.

- UK Government. "Artificial Intelligence Playbook for the UK Government (HTML)." *GOV.UK*, February 10, 2025. https://www.gov.uk/government/publications/ai-playbook-for-the-uk-government/artificial-intelligence-playbook-for-the-uk-government-html.
- UK Government. "Automated Vehicles Act 2024." *GOV.UK*, 2024. https://www.legislation.gov.uk/ukpga/2024/10/contents.
- UK Government. "Online Safety Act 2023." *GOV.UK*, October 26, 2023. https://www.legislation.gov.uk/ukpga/2023/50.
- UNESCO. "UNESCO Survey: Less than 10% of Schools and Universities Have Formal Guidance on AI." *UNESCO*, June 1, 2023. Last updated September 18, 2024. https://www.unesco.org/en/articles/unesco-survey-less-10-schools-and-universities-have-formal-guidance-ai.
- Unicorn – Energy Solutions. "New Detail." *Unicorn*, n.d. https://unicornsystems.eu/energy/news-detail?article=how-artificial-intelligence-is-changing-the-energy-industry&newsArticleId=67ab35c18c1591cc785b5313.
- University of Cambridge Communications Team. "AI Chatbots Have Shown They Have an 'Empathy Gap' That Children Are." *The University of Cambridge*, July 15, 2024. https://www.cam.ac.uk/research/news/ai-chatbots-have-shown-they-have-an-empathy-gap-that-children-are-likely-to-miss.
- US Congress. "S.146 - 119th Congress (2025–2026): TAKE IT DOWN Act." *Congress.gov*, May 19, 2025. https://www.congress.gov/bill/119th-congress/senate-bill/146.
- Vassilev, Apostol, Alina Oprea, Alie Fordyce, Hyrum Anderson, Xander Davies, and Maia Hamin. *NIST Trustworthy and Responsible AI: NIST AI 100-2e 2025 — Adversarial Machine Learning: A Taxonomy and Terminology of Attacks and Mitigations.* National Institute of Standards and Technology, March 2025.
- Velasquez, S. J. "How AI Is Resurrecting Dead Actors." *BBC News*, July 19, 2023. https://www.bbc.com/future/article/20230718-how-ai-is-bringing-film-stars-back-from-the-dead.
- VentureRadar. "Top Symbolic AI Companies." *VentureRadar*, Accessed November 5, 2025. https://www.ventureradar.com/keyword/symbolic%20AI.
- Vermeer, Michael J.D. "Could AI Really Kill off Humans?" *Scientific American*, May 6, 2025. https://www.scientificamerican.com/article/could-ai-really-kill-off-humans.
- Vijayan, Jai. "Samsung Engineers Feed Sensitive Data to ChatGPT, Sparking Workplace AI Warnings." *Dark Reading*, April 11, 2023. https://www.darkreading.com/vulnerabilities-threats/samsung-engineers-sensitive-data-chatgpt-warnings-ai-use-workplace.
- Villalobos, Pablo, Anson Ho, Jaime Sevilla, Tamay Besiroglu, Lennart Heim, and Marius Hobbhahn. "Will We Run Out of Data? Limits of LLM Scaling Based on

Human-generated Data." *arXiv:2211.04325v2*, June 4, 2024. https://arxiv.org/html/2211.04325v2.

- Vincent, James. "The AI Hallucination Problem: Why LLMs Make Things Up." *The Verge,* May 10, 2025. https://www.theverge.com/2025/05/10/ai-hallucinations-llms.
- Visual Storytelling Team, and Madhumita Murgia. "Generative AI Exists Because of the Transformer." *Financial Times,* September 12, 2023. https://ig.ft.com/generative-ai.
- Vizard, Mike. "Survey: AI Tools Are Increasing Amount of Bad Code Needing to Be Fixed." *DevOps.com,* January 10, 2025.
- Wagner, Isaac, and Kaustubh Chakradeo. "Human AI Complementarity in Diagnostic Radiology: The Case of Double Reading." *Philosophy & Technology 38,* no. 2 (2025). https://doi.org/10.1007/s13347-025-00886-5.
- Wallace, Michael, and George Dunlop. "Eliza, a Chatbot Therapist." n.d. https://web.njit.edu/~ronkowit/eliza.html.
- Walsh, Dylan. "A New Look at the Economics of AI." *MIT Sloan,* January 21, 2025. https://mitsloan.mit.edu/ideas-made-to-matter/a-new-look-economics-ai.
- Wang, Li, Xi Chen, XiangWen Deng, Hao Wen, MingKe You, WeiZhi Liu, Qi Li, and Jian Li. "Prompt Engineering in Consistency and Reliability with the Evidence-Based Guideline for LLMs." *npj Digital Medicine 7,* no. 1 (February 20, 2024). https://doi.org/10.1038/s41746-024-01029-4.
- Wang, Spencer. "Bias in Code: Algorithm Discrimination in Financial Systems." *Robert F. Kennedy Human Rights,* January 28, 2025. https://rfkhumanrights.org/our-voices/bias-in-code-algorithm-discrimination-in-financial-systems.
- Waseda University. "Humanoid History - WABOT." *Waseda University,* n.d. https://www.humanoid.waseda.ac.jp/booklet/kato_2.html.
- Waymo. "Autonomous Ride-Hailing – Get a Ride in San Francisco, CA." Accessed November 5, 2025. https://waymo.com/rides/san-francisco.
- Weinman, Sam. "11 Images That Prove AI Can Design Basically Any Golf Course You Want." *GolfDigest75*, n.d. https://www.golfdigest.com/story/ai-golf-courses.
- Werner, John. "The Big AI Slowdown." *Forbes*, November 15, 2024. https://www.forbes.com/sites/johnwerner/2024/11/15/the-big-ai-slowdown.
- Whittaker, Tom. "A Cautionary Tale of Using AI in Law; UK Case Finds That AI Generated Fake Case Law Citations." *Burges Salmon,* December 10, 2023. https://www.burges-salmon.com/articles/102ivgu/a-cautionary-tale-of-using-ai-in-law-uk-case-finds-that-ai-generated-fake-case-l.
- Wiggers, Kyle. "Understanding AI Hallucinations in Large Language Models." *VentureBeat*, May 15, 2025. https://venturebeat.com/2025/05/15/understanding-ai-hallucinations-llms.

- Wikipedia contributors. "AlphaFold." *Wikipedia*. Last updated November 3, 2025. https://en.wikipedia.org/wiki/AlphaFold.
- Wikipedia contributors. "List of Countries by Traffic-Related Death Rate." *Wikipedia*, n.d. https://en.wikipedia.org/wiki/List_of_countries_by_traffic-related_death_rate.
- Wikipedia Contributors. "List of Tesla Autopilot Crashes." *Wikipedia*. n.d. https://en.wikipedia.org/wiki/List_of_Tesla_Autopilot_crashes#Williston,_Florida,_USA_(May_7,_2016).
- Wikipedia contributors. "Vivino." *Wikipedia*. Last updated October 26, 2025. https://en.wikipedia.org/wiki/Vivino.
- Wilkins, Joe. "OpenAI Usage Plummets in the Summer, When Students Aren't Cheating on Homework." *Futurism*, August 8, 2025. https://futurism.com/openai-use-cheating-homework.
- Wilkins, Joe. "The More Scientists Work With AI, the Less They Trust It." *Futurism*, October 13, 2025. https://futurism.com/artificial-intelligence/ai-research-scientists-hype.
- Williams, Ryan. "Shaking up the Earth: The AI Revolution in Seismic Interpretation." *GeoExpro*, January 22, 2024. https://geoexpro.com/shaking-up-the-earth-the-ai-revolution-in-seismic-interpretation.
- Wilson, Kyra, and Aylin Caliskan. "Gender, Race, and Intersectional Bias in Resume Screening via Language Model Retrieval." *Proceedings of the Seventh AAAI/ACM Conference on AI, Ethics, and Society* (AIES 2024): 1578–1590. https://ojs.aaai.org/index.php/AIES/article/view/31748/33915.
- WRITER. Generative AI Adoption in the Enterprise. *WRITER*, 2025. https://go.writer.com/enterprise-ai-adoption-survey.
- Wojtak, Weronika. "Why Asimov's Three Laws of Robotics Fail in the Real World." *Medium*, May 28, 2025. https://medium.com/@w.wojtak/why-asimovs-three-laws-of-robotics-fail-in-the-real-world-0685e5b53a3f.
- Wong, Andrew, Erkin Otles, John P. Donnelly, Andrew Krumm, Jeffrey McCullough, Olivia DeTroyer-Cooley, Justin Pestrue, Marie Phillips, Judy Konye, Carleen Penoza, Muhammad Ghous, Karandeep Singh. "External Validation of a Widely Implemented Proprietary Sepsis Prediction Model in Hospitalized Patients." *JAMA Internal Medicine 181*, no. 8 (2021): 1065–1070. https://doi.org/10.1001/jamainternmed.2021.2626.
- Wood, Matt. "The Fearless Future: 2025 Global AI Jobs Barometer." PwC, June 3, 2025. https://www.pwc.com/gx/en/issues/artificial-intelligence/ai-jobs-barometer.html.
- World Health Organization (WHO). "Road Traffic Injuries." *World Health Organization*, December 13, 2023. https://www.who.int/news-room/fact-sheets/detail/road-traffic-injuries.

- World Health Organization: WHO. "Ageing and Health." *World Health Organization,* October 1, 2025. https://www.who.int/news-room/fact-sheets/detail/ageing-and-health.
- World Intellectual Property Organization. "Berne Convention for the Protection of Literary and Artistic Works (as amended on September 28, 1979)." *TRT/BERNE/001.* n.d. https://www.wipo.int/wipolex/en/text/283698.
- Xiang, Chloe. "'He Would Still Be Here': Man Dies by Suicide after Talking with AI Chatbot, Widow Says." *VICE,* July 27, 2024. https://www.vice.com/en/article/man-dies-by-suicide-after-talking-with-ai-chatbot-widow-says.
- Xu, Frank F., Yufan Song, Boxuan Li, Yuxuan Tang, Kritanjali Jain, Mengxue Bao, Zora Z. Wang, Xuhui Zhou, Zhitong Guo, Murong Cao, Mingyang Yang, Hao Yang Lu, Amaad Martin, Zhe Su, Leander Melroy Maben, Raj Mehta, Wayne Chi, Lawrence Jang, Yiqing Xie, Shuyan Zhou, and Graham Neubig. "TheAgentCompany: Benchmarking LLM Agents on Consequential Real World Tasks." *arXiv (preprint),* December 18, 2024. https://arxiv.org/pdf/2412.14161.
- Yagoda, Maria. "Airline Held Liable for Its Chatbot Giving Passenger Bad Advice - What This Means for Travellers." *BBC News,* February 23, 2024. https://www.bbc.com/travel/article/20240222-air-canada-chatbot-misinformation-what-travellers-should-know.
- Yang, Amy, and Bob Li. "AI Watch: Global Regulatory Tracker – China." *White & Case LLP International Law Firm, Global Law Practice,* September 22, 2025. https://www.whitecase.com/insight-our-thinking/ai-watch-global-regulatory-tracker-china.
- Young, Bryan. "The First 'Killer Robot' Was Around Back in 1979." *HowStuffWorks,* August 15, 2023. https://science.howstuffworks.com/first-killer-robot-was-around-back-in-1979.htm.
- Zeff, Maxwell. "OpenAI's New Reasoning AI Models Hallucinate More." *TechCrunch,* April 18, 2025. https://techcrunch.com/2025/04/18/openais-new-reasoning-ai-models-hallucinate-more.
- Zewe, Adam. "AI-Enabled Control System Helps Autonomous Drones Stay on Target in Uncertain Environments." *MIT News,* June 9, 2025. https://news.mit.edu/2025/ai-enabled-control-system-helps-autonomous-drones-uncertain-environments-0609.
- Zewe, Adam. "Explained: Generative AI's Environmental Impact." *MIT News | Massachusetts Institute of Technology,* January 17, 2025. https://news.mit.edu/2025/explained-generative-ai-environmental-impact-0117.
- Zheng, Zifan, Yezhaohui Wang, Yuxin Huang, Shichao Song, Mingchuan Yang, Bo Tang, Feiyu Xiong, and Zhiyu Li. "Attention Heads of Large Language Models." *Patterns 6,* no. 2 (February 14, 2025): 101176. https://www.sciencedirect.com/science/article/pii/S2666389925000248.

- Zhou, Lexin, Wout Schellaert, Fernando Martínez-Plumed, Yael Moros-Daval, Cèsar Ferri, and José Hernández-Orall. "Larger and More Instructable Language Models Become Less Reliable." *Nature 634,* no. 8032 (September 25, 2024): 61–68. https://doi.org/10.1038/s41586-024-07930-y.
- Zhou, Yujia, Yan Liu, Xiaoxi Li, Jiajie Jin, Hongjin Qian, Zheng Liu, Chaozhuo Li, Zhicheng Dou, Tsung-Yi Ho, and Philip S. Yu. "Trustworthiness in Retrieval-Augmented Generation Systems: A Survey." *arXiv:2409.10102v1,* September 16, 2024. https://arxiv.org/html/2409.10102v1.
- Zhu, Kexin, Jiajie Zhang, Anton Klishin, Mario Esser, William A Blumentals, Juhaeri Juhaeri, Corinne Jouquelet-Royer, Sarah-Jo Sinnott, "Evaluating the Accuracy of Responses by Large Language Models for Information on Disease Epidemiology." *Pharmacoepidemiology and Drug Safety 34,* no. 2 (February 1, 2025): e70111.
- Zirar, Araz, Syed Imran Ali, and Nazrul Islam. "Worker and Workplace Artificial Intelligence (AI) Coexistence: Emerging Themes and Research Agenda." *Technovation 124* (June 2023): 102747. https://doi.org/10.1016/j.technovation.2023.102747.
- Zoria, Yuri. "Ukraine Unveils VATAG — a Battlefield Ground Drone That Can Haul Over 2 Tons and Stay Quiet Doing It." *EuroMaidan Press,* September 16, 2025

About the Author

Andy Hayler is an established software industry authority, advising corporations, software companies, and venture capital firms. He was the founder of software vendor Kalido, which, under his leadership, was the fastest-growing business intelligence vendor in the world in 2001. Kalido was recognised as an innovator in data warehousing and then launched arguably the first true multi-domain master data management product. Andy was the only European named in Red Herring's "Top 10 Innovators of 2002".

Andy started his career with Esso, working in a number of technology roles before moving to Shell. He was Technology Planning Manager of Shell UK, then Principal Technology Consultant for Shell International. He later established a global information management consultancy, which under his leadership grew to 300 staff. Since 2007, Andy has been an independent industry analyst, CEO and co-founder of analyst firm The Information Difference Ltd, and a regular speaker at international conferences. For the last three years, he has been immersed in the world of artificial intelligence.

Andy is also a restaurant critic and the author of The London Transport Restaurant Guide (Boxtree Ltd, 1995).

Endnotes

1 Jeremy Hsu, "AI Hallucinations Are Getting Worse – and They're Here to Stay," New Scientist, May 9, 2025, https://www.newscientist.com/article/2479545-ai-hallucinations-are-getting-worse-and-theyre-here-to-stay.

2 Blake Montgomery, "Nvidia Becomes First Company to Reach $4tn in Market Value," The Guardian, July 10, 2025, https://www.theguardian.com/technology/2025/jul/09/nvidia-first-company-4-trillion.

3 Zara Abrams, "Using Generic AI Chatbots for Mental Health Support: A Dangerous Trend," APA Services, March 12, 2025, https://www.apaservices.org/practice/business/technology/artificial-intelligence-chatbots-therapists.

4 Maggie Harrison Dupré, "First AI Psychosis Case Ends in Murder-Suicide," Futurism via Yahoo News, August 29, 2025, https://ca.news.yahoo.com/man-suffers-chatgpt-psychosis-murders-155857953.html.

5 Sheryl Estrada, "MIT Report: 95% of Generative AI Pilots at Companies Are Failing," Fortune, August 27, 2025, https://fortune.com/2025/08/18/mit-report-95-percent-generative-ai-pilots-at-companies-failing-cfo.

6 Ai Katana, "The Legacy of Japan's Fifth Generation Computer Systems (FGCS) Project on AI," AI KATANA, September 8, 2024, https://www.aikatana.com/p/legacy-japans-fifth-generation-computer-systems-fgcs-project-ai.

7 Ibid.

8 Carl S. Gibson et al., "VAX 9000 Series," Digital Technical Journal of Digital Equipment Corporation 2, no. 4 (Fall 1990): 118–129.

9 Julia Love, "AI Researcher Who Helped Write Landmark Paper Is Leaving Google," Yahoo Finance, July 11, 2023, https://finance.yahoo.com/news/ai-researcher-helped-write-landmark-030025546.html; Cole Stryker and Dave Bergmann, "Transformer Model," IBM, October 16, 2025, https://www.ibm.com/think/topics/transformer-model.

10 B.J. Copeland, "MYCIN | Expert System, Medical Diagnosis & Treatment," Encyclopaedia Britannica, October 7, 2008, https://www.britannica.com/technology/MYCIN.

11 "Aegis Combat System," Lockheed Martin, n.d., https://www.lockheedmartin.com/en-us/products/aegis-combat-system.html.

12 David Georgyan, "AlphaZero vs Stockfish 8: A Landmark Battle of Human and Artificial Intelligence in Chess," Medium, February 20, 2023, https://medium.com/@

david_georgyan/alphazero-vs-stockfish-8-a-landmark-battle-of-human-and-artificial-intelligence-in-chess-ac6250b2355c.

13 Daniel Cossins, "Discriminating Algorithms: 5 Times AI Showed Prejudice," New Scientist, April 27, 2018, https://www.newscientist.com/article/2166207-discriminating-algorithms-5-times-ai-showed-prejudice.

14 Grant Harvey, "This New AI is 100x Faster at Reasoning Than ChatGPT," Tech Republic, July 30, 2025, https://www.techrepublic.com/article/news-ai-hierarchical-reasoning-model.

15 Andy Hayler, "AI Use Cases – the Good, the Bad and the Ugly," The Information Difference, May 23, 2025, https://www.informationdifference.com/ai-the-good-bad-ugly.

16 Aaron Drapkin, "AI Gone Wrong: The Errors, Mistakes, and Hallucinations of AI (2023 – 2025)," Tech.co, September 26, 2025, https://tech.co/news/list-ai-failures-mistakes-errors.

17 GothamChess, "HILARIOUS AI CHESS CHAMPIONSHIP," YouTube, August 5, 2025, https://www.youtube.com/watch?v=S2KmStTbL6c.

18 Google, "Overview of GAN Structure," Google for Developers, n.d., https://developers.google.com/machine-learning/gan/gan_structure; Diederik P. Kingma and Max Welling, "An Introduction to Variational Autoencoders," Foundations and Trends® in Machine Learning 12, no. 4 (January 1, 2019): 307–92, https://doi.org/10.1561/2200000056.

19 Microsoft, "What Are AI Tokens?" Microsoft Copilot, March 24, 2025, https://www.microsoft.com/en-us/microsoft-copilot/for-individuals/do-more-with-ai/general-ai/what-are-ai-tokens?form=MY02PE.

20 Visual Storytelling Team and Madhumita Murgia, "Generative AI Exists Because of the Transformer," Financial Times, September 12, 2023, https://ig.ft.com/generative-ai.

21 Henning Bartsch, Ole Jorgensen, Domenic Rosati, Jason Hoelscher-Obermaier, and Jacob Pfau, "Self-Consistency of Large Language Models under Ambiguity," Proceedings of the 6th BlackboxNLP Workshop: Analyzing and Interpreting Neural Networks for NLP (January 1, 2023): 89–105, https://doi.org/10.18653/v1/2023.blackboxnlp-1.7.

22 Steven Rogulsky, Nicholas Popovic, and Michael Färber, "The Effects of Hallucinations in Synthetic Training Data for Relation Extraction," Knowledge Base Construction from Pre-trained Language Models Workshop at ISWC 2024 (October 2024), https://arxiv.org/html/2410.08393v1.

23 Nicola Jones, "AI Hallucinations Can't Be Stopped—but These Techniques Can Limit Their Damage," Nature 637, no. 8047 (January 21, 2025): 778–80, https://doi.org/10.1038/d41586-025-00068-5; Ankush Ramprakash Gautam, "Impact of High

Data Quality on LLM Hallucinations," International Journal of Computer Applications 187, no. 4 (May 2025): 35–39, https://www.ijcaonline.org/archives/volume187/number4/impact-of-high-data-quality-on-llm-hallucinations.

24 Maggie Harrison Dupré, "Huge Proportion of Internet Is AI-Generated Slime, Researchers Find," Futurism, January 19, 2024, https://futurism.com/the-byte/internet-ai-generated-slime.

25 Ryan Law, Xibeijia Guan, and Tim Soulo, "74% of New Webpages Include AI Content (Study of 900k Pages)," Ahrefs, May 19, 2025, https://ahrefs.com/blog/what-percentage-of-new-content-is-ai-generated.

26 Steven Rogulsky, Nicholas Popovic, and Michael Färber, "The Effects of Hallucinations in Synthetic Training Data for Relation Extraction," Knowledge Base Construction from Pre-trained Language Models Workshop at ISWC 2024 (October 2024), https://arxiv.org/html/2410.08393v1.

27 Dan Milmo, "Mushroom Pickers Urged to Avoid Foraging Books on Amazon That Appear to Be Written by AI," The Guardian, September 1, 2023, https://www.theguardian.com/technology/2023/sep/01/mushroom-pickers-urged-to-avoid-foraging-books-on-amazon-that-appear-to-be-written-by-ai.

28 Mishcon de Reya, "Generative AI – IP Cases and Policy Tracker," Mishcon De Reya LLP, n.d., https://www.mishcon.com/generative-ai-intellectual-property-cases-and-policy-tracker; Damien Charlotin, "AI Hallucination Cases Database," Artificial Authority, n.d., https://www.damiencharlotin.com/hallucinations/?ref=nucleo.jor.br&page=2&page=3&page=4&page=5.

29 SoHornyBeaver, "I asked ChatGPT to list the 47 presidents' portraits in order. It had other ideas," Reddit, April 14, 2025, https://www.reddit.com/r/ChatGPT/comments/1jz5ftd/i_asked_chatgpt_to_list_the_47_presidents.

30 Mikaël Chelli, Jules Descamps, Vincent Lavoué, Christophe Trojani, Michel Azar, Marcel Deckert, Jean-Luc Raynier, Gilles Clowez, Pascal Boileau, and Caroline Ruetsch-Chelli, "Hallucination Rates and Reference Accuracy of ChatGPT and Bard for Systematic Reviews: Comparative Analysis," Journal of Medical Internet Research 26 (May 22, 2024): e53164. https://doi.org/10.2196/53164.

31 Cem Dilmegani and Aleyna Daldal, "AI Hallucination: Comparison of the Popular LLMs," AIMultiple, October 20, 2025, https://research.aimultiple.com/ai-hallucination.

32 Cade Metz and Karen Weise, "A.I. Is Getting More Powerful, but Its Hallucinations Are Getting Worse," The New York Times, May 6, 2025, https://www.nytimes.com/2025/05/05/technology/ai-hallucinations-chatgpt-google.html

33 Vectara, "GitHub - Vectara/Hallucination-leaderboard: Leaderboard Comparing LLM Performance at Producing Hallucinations When Summarizing Short Documents," GitHub, n.d., https://github.com/vectara/hallucination-leaderboard.

34 Ross Kelly, "OpenAI's Sam Altman: Hallucinations are part of the "magic" of generative AI," IT Pro, September 13, 2023, https://www.itpro.com/technology/artificial-intelligence/openais-sam-altman-hallucinations-are-part-of-the-magic-of-generative-ai.

35 Andy Hayler, "AI Use Cases – the Good, the Bad and the Ugly," The Information Difference, May 23, 2025, https://www.informationdifference.com/ai-the-good-bad-ugly.

36 Robert Booth, "High Court Tells UK Lawyers to Stop Misuse of AI After Fake Case-law Citations," The Guardian, June 6, 2025, https://www.theguardian.com/technology/2025/jun/06/high-court-tells-uk-lawyers-to-urgently-stop-misuse-of-ai-in-legal-work.

37 Pack-Logix, "Leading the Industry: Why Our Low .05% Acceptable Failure Rate Matters," Pack-Logix, October 13, 2025, https://pack-logix.com/blog/leading-the-industry-why-our-low-05-acceptable-failure-rate-matters.

38 Adam Tauman Kalai Ofir Nachum, Santosh S. Vempala, and Edwin Zhang, "Why Language Models Hallucinate," arXiv.org, September 4, 2025, https://arxiv.org/abs/2509.04664.

39 ByteBridge, "GPU and TPU Comparative Analysis Report," Medium, February 18, 2024, https://bytebridge.medium.com/gpu-and-tpu-comparative-analysis-report-a5268e4f0d2a.

40 Quantic School of Business and Technology, "How Business Analytics Shapes the Future of AI and Big Data," Quantic School of Business and Technology, August 25, 2025, https://quantic.edu/blog/2025/08/25/how-business-analytics-shapes-the-future-of-ai-and-big-data.

41 International Energy Agency, "AI is set to drive surging electricity demand from data centres while offering the potential to transform how the energy sector works," International Energy Agency, April 10, 2025, https://www.iea.org/news/ai-is-set-to-drive-surging-electricity-demand-from-data-centres-while-offering-the-potential-to-transform-how-the-energy-sector-works.

42 Andy Hayler, "From Data to Droughts – AI and the Environment," The Information Difference, September 15, 2025, https://www.informationdifference.com/from-data-to-droughts-ai-and-the-environment.

43 Luke Barratt, Costanza Gambarini, Andrew Witherspoon, and Aliya Uteuova, "Revealed: Big Tech's New Datacentres Will Take Water From the World's Driest Areas," The Guardian, April 9, 2025, https://www.theguardian.com/environment/2025/apr/09/big-tech-datacentres-water.

44 Aaron Bubley, "Global Crossing Is Reborn...," Praetorian Capital, August 20, 2025, https://pracap.com/global-crossing-reborn.

45 Andy Hayler, "Blowing Bubbles? – the Economic Impact of AI," The Information Difference, August 23, 2025, https://www.informationdifference.com/blowing-bubbles-the-economic-impact-of-ai.

46 Emilia DiFabrizio, "Demystifying Vectors and Embeddings in AI: A Beginner's Guide," Sidecar, June 27, 2024, https://sidecar.ai/blog/demystifying-vectors-and-embeddings-in-ai-a-beginners-guide.

47 Leah A. Wasser, "The Basics of LiDAR - Light Detection and Ranging - Remote Sensing | NSF NEON | Open Data to Understand Our Ecosystems," Neon Science, September 13, 2024, https://www.neonscience.org/resources/learning-hub/tutorials/lidar-basics.

48 Microsoft, "What Are AI Tokens?" Microsoft Copilot, March 24, 2025, https://www.microsoft.com/en-us/microsoft-copilot/for-individuals/do-more-with-ai/general-ai/what-are-ai-tokens?form=MY02PE.

49 Andy Hayler, "When Algorithms Dream: AI Hallucinations in Depth," The Information Difference, August 19, 2025, https://www.informationdifference.com/when-algorithms-dream-ai-hallucinations-in-depth.

50 Andy Hayler, "When AI Picks Sides – AI Bias and Discrimination," The Information Difference, September 2, 2025, https://www.informationdifference.com/when-ai-picks-sides-ai-bias-and-discrimination.

51 Andy Hayler, "AI, A Security Trojan Horse," The Information Difference, June 25, 2025, https://www.informationdifference.com/security-trojan-horse.

52 Swagath Bandhakavi, "Multimodal AI Models Pose Increased Risks for Abuse and Harmful Content, Study Finds," Tech Monitor, May 9, 2025, https://www.techmonitor.ai/digital-economy/ai-and-automation/multimodal-ai-models-increased-risks-abuse-harmful-content.

53 Radhika Rajkumar, "Multimodal AI Poses New Safety Risks, Creates CSEM and Weapons Info," ZDNET, May 8, 2025, https://www.zdnet.com/article/multimodal-ai-poses-new-safety-risks-creates-csem-and-weapons-info.

54 Lingjiao Chen, Matei Zaharia, and James Zou, "How Is ChatGPT's Behavior Changing over Time?", Harvard Data Science Review, March 13, 2024, https://hdsr.mitpress.mit.edu/pub/y95zitmz/release/2.

55 Lauren Leffer, "Yes, AI Models Can Get Worse Over Time," Scientific American, August 2, 2023, https://www.scientificamerican.com/article/yes-ai-models-can-get-worse-over-time.

56 Chris Stokel-Walker, "AIs Get Worse at Answering Simple Questions as They Get Bigger," New Scientist, September 25, 2024, https://www.newscientist.com/article/2449427-ais-get-worse-at-answering-simple-questions-as-they-get-bigger.

57 Lexin Zhou, Wout Schellaert, Fernando Martínez-Plumed, Yael Moros-Daval, Cèsar Ferri, and José Hernández-Orallo, "Larger and More Instructable Language Models

Become Less Reliable," Nature 634, no. 8032 (September 25, 2024): 61–68, https://doi.org/10.1038/s41586-024-07930-y.

58 Jeremy Hsu, "AI Hallucinations Are Getting Worse – and They're Here to Stay," New Scientist, May 9, 2025, https://www.newscientist.com/article/2479545-ai-hallucinations-are-getting-worse-and-theyre-here-to-stay.

59 Vectara, "DeepSeek-R1 Hallucinates More Than DeepSeek-V3," Vectara, September 25, 2025, https://www.vectara.com/blog/deepseek-r1-hallucinates-more-than-deepseek-v3.

60 Charlie Guo, "LLMs Are Getting Dumber and We Have No Idea Why," Artificial Ignorance, September 5, 2024, https://www.ignorance.ai/p/llms-are-getting-dumber-and-we-have.

61 Kevin Okemwa, "Sam Altman indicated it's impossible to create ChatGPT without copyrighted material, but a new study claims 57% of the content on the internet is AI-generated and is subtly killing quality search results," Windows Central, September 3, 2024, https://www.windowscentral.com/software-apps/sam-altman-indicated-its-impossible-to-create-chatgpt-without-copyrighted-material.

62 Ilia Shumailov, Zakhar Shumaylov, Yiren Zhao, Nicolas Papernot, Ross Anderson, and Yarin Gal, "AI Models Collapse When Trained on Recursively Generated Data," Nature 631, no. 8022 (July 24, 2024): 755–59, https://doi.org/10.1038/s41586-024-07566-y.

63 Ben Lutkevich, "Model Collapse Explained: How Synthetic Training Data Breaks AI," Tech Target, July 7, 2023, https://www.techtarget.com/whatis/feature/Model-collapse-explained-How-synthetic-training-data-breaks-AI.

64 Andy Hayler, "Code of Silence – the Hidden Risks of AI-Generated Code," The Information Difference, April 24, 2025, https://www.informationdifference.com/code-of-silence-the-hidden-risks-of-ai-generated-code.

65 Anthropic, "Join Our Team," n.d., https://www.anthropic.com/jobs?team=4002061008.

66 Gil Press, "Are We at Peak AI Bubble and the Cusp of 'AI Moment'?" Forbes, March 30, 2025, https://www.forbes.com/sites/gilpress/2025/03/30/are-we-at-peak-ai-bubble-and-the-cusp-of-ai-moment.

67 Bryan McMahon, "Bubble Trouble," The American Prospect, March 25, 2025, https://prospect.org/2025/03/25/2025-03-25-bubble-trouble-ai-threat.

68 Al Gore, "An Inconvenient Truth," n.d., https://algore.com/library/an-inconvenient-truth.

69 Sara Braun, "CEOs Say That Just a Fraction of AI Initiatives Are Actually Delivering the Return on Investment They Expected," Fortune, May 12, 2025, https://fortune.com/article/ceos-ai-initiatves-fraction-deliver-return-on-investment-roi-study.

70 Joe Wilkins, “Company Regrets Replacing All Those Pesky Human Workers With AI, Just Wants Its Humans Back,” Futurism, May 13, 2025, https://futurism.com/klarna-openai-humans-ai-back.

71 jeffreychristIsAlive, “Dobie Gray - Drift Away (Original Official Video),” YouTube, September 6, 2010, https://www.youtube.com/watch?v=NIuyDWzctgY.

72 Charlie Guo, “LLMs Are Getting Dumber and We Have No Idea Why,” Artificial Ignorance, September 5, 2024, https://www.ignorance.ai/p/llms-are-getting-dumber-and-we-have.

73 Alan Weissberger, “AI Is Getting Smarter, but Hallucinations Are Getting Worse,” IEEE ComSoc Technology Blog, May 10, 2025, https://techblog.comsoc.org/2025/05/10/nyt-ai-is-getting-smarter-but-hallucinations-are-getting-worse.

74 June-Hao Hou, “Comparing AI-Generated images two years apart—2022 vs. 2024,” Medium, April 17, 2024, https://medium.com/@junehao/comparing-ai-generated-images-two-years-apart-2022-vs-2024-6c3c4670b905.

75 Sven-Erik Jonsson, “The Current State of AI Image Generation (Early 2025),” GetaDigital, February 25, 2025, https://www.getadigital.com/blog/the-current-state-of-ai-image-generation-as-of-early-2025.

76 Bernard Marr, “The Amazing Ways Coca-Cola Uses Generative AI in Art and Advertising,” Forbes, September 8, 2023, https://www.forbes.com/sites/bernardmarr/2023/09/08/the-amazing-ways-coca-cola-uses-generative-ai-in-art-and-advertising; Jacques van der Wilt, “11 Best AI Advertising Examples of 2025,” DataFeedWatch, 2025, https://www.datafeedwatch.com/blog/best-ai-advertising-examples

77 Rob Alderson, “Graphic design among most at-risk jobs from AI – report,” Design Week, January 13, 2025, https://www.designweek.co.uk/graphic-design-among-most-at-risk-jobs-from-ai-report/

78 Gaurav Sharma, “The Impact of AI Technology on the Filmmaking Industry,” Raindance, February 14, 2025, https://raindance.org/the-impact-of-ai-technology-on-the-filmmaking-industry.

79 Caroline Nourry, “AI is creating fake legal cases and making its way into real courtrooms, with disastrous results,” The Conversation, March 12, 2024, https://theconversation.com/ai-is-creating-fake-legal-cases-and-making-its-way-into-real-courtrooms-with-disastrous-results-225080.

80 Ellen Jennings-Trace, “Agentic AI Has Issues With Security and Privacy, Signal President Says,” TechRadar, March 10, 2025, https://www.techradar.com/pro/security/agentic-ai-has-profound-issues-with-security-and-privacy-signal-president-says.

81 Charlie Guo, "LLMs Are Getting Dumber and We Have No Idea Why," Artificial Ignorance, September 5, 2024, https://www.ignorance.ai/p/llms-are-getting-dumber-and-we-have.

82 Jeffrey Dastin, "Insight - Amazon scraps secret AI recruiting tool that showed bias against women," Reuters, October 11, 2018, https://www.reuters.com/article/world/insight-amazon-scraps-secret-ai-recruiting-tool-that-showed-bias-against-women-idUSKCN1MK0AG/

83 Craft Law Firm, "Data Analysis: Self-Driving Car Accidents [2019-2024]," Craft Law Firm, June 30, 2025, https://www.craftlawfirm.com/autonomous-vehicle-accidents-2019-2024-crash-data/

84 Bryson Masse, "A Chevy for $1? Car dealer chatbots show perils of AI for customer service," Venture Beat, December 19, 2023, https://venturebeat.com/ai/a-chevy-for-1-car-dealer-chatbots-show-perils-of-ai-for-customer-service.

85 Kung-Hsiang Huang, Akshara Prabhakar, Onkar Thorat, Divyansh Agarwal, Prafulla Kumar Choubey, Yixin Mao, Silvio Savarese, Caiming Xiong, and Chien-Sheng Wu, "CRMArena-Pro: Holistic Assessment of LLM Agents Across Diverse Business Scenarios and Interactions," arXiv:2505.18878, May 24, 2025. https://arxiv.org/abs/2505.18878.

86 Rogerio Bonatti, Dan Zhao, Francesco Bonacci, Dillon Dupont, Sara Abdali, Yinheng Li, Yadong Lu, Justin Wagle, Kazuhito Koishida, Arthur Bucker, Lawrence Jang, and Zack Hui, "Windows Agent Arena: Evaluating Multi-modal OS Agents at Scale," Microsoft Github, n.d., https://microsoft.github.io/WindowsAgentArena.

87 Parshin Shojaee, Iman Mirzadeh, Keivan Alizadeh, Maxwell Horton, Samy Bengio, and Mehrdad Farajtabar, "The Illusion of Thinking: Understanding the Strengths and Limitations of Reasoning Models via the Lens of Problem Complexity," Apple Machine Learning Research, June 2025, https://machinelearning.apple.com/research/illusion-of-thinking.

88 Ernest Davis and Gary Marcus, "Reports of LLMs Mastering Math Have Been Greatly Exaggerated," Marcus on AI, April 5, 2025, https://garymarcus.substack.com/p/reports-of-llms-mastering-math-have.

89 Gary Marcus, "When Billion-dollar AIs Break Down Over Puzzles a Child Can Do, It's Time to Rethink the Hype," The Guardian, June 10, 2025, https://www.theguardian.com/commentisfree/2025/jun/10/billion-dollar-ai-puzzle-break-down.

90 Wilma C. M. Resing, Bart Vogelaar, and Julian G. Elliott, "Children's Solving of 'Tower of Hanoi' Tasks: Dynamic Testing With the Help of a Robot," Educational Psychology 40, no. 9 (November 20, 2019): 1136–63, https://doi.org/10.1080/01443410.2019.1684450.

91 Allen Newell, A Guide to the General Problem-Solver Program GPS-2-2 (The RAND Corporation, 1963), https://stacks.stanford.edu/file/druid:zk239tp3547/zk239tp3547.pdf.

92 Andy Hayler, "Drifting Away? AI Model Performance Over Time," The Information Difference, May 21, 2025, https://www.informationdifference.com/ai-model-performance.

93 Ibid.

94 Anthropic, "Project Vend: Can Claude Run a Small Shop? (and Why Does That Matter?)," Anthropic, June 27, 2025, https://www.anthropic.com/research/project-vend-1.

95 Andy Hayler, "Drifting Away? AI Model Performance Over Time," The Information Difference, May 21, 2025, https://www.informationdifference.com/ai-model-performance.

96 Bryson Masse, "A Chevy for $1? Car dealer chatbots show perils of AI for customer service," Venture Beat, December 19, 2023, https://venturebeat.com/ai/a-chevy-for-1-car-dealer-chatbots-show-perils-of-ai-for-customer-service.

97 Jeremy Hsu, "AI Hallucinations Are Getting Worse – and They'Re Here to Stay," New Scientist, May 9, 2025, https://www.newscientist.com/article/2479545-ai-hallucinations-are-getting-worse-and-theyre-here-to-stay.

98 Alternative_Hall_839, "From OpenAI's demo of their agent tool: a map that's supposed to show a travel itinerary for all 30 MLB stadiums. Even in their own staged advertisement ChatGPT spits out unusable slop," Reddit, July 17, 2025, https://www.reddit.com/r/BetterOffline/comments/1m2g42y/from_openais_demo_of_their_agent_tool_a_map_thats.

99 Xuezhi Wang, Jason Wei, Dale Schuurmans, Quoc Le, Ed Chi, Sharan Narang, Aakanksha Chowdhery, and Denny Zhou, "Self-Consistency Improves Chain of Thought Reasoning in Language Models," arXiv:2203.11171, March 21, 2022, https://arxiv.org/abs/2203.11171.

100 Jason Wei, Xuezhi Wang, Dale Schuurmans, Maarten Bosma, Brian Ichter, Fei Xia, Ed Chi, Quoc Le, and Denny Zhou, "Chain-of-Thought Prompting Elicits Reasoning in Large Language Models," arXiv.2201.11903, January 28, 2022, https://arxiv.org/abs/2201.11903.

101 Alice Rueda, Mohammed S. Hassan, Argyrios Perivolaris, Bazen G. Teferra, Reza Samavi, Sirisha Rambhatla, Yuqi Wu, Yanbo Zhang, Bo Cao, Divya Sharma, Sridhar Krishnan, and Venkat Bhat, "Understanding LLM Scientific Reasoning through Promptings and Model's Explanation on the Answers," arXiv:2505.01482v1, May 2, 2025, https://arxiv.org/html/2505.01482v1.

102 Dina Genkina, "AI Prompt Engineering Is Dead," IEEE Spectrum, May 16, 2025, https://spectrum.ieee.org/prompt-engineering-is-dead.

103 Abel Salinas and Fred Morstatter, "The Butterfly Effect of Altering Prompts: How Small Changes and Jailbreaks Affect Large Language Model Performance." In Findings of the Association for Computational Linguistics: ACL 2024 (Association for Computational Linguistics, 2024): 4629–4651, https://doi.org/10.18653/v1/2024.findings-acl.275.

104 Andy Hayler, "AI Use Cases – the Good, the Bad and the Ugly," The Information Difference, May 23, 2025, https://www.informationdifference.com/ai-the-good-bad-ugly.

105 Andy Hayler, "The Elephant in the Room – AI Image Generation," The Information Difference, July 8, 2025. https://www.informationdifference.com/elephant-ai-image-generation.

106 Frank Landymore, "AI Models Can Send "Subliminal" Messages to Each Other That Make Them More Evil," Futurism, July 26, 2025, https://futurism.com/ai-models-subliminal-messages-evil.

107 Pablo Villalobos, Anson Ho, Jaime Sevilla, Tamay Besiroglu, Lennart Heim, and Marius Hobbhahn, "Will We Run Out of Data? Limits of LLM Scaling Based on Human-generated Data," arXiv:2211.04325v2, June 4, 2024, https://arxiv.org/html/2211.04325v2.

108 Melissa Heikkilä, "This New Data Poisoning Tool Lets Artists Fight Back Against Generative AI," MIT Technology Review, October 23, 2023, https://www.technologyreview.com/2023/10/23/1082189/data-poisoning-artists-fight-generative-ai.

109 Bart Lenaerts-Bergmans, "What Is Data Poisoning?" CrowdStrike, March 19, 2025, https://www.crowdstrike.com/en-gb/cybersecurity-101/cyberattacks/data-poisoning.

110 Marcelo Tibau, "LLMs Are Hitting the Wall: What's Next," Medium, November 13, 2024, https://medium.com/@marcelo_tibau/llms-are-hitting-the-wall-whats-next-cb49a53c9919

111 Jeremy Hsu, "AI Hallucinations Are Getting Worse – and They're Here to Stay," New Scientist, May 9, 2025, https://www.newscientist.com/article/2479545-ai-hallucinations-are-getting-worse-and-theyre-here-to-stay.

112 Ben Dickson, "New AI architecture delivers 100x faster reasoning than LLMs with just 1,000 training examples," Venture Beat, July 26, 2025, https://venturebeat.com/ai/new-ai-architecture-delivers-100x-faster-reasoning-than-llms-with-just-1000-training-examples.

113 Andy Hayler, "Chatbots on the Couch: AI in Therapy," The Information Difference, August 18, 2025, https://www.informationdifference.com/chatbots-on-the-couch-

ai-in-therapy/; Rachel Hall, "'Sliding Into an Abyss': Experts Warn Over Rising Use of AI for Mental Health Support," The Guardian, August 30, 2025, https://www.theguardian.com/society/2025/aug/30/therapists-warn-ai-chatbots-mental-health-support.

114 Visual Storytelling Team and Madhumita Murgia, "Generative AI Exists Because of the Transformer," Financial Times, September 12, 2023, https://ig.ft.com/generative-ai.

115 Microsoft, "Understand Tokens," Microsoft Learn, May 29, 2025, https://learn.microsoft.com/en-us/dotnet/ai/conceptual/understanding-tokens.

116 Andy Hayler, "When AI Picks Sides – AI Bias and Discrimination," The Information Difference, September 2, 2025, https://www.informationdifference.com/when-ai-picks-sides-ai-bias-and-discrimination.

117 Andy Hayler, "When Algorithms Dream: AI Hallucinations in Depth," The Information Difference, August 19, 2025, https://www.informationdifference.com/when-algorithms-dream-ai-hallucinations-in-depth.

118 Sumant R. Ranji, "Large Language Models—Misdiagnosing Diagnostic Excellence?" JAMA Network Open 7, no. 10 (2024): e2440901. https://doi.org/10.1001/jamanetworkopen.2024.40901.

119 Damien Charlotin, "AI Hallucination Cases Database," Artificial Authority, n.d., https://www.damiencharlotin.com/hallucinations/?ref=nucleo.jor.br&page=2&page=3&page=4&page=5.

120 Robert Booth, "High Court Tells UK Lawyers to Stop Misuse of AI After Fake Case-law Citations," The Guardian, June 6, 2025, https://www.theguardian.com/technology/2025/jun/06/high-court-tells-uk-lawyers-to-urgently-stop-misuse-of-ai-in-legal-work.

121 Vytenis Kaubrė, "LLM Training Data: The 8 Main Public Data Sources," Oxylabs, September 27, 2024, https://oxylabs.io/blog/llm-training-data.

122 Common Crawl, "Open Repository of Web Crawl Data," Common Crawl, n.d., https://commoncrawl.org.

123 GitHub, "Build and Ship Software on a Single, Collaborative Platform," GitHub, 2025, https://github.com.

124 Kaggle, "Your Machine Learning and Data Science Community," Kaggle (home page), n.d., https://www.kaggle.com.

125 Marcus Lu, "Ranked: The Most Cited Websites by AI Models," Visual Capitalist, August 18, 2025, https://www.visualcapitalist.com/ranked-the-most-cited-websites-by-ai-models.

126 Cristina Improta, Rosalia Tufano, Pietro Liguori, Domenico Cotroneo, and Gabriele Bavota, "Quality In, Quality Out: Investigating Training Data's Role in

AI Code Generation," arXiv:2503.11402v1, March 14, 2025, https://arxiv.org/html/2503.11402v1.

127 Yujia Zhou, Yan Liu, Xiaoxi Li, Jiajie Jin, Hongjin Qian, Zheng Liu, Chaozhuo Li, Zhicheng Dou, Tsung-Yi Ho, and Philip S. Yu, "Trustworthiness in Retrieval-Augmented Generation Systems: A Survey," arXiv:2409.10102v1, September 16, 2024, https://arxiv.org/html/2409.10102v1.

128 Jeffrey Ip, "RAG Evaluation Metrics: Assessing Answer Relevancy, Faithfulness, Contextual Relevancy, and More," Confident AI, October 10, 2025, https://www.confident-ai.com/blog/rag-evaluation-metrics-answer-relevancy-faithfulness-and-more.

129 Skylar Payne, "Why RAG Is (Still) Not Dead – Skylar Payne," Skylar Payne, April 6, 2025, https://skylarbpayne.com/posts/rag-not-dead.

130 Precisely, "New Global Research Points to Lack of Data Quality and Governance as Major Obstacles to AI Readiness," Precisely, September 18, 2024, https://www.precisely.com/press-release/new-global-research-points-to-lack-of-data-quality-and-governance-as-major-obstacles-to-ai-readiness.

131 David Curry, "75% of Executives Don't Trust Their Data," RTInsights, February 22, 2022, https://www.rtinsights.com/executives-dont-trust-data.

132 The Economist Group, Unlocking Enterprise AI: Opportunities and Strategies (Databricks, 2024), https://www.databricks.com/resources/analyst-research/unlocking-enterprise-ai-opportunities-and-strategies.

133 Sylvain Duranton, "Are Coders' Jobs at Risk? AI's Impact on the Future of Programming," Forbes, April 15, 2024, https://www.forbes.com/sites/sylvainduranton/2024/04/15/are-coders-jobs-at-risk-ais-impact-on-the-future-of-programming.

134 Stanford University, "Dan Boneh and Team Find Relying on AI Is More Likely to Make Your Code Buggier," Stanford University Department of Electrical Engineering, January 2023, https://ee.stanford.edu/dan-boneh-and-team-find-relying-ai-more-likely-make-your-code-buggier.

135 Yujia Fu, Peng Liang, Amjed Tahir, Zengyang Li, Mojtaba Shahin, Jiaxin Yu, and Jinfu Chen, "Security Weaknesses of Copilot Generated Code in GitHub," arXiv:2310.02059v2l, April 4, 2024, https://arxiv.org/html/2310.02059v2.

136 Namanyayg Goel, "Vibe Coding Is a Dangerous Fantasy," N's Blog, March 20, 2025, https://nmn.gl/blog/vibe-coding-fantasy.

137 Gene Marks, "Business Tech News: Zuckerberg Says AI Will Replace Mid-Level Engineers Soon," Forbes, January 26, 2025, https://www.forbes.com/sites/quickerbettertech/2025/01/26/business-tech-news-zuckerberg-says-ai-will-replace-mid-level-engineers-soon.

138 Sylvain Duranton, "Are Coders' Jobs at Risk? AI's Impact on the Future of Programming," Forbes, April 15, 2024, https://www.forbes.com/sites/sylvainduranton/2024/04/15/are-coders-jobs-at-risk-ais-impact-on-the-future-of-programming.

139 Neeraj Kumar Singh, "The Evolution of Software Development Tools: A Historical Comparison of Capabilities and Paradigm," Medium, February 16, 2025, https://neerazz.medium.com/the-evolution-of-software-development-tools-a-historical-comparison-of-capabilities-and-paradigms-70ef56d414bb.

140 The Economist editors, "Why AI hasn't taken your job," The Economist, May 26, 2025, https://www.economist.com/finance-and-economics/2025/05/26/why-ai-hasnt-taken-your-job.

141 Esteban Sanchez, "Software Maintenance Cost," Galorath, December 18, 2024, https://galorath.com/blog/software-maintenance-costs.

142 Mike Vizard, "Survey: AI Tools are Increasing Amount of Bad Code Needing to be Fixed," DevOps.com, January 10, 2025, https://devops.com/survey-ai-tools-are-increasing-amount-of-bad-code-needing-to-be-fixed.

143 METR, "Measuring the Impact of Early-2025 AI on Experienced Open-Source Developer Productivity," METR, July 10, 2025, https://metr.org/blog/2025-07-10-early-2025-ai-experienced-os-dev-study.

144 Legit Security, "AI Code Generation: The Risks and Benefits of AI in Software," Legit Security, January 21, 2025, https://www.legitsecurity.com/aspm-knowledge-base/ai-code-generation-benefits-and-risks; Neil Perry, Megha Srivastava, Deepak Kumar, and Dan Boneh, "Do Users Write More Insecure Code with AI Assistants?" arXiv:2211.03622, Last Updated December 18, 2023, https://arxiv.org/abs/2211.03622.

145 Spiral Compute Limited, "The Future of AI in Software Engineering 2025: Beyond the Hype," Spiral Compute Limited, June 14, 2025, https://www.spiralcompute.co.nz/the-future-of-ai-in-software-engineering-2025-beyond-the-hype.

146 Generative AI Adoption in the Enterprise (WRITER, 2025), https://go.writer.com/enterprise-ai-adoption-survey.

147 Sander Schulhoff, "Limitations of LLMs: Bias, Hallucinations, and More," Learn Prompting, March 6, 2025, https://learnprompting.org/docs/basics/pitfalls.

148 Dan Russell, "Answer: So what ARE LLMs good at? What are they bad at?" July 17, 2025, https://searchresearch1.blogspot.com/2025/07/answer-so-what-are-llms-good-at-what.html.

149 Swaroop Dora, Deven Lunkad, Naziya Aslam, and S. Venkatesan, "The Hidden Risks of LLM-Generated Web Application Code: A Security-Centric Evaluation of Code

Generation Capabilities in Large Language Models," arXiv:2504.20612v1, April 29, 2025, https://arxiv.org/html/2504.20612v1

150 Cem Dilmegani and Aleyna Daldal, "AI Hallucination: Comparison of the Popular LLMs," AIMultiple, October 20, 2025, https://research.aimultiple.com/ai-hallucination.

151 Jeremy Hsu, "AI Hallucinations Are Getting Worse – and They're Here to Stay," New Scientist, May 9, 2025, https://www.newscientist.com/article/2479545-ai-hallucinations-are-getting-worse-and-theyre-here-to-stay.

152 Thomas Claburn, "AI bots hallucinate software packages and devs download them," The Register, March 28, 2024, https://www.theregister.com/2024/03/28/ai_bots_hallucinate_software_packages.

153 Sead Fadilpašić, "'Slopsquatting'; Attacks Are Using AI-hallucinated Names Resembling Popular Libraries to Spread Malware," TechRadar, April 14, 2025, https://www.techradar.com/pro/security/ai-hallucinated-names-resembling-popular-libraries-created-for-slopsquatting-attacks.

154 Farhad Manjoo, "It's the End of Computer Programming as We Know It. (And I Feel Fine.)," The New York Times, June 2, 2023, https://www.nytimes.com/2023/06/02/opinion/ai-coding.html.

155 Andy Hayler, "Agents of Change or Agents of Chaos? The Reality of Agentic AI," The Information Difference, April 22, 2025, https://www.informationdifference.com/the-reality-of-agentic-ai.

156 Andy Hayler, "The Domino Effect – Benchmarking Agentic AI," The Information Difference, June 17, 2025, https://www.informationdifference.com/benchmarking-agentic-ai.

157 Andy Hayler, "MCP – Multiple Security Pitfalls?" The Information Difference, June 10, 2025, https://www.informationdifference.com/security-pitfalls.

158 Department for Science, Innovation and Technology, "AI Cyber Security Code of Practice," GOV.UK, January 31, 2025, https://www.gov.uk/government/publications/ai-cyber-security-code-of-practice.

159 SoSafe, Cybercrime Trends 2025 (SoSafe, 2025), https://sosafe-awareness.com/resources/reports/cybercrime-trends.

160 IBM, Cost of a Data Breach 2025 (IBM, 2025), https://www.ibm.com/reports/data-breach.

161 Crowdstrike, CrowdStrike 2024 Global Threat Report (Crowdstrike, 2024), https://www.crowdstrike.com/en-us/resources/reports/crowdstrike-2024-global-threat-report.

162 Dan Milmo, "UK Engineering Firm Arup Falls Victim to £20m Deepfake Scam," The Guardian, May 17, 2024, https://www.theguardian.com/technology/article/2024/may/17/uk-engineering-arup-deepfake-scam-hong-kong-ai-video.

163 Nick Robins-Early, "CEO of World's Biggest Ad Firm Targeted by Deepfake Scam," The Guardian, May 10, 2024, https://www.theguardian.com/technology/article/2024/may/10/ceo-wpp-deepfake-scam.

164 ISO, ISO/IEC 27001:2022: Information security, cybersecurity and privacy protection—Information security management systems—Requirements (ISO, 2022), https://www.iso.org/standard/27001.

165 Shelton Fitch, "The Surprising Power of Next Word Prediction: Large Language Models Explained, Part 1," Center for Security and Emerging Technology, March 8, 2024, https://cset.georgetown.edu/article/the-surprising-power-of-next-word-prediction-large-language-models-explained-part-1.

166 Pierre-Carl Langlais, Carlos Rosas Hinostroza, Mattia Nee, Catherine Arnett, Pavel Chizhov, Eliot Krzystof Jones, Irène Girard, David Mach, Anastasia Stasenko, and Ivan P. Yamshchikov, "Common Corpus: The Largest Collection of Ethical Data for LLM Pre-Training," arXiv:2506.01732, June 2, 2025, https://arxiv.org/abs/2506.01732.

167 IBM, "What is gradient descent?" IBM, https://www.ibm.com/think/topics/gradient-descent.

168 Avril Aysha, "Data Bias in LLM and Generative AI Applications," MOSTLY AI, December 13, 2024, https://mostly.ai/blog/data-bias-types.

169 BBC News, "Amazon Scrapped 'sexist AI' Tool," BBC News, October 10, 2018, https://www.bbc.com/news/technology-45809919.

170 Andy Hayler, "Scraping by – AI and Copyright Law," The Information Difference, August 18, 2025, https://www.informationdifference.com/scraping-by-ai-and-copyright-law.

171 https://www.technologyreview.com/2023/10/23/1082189/data-poisoning-artists-fight-generative-ai/

172 Shawn Shan, Wenxin Ding, Josephine Passananti, Stanley Wu, Haitao Zheng, and Ben Y. Zhao, "Nightshade: Prompt-Specific Poisoning Attacks on Text-to-Image Generative Models," arXiv:2310.13828, October 20, 2023, https://arxiv.org/abs/2310.13828.

173 Melissa Heikkilä, "This New Data Poisoning Tool Lets Artists Fight Back Against Generative AI," MIT Technology Review, October 23, 2023, https://www.technologyreview.com/2023/10/23/1082189/data-poisoning-artists-fight-generative-ai.

174 Kapersky, "What Is Steganography & How Does It Work?" Kapersky, February 8, 2023, https://www.kaspersky.com/resource-center/definitions/what-is-steganography.

175 Institut Català d'Investigació Química, "Invisible Ink," ICIQ, December 11, 2024, https://iciq.org/experiment/invisible-ink.

176 David Tidmarsh, "A Guide to Steganography: Meaning, Types, Tools, &Amp; Techniques," Cybersecurity Exchange, April 12, 2025, https://www.eccouncil.org/

cybersecurity-exchange/ethical-hacking/what-is-steganography-guide-meaning-types-tools.

177 Onn Nir, "Magecart Evolves Again: A New Case Study," Reflectiz, August 8, 2024, https://www.reflectiz.com/blog/magecart-case-study-2023.

178 Bruce Schneier, "Real-World Steganography," Schneier on Security, January 20, 2023, https://www.schneier.com/blog/archives/2023/01/real-world-steganography.html.

179 Ravie Lakshmanan, "Hackers Hide Malware in Images to Deploy VIP Keylogger and 0bj3ctivity Stealer," The Hacker News, January 16, 2025, https://thehackernews.com/2025/01/hackers-hide-malware-in-images-to.html.

180 Digital Watch Observatory, "Hackers Use Steganography to Evade Windows Defences," Digital Watch Observatory, August 5, 2025, https://dig.watch/updates/hackers-use-steganography-to-evade-windows-defences.

181 Daniel Alexander Alber, Zihao Yang, Anton Alyakin, Eunice Yang, Sumedha Rai, Aly A. Valliani, Jeff Zhang, et al., "Medical Large Language Models Are Vulnerable to Data-poisoning Attacks," Nature Medicine 31 (2025): 618–626, https://doi.org/10.1038/s41591-024-03445-1.

182 "The Pile" (home page), n.d., https://pile.eleuther.ai.

183 "PubMed" (home page), n.d., https://pubmed.ncbi.nlm.nih.gov.

184 Andy Hayler, "When Algorithms Dream: AI Hallucinations in Depth," The Information Difference, August 19, 2025, https://www.informationdifference.com/when-algorithms-dream-ai-hallucinations-in-depth.

185 Thomas E. Armstrong, "Slopsquatting Assurance," EDPACS, The EDP Audit, Control, and Security Newsletter, June 2, 2025, 1–9, https://doi.org/10.1080/07366981.2025.2510097.

186 Kathrin Grosse and Alexandre Alahi, "A qualitative AI security risk assessment of autonomous vehicles," Transportation Research Part C: Emerging Technologies 169 (December 2024): 104797, https://doi.org/10.1016/j.trc.2024.104797.

187 Alessandro Mascellino, "New ConfusedPilot Attack Targets AI Systems With Data Poisoning," Infosecurity Magazine, October 15, 2025, https://www.infosecurity-magazine.com/news/confusedpilot-attack-targets-ai.

188 Xinran Li and Zichi Wang, "Vaccine for Digital Images Against Steganography," Scientific Reports 14, no. 1 (September 12, 2024), https://doi.org/10.1038/s41598-024-72693-5.

189 Dan Crum, "Hidden Threats in AI Data: Protecting Against Embedded Steganography," Owl Cyber Defense, November 19, 2024, https://owlcyberdefense.com/blog/hidden-threats-in-ai-data-protecting-against-steganography.

190 Apostol Vassilev, Alina Oprea, Alie Fordyce, Hyrum Anderson, Xander Davies, and Maia Hamin, NIST Trustworthy and Responsible AI NIST AI 100-2e2025: Adversarial

Machine Learning A Taxonomy and Terminology of Attacks and Mitigations (National Institute of Standards and Technology, March 2025).

191 Ilia Shumailov, Zakhar Shumaylov, Yiren Zhao, Nicolas Papernot, Ross Anderson, and Yarin Gal, "AI Models Collapse When Trained on Recursively Generated Data," Nature 631, no. 8022 (July 24, 2024): 755–59, https://doi.org/10.1038/s41586-024-07566-y.

192 Phil Swatton and Margaux Leblanc, "What are deepfakes and how can we detect them?" The Alan Turing Institute, June 7, 2024, https://www.turing.ac.uk/blog/what-are-deepfakes-and-how-can-we-detect-them.

193 GeeksforGeeks, "How to Calculate Optimal Batch Size for Training Neural Networks," GeeksforGeeks, July 23, 2025, https://www.geeksforgeeks.org/deep-learning/how-to-calculate-optimal-batch-size-for-training-neural-networks.

194 Fazeela Siddiqui, Jiachen Yang, Shuai Xiao, and Muhammad Fahad, "Diffusion Model in Modern Detection: Advancing Deepfake techniques," Knowledge-based Systems 325 (5 September 2025): 113922, https://www.sciencedirect.com/science/article/abs/pii/S0950705125009670.

195 Eric Szeto, "Dutch Politicians Join Calls to Extradite Canadian Behind Notorious AI Porn Site," CBC, August 13, 2025, https://www.cbc.ca/news/canada/mrdeepfakes-extradition-netherlands-david-do-1.7608257; James Chater, "AI Deepfake Porn Humiliated Me, Says Penny Mordaunt," BBC News, July 23, 2025, https://bbc.co.uk/news/articles/ckg3r3vm1d0o.

196 Heather Chen and Kathleen Magramo, "Finance worker pays out $25 million after video call with deepfake 'chief financial officer'," CNN, February 4, 2024, https://edition.cnn.com/2024/02/04/asia/deepfake-cfo-scam-hong-kong-intl-hnk; Dan Milmo, "UK Engineering Firm Arup Falls Victim to £20m Deepfake Scam," The Guardian, May 17, 2024, https://www.theguardian.com/technology/article/2024/may/17/uk-engineering-arup-deepfake-scam-hong-kong-ai-video.

197 Dan Milmo and Alex Hern, "From Pope's Jacket to Napalm Recipes: How Worrying Is AI's Rapid Growth?" The Guardian, April 23, 2023, https://www.theguardian.com/technology/2023/apr/23/pope-jacket-napalm-recipes-how-worrying-is-ai-rapid-growth.

198 Accelerated Capability Environment, "Innovating to Detect Deepfakes and Protect the Public," GOV.UK, February 5, 2025, https://www.gov.uk/government/case-studies/innovating-to-detect-deepfakes-and-protect-the-public.

199 Ameer Owda, "Top 10 AI Deepfake Detection Tools to Combat Digital Deception in 2025," SOCRadar® Cyber Intelligence Inc., October 21, 2025, https://socradar.io/top-10-ai-deepfake-detection-tools-2025.; Rachel Leingang, "How to Spot a Deepfake: The Maker of a Detection Tool Shares the Key Giveaways," The Guardian, June 7,

2024, https://www.theguardian.com/us-news/article/2024/jun/07/how-to-spot-a-deepfake.

200 Ibid.

201 Tamara Cohen, "Warning to UK Politicians Over Risk of Audio Deepfakes That Could Derail the Election," Sky News, June 2, 2024, https://news.sky.com/story/warning-to-uk-politicians-over-risk-of-audio-deepfakes-that-could-derail-the-general-election-13146573.

202 Robert Tait, "US Senator Targeted by Deepfake Caller Posing as Ukrainian Diplomat," The Guardian, September 26, 2024, https://www.theguardian.com/us-news/2024/sep/26/ben-cardin-dmytro-kuleba-deepfake-ukraine.

203 Tamara Cohen, "Warning to UK Politicians Over Risk of Audio Deepfakes That Could Derail the Election," Sky News, June 2, 2024. https://news.sky.com/story/warning-to-uk-politicians-over-risk-of-audio-deepfakes-that-could-derail-the-general-election-13146573.

204 Samuel Osborne, "Fake AI-generated Joe Biden Robocall Tells People in New Hampshire Not to Vote," Sky News, January 23, 2024, https://news.sky.com/story/fake-ai-generated-joe-biden-robocall-tells-people-in-new-hampshire-not-to-vote-13054446.

205 UK Government, Online Safety Act 2023, October 26, 2023, https://www.legislation.gov.uk/ukpga/2023/50.

206 European Parliament, "EU AI Act: First Regulation on Artificial Intelligence," European Parliament, August 6, 2023, https://www.europarl.europa.eu/topics/en/article/20230601STO93804/eu-ai-act-first-regulation-on-artificial-intelligence.

207 US Congress, "S.146 - 119th Congress (2025-2026): TAKE IT DOWN Act," Congress.gov., May 19, 2025. https://www.congress.gov/bill/119th-congress/senate-bill/146.

208 Bruce D. Sokler, Alexander Hecht, Christian Tamotsu Fjeld, and Matthew Tikhonovsky, "President Trump Signs AI Deepfake Act Into Law and House Passes AI Measures—AI: The Washington Report," Mintz, May 22, 2025, https://www.mintz.com/insights-center/viewpoints/54731/2025-05-22-president-trump-signs-ai-deepfake-act-law-and-house.

209 Transparency Coalition, "2025 AI Deepfake Bills—Transparency Coalition. Legislation for Transparency in AI Now," Transparency Coalition, April 28, 2025, https://www.transparencycoalition.ai/news/2025-ai-deepfake-bills.

210 Miranda Bryant, "Denmark to Tackle Deepfakes by Giving People Copyright to Their Own Features," The Guardian, June 27, 2025, https://www.theguardian.com/technology/2025/jun/27/deepfakes-denmark-copyright-law-artificial-intelligence.

211 Lewis Maddison, "Samsung Workers Made a Major Error by Using ChatGPT," TechRadar, April 4, 2023, https://www.techradar.com/news/samsung-workers-leaked-company-secrets-by-using-chatgpt.

212 Kate Park, "Samsung Bans Use of Generative AI Tools Like ChatGPT After April Internal Data Leak," TechCrunch, May 3, 2023, https://techcrunch.com/2023/05/02/samsung-bans-use-of-generative-ai-tools-like-chatgpt-after-april-internal-data-leak.

213 Alex Scroxton, "Many UK Organisations Considering ChatGPT Bans on Employee Devices," Computer Weekly, August 8, 2023, https://www.computerweekly.com/news/366547400/Many-UK-organisations-considering-ChatGPT-bans-on-employee-devices.

214 Admin, "Companies That Have Banned ChatGPT," Jaxon, March 12, 2024, https://jaxon.ai/list-of-companies-that-have-banned-chatgpt.

215 Sourabhkv, "Make Your Own Private ChatGPT," Microsoft Tech Community, December 28, 2024, https://techcommunity.microsoft.com/blog/educatordeveloperblog/make-your-own-private-chatgpt/4357607.

216 William Kwan Fbcs, "Navigating the Risks of 'Shadow AI'," British Computer Society, July 8, 2025, https://www.bcs.org/articles-opinion-and-research/navigating-the-risks-of-shadow-ai.

217 Adriel Sanchez, "New WalkMe Survey Shows Shadow AI Is Rampant; Training Gaps Undermine AI ROI," SAP News Center, August 27, 2025, https://news.sap.com/2025/08/new-walkme-survey-shadow-ai-rampant-training-gaps-undermine-roi.

218 Scarlett Evans, "Shadow AI a Major Concern Across Enterprise IT, Study Finds," AI Business, June 5, 2025, https://aibusiness.com/responsible-ai/shadow-ai-a-major-concern-across-enterprise-it-study-finds.

219 Stephanie Tully, Chiara Longoni, and Gil Appel, "EXPRESS: Lower Artificial Intelligence Literacy Predicts Greater AI Receptivity," Journal of Marketing 8, no. 5 (January 13, 2025), 1–20, https://doi.org/10.1177/00222429251314491.

220 David Rowlands and Nicole Gillespie, "Global Study Reveals Trust of AI Remains a Critical Challenge Reflecting Tension Between Benefits and Risks," KPMG, April 2024, https://kpmg.com/xx/en/media/press-releases/2025/04/trust-of-ai-remains-a-critical-challenge.html; Joe Wilkins, "The More Scientists Work With AI, the Less They Trust It," Futurism, October 13, 2025, https://futurism.com/artificial-intelligence/ai-research-scientists-hype.

221 Andy Hayler, "Finding the Goldilocks Zone for AI-Generated Code," The Information Difference, August 12, 2025, https://www.informationdifference.com/ai-generated-code.

222 Andy Hayler, "When Algorithms Dream: AI Hallucinations in Depth," The Information Difference, August 19, 2025, https://www.informationdifference.com/when-algorithms-dream-ai-hallucinations-in-depth.

223 Lexin Zhou, Wout Schellaert, Fernando Martínez-Plumed, Yael Moros-Daval, Cèsar Ferri, and José Hernández-Orall, "Larger and More Instructable Language Models Become Less Reliable," Nature 634, no. 8032 (September 25, 2024): 61–68, https://doi.org/10.1038/s41586-024-07930-y.

224 OWASP Top 10 for LLM & Generative AI Security, "LLM01:2025 Prompt Injection," OWASP Gen AI Security Project, 2025, https://genai.owasp.org/llmrisk/llm01-prompt-injection.

225 Check Point Research, "AI Security Report 2025: Understanding Threats and Building Smarter Defenses," Check Point Blog, April 30, 2025, https://blog.checkpoint.com/research/ai-security-report-2025-understanding-threats-and-building-smarter-defenses.

226 Andy Hayler, "Hiding in Plain Sight – AI Data Poisoning," The Information Difference, August 27, 2025, https://www.informationdifference.com/hiding-in-plain-sight-ai-data-poisoning.

227 Jay Chen and Royce Lu, "Deceptive Delight: Jailbreak LLMs Through Camouflage and Distraction," Unit 42, October 23, 2024, https://unit42.paloaltonetworks.com/jailbreak-llms-through-camouflage-distraction.

228 Rachyl Jones, "It's Time To Get Serious About AI Hallucinations," Fortune, January 17, 2024, https://fortune.com/2024/01/17/ai-hallucination-aporia-survey.

229 Amy Dawson, "87% of UK Organisations Are Vulnerable to Cyberattacks in the Age of AI," Microsoft UK Stories, April 18, 2024, https://ukstories.microsoft.com/features/87-of-uk-organisations-are-vulnerable-to-cyberattacks-in-the-age-of-ai-research-reveals.

230 Julia Kollewe, "More Than 25% of UK Businesses Hit by Cyber-attack in Last Year, Report Finds," The Guardian, June 30, 2025, https://www.theguardian.com/business/2025/jun/30/uk-businesses-hit-by-cyber-attack-last-year-report.

231 Matthew Kosinski, "What is black box AI?", IBM, https://www.ibm.com/think/topics/black-box-ai.

232 Zifan Zheng, Yezhaohui Wang, Yuxin Huang, Shichao Song, Mingchuan Yang, Bo Tang, Feiyu Xiong, and Zhiyu Li, "Attention heads of large language models," Patterns 6, no. 2 (14 February 2025), 101176, https://www.sciencedirect.com/science/article/pii/S2666389925000248.

233 "Deterministic system", Taylor & Francis, n.d. https://taylorandfrancis.com/knowledge/Engineering_and_technology/Systems_%26_control_engineering/Deterministic_system.

234 Ljubiša Bojić, Olga Zagovora, Asta Zelenkauskaite, Vuk Vuković, Milan Čabarkapa, Selma Veseljević Jerković, and Ana Jovančević, "Comparing Large Language Models and Human Annotators in Latent Content Analysis of Sentiment, Political Leaning, Emotional Intensity and Sarcasm," Scientific Reports 15, no. 1 (April 3, 2025), https://doi.org/10.1038/s41598-025-96508-3; Li Wang, Xi Chen, XiangWen Deng, Hao Wen, MingKe You, WeiZhi Liu, Qi Li, and Jian Li, "Prompt Engineering in Consistency and Reliability With the Evidence-based Guideline for LLMs," npj Digital Medicine 7, no. 1 (February 20, 2024), https://doi.org/10.1038/s41746-024-01029-4.

235 Angel Buendia, "CSV Vs. CSA: What Are the Main Differences?" Scilife, April 9, 2025, https://www.scilife.io/blog/csv-csa-main-differences.

236 Gerry Creaner and Donagh Fitzgerald, "What Is Computer System Validation (CSV)?" GetReskilled, August 2024, https://www.getreskilled.com/what-is-computer-systems-validation-csv.

237 Henning Heyen, Amy Widdicombe, Noah Y. Siegel, Maria Perez-Ortiz, and Philip Treleaven, "The Effect of Model Size on LLM Post-hoc Explainability via LIME," arXiv:2405.05348, May 8, 2024, https://arxiv.org/abs/2405.05348.

238 SHAP, "An introduction to explainable AI with Shapley values," SHAP, https://shap.readthedocs.io/en/latest/example_notebooks/overviews/An%20introduction%20to%20explainable%20AI%20with%20Shapley%20values.html

239 Fazl Barez, Tung-Yu Wu, Iván Arcuschin, Michael Lan, Vincent Wang, Noah Siegel, Nicolas Collignon, Clement Neo, Isabelle Lee, Alasdair Paren, Adel Bibi, Robert Trager, Damiano Fornasiere, Mila John Yan, Yanai Elazar, and Yoshua Bengio Mila, "Chain-of-Thought Is Not Explainability," Oxford Martin AIGI, July 2025.

240 Miles Turpin, Julian Michael, Ethan Perez, Samuel R. Bowman, "Language Models Don't Always Say What They Think: Unfaithful Explanations in Chain-of-Thought Prompting," arXiv:2305.04388, May 7, 2023, https://arxiv.org/abs/2305.04388

241 Robert Booth, "High Court Tells UK Lawyers to Stop Misuse of AI After Fake Case-law Citations," The Guardian, June 6, 2025, https://www.theguardian.com/technology/2025/jun/06/high-court-tells-uk-lawyers-to-urgently-stop-misuse-of-ai-in-legal-work.

242 Raksha Sharma, "AI Plagiarism Detection Market Research Report 2033," Growth Market Reports, August 29, 2025, https://growthmarketreports.com/report/ai-plagiarism-detection-market.

243 Shalwa, "AI Plagiarism Statistics 2025: Transforming Academic Integrity," ARTSMART AI, February 23, 2025, https://artsmart.ai/blog/ai-plagiarism-statistics.

244 Michael Goodier, "Revealed: Thousands of UK University Students Caught Cheating Using AI," The Guardian, September 15, 2025, https://www.theguardian.com/

education/2025/jun/15/thousands-of-uk-university-students-caught-cheating-using-ai-artificial-intelligence-survey.

245 Federal Trade Commission, "FTC Order Requires Workado to Back up Artificial Intelligence Detection Claims," Federal Trade Commission, April 28, 2025, https://www.ftc.gov/news-events/news/press-releases/2025/04/ftc-order-requires-workado-back-artificial-intelligence-detection-claims.

246 Emily Barnes, "Do AI Plagiarism Detectors Work? Here's What the Research Says," VKTR.com, May 14, 2025, https://www.vktr.com/ai-ethics-law-risk/do-ai-plagiarism-detectors-work-heres-what-the-research-says.

247 Chandra Steele, "Can You Spot AI-Generated Images? Take Our Quiz to Test Your Skills," PCMag UK, February 10, 2025, https://uk.pcmag.com/ai/148429/how-to-detect-ai-created-images.

248 Andy Hayler, "Fake It 'Til You Make It – AI Deepfakes," The Information Difference, September 2, 2025, https://www.informationdifference.com/fake-it-til-you-make-it-ai-deepfakes.

249 Sarah Shaffi, "'It's The Opposite of Art': Why Illustrators Are Furious About AI," The Guardian, January 23, 2023, https://www.theguardian.com/artanddesign/2023/jan/23/its-the-opposite-of-art-why-illustrators-are-furious-about-ai.

250 Andy Hayler, "Silicon Dragon – the Rise of AI in China," The Information Difference, August 26, 2025, https://www.informationdifference.com/silicon-dragon-the-rise-of-ai-in-china.

251 Digital Watch Observatory, "AI-generated Media Must Now Carry Labels in China," Digital Watch Observatory, September 2, 2025, https://dig.watch/updates/ai-generated-media-must-now-carry-labels-in-china.

252 Lev Craig, "AI Watermarking," Search Enterprise AI, October 31, 2023, https://www.techtarget.com/searchenterpriseai/definition/AI-watermarking.

253 Melissa Heikkilä, "It's Easy To Tamper With Watermarks From AI-generated Text," MIT Technology Review, March 29, 2024, https://www.technologyreview.com/2024/03/29/1090310/its-easy-to-tamper-with-watermarks-from-ai-generated-text.

254 Arwa Mahdawi, "AI-generated 'Slop' Is Slowly Killing the Internet, so Why Is Nobody Trying to Stop It?" The Guardian, January 8, 2025, https://www.theguardian.com/global/commentisfree/2025/jan/08/ai-generated-slop-slowly-killing-internet-nobody-trying-to-stop-it.

255 Andy Hayler, "Feeding the Ravenous AI Beast," The Information Difference, August 11, 2025, https://www.informationdifference.com/feeding-the-beast.

256 Sean Ross, "Financial Services: Sizing the Sector in the Global Economy," Investopedia, August 15, 2024, https://www.investopedia.com/ask/answers/030515/what-percentage-global-economy-comprised-financial-services-sector.asp.

257 Elyse Cuttler, "Inside the algorithm: How gen AI and graph technology are cracking down on card sharks," Mastercard, July 18, 2024, https://www.mastercard.com/news/perspectives/2024/inside-the-algorithm-how-gen-ai-and-graph-technology-are-cracking-down-on-card-sharks/

258 Cem Dilmegani and Sena Sezer, "Top 25 Generative AI Finance Use Cases & Case Studies," AIMultiple, September 30, 2025, https://research.aimultiple.com/generative-ai-finance.

259 Pham The Anh, "[AI & Algorithmic Trading] High-Frequency Trading (HFT): The Lightning-Fast World of Algorithmic Trading," Where AI And Quant Meet Funny—Humor, July 27, 2024, https://medium.com/funny-ai-quant/high-frequency-trading-hft-the-lightning-fast-world-of-algorithmic-trading-7512c825d9b3

260 Tim Parker, "Has High Frequency Trading Ruined the Stock Market for the Rest of Us?" Investopedia, September 18, 2022, https://www.investopedia.com/financial-edge/0113/has-high-frequency-trading-ruined-the-stock-market-for-the-rest-of-us.aspx.

261 CFI Team, "2010 Flash Crash: The Stock Market Crash of March 6, 2010," Corporate Finance Institute, https://corporatefinanceinstitute.com/resources/equities/2010-flash-crash.

262 "Stripe" (home page), n.d., https://stripe.com/en-fr.

263 "Tencent" (home page), n.d., https://www.tencent.com/en-us/business.html.

264 "Revolut" (home page), n.d., https://www.revolut.com.

265 "Chime" (home page), n.d., https://app.chime.com/login.

266 "Ant Group" (home page), n.d., https://www.antgroup.com/en.

267 Kep Lee, "The Real Cost of Fraud for Financial Institutions Explained," Abrigo, July 24, 2025, https://www.abrigo.com/blog/blog-the-true-cost-of-fraud.

268 Yanya Ruan and József Mezei, "When Do AI Chatbots Lead to Higher Customer Satisfaction Than Human Frontline Employees in Online Shopping Assistance? Considering Product Attribute Type," Journal of Retailing and Consumer Services 68 (June 25, 2022): 103059, https://doi.org/10.1016/j.jretconser.2022.103059.

269 Chrystal R. China and Michael Goodwin, "What is COBOL?" IBM, https://www.ibm.com/think/topics/cobol.

270 Bos Communications, "8 Most Popular Programming Languages Used in Banking/Finance," BOS Fintech, January 23, 2023, https://bosfintech.com/8-most-popular-programming-languages-used-in-banking-finance.

271 Andy Hayler, "Finding the Goldilocks Zone for AI-Generated Code," The Information Difference, August 12, 2025, https://www.informationdifference.com/ai-generated-code.

272 The Economist writers, "How AI-powered hackers are stealing billions," The Economist, August 19, 2025, https://www.economist.com/business/2025/08/19/how-ai-powered-hackers-are-stealing-billions.

273 Charlie Lewis, Ida Kristensen, and Jeffrey Caso with Julian Fuchs, "AI is the greatest threat—and defense—in cybersecurity today. Here's why," McKinsey, May 15, 2025, https://www.mckinsey.com/about-us/new-at-mckinsey-blog/ai-is-the-greatest-threat-and-defense-in-cybersecurity-today.

274 Spencer Wang, "Bias in Code: Algorithm Discrimination in Financial Systems," Robert F. Kennedy Human Rights, January 28, 2025, https://rfkhumanrights.org/our-voices/bias-in-code-algorithm-discrimination-in-financial-systems.

275 Robert Bartlett, Adair Morse, Richard Stanton, and Nancy Wallace, "Consumer-lending discrimination in the FinTech Era," Journal of Financial Economics 143, no. 1 (January 2022): 30–56, https://www.sciencedirect.com/science/article/abs/pii/S0304405X21002403.

276 European Parliament Think Tank, "Algorithmic Discrimination Under the AI Act and the GDPR," European Parliament Think Tank, February 26, 2025, https://www.europarl.europa.eu/thinktank/en/document/EPRS_ATA(2025)769509.

277 Andy Hayler, "Thinking Outside the Bot," The Information Difference, August 14, 2025, https://www.informationdifference.com/thinking-outside-the-bot.

278 Andy Hayler, "Feeding the Ravenous AI Beast," The Information Difference, August 11, 2025, https://www.informationdifference.com/feeding-the-beast.

279 Lucas Hasler, "The Complete Guide to Lottery in Lichtenstein," Lott, https://www.lott.li/en.

280 Statista, "Gambling – Worldwide," Statista, https://www.statista.com/outlook/amo/gambling/worldwide

281 Grand View Research, "Online Gambling Market (2025 - 2030)," Grand View Research, n.d., https://www.grandviewresearch.com/industry-analysis/online-gambling-market.

282 "Gambling Statistics", Bet Victor, https://www.betvictor.com/blog/gambling-statistics.

283 Drishya, "The Biggest Gambling Countries in the World in 2025," KYC Hub, September 9, 2025, https://www.kychub.com/blog/biggest-gambling-countries-in-the-world.

284 Carson, "The Role of AI in Detecting Cheating and Collusion in Online Poker Games," The Future of Things, November 25, 2024, https://thefutureofthings.com/23725-the-role-of-ai-in-detecting-cheating-and-collusion-in-online-poker-games.

285 Charles Rettmuller, "PokerStars PLO Bot Ring Under Investigation," PokerTube, n.d., https://www.pokertube.com/article/458-pokerstars-plo-bot-ring-under-investigation.

286 “Applications of AI in the Gambling Industry,” Bird & Bird, 2004, https://www.twobirds.com/en/insights/2024/uk/applications-of-ai-in-the-gambling-industry.

287 Elle Todd, Casey H. Yang, and Sam Hill, “Gambling | Entertainment and Media Guide to AI | Perspectives,” Reed Smith LLP, February 5, 2024, https://www.reedsmith.com/en/perspectives/ai-in-entertainment-and-media/2024/02/gambling.

288 Ibid.

289 “The Rise of AI and VR in the Best New Online Casinos,” Graphisoft Hong Kong, n.d., https://www.graphisoft.com/hk/the-rise-of-ai-and-vr-in-the-best-new-online-casinos.

290 “Leveraging Virtual Reality for Immersive Casino Gaming Experiences,” Smartico, n.d., https://www.smartico.ai/blog-post/virtual-reality-immersive-casino-gaming-experiences

291 The Royal Swedish Academy of Sciences, “Press release: Nobel Prize in Chemistry 2024,” NobelPrize.org, October 9, 2024, https://www.nobelprize.org/prizes/chemistry/2024/press-release.

292 Dave Bergmann, “What is deep learning?” IBM, n.d., https://www.ibm.com/think/topics/deep-learning.

293 Wikipedia contributors, “AlphaFold,” Wikipedia, Last updated November 3, 2025, https://en.wikipedia.org/wiki/AlphaFold.

294 EMBL-EBI, “What is the protein folding problem?” EMBL-EBI, n.d., https://www.ebi.ac.uk/training/online/courses/alphafold/an-introductory-guide-to-its-strengths-and-limitations/what-is-the-protein-folding-problem/

295 Embl-Ebi, “What is AlphaFold?” EMBL-EBI, n.d., https://www.ebi.ac.uk/training/online/courses/alphafold/an-introductory-guide-to-its-strengths-and-limitations/what-is-alphafold.

296 Samuel Hume, “AI May Help Us Cure Countless Diseases – and Usher in a New Golden Age of Medicine,” The Guardian, March 28, 2025, https://www.theguardian.com/commentisfree/ng-interactive/2025/mar/28/ai-alphafold-biology-protein-structure; John Jumper, Richard Evans, Alexander Pritzel, Tim Green, Michael Figurnov, Olaf Ronneberger, Kathryn Tunyasuvunakool, et al., “Highly Accurate Protein Structure Prediction With AlphaFold,” Nature 596, no. 7873 (July 15, 2021): 583–89, https://doi.org/10.1038/s41586-021-03819-2.

297 James Gallagher, “AI Designs New Superbug-killing Antibiotics for Gonorrhoea and MRSA,” BBC News, August 14, 2025, https://www.bbc.co.uk/news/articles/cgr94xxye2lo.

298 NHS, “Antibiotic Resistance,” nhs.uk, November 18, 2022, https://www.nhs.uk/medicines/antibiotics/antibiotic-antimicrobial-resistance.

299 NHS, “MRSA,” nhs.uk, Last reviewed May 19, 2023, https://www.nhs.uk/conditions/mrsa.

300 Derek Lowe, "AI Drugs So Far," Science, May 13, 2024, https://www.science.org/content/blog-post/ai-drugs-so-far.

301 Cancer Research UK, "Phases of Clinical Trials," Cancer Research UK, Last reviewed May 26, 2025, https://www.cancerresearchuk.org/about-cancer/find-a-clinical-trial/what-clinical-trials-are/phases-of-clinical-trials.

302 Statista, "Average Length of a Clinical Trial Cycle 2020-2024," Statista, May 2, 2025, https://www.statista.com/statistics/1419920/biopharma-clinical-trial-cycle-time.

303 Matthew Hutson, "How AI Is Being Used to Accelerate Clinical Trials," Nature 627, no. 8003 (March 13, 2024): S2–5, https://doi.org/10.1038/d41586-024-00753-x.

304 Andrew Mulcahy, Stephanie Rennane, Daniel Schwam, Reid Dickerson, Lawrence Baker, and Kanaka Shetty, "Use of Clinical Trial Characteristics to Estimate Costs of New Drug Development," JAMA Network Open 8, no. 1 (2025):e2453275. doi:10.1001/jamanetworkopen.2024.53275

305 Eungdo Kim, Jaehoon Yang, Sungjin Park, and Kwangsoo Shin, "Factors Affecting Success of New Drug Clinical Trials," Therapeutic Innovation & Regulatory Science 57, no. 4 (May 11, 2023): 737–50, https://doi.org/10.1007/s43441-023-00509-1.

306 Preston Fore, "Microsoft Researchers Have Revealed the 40 Jobs Most Exposed to AI—and Even Teachers Make the List," Fortune, July 31, 2025, https://fortune.com/2025/07/31/microsoft-research-generative-ai-occupational-impact-jobs-most-and-least-likely-to-impact-teaching-office-jobs-college-gen-z-grads.

307 Martin Reed, "SoA Survey Reveals a Third of Translators and Quarter of Illustrators Losing Work to AI," The Society of Authors, April 11, 2024, https://societyofauthors.org/2024/04/11/soa-survey-reveals-a-third-of-translators-and-quarter-of-illustrators-losing-work-to-ai.

308 Charis McGowan, "'One Day I Overheard My Boss Saying: Just Put It in ChatGPT': The Workers Who Lost Their Jobs to AI," The Guardian, May 31, 2025, https://www.theguardian.com/technology/2025/may/31/the-workers-who-lost-their-jobs-to-ai-chatgpt.

309 Regan Morris, "AI Helped Cause Hollywood Strikes. Now It's in Oscar-winning Films," BBC News, March 31, 2025, https://www.bbc.com/news/articles/ce303x19dwgo.

310 Mark Sweney, "The 'Death of Creativity'? AI Job Fears Stalk Advertising Industry," The Guardian, June 9, 2025, https://www.theguardian.com/technology/2025/jun/09/ai-advertising-industry-google-facebook-meta-ads.

311 LLLLITL, "Coca-Cola - Secret Santa (AI-Generated Christmas Ad 2024)," YouTube, November 15, 2024, https://www.youtube.com/watch?v=lQWUKWM2JrQ.

312 Zoe Kleinman, "How an AI-written Book Shows Why the Tech 'terrifies' Creatives," BBC News, January 31, 2025, https://www.bbc.com/news/articles/cp8k5gezykyo.

313 Dan Milmo, "Mushroom Pickers Urged to Avoid Foraging Books on Amazon That Appear to Be Written by AI," The Guardian, September 2, 2023, https://www.theguardian.com/technology/2023/sep/01/mushroom-pickers-urged-to-avoid-foraging-books-on-amazon-that-appear-to-be-written-by-ai.

314 Anthony Cuthbertson, "Hundreds of AI-written Books Flood Amazon," The Independent, February 22, 2023, https://www.independent.co.uk/tech/ai-author-books-amazon-chatgpt-b2287111.html.

315 Ella Creamer, "Amazon Removes Books 'Generated by AI' for Sale Under Author's Name," The Guardian, August 9, 2023, https://www.theguardian.com/books/2023/aug/09/amazon-removes-books-generated-by-ai-for-sale-under-authors-name.

316 Robert Booth, "High Court Tells UK Lawyers to Stop Misuse of AI After Fake Case-law Citations," The Guardian, June 6, 2025, https://www.theguardian.com/technology/2025/jun/06/high-court-tells-uk-lawyers-to-urgently-stop-misuse-of-ai-in-legal-work.

317 Dan Milmo, "UK Engineering Firm Arup Falls Victim to £20m Deepfake Scam," The Guardian, May 17, 2024, https://www.theguardian.com/technology/article/2024/may/17/uk-engineering-arup-deepfake-scam-hong-kong-ai-video.

318 Shraddha Nair, "German Artist Mario Klingemann on His Creation 'Botto', an NFT Revolution," Stir World, March 10, 2022, https://www.stirworld.com/see-features-german-artist-mario-klingemann-on-his-creation-botto-an-nft-revolution.

319 Theresa M. Weisenberger, Diana C. Milton and Harrison A. Enright, "Case Tracker: Artificial Intelligence, Copyrights and Class Actions," BakerHostetler, n.d., https://www.bakerlaw.com/services/artificial-intelligence-ai/case-tracker-artificial-intelligence-copyrights-and-class-actions.

320 Blake Brittain, "Judge rejects Anthropic bid to appeal copyright ruling, postpone trial," Reuters, August 12, 2025, https://www.reuters.com/legal/litigation/judge-rejects-anthropic-bid-appeal-copyright-ruling-postpone-trial-2025-08-12.

321 Cooley Alert, "Copyright Ownership of Generative AI Outputs Varies Around the World," Cooley, January 29, 2024, https://www.cooley.com/news/insight/2024/2024-01-29-copyright-ownership-of-generative-ai-outputs-varies-around-the-world.

322 Zhengyuan Jiang, Moyang Guo, Yuepeng Hu, and Neil Zhenqiang Gong, "Watermark-based Attribution of AI-Generated Content," arXiv:2404.04254, https://arxiv.org/abs/2404.04254.

323 Joe Wilkins, "OpenAI Usage Plummets in the Summer, When Students Aren't Cheating on Homework," Futurism, August 8, 2025, https://futurism.com/openai-use-cheating-homework; Douglas Mark, ""Analysis: Did the Demand for ChatGPT Plunge Because Students Left for Summer Break?", Online Education, n.d., https://www.onlineeducation.com/features/chatgpt-demand-declines-in-the-summer.

324 Alistair Barr, "School's Out for Summer, and If ChatGPT Usage Is Falling Because Students Are Off, That's a Bad Sign for OpenAI," Business Insider, July 14, 2023, https://www.businessinsider.com/chatgpt-usage-falling-students-summer-break-bad-sign-openai-microsoft-2023-7.

325 "Student Generative AI Survey 2025," HEPI, August 27, 2025, https://www.hepi.ac.uk/reports/student-generative-ai-survey-2025.

326 Educate Ventures, "The Beyond the Hype Report," Educate Ventures Research, n.d., https://www.educateventures.com/beyond-the-hype.

327 UNESCO, "UNESCO survey: Less than 10% of schools and universities have formal guidance on AI," UNESCO, June 1, 2023, Last updated September 18, 2024, https://www.unesco.org/en/articles/unesco-survey-less-10-schools-and-universities-have-formal-guidance-ai.

328 Michael Goodier, "Revealed: Thousands of UK University Students Caught Cheating Using AI," The Guardian, September 15, 2025, https://www.theguardian.com/education/2025/jun/15/thousands-of-uk-university-students-caught-cheating-using-ai-artificial-intelligence-survey.

329 Aviva Legatt, "Students Are Already Using AI. Are Colleges Teaching AI Literacy?" Forbes, June 11, 2025, https://www.forbes.com/sites/avivalegatt/2025/06/11/students-are-already-using-ai-are-colleges-teaching-ai-literacy.

330 FT Team, "How AI-powered tools are enhancing personalised learning for students," Financial Times, n.d., https://www.ft.com/partnercontent/isp/how-ai-powered-tools-are-enhancing-personalised-learning-for-students.html

331 Kristjan-Julius Laak and Jaan Aru, "AI and personalized learning: bridging the gap with modern educational goals," arXiv:2404.02798v2, March 21, 2025, https://arxiv.org/html/2404.02798v2.

332 Hazel Shearing, "Teachers Can Use AI to Save Time on Marking, New Guidance Says," BBC News, June 10, 2025, https://www.bbc.com/news/articles/c1kvyj7dkp0o.

333 "Plagiarism Checker Software Market Size, Forecast to 2033," Business Research Insights, n.d., https://www.businessresearchinsights.com/market-reports/plagiarism-checker-software-market-115791.

334 Michaela G. Murdock and Aditya Tadinada, "Can AI Tools Reliably and Effectively Detect Plagiarism in Scientific Writing?" Cureus 17, no. 1 (May 11, 2025), https://doi.org/10.7759/cureus.83924.

335 Adam Rowe, "Yet Another Study Finds That AI Is Making Us Dumb," Tech.co, June 17, 2025, https://tech.co/news/another-study-ai-making-us-dumb.

336 Michael Gerlich, "AI Tools in Society: Impacts on Cognitive Offloading and the Future of Critical Thinking," SSRN (January 3, 2025). http://dx.doi.org/10.2139/ssrn.5082524.

337 Silvia García-Méndez, Francisco De Arriba-Pérez, and María Del Carmen Somoza-López, "A Review on the Use of Large Language Models as Virtual Tutors," Science & Education 34 (2025): 877–892. https://doi.org/10.1007/s11191-024-00530-2.

338 "Khanmigo for Learners: Always-available Tutor, Powered by AI," Khanmigo, n.d., https://www.khanmigo.ai/learners.

339 Monica Earle, "Duolingo Introduces AI-Powered Innovations at Duocon 2024," Duolingo, September 2024, https://investors.duolingo.com/news-releases/news-release-details/duolingo-introduces-ai-powered-innovations-duocon-2024.

340 Rose Luckin, "Yes, AI Could Profoundly Disrupt Education. But Maybe That's Not a Bad Thing," The Guardian, June 4, 2025, https://www.theguardian.com/commentisfree/2023/jul/14/ai-artificial-intelligence-disrupt-education-creativity-critical-thinking.

341 Andy Hayler, "When Algorithms Dream: AI Hallucinations in Depth," The Information Difference, August 19, 2025, https://www.informationdifference.com/when-algorithms-dream-ai-hallucinations-in-depth.

342 R.A. Miller, "A History of the INTERNIST-1 and Quick Medical Reference (QMR) Computer-Assisted Diagnosis Projects, with Lessons Learned," Yearbook of Medical Informatics (2009): 121–36, https://www.thieme-connect.com/products/ejournals/pdf/10.1055/s-0038-1638702.pdf?OR=Word

343 "Using decision support to help explain clinical manifestations of disease," DXplain, The Laboratory of Computer Science, n.d., https://www.mghlcs.org/projects/dxplain.

344 Reed T. Sutton, David Pincock, Daniel C. Baumgart, Daniel C. Sadowski, Richard N. Fedorak, and Karen I. Kroeker, "An overview of clinical decision support systems: benefits, risks, and strategies for success," NPJ Digital Medicine 3, (2020): 17.

345 Henrico Dolfing, "Case Study 20: The $4 Billion AI Failure of IBM Watson for Oncology," Henrico Dolfing, December 7, 2024, https://www.henricodolfing.com/2024/12/case-study-ibm-watson-for-oncology-failure.html.

346 Andrew Wong, Erkin Otles, John P. Donnelly, Andrew Krumm, Jeffrey McCullough, Olivia DeTroyer-Cooley, Justin Pestrue, Marie Phillips, Judy Konye, Carleen Penoza, Muhammad Ghous, Karandeep Singh, "External Validation of a Widely Implemented Proprietary Sepsis Prediction Model in Hospitalized Patients," JAMA Intern Med. 181, no. 8 (2021): 1065–1070, doi:10.1001/jamainternmed.2021.2626

347 Derek Smith, "Widely used AI tool for early sepsis detection may be cribbing doctors' suspicions," UMich News, February 15, 2024, https://news.umich.edu/widely-used-ai-tool-for-early-sepsis-detection-may-be-cribbing-doctors-suspicions.

348 European Commission, "Artificial Intelligence in Healthcare," European Commission, n.d., https://health.ec.europa.eu/ehealth-digital-health-and-care/artificial-intelligence-healthcare_en.

349 Mingyang Chen, Yuting Wang, Qiankun Wang, Jingyi Shi, Huike Wang, Zichen Ye, Peng Xue, and Youlin Qiao, "Impact of Human and Artificial Intelligence Collaboration on Workload Reduction in Medical Image Interpretation," NPJ Digital Medicine 7, no. 1 (November 30, 2024), https://doi.org/10.1038/s41746-024-01328-w.

350 Jonathan Govette, "Why AI in Healthcare Has Failed in 2024," Oatmeal Health, December 14, 2024, https://oatmealhealth.com/why-has-ai-failed-so-far-in-healthcare-despite-billions-of-investment.

351 FunctionalMind, "FunctionalMindTM – AI Tool for Functional & Integrative Medicine Clinicians," FunctionalMind, n.d., https://go.functionalmind.ai/home.

352 Andy Hayler, "The Elephant in the Room – AI Image Generation," The Information Difference, July 8, 2025. https://www.informationdifference.com/elephant-ai-image-generation.

353 Robert Booth, "High Court Tells UK Lawyers to Stop Misuse of AI After Fake Case-law Citations," The Guardian, June 6, 2025, https://www.theguardian.com/technology/2025/jun/06/high-court-tells-uk-lawyers-to-urgently-stop-misuse-of-ai-in-legal-work; Sam Tobin, "Lawyers face sanctions for citing fake cases with AI, warns UK judge," Reuters, June 6, 2025, https://www.reuters.com/world/uk/lawyers-face-sanctions-citing-fake-cases-with-ai-warns-uk-judge-2025-06-06/

354 "AlphaFold," Google DeepMind, n.d., https://deepmind.google/science/alphafold.

355 John Jumper, Richard Evans, Alexander Pritzel, Tim Green, Michael Figurnov, Olaf Ronneberger, Kathryn Tunyasuvunakool, Russ Bates, Augustin Žídek, Anna Potapenko et al., "Highly accurate protein structure prediction with AlphaFold," Nature 596 (2021): 583–589, https://doi.org/10.1038/s41586-021-03819-2.

356 Bing Hu, Ashish Saragadam, Anita Layton, and Helen Chen, "Synthetic Data from Diffusion Models Improve Drug Discovery Prediction," arXiv:2405.03799, May 6, 2024, https://arxiv.org/abs/2405.03799.

357 Derek Lowe, "AI Drugs So Far," Science, May 13, 2024, https://www.science.org/content/blog-post/ai-drugs-so-far; Drug Target Review, "First AI-designed Drug, Rentosertib, Officially Named by USAN," Drug Target Review, March 14, 2025, https://www.drugtargetreview.com/news/157365/first-ai-designed-drug-rentosertib-named-by-usan.

358 Ashwin Telang, "Artificial Intelligence at Merck – Two Use Cases," Emerj, February 10, 2025, https://emerj.com/artificial-intelligence-at-merck.

359 Philip Ball, "The Dangers of So-called AI Experts Believing Their Own Hype," New Scientist, July 2, 2025, https://www.newscientist.com/article/mg26635500-100-the-dangers-of-so-called-ai-experts-believing-their-own-hype.

360 Ben Rand, "When AI Chatbots Help People Act More Human," Harvard Business School, May 27, 2025, https://www.library.hbs.edu/working-knowledge/when-ai-chatbots-help-people-be-more-human.

361 David Batty, "'She Helps Cheer Me Up: The People Forming Relationships With AI Chatbots," The Guardian, April 15, 2025, https://www.theguardian.com/technology/2025/apr/15/she-helps-cheer-me-up-the-people-forming-relationships-with-ai-chatbots.

362 "Replika" (home page), n.d., https://replika.com/?srsltid=AfmBOoq7_e8-RJry4nfOO-zxgmCbIewStyCQQRaoE_5ORL57gs1NT1RG.

363 "My Anima" (home page), n.d., https://myanima.ai.

364 "Nomi" (home page), n.d., https://nomi.ai.

365 "Kindroid" (home page), n.d., https://landing.kindroid.ai.

366 Helmholtz Munich, "AI That Thinks Like Us: New Model Predicts Human Decisions With Startling Accuracy," Scitech Daily, July 6, 2025, https://scitechdaily.com/ai-that-thinks-like-us-new-model-predicts-human-decisions-with-startling-accuracy.

367 Marcel Binz, Elif Akata, Matthias Bethge, Franziska Brändle, Fred Callaway, Julian Coda-Forno, Peter Dayan, Can Demircan, Maria K. Eckstein, Noémi Éltető, Thomas L. Griffiths, Susanne Haridi, Akshay K. Jagadish, Li Ji-An, Alexander Kipnis, Sreejan Kumar, et al., "A foundation model to predict and capture human cognition," Nature 644 (2025): 1002–1009. https://doi.org/10.1038/s41586-025-09215-4.

368 Nigel Mulligan, "Ghostbots: AI versions of deceased loved ones could be a serious threat to mental health," The Conversation, March 14, 2024, https://theconversation.com/ghostbots-ai-versions-of-deceased-loved-ones-could-be-a-serious-threat-to-mental-health-224984.

369 Alexander Mafi, "The Risks and Benefits of AI Therapy Tools," BMJ 389 (May 8, 2025): r821, https://doi.org/10.1136/bmj.r821.

370 Matthew Smith, "What Do Britons Think AI Chatbots Are Good At?" YouGov, April 24, 2025, https://yougov.co.uk/technology/articles/52062-what-do-britons-think-ai-chatbots-are-good-at.

371 Susie Alegre, "Need for Regulation Is Urgent as AI Chatbots Are Being Rolled Out to Support Mental Health," Centre for International Governance Innovation, July 18, 2025, https://www.cigionline.org/articles/need-for-regulation-is-urgent-as-ai-chatbots-are-being-rolled-out-to-support-mental-health.

372 Staff Writer, "NEDA Suspends AI Chatbot for Giving Harmful Eating Disorder Advice," Psychiatrist.com, June 5, 2023, https://www.psychiatrist.com/news/neda-suspends-ai-chatbot-for-giving-harmful-eating-disorder-advice.

373 Craig S. Smith, "How Bad Traits Can Spread Unseen in AI," Forbes, July 25, 2025, https://www.forbes.com/sites/craigsmith/2025/07/25/how-bad-traits-can-spread-unseen-in-ai.

374 Chloe Xiang and Chloe Xiang, "'He Would Still Be Here': Man Dies by Suicide After Talking With AI Chatbot, Widow Says," VICE, July 27, 2024, https://www.vice.com/en/article/man-dies-by-suicide-after-talking-with-ai-chatbot-widow-says.

375 The University of Cambridge Communications team, "AI Chatbots Have Shown They Have an 'Empathy Gap' That Children Are," The University of Cambridge, July 15, 2024, https://www.cam.ac.uk/research/news/ai-chatbots-have-shown-they-have-an-empathy-gap-that-children-are-likely-to-miss.

376 Rachel Gardner, "The Robots Assessing Children's Mental Wellbeing," The University of Cambridge, Department of Computer Science and Technology, September 1, 2022, https://www.cst.cam.ac.uk/news/robots-assessing-childrens-mental-wellbeing.

377 Bernard D. Beitman MD, "AI Chatbots May Mirror Narcissism—clinical Insights and Research Converge," Psychology Today, April 21, 2025, https://www.psychologytoday.com/gb/blog/connecting-with-coincidence/202504/are-chatbots-too-certain-and-too-nice.

378 Linn Freedman, "Illinois Enacts Act Prohibiting AI Therapy," JD Supra, August 11, 2025, https://www.jdsupra.com/legalnews/illinois-enacts-act-prohibiting-ai-9166547/

379 Susie Alegre, "Need for Regulation Is Urgent as AI Chatbots Are Being Rolled Out to Support Mental Health," Centre for International Governance Innovation, July 18, 2025, https://www.cigionline.org/articles/need-for-regulation-is-urgent-as-ai-chatbots-are-being-rolled-out-to-support-mental-health.

380 Stuart D. Levi, Pramode Chiruvolu, Mana Ghaemmaghami, and Shannon N. Morgan, "Fair Use and AI Training: Two Recent Decisions Highlight the Complexity of This Issue," Skadden, Arps, Slate, Meagher & Flom LLP, July 8, 2025, https://www.skadden.com/insights/publications/2025/07/fair-use-and-ai-training.

381 World Intellectual Property Organization, "Berne Convention for the Protection of Literary and Artistic Works (as amended on September 28, 1979), TRT/BERNE/001," World Intellectual Property Organization, n.d., https://www.wipo.int/wipolex/en/text/283698.

382 Ashley Belanger, "AI Industry Horrified to Face Largest Copyright Class Action Ever Certified," Ars Technica, August 8, 2025, https://arstechnica.com/tech-policy/2025/08/ai-industry-horrified-to-face-largest-copyright-class-action-ever-certified.

383 Andy Hayler, "AI's Copyright Crossroads – Anthropic Settles Landmark Lawsuit," The Information Difference, August 28, 2025, https://www.informationdifference.com/ais-copyright-crossroads-anthropic-settles-landmark-lawsuit.

384 Damien Charlotin, "AI Hallucination Cases Database," Artificial Authority, n.d., https://www.damiencharlotin.com/hallucinations/?ref=nucleo.jor.br&page=2&page=3&page=4&page=5.

385 Jeremy Hsu, "AI Hallucinations Are Getting Worse – and They're Here to Stay," New Scientist, May 9, 2025, https://www.newscientist.com/article/2479545-ai-hallucinations-are-getting-worse-and-theyre-here-to-stay.

386 Tom Whittaker, "A Cautionary Tale of Using AI in Law; UK Case Finds That AI Generated Fake Case Law Citations," Burges Salmon, December 10, 2023, https://www.burges-salmon.com/articles/102ivgu/a-cautionary-tale-of-using-ai-in-law-uk-case-finds-that-ai-generated-fake-case-l.

387 Nick Henderson, "AI Hallucinations Crisis: Over 50 Fake Cases Cited in July Alone," VinciWorks, August 3, 2025, https://vinciworks.com/blog/ai-hallucinations-crisis-over-50-fake-cases-cited-in-july-alone.

388 Robert Booth, "High Court Tells UK Lawyers to Stop Misuse of AI After Fake Case-law Citations," The Guardian, June 6, 2025, https://www.theguardian.com/technology/2025/jun/06/high-court-tells-uk-lawyers-to-urgently-stop-misuse-of-ai-in-legal-work.

389 Sara Merken, "New York lawyers sanctioned for using fake ChatGPT cases in legal brief," Reuters, June 26, 2023, https://www.reuters.com/legal/new-york-lawyers-sanctioned-using-fake-chatgpt-cases-legal-brief-2023-06-22.

390 Lexis Nexis, "Fast Law: Why Speed Is the Priority for Lawyers Using AI," Lexis Nexis, https://www.lexisnexis.co.uk/insights/fast-law-why-speed-is-the-priority-for-lawyers-using-ai/index.html.

391 "Global AI Law and Policy Tracker," IAPP, May 1, 2025, https://iapp.org/resources/article/global-ai-legislation-tracker.

392 AIPRM, "AI Laws Around the World," AIPRM, n.d., https://www.aiprm.com/en-gb/ai-laws-around-the-world.

393 Netflix, "Machine Learning," Netflix, n.d., https://research.netflix.com/research-area/machine-learning

394 Talo - Real-Time AI Translation for Video-Calls, "Talo Presentation Mode Demo – Real-Time Translation for Webinars," YouTube, June 23, 2025, https://www.youtube.com/watch?v=M1l4LJBdHHk.

395 Arjun Mahajan, Kimia Heydari, and Dylan Powell, "Wearable AI to enhance patient safety and clinical decision-making," npj Digital Medicine 8, no. 176 (2025). https://doi.org/10.1038/s41746-025-01554-w

396 Stefano Canali, Viola Schiaffonati, and Andrea Aliverti, "Challenges and Recommendations for Wearable Devices in Digital Health: Data Quality,

Interoperability, Health Equity, Fairness," PLOS Digital Health 1, no. 10 (October 13, 2022): e0000104, https://doi.org/10.1371/journal.pdig.0000104.

397 Jill McKeon, "61M Fitbit, Apple Users Had Data Exposed in Wearable Device Data Breach," TechTarget, September 16, 2021, https://www.techtarget.com/healthtechsecurity/news/366594948/61M-Fitbit-Apple-Users-Had-Data-Exposed-in-Wearable-Device-Data-Breach.

398 Contentsquare, "4 Sentiment Analysis Examples to Help You Improve CX," Contentsquare, August 12, 2024, https://contentsquare.com/guides/sentiment-analysis/examples.

399 Dean Elphick, "Hotel Dynamic Pricing: Definition, Examples, and Best Software to Use," SiteMinder, June 25, 2025, https://www.siteminder.com/r/hotel-dynamic-pricing.

400 Gamze Tuncay, Kıymet Kaya, Yaren Yılmaz, Yusuf Yaslan, and Şule Gündüz Öğüdücü, "A Reinforcement Learning Based Dynamic Room Pricing Model for Hotel Industry," INFOR: Information Systems and Operational Research 62, no. 2 (2023): 211–31. https://doi.org/10.1080/03155986.2023.2235223

401 BBC News, "Travel Site Orbitz Offers Mac Users More Costly Hotels," BBC News, June 26, 2012, https://www.bbc.co.uk/news/technology-18595347.

402 Kiran Gange, "Leveraging Artificial Intelligence in Pricing," Pricing Society, February 13, 2025, https://www.pricingsociety.com/post/leveraging-artificial-intelligence-in-pricing.

403 Alina Sayapov, "The Future of Assortment Planning: AI-Driven Predictive Analytics," Retalon, August 15, 2025, https://retalon.com/blog/ai-driven-assortment-planning.

404 Yanya Ruan and József Mezei, "When do AI chatbots lead to higher customer satisfaction than human frontline employees in online shopping assistance? Considering product attribute type," Journal of Retailing and Consumer Services 68 (2022): 103059, https://doi.org/10.1016/j.jretconser.2022.103059.

405 Avinash Chandra Das, "The next frontier of customer engagement: AI-enabled customer service," McKinsey & Company, March 27, 2023, https://www.mckinsey.com/capabilities/operations/our-insights/the-next-frontier-of-customer-engagement-ai-enabled-customer-service

406 Maria Yagoda, "Airline Held Liable for Its Chatbot Giving Passenger Bad Advice - What This Means for Travellers," BBC News, February 23, 2024, https://www.bbc.com/travel/article/20240222-air-canada-chatbot-misinformation-what-travellers-should-know.

407 Gene Marks, "Business Tech News: Klarna Reverses on AI, Says Customers Like Talking to People," Forbes, May 18, 2025, https://www.forbes.com/sites/

quickerbettertech/2025/05/18/business-tech-news-klarna-reverses-on-ai-says-customers-like-talking-to-people.

408 Charlie Mitchell, "A Customer Service AI Agent Spits Out Complete Salesforce Records in an Attack by Security Researchers," CX Today, August 18, 2025, https://www.cxtoday.com/crm/a-customer-service-ai-agent-spits-out-complete-salesforce-records-in-an-attack-by-security-researchers; Tamir Ishay Sharbat, "AgentFlayer: When AIjacking Leads to Full Data Exfiltration in Copilot Studio," Zenity Labs, July 7, 2025, https://labs.zenity.io/p/a-copilot-studio-story-2-when-aijacking-leads-to-full-data-exfiltration-bc4a.

409 Lyndon Bell, "Visual Search in Online Shopping: The Future of Retail in 2025," AdLift, January 29, 2025, https://www.adlift.com/blog/visual-search-in-online-shopping-the-future-of-retail-in-2025.

410 Debarun Chakraborty, Aruna Polisetty, Sowmya G, Nripendra P. Rana, and Sangeeta Khorana, "Unlocking the Potential of AI: Enhancing Consumer Engagement in the Beauty and Cosmetic Product Purchases," Journal of Retailing and Consumer Services 79 (April 5, 2024): 103842, https://doi.org/10.1016/j.jretconser.2024.103842.

411 Chanel, "ROUGE ALLURE VELVET LUMINOUS MATTE LIP COLOUR 58 ROUGE VIE 3.5G," Chanel, September 29, 2025, https://www.chanel.com/gb/makeup/virtual-makeup-try-on.

412 Signifyd, "Signifyd | Fraud Protection & Prevention for Ecommerce Retailers," Signifyd, October 23, 2025, https://www.signifyd.com.

413 Andy Hayler, "AI Use Cases – the Good, the Bad and the Ugly," The Information Difference, May 23, 2025, https://www.informationdifference.com/ai-the-good-bad-ugly.

414 International Energy Agency, "The Oil and Gas Industry in Net Zero Transitions: Executive Summary," International Energy Agency, November 23, 2023, https://www.iea.org/reports/the-oil-and-gas-industry-in-net-zero-transitions/executive-summary.

415 Britannica Editors, "Seismic Wave | Earth's Interior Structure & Movement," Encyclopedia Britannica, January 12, 2000, https://www.britannica.com/science/seismic-wave.

416 Ryan Williams, "Shaking up the Earth: The AI Revolution in Seismic Interpretation," GeoExpro, January 22, 2024, https://geoexpro.com/shaking-up-the-earth-the-ai-revolution-in-seismic-interpretation.

417 Nwosu Obinnaya Chikezie Victor and Lucky Oghenechodja Daniel, "Automated Seismic Interpretation: Machine Learning Technologies are Being Used to Develop Automated Seismic Interpretation to Identify Geological Features, Such as Faults and Stratigraphic Horizons," International Journal of Artificial Intelligence and Machine Learning 3, no. 2 (2023): 74–98, doi:10.51483/IJAIML.3.2.2023.74-98.

418 Avi Salzman, "AI is Changing Oil Country—and Pumping Up Profits," Barron's, November 26, 2024, https://www.barrons.com/articles/ai-oil-industry-profit-permian-basin-8adcacdd.

419 International Labmate, "Equipment failure 'caused BP Deepwater Horizon spill'," Petrochemical Chemical & Energy, n.d., https://www.petro-online.com/news/fuel-for-thought/13/breaking-news/equipment-failure-caused-bp-deepwater-horizon-spill/30457.

420 "New Detail," Unicorn – Energy Solutions, n.d., https://unicornsystems.eu/energy/news-detail?article=how-artificial-intelligence-is-changing-the-energy-industry&newsArticleId=67ab35c18c1591cc785b5313.

421 Dunn Sheehan, "The 5 Worst Oil Rig Disasters in History," Dunn Sheehan, December 18, 2024, https://www.dunnsheehan.com/news-insights/the-5-worst-oil-rig-disasters-in-history.

422 GlobalData, "AI And Robotics Unlock Sustainable Efficiency in the Oil and Gas Sector," DirectIndustry e-Magazine, July 12, 2024, https://emag.directindustry.com/2024/07/12/ai-and-robotics-unlock-sustainable-efficiency-in-the-oil-and-gas-sector.

423 Guorui Li, Tuck-Whye Wong, Benjamin Shih, Chunyu Guo, Luwen Wang, Jiaqi Liu, Tao Wang, Xiaobo Liu, Jiayao Yan, Baosheng Wu, Fajun Yu, Yunsai Chen, Yiming Liang, Yaoting Xue, Chengjun Wang, Shunping He, Li Wen, Michael T. Tolley, A-Man Zhang, Cecilia Laschi, and Tiefeng Li, "Bioinspired soft robots for deep-sea exploration," Nature Communications 14 (2023): 7097, https://www.nature.com/articles/s41467-023-42882-3; NOAA Ocean Exploration, "What Is an ROV?" NOAA Ocean Exploration, Last updated December 16, 2020, https://oceanexplorer.noaa.gov/ocean-fact/rov.

424 Amit Shukla and Hamad Karki, "Application of robotics in offshore oil and gas industry—A review Part II," Robotics and Autonomous Systems 75, Part B (January 2016): 508–524, https://doi.org/10.1016/j.robot.2015.09.013.

425 Chrystal R. China, "10 ways the oil and gas industry can leverage digital twin technology," IBM, n.d., https://www.ibm.com/think/topics/digital-twin-for-oil-gas.

426 Wang Jiangang, Shi Lei, Feng Ding, Liang Jinli, Hou Lingxia, and Miao Enming, "A digital twin modeling and application for gear rack drilling rigs lifting system," Scientific Reports 14 (2024): 23711. https://doi.org/10.1038/s41598-024-73954-z.

427 Vinicius Kreischer de Almeida, Douglas Ericson de Oliveira, Claudio Daniel T. de Barros, Gabriel dos Santos Scatena, Asdrubal N. Queiroz Filho, Fabio Levy Siqueira, Anna Helena Reali Costa, Edson Satoshi Gomi, Leonardo A. F. Mendoza, Evelyn C. S. Batista, Cristian E. Muñoz, Isabela Guimarães Siqueira, Rodrigo A. Barreira, Ismael H. F. dos Santos, Carlos Cardoso, Eduardo Ogasawara, and Fabio Porto, "A Digital Twin System for Oil And Gas Industry: A Use Case on Mooring Lines Integrity Monitoring,"

MODELS Companion '24: Proceedings of the ACM/IEEE 27th International Conference on Model Driven Engineering Languages and Systems (2024): 322–331, https://dl.acm.org/doi/10.1145/3652620.3688244.

428 Zahid Habib, Phil Spring, Deborah Walker, Yoshihiro Shimada, Satoshi Nagata, Syed Muhammad Ali Razi, Shannon Wilson, and Spencer Lin, Oil and Gas in the AI Era (IBM, 2025), https://www.ibm.com/thought-leadership/institute-business-value/en-us/report/oil-and-gas-in-ai-era.

429 Andy Hayler, "Thinking Outside the Bot," The Information Difference, August 14, 2025, https://www.informationdifference.com/thinking-outside-the-bot.

430 Zahid Habib, Phil Spring, Deborah Walker, Yoshihiro Shimada, Satoshi Nagata, Syed Muhammad Ali Razi, Shannon Wilson, and Spencer Lin, Oil and Gas in the AI Era (IBM, 2025), https://www.ibm.com/thought-leadership/institute-business-value/en-us/report/oil-and-gas-in-ai-era.

431 Ariana Hurtado, "Survey Reveals Biggest Challenge in Implementing AI Technologies in Offshore Oil and Gas Sector," Offshore Magazine, June 5, 2025, https://www.offshore-mag.com/special-reports/article/55295135/survey-reveals-biggest-challenge-in-implementing-ai-technologies-in-offshore-oil-and-gas-sector.

432 Andy Hayler, "Stop AI Becoming a Security Trojan Horse," The Information Difference, June 25, 2025, https://www.informationdifference.com/security-trojan-horse.

433 The Economist team, "The world's most valuable resource is no longer oil, but data," The Economist, May 6, 2017, https://www.economist.com/leaders/2017/05/06/the-worlds-most-valuable-resource-is-no-longer-oil-but-data.

434 Statista, "Mining - Worldwide | Statista Market Forecast," Statista, n.d., https://www.statista.com/outlook/io/mining/worldwide.

435 Statista, "Net Profit Margin of the Top Mining Companies 2002-2025," Statista, 2025, https://www.statista.com/statistics/208725/net-profit-margin-of-the-top-mining-companies.

436 GlobalData, "Case Studies: AI in Mining," Mine, September 30, 2024, https://mine.nridigital.com/mine_oct24/case-studies-ai-mining.

437 https://www.sciencedirect.com/science/article/pii/S2214790X24000388

438 Zoe Corbyn, "Autonomous Vehicles: How Mines Control Driverless Trucks," BBC News, November 8, 2024, https://www.bbc.com/news/articles/cgej7gzg8l0o.

439 Caitlin C. Corrigan and Svetlana A. Ikonnikova, "A review of the use of AI in the mining industry: Insights and ethical considerations for multi-objective optimization," The Extractive Industries and Society 17 (March 2024): 101440, https://www.sciencedirect.com/science/article/pii/S2214790X24000388

440 GlobalData, "Applications of AI in the mining sector," Mine, October 14, 2014, https://mine.nridigital.com/mine_oct24/case-studies-ai-mining.

441 Carly Leonida, "AI: Bringing Mining Companies Closer to Their Data," Engineering and Mining Journal, April 2025, https://www.e-mj.com/features/ai-bringing-mining-companies-closer-to-their-data.

442 BHP, "BHP unveils world-first automated shiploaders," BHP, July 2022, https://www.bhp.com/news/media-centre/releases/2022/06/bhp-unveils-world-first-automated-shiploaders.

443 "Demolition Man (1993)," IMDB.com, https://www.imdb.com/title/tt0106697.

444 Commander JedoMeta, "Total Recall - Johnny Cab," YouTube, August 14, 2016, https://www.youtube.com/watch?v=eWgrvNHjKkY.

445 Wikipedia contributors, "List of Countries by Traffic-related Death Rate," Wikipedia, n.d., https://en.wikipedia.org/wiki/List_of_countries_by_traffic-related_death_rate.

446 Carl Engelking, "The 'Driverless' Car Era Began More Than 90 Years Ago," Discover Magazine, December 13, 2017, https://www.discovermagazine.com/the-driverless-car-era-began-more-than-90-years-ago-1327.

447 "Autonomous 'Self-Driving' Vehicles," Robotics Institute Carnegie Mellon University, 2024, https://www.ri.cmu.edu/autonomous-vehicles.

448 Tobias Nothdurft, Peter Hecker, Sebastian Ohl, Falko Saust, Markus Maurer, Andreas Reschka, and Jurgen Rüdiger Böhmer, "Stadtpilot: First Fully Autonomous Test Drives in Urban Traff," Conference Record - IEEE Conference on Intelligent Transportation Systems (November 2011), https://www.tu-braunschweig.de/fileadmin/Redaktionsgruppen/Institute_Fakultaet_5/IFR/Dateien_EFS/Publikationen/Stadtpilot_FirstFullyAutonomous.pdf

449 Samuel Gibbs, "Driverless Cars to Be Tested in UK," The Guardian, January 1, 2015, https://www.theguardian.com/technology/2015/jan/01/driverless-cars-tested-uk-bristol-coventry-milton-keynes-greenwich.

450 Wikipedia contributors, "List of Tesla Autopilot Crashes," Wikipedia, n.d., https://en.wikipedia.org/wiki/List_of_Tesla_Autopilot_crashes#Williston,_Florida,_USA_(May_7,_2016).

451 "Safety Impact," Waymo, n.d., https://waymo.com/safety/impact.

452 Sarah Edwards, "Self Driving Car Accidents Trend Chart (2025)," ConsumerShield, October 9, 2025, https://www.consumershield.com/articles/self-driving-car-accidents-trends.

453 Nagler, "Standing still," RAC Foundation, June 8, 2021, https://www.racfoundation.org/research/mobility/still-standing-still.

454 Lisa D. Sparks, "Self-driving cars can tap into 'AI-powered social network' to talk to each other while on the road," LiveScience, May 2, 2025, https://www.livescience.com/technology/electric-vehicles/self-driving-cars-can-tap-into-ai-powered-social-network-to-talk-to-each-other-while-on-the-road.

455 "Driving Directions, Live Traffic & Road Conditions Updates," Waze, n.d., https://www.waze.com/en-GB/live-map.

456 Jonas Binding, "The misguided dilemma of the trolley problem: Why you shouldn't worry about autonomous vehicles solving ethics riddles," Volvo, January 22, 2024, https://www.volvoautonomoussolutions.com/en-en/news-and-insights/insights/articles/2024/jan/the-misguided-dilemma-of-the-trolley-problem-.html.

457 David Ingram, "Why Waymo cars became sitting ducks during the L.A. protests," NBC News, June 14, 2025, https://www.nbcnews.com/tech/innovation/waymo-cars-set-fire-sitting-ducks-la-protests-rcna212426.

458 Abené Clayton, "Protesters Develop Novel Way to Build Cone-sensus Against Driverless Cars," The Guardian, July 8, 2023, https://www.theguardian.com/technology/2023/jul/07/san-francisco-autonomous-cars-protest-cone.

459 Majid Ismailzada, "How Many Self-driving Cars Have Crashed," G&M Direct Hire, October 11, 2025, https://gmdirecthire.co.uk/blog/self-driving-cars-crashes.

460 Johannes Deichmann, Autonomous driving's future: Convenient and connected (McKinsey & Company, 2023), https://www.mckinsey.com/industries/automotive-and-assembly/our-insights/autonomous-drivings-future-convenient-and-connected.

461 UK Government, "Automated Vehicles Act 2024," GOV.UK, 2024, https://www.legislation.gov.uk/ukpga/2024/10/contents.

462 "Radioplane OQ-2A Drone," Air Zoo Aerospace & Science Museum, n.d., https://www.airzoo.org/wwii/airplanes-3/radioplane-drone.

463 JOUAV, "How Far Can a Drone Fly? Maximum Ranges and Legal Limits," Last updated October 28, 2025, https://www.jouav.com/blog/how-far-can-a-drone-fly.html

464 Defensemirror.com bureau, "Bayraktar TB2T-AI Breaks Altitude Record With 37,096 Feet During Test Flight," Defense Mirror, May 7, 2025, https://defensemirror.com/news/39440/Bayraktar_TB2T_AI_Breaks_Altitude_Record_with_37_096_Feet_During_Test_Flight.

465 Mark Boris Andrijanič, "A Western-funded Drone Surge Could End Russia's Invasion of Ukraine," Atlantic Council, July 14, 2025, https://www.atlanticcouncil.org/blogs/ukrainealert/a-western-funded-drone-surge-could-end-russias-invasion-of-ukraine.

466 Thomas Newdick, "Ukraine Sinks Russian Cargo Ship in Caspian Sea," The War Zone, August 15, 2025, https://www.twz.com/air/ukraine-sinks-russian-cargo-ship-in-caspian-sea.

467 Peter Dickinson, "Ukraine Is Shaping the Future of Drone Warfare at Sea as Well as on Land - Atlantic Council," Atlantic Council, June 12, 2025, https://www.atlanticcouncil.org/blogs/ukrainealert/ukraine-is-shaping-the-future-of-drone-warfare-at-sea-as-well-as-on-land.

468 Jason Sherman, "Drone-on-Drone Combat in Ukraine Marks a New Era of Aerial Warfare," Scientific American, April 3, 2023, https://www.scientificamerican.com/article/drone-on-drone-combat-in-ukraine-marks-a-new-era-of-aerial-warfare.

469 Andy Hayler, "Droning on – AI in the Defence Industry," The Information Difference, August 20, 2025, https://www.informationdifference.com/droning-on-ai-in-the-defence-industry.

470 Tania Myronyshena, "Ukraine's New Ground Drones Are Hitting the Battlefield in Ever-increasing Numbers," The Kyiv Independent, July 16, 2025, https://kyivindependent.com/ukraine-approves-new-ground-robots-to-relieve-infantry-strained-by-mobilization-crisis.

471 Daniel Boffey, "Killing Machines: How Russia and Ukraine's Race to Perfect Deadly Pilotless Drones Could Harm Us All," The Guardian, June 25, 2025, https://www.theguardian.com/world/2025/jun/25/ukraine-russia-autonomous-drones-ai.

472 Adam Zewe, "AI-enabled Control System Helps Autonomous Drones Stay on Target in Uncertain Environments," MIT News, June 9, 2025, https://news.mit.edu/2025/ai-enabled-control-system-helps-autonomous-drones-uncertain-environments-0609.

473 Artem Mazhulin, Oliver Holmes, Lucy Swan, Laure Boulinier, and Arnel Hecimovic, "Operation Spiderweb: A Visual Guide to Ukraine's Destruction of Russian Aircraft," The Guardian, June 11, 2025, https://www.theguardian.com/world/2025/jun/02/operation-spiderweb-visual-guide-ukraine-drone-attack-russian-aircraft.

474 Alexander Blanchard, "The Road Less Travelled: Ethics in the International Regulatory Debate on Autonomous Weapon Systems," Humanitarian Law & Policy Blog, April 25, 2024, https://blogs.icrc.org/law-and-policy/2024/04/25/the-road-less-travelled-ethics-in-the-international-regulatory-debate-on-autonomous-weapon-systems.

475 "Stop Killer Robots – Less Autonomy, More Humanity," Stop Killer Robots, n.d., https://www.stopkillerrobots.org.

476 Jeff Davis, "Phalanx CIWS: Everything You Need to Know About the Navy's Automated, Missile-munching Gatling Gun," n.d., Phalanx, https://ig.space/commslink/phalanx-ciws-everything-you-need-to-know-about-the-gatlin-gun-navy-ship-defense.

477 Joe Hernandez, "A Military Drone With a Mind of Its Own Was Used in Combat, U.N. Says," NPR, June 1, 2021, https://www.npr.org/2021/06/01/1002196245/a-u-n-report-suggests-libya-saw-the-first-battlefield-killing-by-an-autonomous-d.

478 Sarah Scoles, "The Technology for Autonomous Weapons Exists. What Now?" Undark Magazine, November 26, 2025, https://undark.org/2024/11/26/unleashed-autonomous-weapons.

479 Andy Hayler, "Thinking Outside the Bot," The Information Difference, August 14, 2024, https://www.informationdifference.com/thinking-outside-the-bot.

480 Rebecca Pool, "Saab's Robert Lindegren on Drone Swarms, Edge AI, and the Future of Autonomous Warfare," EE Times, March 5, 2025, https://www.eetimes.eu/saab-robert-lindegren-on-drone-swarms-edge-ai-and-the-future-of-autonomous-warfare.

481 "Metalhead (2017)," IMDb, n.d., https://www.imdb.com/title/tt5710984/reference.

482 "The Turing-Welchman Bombe," The National Museum of Computing, n.d., https://www.tnmoc.org/bombe.

483 Jason N. Adler, "Modernizing Military Decision-Making: Integrating AI into Army Planning," Army University Press, August 2025, https://www.armyupress.army.mil/Journals/Military-Review/Online-Exclusive/2025-OLE/Modernizing-Military-Decision-Making.

484 Benjamin Jensen and Jake S. Kwon, "The U.S. Army, Artificial Intelligence, and Mission Command," War on the Rocks, March 10, 2025, https://warontherocks.com/2025/03/the-u-s-army-artificial-intelligence-and-mission-command.

485 "AI Technology Is Changing How Wars Are Won," TE Connectivity, n.d., https://www.te.com/en/industries/defense-military/insights/ai-in-warfare-and-military-applications.html

486 Nick Robins-Early, "AI's 'Oppenheimer Moment': Autonomous Weapons Enter the Battlefield," The Guardian, November 14, 2024, https://www.theguardian.com/technology/article/2024/jul/14/ais-oppenheimer-moment-autonomous-weapons-enter-the-battlefield.

487 OWASP Top 10 for LLM & Generative AI Security, "LLM01:2025 Prompt Injection," OWASP Gen AI Security Project, n.d., https://genai.owasp.org/llmrisk/llm01-prompt-injection.

488 Yuri Zoria, "Ukraine unveils VATAG—a battlefield ground drone that can haul over 2 tons and stay quiet doing it," EuroMaidan Press, September 16, 2025, https://euromaidanpress.com/2025/09/16/ukraine-unveils-vatag-a-battlefield-ground-drone-that-can-haul-over-2-tons-and-stay-quiet-doing-it.

489 Claire Penketh, "AI In Defence: Ethics, Risks, and the Future of Autonomous Warfare," British Computer Society, April 7, 2025, https://www.bcs.org/articles-opinion-and-research/ai-in-defence-ethics-risks-and-the-future-of-autonomous-warfare.

490 "HAROP: Long Range Loitering Munition," IAI, https://www.iai.co.il/p/harop.

491 "Stop Killer Robots – Less Autonomy, More Humanity," Stop Killer Robots, n.d., https://www.stopkillerrobots.org.

492 The Editors of Encyclopaedia Britannica, "The Mechanical Turk: AI Marvel or Parlor Trick?" Encyclopedia Britannica, n.d., https://www.britannica.com/story/the-mechanical-turk-ai-marvel-or-parlor-trick; Primal Space, "The Robot Chess Player Scam," YouTube, June 26, 2024, https://www.youtube.com/watch?v=Xosn4ManeD4.

493 "Unimate," Encyclopedia Britannica, n.d., https://www.britannica.com/technology/Unimate.

494 SRI International, "Shakey the Robot," SRI, n.d., https://www.sri.com/hoi/shakey-the-robot.

495 Michael Wallace and George Dunlop, "Eliza, a Chatbot Therapist," Eliza, n.d., https://web.njit.edu/~ronkowit/eliza.html.

496 Robert K. Lindsay Jr., Bruce G. Buchanan, Edward A. Feigenbaum, and Joshua Lederberg, "DENDRAL: A Case Study of the First Expert System for Scientific Hypothesis Formation," Artificial Intelligence 61 (1993): 209–261, https://web.mit.edu/6.034/www/6.s966/dendral-history.pdf.

497 Waseda University, "Humanoid History -WABOT-," Waseda University, n.d., https://www.humanoid.waseda.ac.jp/booklet/kato_2.html.

498 Kate Ng, "How The Furby Took Over the World," The Independent, August 23, 2023, https://www.independent.co.uk/life-style/furby-history-toys-b2397147.html.

499 NASA, "Mars Pathfinder - Mars Missions," NASA Jet Propulsion Laboratory (JPL), n.d., https://www.jpl.nasa.gov/missions/mars-pathfinder-sojourner-rover.

500 PRNewswire, "iRobot Introduces RoombaTM Intelligent FloorVac - the First Automatic Floor Cleaner in the U.S.," iRobot MediaKit, September 18, 2002, https://media.irobot.com/2002-09-18-iRobot-Introduces-Roomba-Intelligent-FloorVac-The-First-Automatic-Floor-Cleaner-In-The-U-S.

501 International Federation of Robotics, "Record of 4 Million Robots in Factories Worldwide," International Federation of Robotics, n.d., https://ifr.org/ifr-press-releases/news/record-of-4-million-robots-working-in-factories-worldwide.

502 NOAA, "What Is Lidar," National Ocean Service, n.d., https://oceanservice.noaa.gov/facts/lidar.html.

503 Amazon Web Services, "What Is Reinforcement Learning? - Reinforcement Learning Explained - AWS," Amazon Web Services, Inc., n.d., https://aws.amazon.com/what-is/reinforcement-learning; "Starting on the Right Foot With Reinforcement Learning," Boston Dynamics, n.d., https://bostondynamics.com/blog/starting-on-the-right-foot-with-reinforcement-learning.

504 Sky News, "Robot Outperforms Human Surgeons in Pig Gut Op," Sky News, May 5, 2016, https://news.sky.com/story/robot-outperforms-human-surgeons-in-pig-gut-op-10269870.

505 Péter Fankhauser, "Pioneering Autonomous Inspection for Enhanced Nuclear Safety at Onkalo," ANYbotics, n.d., https://www.anybotics.com/news/autonomous-inspection-for-enhanced-nuclear-safety-at-onkalo.

506 Melissa Ryan, Karl McLetchie, and Philip Hoffman, "Ocean Exploration Technology: How Robots Are Uncovering the Mysteries of the Deep," NOAA Ocean Exploration, June 9, 2023, https://oceanexplorer.noaa.gov/explainers/technology.

507 NASA, "Robonaut2," NASA, July 14, 2025, https://www.nasa.gov/robonaut2.

508 Ben Morris, "How Robots Are Taking Over Warehouse Work," BBC News, April 23, 2024, https://www.bbc.co.uk/news/business-68639533.

509 Scott Dresser, "Amazon Deploys Over 1 Million Robots and Launches New AI Foundation Model," Amazon, July 1, 2025, https://www.aboutamazon.com/news/operations/amazon-million-robots-ai-foundation-model.

510 Joe Kucinski, "Tesla Has the Highest Fatal Accident Rate of All Auto Brands, Study Finds," Road and Track, November 15, 2024, https://www.roadandtrack.com/news/a62919131/tesla-has-highest-fatal-accident-rate-of-all-auto-brands-study/; Craft Law Firm, "Data Analysis: Self-Driving Car Accidents [2019-2024]," Craft Law Firm, n.d., https://www.craftlawfirm.com/autonomous-vehicle-accidents-2019-2024-crash-data.

511 Andy Hayler, "Braking News – AI in Autonomous Vehicles," The Information Difference, August 21, 2025, https://www.informationdifference.com/braking-news-ai-in-autonomous-vehicles.

512 Weronika Wojtak, "Why Asimov's Three Laws of Robotics Fail in the Real World," Medium,

May 28, 2025, https://medium.com/@w.wojtak/why-asimovs-three-laws-of-robotics-fail-in-the-real-world-0685e5b53a3f; The Editors of Encyclopaedia Britannica, "Three Laws of Robotics," Encyclopedia Britannica, n.d., https://www.britannica.com/topic/Three-Laws-of-Robotics.

513 Sara Brown, "A New Study Measures the Actual Impact of Robots on Jobs. It's Significant," MIT Sloan, July 29, 2020, https://mitsloan.mit.edu/ideas-made-to-matter/a-new-study-measures-actual-impact-robots-jobs-its-significant.

514 Daisuke Adachi, "Robots and Wage Polarisation," i, August 18, 2024, https://cepr.org/voxeu/columns/robots-and-wage-polarisation.

515 The Economist, "Economists are revising their views on robots and jobs," The Economist, January 22, 2022, https://www.economist.com/finance-and-economics/2022/01/22/economists-are-revising-their-views-on-robots-and-jobs.

516 World Health Organization, "Ageing and Health," World Health Organization, October 1, 2025, https://www.who.int/news-room/fact-sheets/detail/ageing-and-health.

517 Amy Hawkins, "Box, Run, Crash: China's Humanoid Robot Games Show Advances and Limitations," The Guardian, August 15, 2025, https://www.theguardian.com/world/2025/aug/15/china-world-humanoid-robot-games-advances-limitations.

518 Pamela Smith, "Chop, Chop: Improving Food Prep With the Power of AI," College of Engineering at Carnegie Mellon University, n.d., https://engineering.cmu.edu/news-

events/news/2023/11/29-robochop.html; Samantha Kelly, "Laundry-Folding-Robotics Company Attracts $400M From Jeff Bezos and OpenAI," CNET, November 14, 2024, https://www.cnet.com/tech/services-and-software/laundry-folding-robotics-company-attracts-400m-from-jeff-bezos-and-openai.

519 Robert Lea, "Autonomous Robot Swarms Come Together to Perform a Variety of Missions," Advanced Science News, November 19, 2024, https://www.advancedsciencenews.com/autonomous-robot-swarms-come-together-to-perform-a-variety-of-missions.

520 Andy Hayler, "Droning on – AI in the Defence Industry," The Information Difference, August 20, 2025, https://www.informationdifference.com/droning-on-ai-in-the-defence-industry.

521 Ministry of Defence, "British Soldiers Take Down Drone Swarm in Groundbreaking Use of Radio Wave Weapon," GOV.UK, April 17, 2025, https://www.gov.uk/government/news/british-soldiers-take-down-drone-swarm-in-groundbreaking-use-of-radio-wave-weapon.

522 "Robotics Market Size, Share, Growth, Trends, Report, 2033," IMARC, n.d., https://www.imarcgroup.com/robotics-market.

523 IFR International Federation of Robotics, "China: Robot Installations Grew by 44 Percent," IFR International Federation of Robotics, n.d., https://ifr.org/news/china-robot-installations-grew-by-44-percent.

524 Paul Karp, "Deloitte Accused of Erroneous Citations, Leading to Suspected AI Use in Major Report on Welfare," Australian Financial Review, August 22, 2025, https://www.afr.com/companies/professional-services/academics-raise-alarm-over-suspected-ai-use-in-deloitte-report-20250822-p5mp0f.; Department of Employment and Workplace Relations, Australia, Targeted Compliance Framework Assurance Review – Final Report (Department of Employment and Workplace Relations, 2025), https://www.dewr.gov.au/assuring-integrity-targeted-compliance-framework/resources/targeted-compliance-framework-assurance-review-final-report

525 Andy Hayler, "Scraping by – AI and Copyright Law," The Information Difference, August 18, 2025, https://www.informationdifference.com/scraping-by-ai-and-copyright-law.

526 Andy Hayler, "When Algorithms Dream: AI Hallucinations in Depth," The Information Difference, August 19, 2025, https://www.informationdifference.com/when-algorithms-dream-ai-hallucinations-in-depth.

527 Jeremy Hsu, "AI Hallucinations Are Getting Worse – and They're Here to Stay," New Scientist, May 9, 2025, https://www.newscientist.com/article/2479545-ai-hallucinations-are-getting-worse-and-theyre-here-to-stay.

528 Dan Milmo, "Mushroom Pickers Urged to Avoid Foraging Books on Amazon That Appear to Be Written by AI," The Guardian, September 1, 2023, https://www.theguardian.com/technology/2023/sep/01/mushroom-pickers-urged-to-avoid-foraging-books-on-amazon-that-appear-to-be-written-by-ai.

529 The Authors Guild, "AI Is Driving a New Surge of Sham 'Books' on Amazon," The Authors Guild, March 15, 2024, https://authorsguild.org/news/ai-driving-new-surge-of-sham-books-on-amazon.

530 Kevin Maimann, "Authors Fighting Deluge of Fake Writers and AI-generated Books," CBC, September 12, 2024, https://www.cbc.ca/news/entertainment/ai-generated-books-amazon-1.7319018.

531 Andy Hayler, "Scraping by – AI and Copyright Law," The Information Difference, August 18, 2025, https://www.informationdifference.com/scraping-by-ai-and-copyright-law.

532 Andy Hayler, "AI's Copyright Crossroads – Anthropic Settles Landmark Lawsuit," The Information Difference, August 28, 2025, https://www.informationdifference.com/ais-copyright-crossroads-anthropic-settles-landmark-lawsuit.

533 Clwyd Probert, "The Revolutionary Impact of AI on the Consulting Industry," Whitehat SEO, August 10, 2024, https://blog.whitehat-seo.co.uk/ai-impact-on-consulting.

534 "Big Five Consulting: Betting Billions on AI Partnerships," Virtasant, April 15, 2025, https://www.virtasant.com/ai-today/big-five-consulting-betting-billions-on-ai-partnerships.

535 Andy Hayler, "Stop AI Becoming a Security Trojan Horse," The Information Difference, June 25, 2025, https://www.informationdifference.com/security-trojan-horse.

536 Medha Mehta, "AI Bias: 14 Real AI Bias Examples & Mitigation Guide," Crescendo, August 19, 2025, https://www.crescendo.ai/blog/ai-bias-examples-mitigation-guide.

537 Andy Hayler, "Drifting Away? AI Model Performance Over Time," The Information Difference, May 21, 2025, https://www.informationdifference.com/ai-model-performance.

538 Peter Bondarenko, "Enron Scandal," Encyclopedia Britannica, Last updated September 26, 2025, https://www.britannica.com/event/Enron-scandal.; Denis Collins, "Arthur Andersen," Encyclopedia Britannica, n.d., https://www.britannica.com/money/Arthur-Andersen.

539 Charlie Mitchell, "A Customer Service AI Agent Spits Out Complete Salesforce Records in an Attack by Security Researchers," CX Today, August 18, 2025, https://www.cxtoday.com/crm/a-customer-service-ai-agent-spits-out-complete-salesforce-records-in-an-attack-by-security-researchers.

540 Aimée Look, "Top Consulting Firms Are Being Hit by an AI Reckoning," The Logic, July 24, 2025, https://thelogic.co/news/ai-consultant-reckoning.

541 Barney Macintyre, "Big Four Cut Jobs for Graduates as AI Adds to Consulting Crisis," The Observer, July 20, 2025, https://observer.co.uk/news/business/article/big-four-cut-jobs-for-graduates-as-ai-adds-to-consulting-crisis.

542 Jan Conway, "Topic: Global Wine Market," Statista, September 19, 2025, https://www.statista.com/topics/7802/global-wine.

543 Lauren Eads, "AI And Wine: A Taste of the Future?" Decanter, March 28, 2024, https://www.decanter.com/wine/ai-and-wine-a-taste-of-the-future-523210.

544 Jane Anson, "How Accurate Are the Figures on Wine Fraud?" Jane Anson - Inside Bordeaux, October 5, 2022, https://janeanson.com/how-accurate-are-the-figures-on-wine-fraud?srsltid=AfmBOorSTgPdVPXs2FvVdRWAy-85VIpNklAKHsMxmnwYxTgT9lVQ66CT.

545 L'Atelier Du Vin, "Corked Wine, Cork Taint, Musty Odours: What to Do," L'Atelier Du Vin, March 13, 2023, https://www.atelierduvin.com/en/corked-wine-a-definition-and-practical-guide/?srsltid=AfmBOooT0oniYfZqtdryNLiZzxAhuWHNG-hohxXKCX3jlD6cwycMZwa3.

546 Andy Hayler, "Uncorking the Future – AI in the Wine Industry," The Information Difference, September 1, 2025, https://www.informationdifference.com/uncorking-the-future-ai-in-the-wine-industry.

547 "Cork Supply's AI Driven and Patented X100 Technology Gains International Recognition," Newsworthy.ai, February 19, 2025, https://www.newsworthy.ai/news/202502191435/cork-supplys-ai-driven-and-patented-x100-technology-gains-international-recognition.

548 "Preferabli," Preferabli, n.d., https://preferabli.com.

549 Richard Siddle, "How M&S's New AI Wine Finder Tool From Preferabli Is Going to Work," The Buyer, February 26, 2025, https://www.the-buyer.net/insight/how-m-and-s-s-new-ai-wine-finder-tool-from-preferabli-is-going-to-work.

550 "Tastry | Know What Consumers Want With Wine AI," Tastry, n.d., https://tastry.com.

551 Wikipedia contributors, "Vivino," Wikipedia, Last updated October 26, 2025, https://en.wikipedia.org/wiki/Vivino.

552 "Aerial Vineyard Mapping - Vigor & Grapevine Disease," VineView, n.d., https://vineview.com.

553 Matt Alderton, "Are Flying Vineyard Drones Creating Better Wine?" Wine Enthusiast, Last updated May 4, 2023, https://www.wineenthusiast.com/culture/wine/are-flying-vineyard-drones-creating-better-wine/?srsltid=AfmBOooaowBacwVDHxmpCRkbONIqmMbHOxm7ffMmJbLA4TKEsrmLI9NW.

554 Lauren Eads, "AI And Wine: A Taste of the Future?" Decanter, March 28, 2024, https://www.decanter.com/wine/ai-and-wine-a-taste-of-the-future-523210.

555 "Vins Du Languedoc Modernes Et Engagés," Aubert et Mathieu, n.d., https://aubertetmathieu.com.

556 "How do I become a Master of Wine?" Financial Times, August 23, 2023, https://www.ft.com/content/bad75369-e81a-462e-ad29-4487608a1520.

557 Jing Cao, "AI: A New and Impactful Player in the Quality Evaluation of Wine," Harvard Data Science Review 7, no. 1 (January 30, 2025), https://doi.org/10.1162/99608f92.be44bdad.

558 "Metropolis (1927)," IMDb, n.d., https://www.imdb.com/title/tt0017136/reference/?ref_=nv_sr_srsg_0_tt_8_nm_0_in_0_q_metropolis.

559 "Blade Runner (1982)," IMDb, n.d., https://www.imdb.com/title/tt0083658.

560 "The Matrix (1999)," IMDb, n.d., https://www.imdb.com/title/tt0133093/reference/?ref_=fn_all_ttl_1.

561 "The Terminator (1984)," i, n.d., https://www.imdb.com/title/tt0088247/reference/?ref_=nv_sr_srsg_0_tt_8_nm_0_in_0_q_th%2520terminato

562 "I, Robot (2004)," IMDb, n.d., https://www.imdb.com/title/tt0343818/reference/?ref_=fn_all_ttl_1.

563 "A.I. Artificial Intelligence (2001)," IMDb, n.d., https://www.imdb.com/title/tt0212720/reference/?ref_=nv_sr_srsg_1_tt_3_nm_4_in_0_q_ai.

564 "Short Circuit (1986)," IMDb, n.d., https://www.imdb.com/title/tt0091949/reference/?ref_=nv_sr_srsg_0_tt_7_nm_1_in_0_q_short%2520circuit.

565 "Her (2013), IMDb, n.d., https://www.imdb.com/title/tt1798709/reference/?ref_=nv_sr_srsg_3_tt_5_nm_3_in_0_q_her.

566 "Ex Machina (2014)," IMDb, n.d., https://www.imdb.com/title/tt0470752/reference/?ref_=nv_sr_srsg_0_tt_7_nm_1_in_0_q_ex%2520mach.

567 Andrew Pulver, "London Premiere of Movie With AI-generated Script Cancelled After Backlash," The Guardian, June 20, 2024, https://www.theguardian.com/film/article/2024/jun/20/premiere-movie-ai-generated-script-cancelled-backlash-the-last-screenwriter-prince-charles-cinema.

568 Scott Myers, "Hitchcock's Storyboards from 13 Classic Films," Go Into the Story (Official Screenwriting Blog of The Black List), Medium, November 11, 2010, https://gointothestory.blcklst.com/hitchcocks-storyboards-from-13-classic-films-239a2a40f2de

569 Dominic Lees, "2024: The Year in AI," BFI, December 12, 2024, https://www.bfi.org.uk/sight-and-sound/features/2024-year-ai.

570 "Hooroo Jackson," IMDb, n.d., https://www.imdb.com/name/nm6224020/?ref_=nv_sr_srsg_0_tt_5_nm_2_in_1_q_hooroo.

571 "Window Seat (2023)," IMDb, n.d., https://www.imdb.com/title/tt28442424.

572 Hooroo Jackson, "Window Seat (2023) the First Fully AI Feature Film in the History of Cinema! // HD," YouTube, August 22, 2023, https://www.youtube.com/watch?v=WxVUxf1gcQw.

573 Ryan Morrison and Amanda Caswell, "I've Spent 200 Hours Testing the Best AI Video Generators—Here's My Top Picks," Tom's Guide, Last updated July 18, 2025, https://www.tomsguide.com/features/5-best-ai-video-generators-tested-and-compared.

574 "Sora" (home page), https://openai.com/sora.

575 Andy Hayler, "Scraping by – AI and Copyright Law," The Information Difference, August 18, 2025, https://www.informationdifference.com/scraping-by-ai-and-copyright-law.

576 S.J. Velasquez, "How AI Is Resurrecting Dead Actors," BBC News, July 19, 2023, https://www.bbc.com/future/article/20230718-how-ai-is-bringing-film-stars-back-from-the-dead.

577 Seth Abramovitch, "How Did 'Alien: Romulus' Create Its Most Controversial Character?" The Hollywood Reporter, August 23, 2024, https://www.hollywoodreporter.com/movies/movie-features/alien-romulus-ian-holm-rook-ash-ai-1235982350.

578 Laura Harman, "7 Dead Movie Stars Who've Been Brought Back to Life on Screen With CGI," Metro, August 24, 2024, https://metro.co.uk/2024/08/24/7-dead-movie-stars-whove-brought-back-life-screen-cgi-21471594.

579 Felicity Cross, "New Law Passed on Controversial Use of AI to 'Bring Back' Dead Actors After Christopher Reeve's Family's Outrage," The Sun, September 1, 2024, https://www.thesun.co.uk/tvandshowbiz/30202718/law-ai-dead-actors-christopher-reeve.

580 Mike McGee, "How We Resurrected Audrey HepburnTM for the Galaxy Chocolate Ad," The Guardian, October 8, 2014, https://www.theguardian.com/media-network/media-network-blog/2014/oct/08/how-we-made-audrey-hepburn-galaxy-ad.

581 "Writers Guild of America West" (home page), https://www.wga.org.

582 Screen Actors Guild–American Federation of Television and Radio Artists "SAG-AFTRA" (home page), https://www.sagaftra.org.

583 Andy Hayler, "'I'm Sorry Dave' – Is AI An Existential Threat?" The Information Difference, August 17, 2025, https://www.informationdifference.com/im-sorry-dave-is-ai-an-existential-threat.

584 Embedur, "A Deep Dive Into Wearable AI Devices in the Sports Industry," embedUR, n.d., https://www.embedur.ai/a-deep-dive-into-wearable-ai-devices-in-the-sports-industry.

585 E.D. Gibson, "The Tech Revolution in Sport," Deconch 30, May 19, 2025, https://deconch30.medium.com/the-tech-revolution-in-sports-9bcf1fc9dce3.

586 William Johnston, Cailbhe Doherty, Fionn Cleirigh Büttner, and Brian Caulfield, "Wearable sensing and mobile devices: the future of post-concussion monitoring?" Concussion 2, no. 1 (2017): CNC28, doi:10.2217/cnc-2016-0025.

587 "Hawk-Eye | A Global Leader in the Live Sports Arena," Hawkeye Innovations, n.d., https://www.hawkeyeinnovations.com.

588 Matt Astbury, "Euro 2024: What is snickometer technology? How does snicko work?" DAZN, June 21, 2024, https://www.dazn.com/en-GB/news/football/euro-2024-what-is-snickometer-technology-how-does-snicko-work/16oifal9vx87l102zxnl2vt2v1.

589 James Darley, "The 148-Year Tradition Wimbledon is Breaking with Technology," AI Magazine, June 30, 2025, https://aimagazine.com/articles/the-148-year-tradition-wimbledon-is-breaking-with-technology.

590 Matt Hughes, "Premier League to Bring in AI-powered Camera System to Speed up VAR Process," The Guardian, August 13, 2025, https://www.theguardian.com/football/article/2024/aug/13/premier-league-to-introduce-revolutionary-camera-system-to-aid-var-process.; BBC Sport, "Semi-automated Offside: Premier League to Introduce Technology on 12 April," BBC Sport, April 1, 2025, https://www.bbc.co.uk/sport/football/articles/cgenyp53plpo.

591 "Football Radar" (home page), https://www.footballradar.com.

592 "Veo Sports Technology: AI Video Analysis for Teams" (home page), https://www.veo.co.

593 Paul-Antoine Girard, "AI In Sports: The Shift From Intuition to AI-Driven Coaching," The AI Journal, 2025, https://aijourn.com/ai-in-sports-the-shift-from-intuition-to-ai-driven-coaching.

594 Anuraag Jain, "AI In Sports - Revolutionizing Training and Performance," Oyelabs, September 12, 2025, https://oyelabs.com/ai-in-sports-revolutionizing-training-and-performance.

595 Bloodline Golf, "AI Drives a New Era in Golf," Bloodline Golf, October 17, 2024, https://bloodline.golf/blogs/top-news/ai-drives-a-new-era-in-golf?srsltid=AfmBOor9nY3pzkPkERYA8QkGZgTKI-Oscg7ErAGGvrX2S-yOkA1Ilgia.

596 Sam Weinman, "11 images that prove AI can design basically any golf course you want," GolfDigest75, n.d., https://www.golfdigest.com/story/ai-golf-courses.

597 Andy Hayler, "Athletes and Algorithms – AI in Sports," The Information Difference, September 9, 2025, https://www.informationdifference.com/athletes-and-algorithms.

598 Seb Coe and Nick Jennings, "AI In Sport – Opportunity, Excitement, Progression and Acceleration – Vice-Chancellor's Communications," Blogs Lbroro, March 19, 2025, https://blog.lboro.ac.uk/vice-chancellor/2025/03/19/ai-in-sport-opportunity-excitement-progression-and-acceleration.

599 Shane Sale, "Artificial Intelligence Will Revolutionise Football," October 14, 2019, https://www.linkedin.com/pulse/artificial-intelligence-revolutionise-football-shane-sale.

600 John Peters, Beth Keating, Nita Wang, Hayley Darukhanavala, and Ilan Geller, "ESPN scores with generative AI," Accenture, 2025, https://www.accenture.com/gb-en/case-studies/data-ai/espn-scores-with-generative-ai.

601 Michael Burns, "Storytelling, Monetisation and Engagement: Making the Pitch for AI in Sports Broadcasting," SVG Europe, May 12, 2025, https://www.svgeurope.org/blog/headlines/storytelling-monetisation-and-engagement-making-the-pitch-for-ai-in-sports-broadcasting.

602 Scott Mansell, "AI and Machine Learning in Motorsport," Fluid Jobs, n.d., https://fluidjobs.com/blog/how-is-ai-and-machine-learning-is-changing-motorsport.

603 Jags Kandasamy, "Defense-Grade AI Scores a Strike: Transforming Bowling and Beyond With Edge Computing," RTInsights, April 16, 2025, https://www.rtinsights.com/defense-grade-ai-scores-a-strike-transforming-bowling-and-beyond-with-edge-computing.

604 Magnifi, "How Niche Sports Are Finding Their Spotlight with AI," Magnifi, n.d., https://magnifi.ai/insights/how-niche-sports-are-finding-their-spotlight-with-ai.

605 IBM, "What is homomorphic encryption?" IBM, n.d., https://www.ibm.com/think/topics/homomorphic-encryption.

606 Jae-Hak Kim, Janghyeon Kim, Hoseok Kang, and Bo-Young Youn, "Ethical implications of artificial intelligence in sport: A systematic scoping review," Journal of Sport and Health Science 14 (December 2025): 101047, https://doi.org/10.1016/j.jshs.2025.101047; Andy Hayler, "When AI Picks Sides – AI Bias and Discrimination," The Information Difference, September 2, 2025, https://www.informationdifference.com/when-ai-picks-sides-ai-bias-and-discrimination.

607 Piers Kelly, "How Governments Are Using AI: 8 Real-World Case Studies," Govnet Technology, February 19, 2025, https://blog.govnet.co.uk/technology/ai-in-government-case-studies.

608 "Virtual Intelligent Chat Assistant (VICA)" (home page), n.d., https://www.vica.gov.sg.

609 Department for Science, Innovation and Technology, "Government's Experimental AI Chatbot to Help People Set up Small Businesses and Find Support," GOV.UK, November 5, 2024, https://www.gov.uk/government/news/governments-experimental-ai-chatbot-to-help-people-set-up-small-businesses-and-find-support.

610 Arantxa Herranz, "Success story: Smart litter bins in Seoul," Tomorrow. City, November 15, 2020, https://www.tomorrow.city/success-story-smart-litter-bins-in-seoul.

611 Umberto Bacchi, "EU's lie-detecting virtual border guards face court scrutiny," Reuters, February 12, 2021, https://www.reuters.com/article/technology/eus-lie-detecting-virtual-border-guards-face-court-scrutiny-idUSL8N2KB2GT.

612 Andy Hayler, "Generative AI Works in a Mysterious Way – Explainability in AI," The Information Difference, September 12, 2025. https://www.informationdifference.com/explainability-in-ai.

613 Andy Hayler, "When AI Picks Sides – AI Bias and Discrimination," The Information Difference, September 2, 2025, https://www.informationdifference.com/when-ai-picks-sides-ai-bias-and-discrimination.

614 Andy Hayler, "When Algorithms Dream: AI Hallucinations in Depth," The Information Difference, August 19, 2025, https://www.informationdifference.com/when-algorithms-dream-ai-hallucinations-in-depth.

615 Andy Hayler, "The AI Trust Gap," The Information Difference, August 4, 2025, https://www.informationdifference.com/the-ai-trust-gap.

616 "Artificial Intelligence Playbook for the UK Government (HTML)," GOV.UK, February 10, 2025, https://www.gov.uk/government/publications/ai-playbook-for-the-uk-government/artificial-intelligence-playbook-for-the-uk-government-html.

617 Guy Delauney, "World's First AI Minister Will Eliminate Corruption, Says Albania's PM," BBC News, September 12, 2025, https://www.bbc.com/news/articles/cm2znzgwj3xo.

618 Andy Hayler, "'I, Claudius' – an Agentic AI Experiment," The Information Difference, June 10, 2025, https://www.informationdifference.com/i-claudius-an-agentic-ai-experiment.

619 Frank Landymore, "Car Dealership Disturbed When Its AI Is Caught Offering Chevys for $1 Each," Futurism, December 21, 2023, https://futurism.com/the-byte/car-dealership-ai.

620 Sheryl Estrada, "MIT Report: 95% of Generative AI Pilots at Companies Are Failing," Fortune, August 18, 2025, https://fortune.com/2025/08/18/mit-report-95-percent-generative-ai-pilots-at-companies-failing-cfo.

621 charlirobey, "Imagine a hippo as your surgeon! Google AI is ridiculous," Reddit, March 4, 2025, https://www.reddit.com/r/mildlyinfuriating/comments/1j3azit/imagine_a_hippo_as_your_surgeon_google_ai_is.

622 ClaudeLog, "ClaudeLog - Claude Code Docs, Guides, Tutorials & Best Practices," ClaudeLog, Last updated November 1, 2025, https://claudelog.com/claude-code-pricing.

623 Maria Yagoda, "Airline Held Liable for Its Chatbot Giving Passenger Bad Advice - What This Means for Travellers," BBC News, February 23, 2024, https://www.bbc.com/

travel/article/20240222-air-canada-chatbot-misinformation-what-travellers-should-know.

624 Alfred "Coach Fred" Farrington II, "The Cost Per Query For An AI Chatbot Can Be As Much As 10 Times The Cost Of A Conventional Google Search," Medium, March 16, 2024, https://alfredfarrington.medium.com/the-cost-per-query-for-an-ai-chatbot-can-be-as-much-as-10-times-the-cost-of-a-conventional-google-dd5dd44a7745.

625 Sara Braun, "CEOs Say That Just a Fraction of AI Initiatives Are Actually Delivering the Return on Investment They Expected," Fortune, May 12, 2025, https://fortune.com/article/ceos-ai-initiatves-fraction-deliver-return-on-investment-roi-study.

626 Andrea Hill, "Why 95% of AI Pilots Fail, and What Business Leaders Should Do Instead," Forbes, August 21, 2025, https://www.forbes.com/sites/andreahill/2025/08/21/why-95-of-ai-pilots-fail-and-what-business-leaders-should-do-instead; Jeremy Kahn, "Why Did MIT Find 95% of AI Projects Fail? Hint: It Wasn't About the Tech Itself," Fortune, August 21, 2025, https://fortune.com/2025/08/21/an-mit-report-that-95-of-ai-pilots-fail-spooked-investors-but-the-reason-why-those-pilots-failed-is-what-should-make-the-c-suite-anxious.

627 Jorge Dominguez, "The Curious Case of the CHAOS Report 2009," Project Smart, July 1, 2009, Last updated 10 October 2021, https://www.projectsmart.co.uk/it-project-management/the-curious-case-of-the-chaos-report-2009.php.

628 Jakub Szarmach, "STATE OF AI IN BUSINESS 2025," AI Governance Library, September 22, 2025, https://www.aigl.blog/state-of-ai-in-business-2025.

629 James Ryseff, Brandon F. De Bruhl, and Sydne J. Newberry, "The Root Causes of Failure for Artificial Intelligence Projects and How They Can Succeed: Avoiding the Anti-Patterns of AI," RAND, August 13, 2024, https://www.rand.org/pubs/research_reports/RRA2680-1.html.

630 Andy Hayler, "When Algorithms Dream: AI Hallucinations in Depth," The Information Difference, August 19, 2025, https://www.informationdifference.com/when-algorithms-dream-ai-hallucinations-in-depth.

631 Frank F. Xu, Yufan Song, Boxuan Li, Yuxuan Tang, Kritanjali Jain, Mengxue Bao, Zora Z. Wang, Xuhui Zhou, Zhitong Guo, Murong Cao, Mingyang Yang, Hao Yang Lu, Amaad Martin, Zhe Su, Leander Melroy Maben, Raj Mehta, Wayne Chi, Lawrence Jang, Yiqing Xie, Shuyan Zhou, and Graham Neubig, "TheAgentCompany: Benchmarking LLM Agents on Consequential Real World Tasks," arXiv:2412.14161, December 18, 2024, https://arxiv.org/pdf/2412.14161.

632 Andy Hayler, "AI Use Cases – the Good, the Bad and the Ugly," The Information Difference, May 23, 2025, https://www.informationdifference.com/ai-the-good-bad-ugly.

633 Andy Hayler, "Thinking Outside the Bot," The Information Difference, August 14, 2025, https://www.informationdifference.com/thinking-outside-the-bot.

634 World Economic Forum, "A short history of jobs and automation," World Economic Forum, September 3, 2020, https://www.weforum.org/stories/2020/09/short-history-jobs-automation.

635 Timothy Taylor, "Telephone Operators: The Elimination of a Job," Conversable Economist, August 19, 2024, https://conversableeconomist.com/2024/08/19/telephone-operators-the-elimination-of-a-job.

636 Kiran Tomlinson, Sonia Jaffe, Will Wang, Scott Counts, and Siddharth Suri, "Working With AI: Measuring the Applicability of Generative AI to Occupations," Microsoft Research, July 2025, https://www.microsoft.com/en-us/research/publication/working-with-ai-measuring-the-occupational-implications-of-generative-ai; Preston Fore, "Microsoft Researchers Have Revealed the 40 Jobs Most Exposed to AI—and Even Teachers Make the List," Fortune, July 31, 2025, https://fortune.com/2025/07/31/microsoft-research-generative-ai-occupational-impact-jobs-most-and-least-likely-to-impact-teaching-office-jobs-college-gen-z-grads.

637 Tera Alias and Andrew Goodman, "Not yet productive, already disruptive: AI's uneven effects on UK jobs and talent," McKinsey & Company, July 14, 2025, https://www.mckinsey.com/uk/our-insights/the-mckinsey-uk-blog/ai-uneven-effects-on-uk-jobs-and-talent.

638 Sheryl Estrada, "MIT Report: 95% of Generative AI Pilots at Companies Are Failing," Fortune, August 18, 2025, https://fortune.com/2025/08/18/mit-report-95-percent-generative-ai-pilots-at-companies-failing-cfo.

639 Erik Brynjolfsson, Bharat Chandar, and Ruyu Chen, "Canaries in the Coal Mine? Six Facts about the Recent Employment Effects of Artificial Intelligence," August 26, 2025, Stanford Digital Economy Lab, https://digitaleconomy.stanford.edu/wp-content/uploads/2025/08/Canaries_BrynjolfssonChandarChen.pdf.

640 ET Spotlight team, "After Firing 700 Employees for AI, Swedish Company Admits Their Mistake and Plans to Rehire Humans. What Went Wrong," The Economic Times, May 18, 2025, https://economictimes.indiatimes.com/magazines/panache/after-firing-700-employees-for-ai-swedish-company-admits-their-mistake-and-plans-to-rehire-humans-what-happened/articleshow/121252776.cms?from=mdr.

641 Andy Hayler, "Finding the Goldilocks Zone for AI-Generated Code," The Information Difference, August 12, 2025, https://www.informationdifference.com/ai-generated-code.

642 Simon Sharwood, "WS CEO says using AI to replace junior staff is 'Dumbest thing I've ever heard'," The Register, August 21, 2025, https://www.theregister.com/2025/08/21/aws_ceo_entry_level_jobs_opinion.

643 Andy Hayler, "When Algorithms Dream: AI Hallucinations in Depth," The Information Difference, August 19, 2025, https://www.informationdifference.com/when-algorithms-dream-ai-hallucinations-in-depth.

644 Max Roser, "Technology Over the Long Run: Zoom Out to See How Dramatically the World Can Change Within a Lifetime," Our World in Data, February 22, 2023, https://ourworldindata.org/technology-long-run.

645 Ibid.

646 Matt Wood, "The Fearless Future: 2025 Global AI Jobs Barometer," PwC, June 3, 2025, https://www.pwc.com/gx/en/issues/artificial-intelligence/ai-jobs-barometer.html.

647 Isaac Wagner and Kaustubh Chakradeo, "Human-AI Complementarity in Diagnostic Radiology: The Case of Double Reading," Philosophy & Technology 38, no. 2 (2025), https://doi.org/10.1007/s13347-025-00886-5.

648 Araz Zirar, Syed Imran Ali, and Nazrul Islam, "Worker and workplace Artificial Intelligence (AI) coexistence: Emerging themes and research agenda," Technovation 124 (June 2023): 102747, https://doi.org/10.1016/j.technovation.2023.102747.

649 Gené Teare, "Q2 Global Venture Funding Climbs in a Blockbuster Quarter for AI and as Capital Concentrates in Larger Companies," Crunchbase News, July 8, 2025, https://news.crunchbase.com/venture/global-funding-climbs-q2-2025-ai-ma-data.

650 Goldman Sachs, "How Will AI Affect the Global Workforce?" Goldman Sachs, August 13, 2025, https://www.goldmansachs.com/insights/articles/how-will-ai-affect-the-global-workforce.

651 Preston Fore, "Microsoft Researchers Have Revealed the 40 Jobs Most Exposed to AI—and Even Teachers Make the List," Fortune, July 31, 2025, https://fortune.com/2025/07/31/microsoft-research-generative-ai-occupational-impact-jobs-most-and-least-likely-to-impact-teaching-office-jobs-college-gen-z-grads.

652 Statista, "Google: Annual Advertising Revenue 2001-2024," Statista, February 5, 2025, https://www.statista.com/statistics/266249/advertising-revenue-of-google.

653 Andy Tattersall, "AI's Threat To Google Is More About Advertising Income Than Being the Number One Search Engine," Business Reporter, n.d., https://www.business-reporter.co.uk/technology/ais-threat-to-google-is-more-about-advertising-income-than-being-the-number-one-search-engine.

654 Athena Chapekis and Anna Lieb, "Google Users Are Less Likely to Click on Links When an AI Summary Appears in the Results," Pew Research Center, July 22, 2025, https://www.pewresearch.org/short-reads/2025/07/22/google-users-are-less-likely-to-click-on-links-when-an-ai-summary-appears-in-the-results.

655 PPA, "How Google AI Offerings Are Harming Publishers: PPA Submits Recommendations to the Competition and Markets Authority," PPA, August 14, 2025,

https://ppa.co.uk/how-google-ai-offerings-are-harming-publishers-ppa-submits-recommendations-to-the-competition-and-markets-authority.

656 Jared, "Is Google's Advertising Dying? AI Impact Unveiled," Geeklab - Digital Innovators, April 16, 2025, Last updated April 16, 2025, https://geeklab.blog/impact-of-ai-on-googles-search-advertising-and-cloud-business.

657 Natasha Sommerfeld, "Consumer reliance on AI search results signals new era of marketing – Bain & Company," Bain, February 19, 2025, https://www.bain.com/about/media-center/press-releases/20252/consumer-reliance-on-ai-search-results-signals-new-era-of-marketing--bain--company-about-80-of-search-users-rely-on-ai-summaries-at-least-40-of-the-time-on-traditional-search-engines-about-60-of-searches-now-end-without-the-user-progressing-to-a.

658 Dashveenjit Kaur, "Zuckerberg's $15B Bet: How Meta's 'Superintelligence Labs' Became Silicon Valley's Most Expensive AI Talent War," AI News, July 17, 2025, https://www.artificialintelligence-news.com/news/meta-superintelligence-ai-lab-zuckerberg-talent-war.

659 Cal Jeffrey, "Sam Altman says investors are acting irrational in a booming AI bubble," Tech Spot, August 15, 2025, https://www.techspot.com/news/109090-sam-altman-investors-acting-irrational-booming-ai-bubble.html

660 Philipp Carlsson-Szlezak, Paul Swartz, and Francois Candelon, "Why we need to be realistic about generative AI's economic impact," World Economic Forum, August 31, 2023, https://www.weforum.org/stories/2023/08/generative-ai-realistic-economic-impact/

661 Hayden Field, "GPT-5 Failed the Hype Test," The Verge, August 15, 2025, https://www.theverge.com/openai/759755/gpt-5-failed-the-hype-test-sam-altman-openai; Gary Marcus, "GPT-5: Overdue, Overhyped and Underwhelming. And That's Not the Worst of It," Marcus on AI, August 10, 2025, https://garymarcus.substack.com/p/gpt-5-overdue-overhyped-and-underwhelming.

662 Tharin Pillay, "How OpenAI's Sam Altman Is Thinking About AGI and Superintelligence in 2025," TIME, January 8, 2025, https://time.com/7205596/sam-altman-superintelligence-agi.

663 Frank Landymore, "OpenAI'S New AI Agent Takes One Hour to Order Food and Recommends Visiting a Baseball Stadium in the Middle of the Ocean," Futurism, July 20, 2025, https://futurism.com/openai-new-ai-agent-food-stadium.

664 All-In Podcast, "Google DeepMind CEO Demis Hassabis on AI, Creativity, and a Golden Age of Science | All-In Summit," YouTube, September 12, 2025, https://www.youtube.com/watch?v=Kr3Sh2PKA8Y.

665 Chess.com Team and Chess.com Team, "Kasparov Vs. Deep Blue | the Match That Changed History," Chess.com, Last updated October 12, 2018, https://www.chess.com/article/view/deep-blue-kasparov-chess.

666 GothamChess, "HILARIOUS AI CHESS CHAMPIONSHIP," YouTube, August 5, 2025, https://www.youtube.com/watch?v=S2KmStTbL6c.

667 Jeremy Hsu, "AI Hallucinations Are Getting Worse – and They're Here to Stay," New Scientist, May 9, 2025, https://www.newscientist.com/article/2479545-ai-hallucinations-are-getting-worse-and-theyre-here-to-stay.

668 Maria Korolov, "Fast Vs. Slow: The Real Impact of AI Adoption Speed," CIO, January 15, 2025, https://www.cio.com/article/3634175/fast-vs-slow-the-real-impact-of-ai-adoption-speed.html.

669 James Ryseff, Brandon F. De Bruhl, and Sydne J. Newberry, "The Root Causes of Failure for Artificial Intelligence Projects and How They Can Succeed: Avoiding the Anti-Patterns of AI," RAND, August 13, 2024, https://www.rand.org/pubs/research_reports/RRA2680-1.html.

670 Lindsay Kohler, "Fear Isn't Slowing Down AI Adoption at Work. A Lack of Vision Is," Forbes, January 27, 2025, https://www.forbes.com/sites/lindsaykohler/2025/01/27/fear-isnt-slowing-down-ai-adoption-at-work-a-lack-of-vision-is.

671 Maggie Harrison Dupré, "Billion-Dollar AI Company Gives up on AGI While Desperately Fighting to Stop Bleeding Money," Futurism, August 14, 2025, https://futurism.com/billion-dollar-ai-company-gives-up-on-agi.

672 Gabriel Snyder, "Yann LeCun, Pioneer of AI, Thinks Today's LLM's Are Nearly Obsolete," Newsweek, Last updated September 5, 2025, https://www.newsweek.com/nw-ai/ai-impact-interview-yann-lecun-artificial-intelligence-2054237.

673 Marcelo Tibau, "LLMs Are Hitting the Wall: What's Next," Medium, November 13, 2024, https://medium.com/@marcelo_tibau/llms-are-hitting-the-wall-whats-next-cb49a53c9919.

674 Christopher Mims, "Silicon Valley's New Strategy: Move Slow and Build Things," The Wall Street Journal, August 1, 2025, https://www.wsj.com/tech/ai/silicon-valley-ai-infrastructure-capex-cffe0431?st=oLCAcg&reflink=desktopwebshare_permalink

675 Brian Duignan, "Dot-com bubble," Encyclopedia Britannica, n.d., https://www.britannica.com/money/dot-com-bubble.

676 Chris Morris, "Apollo's Chief Economist Warns the AI Bubble Is Even Worse Than the 1999 Dot-com Bubble," Fortune, July 17, 2025, https://fortune.com/2025/07/17/ai-bubble-vs-dot-com-stocks-apollo-economist-torsten-slok.

677 David Meyer, "Alibaba's Chair Issues 'bubble' Warning About U.S. AI Investments," Fortune, March 25, 2025, https://fortune.com/2025/03/25/alibaba-chair-joe-tsai-warns-ai-bubble.

678 John Cassidy, "Is The A.I. Boom Turning Into an A.I. Bubble?" The New Yorker, August 11, 2025, https://www.newyorker.com/news/the-financial-page/is-the-ai-boom-turning-into-an-ai-bubble.

679 QNA, "China Home to 15% of the World's AI Companies," QNA, July 29, 2025, https://qna.org.qa/en/news/news-details?id=china-home-to-15-of-the-worlds-ai-companies&date=29/07/2025

680 The Supreme People's Procuratorate of the People's Republic of China, "Data Security Law of the People's Republic of China," The Supreme People's Procuratorate of the People's Republic of China, June 10, 2021, https://en.spp.gov.cn/2021-06/10/c_948426_2.htm.

681 Statista, "Artificial Intelligence - China | Statista Market Forecast," Statista, https://www.statista.com/outlook/tmo/artificial-intelligence/china.

682 James Pethokoukis, "America's AI Lead Over China: Here's Why It Will Continue," American Enterprise Institute, July 8, 2025, https://www.aei.org/articles/americas-ai-lead-over-china-heres-why-it-will-continue.

683 Gale Pooley, "Why China May Surpass the United States in the AI Supremacy Race," The Daily Economy, February 27, 2025, https://thedailyeconomy.org/article/why-china-may-surpass-the-united-states-in-the-ai-supremacy-race.

684 Will Knight, "China Is the World's Biggest Face Recognition Dealer," WIRED, January 24, 2023, https://www.wired.com/story/china-is-the-worlds-biggest-face-recognition-dealer.

685 Michael Standaert, "Smile for the Camera: The Dark Side of China's Emotion-recognition Tech," The Guardian, March 3, 2021, https://www.theguardian.com/global-development/2021/mar/03/china-positive-energy-emotion-surveillance-recognition-tech.

686 Morgan Stanley, "How China Is Becoming an AI Powerhouse," Morgan Stanley, May 22, 2025, https://www.morganstanley.com/insights/articles/china-ai-becoming-global-leader.

687 Telecom Review. "Inside China's Smart City Boom: Leveraging AI, 5G, and IoT for Urban Innovation," Telecom Review, March 19, 2024.

688 Ni Tao, "China Smart Cities: Digital Evolution at Scale," CKGSB Knowledge, July 17, 2025, https://english.ckgsb.edu.cn/knowledge/article/china-smart-cities-digital-evolution-at-scale.

689 Amy Hawkins, "Humanoid Workers and Surveillance Buggies: 'Embodied AI' Is Reshaping Daily Life in China," The Guardian, April 21, 2025, https://www.theguardian.com/world/2025/apr/21/humanoid-workers-and-surveillance-buggies-embodied-ai-is-reshaping-daily-life-in-china.

690 BBC News, "China Launches Fleet of Self-driving Trucks," BBC News, June 6, 2025, https://www.youtube.com/watch?v=ypj2ii--1Uc.

691 An Ranran X, "Over 50 Chinese Cities Have Brought Out Rules for Self-Driving, Smart Connected Vehicles," YiCai Global, January 15, 2025, https://www.yicaiglobal.com/news/over-50-chinese-cities-issue-self-driving-intelligent-connected-vehicle-rules.

692 Yi-Ling Liu, "China's Vision for a Driverless Future Is Miles Ahead of Everyone Else's," Rest of World, August 12, 2025, https://restofworld.org/2025/china-ai-powered-self-driving-cars.

693 Demetri Sevastopulo, "Donald Trump Freezes Export Controls to Secure Trade Deal with China," Financial Times, July 28, 2025, https://www.ft.com/content/19442dba-c724-4825-9388-26219a12cb8a.

694 Elizabeth Gibney, "China's Cheap, Open AI Model DeepSeek Thrills Scientists," Nature, January 23, 2025, https://doi.org/10.1038/d41586-025-00229-6.

695 Lily Jamali, "It Shocked the US Market but Has China's DeepSeek Changed AI?" BBC News, August 10, 2025, https://www.bbc.com/news/articles/c4gez754mn6o.

696 Reuters, "Chinese AI startup DeepSeek releases upgraded model with domestic chip support," Reuters, August 21, 2025, https://www.reuters.com/world/china/chinese-ai-startup-deepseek-releases-upgraded-model-with-domestic-chip-support-2025-08-21.

697 Ewelina U. Ochab, "'Let China Sleep, for When She Wakes, She Will Shake the World,'" Forbes, Last updated December 10, 2021, https://www.forbes.com/sites/ewelinaochab/2021/01/13/let-china-sleep-for-when-she-wakes-she-will-shake-the-world.

698 Evan Anderson, Jim Holdsworth, and Matthew Kosinski, "What is red teaming?" IBM, 2025, https://www.ibm.com/think/topics/red-teaming.

699 "JailbreakBench/JBB-Behaviors," Hugging Face, n.d., https://huggingface.co/datasets/JailbreakBench/JBB-Behaviors.

700 Yongzhe Huang, Nick Bray, Akshata Rao, Yang Ji, and Wenjun Hu, "How Good Are the LLM Guardrails on the Market? A Comparative Study on the Effectiveness of LLM Content Filtering Across Major GenAI Platforms," Unit 42, June 2, 2025, https://unit42.paloaltonetworks.com/comparing-llm-guardrails-across-genai-platforms.

701 Yongzhe Huang, Yang Ji, and Wenjun Hu, "Investigating LLM Jailbreaking of Popular Generative AI Web Products," Unit 42, February 21, 2025, https://unit42.paloaltonetworks.com/jailbreaking-generative-ai-web-products.

702 Liv McMahon, "AI System Resorts to Blackmail if Told It Will Be Removed," BBC News, May 23, 2025, https://www.bbc.co.uk/news/articles/cpqeng9d20go.

703 Adam Smith, "Threaten an AI Chatbot and It Will Lie, Cheat and 'Let You Die' in an Effort to Stop You, Study Warns," Live Science, June 26, 2025, https://www.

livescience.com/technology/artificial-intelligence/threaten-an-ai-chatbot-and-it-will-lie-cheat-and-let-you-die-in-an-effort-to-stop-you-study-warns.

704 Nicholas Fearn, "'Master of Deception': Current AI Models Already Have the Capacity to Expertly Manipulate and Deceive Humans," Live Science, May 23, 2024, https://www.livescience.com/technology/artificial-intelligence/master-of-deception-current-ai-models-already-have-the-capacity-to-expertly-manipulate-and-deceive-humans.

705 The Editors of Encyclopaedia Britannica, "Three Laws of Robotics," Encyclopedia Britannica, n.d., https://www.britannica.com/topic/Three-Laws-of-Robotics.

706 Nirdiamant, "15 LLM Jailbreaks That Shook AI Safety," Medium, January 28, 2025, https://medium.com/@nirdiamant21/15-llm-jailbreaks-that-shook-ai-safety-981d2796d5c6.

707 Frank Landymore, "Car Dealership Disturbed When Its AI Is Caught Offering Chevys for $1 Each," Futurism, December 21, 2023, https://futurism.com/the-byte/car-dealership-ai.

708 Len Noe, "LLMs Gone Wild: AI Without Guardrails," Cyberark, September 13, 2024, https://www.cyberark.com/resources/blog/llms-gone-wild-ai-without-guardrails.

709 Zhisheng Chen, "Ethics and Discrimination in Artificial Intelligence-enabled Recruitment Practices," Humanities and Social Sciences Communications 10, no. 1 (September 13, 2023), https://doi.org/10.1057/s41599-023-02079-x.

710 Rachel Goodman, "Why Amazon's Automated Hiring Tool Discriminated Against Women," American Civil Liberties Union, October 12, 2018, http://aclu.org/news/womens-rights/why-amazons-automated-hiring-tool-discriminated-against.

711 Arthi Nachiappan, "'I Thought I Was Going Mad': Former Make-up Artist Says She Lost Her Job After Being Marked Down by AI Tool," Sky News, February 1, 2024, https://news.sky.com/story/companies-increasingly-using-ai-for-recruiting-and-why-it-could-cost-you-your-job-13060905.

712 Aylin Caliskan and Kyra Wilson, "Gender, Race, and Intersectional Bias in AI Resume Screening via Language Model Retrieval," Brookings, April 25, 2025, https://www.brookings.edu/articles/gender-race-and-intersectional-bias-in-ai-resume-screening-via-language-model-retrieval.

713 John Sandall and Sophie Carr, "Case Studies: When AI and CV Screening Goes Wrong," Fairness Tales, August 29, 2025, https://www.fairnesstales.com/p/issue-2-case-studies-when-ai-and-cv-screening-goes-wrong.

714 Dave Gershgorn, "Companies are on the hook if their hiring algorithms are biased," Quartz, July 21, 2022, https://qz.com/1427621/companies-are-on-the-hook-if-their-hiring-algorithms-are-biased.

715 Stefan Milne, "AI Tools Show Biases in Ranking Job Applicants' Names According to Perceived Race and Gender," UW News, October 31, 2024, https://www.washington.edu/news/2024/10/31/ai-bias-resume-screening-race-gender.

716 Kyra Wilson and Aylin Caliskan, "Gender, Race, and Intersectional Bias in Resume Screening via Language Model Retrieval," Proceedings of the Seventh AAAI/ACM Conference on AI, Ethics, and Society (AIES 2024): 1578–1590, https://ojs.aaai.org/index.php/AIES/article/view/31748/33915.

717 Michael Kearns and Aaron Roth, The Ethical Algorithm: The Science of Socially Aware Algorithm Design (Oxford University Press USA, 2020).

718 Barbora Korcova, "AI In Recruitment: Balancing Innovation with Legal Risk," EM Law | Commercial Lawyers in Central London, August 22, 2025, https://emlaw.co.uk/ai-in-recruitment-balancing-innovation-with-legal-risk.

719 Jacob Snow, "Amazon's Face Recognition Falsely Matched 28 Members of Congress with Mugshots," American Civil Liberties Union, July 26, 2018, https://www.aclu.org/news/privacy-technology/amazons-face-recognition-falsely-matched-28.

720 Andy Hayler, "Code of Silence – the Hidden Risks of AI-Generated Code," The Information Difference, April 24, 2025, https://www.informationdifference.com/code-of-silence-the-hidden-risks-of-ai-generated-code.

721 BBC News, "Amazon Scrapped 'sexist AI' Tool," BBC News, October 10, 2018, https://www.bbc.com/news/technology-45809919.

722 Cem Dilmegani, "Bias in AI: Examples and 6 Ways to Fix It," AIMultiple, Last updated November 3, 2025, https://research.aimultiple.com/ai-bias.

723 Carla K. Johnson, "Racial Bias in Health Care Software Aids Whites Over Blacks," AP News, October 25, 2019, https://apnews.com/racial-bias-in-health-care-software-aids-whites-over-blacks-b5fb4e1ae6e944fd979568df1fdb6df4.

724 Jeff Larson, Julia Angwin, Lauren Kirchner, and Surya Mattu, "How We Analyzed the COMPAS Recidivism Algorithm," ProPublica, May 26, 2016, https://www.propublica.org/article/how-we-analyzed-the-compas-recidivism-algorithm.

725 Ng S.T. Chong, "The Rise of the Deceptive Machines: When AI Learns to Lie," UNU Campus Computing Centre, January 1, 2025, https://c3.unu.edu/blog/the-rise-of-the-deceptive-machines-when-ai-learns-to-lie.

726 OpenAI, "GPT-4 System Card," report, August 2022, https://cdn.openai.com/papers/gpt-4-system-card.pdf.

727 Anthony Cuthbertson, "ChatGPT Successor Tricks Worker Into Thinking It's Human," The Independent, March 15, 2023, https://www.independent.co.uk/tech/chatgpt-gpt4-ai-openai-b2301523.html.

728 World Health Organization, "Road Traffic Injuries," World Health Organization, December 13, 2023, https://www.who.int/news-room/fact-sheets/detail/road-traffic-injuries.

729 Autonomous Vehicle Industry Association, "Research & Discoveries (R&D): Waymo Reduces Crash Rates Compared to Human Drivers Over 7+ Million AV Miles," Autonomous Vehicle Industry Association, January 17, 2024, https://www.theavindustry.org/blog/waymo-reduces-crash-rates-compared-to-human-drivers.

730 Ernesto Damiani, "Autonomy and Accuracy in Weapon Systems: The Prospects of Artificial Intelligence," ISPI, January 28, 2025, https://www.ispionline.it/en/publication/autonomy-and-accuracy-in-weapon-systems-the-prospects-of-artificial-intelligence-198146.

731 Taylor Jones, "Real-Life Technologies that Prove Autonomous Weapons are Already Here," Future of Life Institute, November 22, 2021, https://futureoflife.org/aws/real-life-technologies-that-prove-autonomous-weapons-are-already-here.

732 European Parliament, "EU AI Act: First Regulation on Artificial Intelligence," European Parliament, Published: August 6, 2023, Last updated February 19, 2025, https://www.europarl.europa.eu/topics/en/article/20230601STO93804/eu-ai-act-first-regulation-on-artificial-intelligence.

733 Abnormal AI, "WormGPT's Demise: What Cybercriminals Are Using Now," Abnormal AI, November 26, 2024, https://abnormal.ai/blog/what-happened-to-wormgpt-cybercriminal-tools.

734 Deeba Ahmed, "Employee Duped by AI-Generated CFO in $25.6M Deepfake Scam," HackRead, February 5, 2024, https://hackread.com/employee-duped-ai-generated-cfo-deepfake-scam.

735 Jai Vijayan, "Samsung Engineers Feed Sensitive Data to ChatGPT, Sparking Workplace AI Warnings," Dark Reading, April 11, 2023, https://www.darkreading.com/vulnerabilities-threats/samsung-engineers-sensitive-data-chatgpt-warnings-ai-use-workplace.

736 Shannon Bond, "How AI Deepfakes Polluted Elections in 2024," NPR, December 21, 2024, https://www.npr.org/2024/12/21/nx-s1-5220301/deepfakes-memes-artificial-intelligence-elections.

737 Thor Olavsrud, "11 Famous AI Disasters," CIO, August 7, 2025, https://www.cio.com/article/190888/5-famous-analytics-and-ai-disasters.html.

738 Dylan Walsh, "A New Look at the Economics of AI," MIT Sloan, January 21, 2025, https://mitsloan.mit.edu/ideas-made-to-matter/a-new-look-economics-ai.

739 Josh Howarth, "Most Visited Websites in the World (August 2025)," Exploding Topics, August 20, 2025, https://explodingtopics.com/blog/most-visited-websites.

740 CV VC, "Where VCs Are Investing in 2025: Blockchain Vs. AI Funding Trends," CV VC, May 9, 2025, https://www.cvvc.com/blogs/where-vcs-are-investing-in-2025-blockchain-vs-ai-funding-trends.

741 KPMG and KPMG International Limited, "Trust, Attitudes and Use of Artificial Intelligence: A Global Study 2025," KPMG, August 13, 2025, https://kpmg.com/se/en/insights/ai/trust-attitudes-and-use-of-ai.html.

742 Damien Charlotin, "AI Hallucination Cases Database," Artificial Authority, n.d., https://www.damiencharlotin.com/hallucinations/?ref=nucleo.jor.br&page=2&page=3&page=4&page=5.

743 "Groundbreaking BBC Research Shows Issues With Over Half the Answers From Artificial Intelligence (AI) Assistants," BBC, February 11, 2025, https://www.bbc.com/mediacentre/2025/bbc-research-shows-issues-with-answers-from-artificial-intelligence-assistants.

744 Jeremy Hsu, "AI Hallucinations Are Getting Worse – and They're Here to Stay," New Scientist, May 9, 2025, https://www.newscientist.com/article/2479545-ai-hallucinations-are-getting-worse-and-theyre-here-to-stay.

745 Marcin Frąckiewicz, "Black Box AI Exposed: Hidden Algorithms, Risks, and Breakthroughs in 2025," TechStock2, July 5, 2025, https://ts2.tech/en/black-box-ai-exposed-hidden-algorithms-risks-and-breakthroughs-in-2025.

746 Adam Zewe, "Explained: Generative AI's Environmental Impact," MIT News | Massachusetts Institute of Technology, January 17, 2025, https://news.mit.edu/2025/explained-generative-ai-environmental-impact-0117.

747 Matt Wood, "The Fearless Future: 2025 Global AI Jobs Barometer," PwC, June 3, 2025, https://www.pwc.com/gx/en/issues/artificial-intelligence/ai-jobs-barometer.html; Till Leopold, "How AI is reshaping the career ladder, and other trends in jobs and skills on Labour Day," World Economic Forum, April 30, 2025, https://www.weforum.org/stories/2025/04/ai-jobs-international-workers-day.

748 Datatron Technologies, "Real-life Examples of Discriminating Artificial Intelligence," Datatron, n.d., https://datatron.com/real-life-examples-of-discriminating-artificial-intelligence/; Django Beatty, Kritsada Masanthia, Teepakorn Kaphol, and Niphan Sethi, "Revealing Hidden Bias in AI: Lessons from Large Language Models," arXiv:2410.16927v1, October 22, 2024, https://arxiv.org/html/2410.16927v1.

749 Kexin Zhu, Jiajie Zhang, Anton Klishin, Mario Esser, William A. Blumentals, Juhaeri Juhaeri, Corinne Jouquelet-Royer, and Sarah-Jo Sinnott, "Evaluating the Accuracy of Responses by Large Language Models for Information on Disease Epidemiology," Pharmacoepidemiology and Drug Safety 34, no. 2 (February 1, 2025): e70111, https://doi.org/10.1002/pds.70111.

750 Li Wang, Xi Chen, XiangWen Deng, Hao Wen, MingKe You, WeiZhi Liu, Qi Li, and Jian Li, "Prompt Engineering in Consistency and Reliability with the Evidence-based Guideline for LLMs," npj Digital Medicine 7, no. 1 (February 20, 2024), https://doi.org/10.1038/s41746-024-01029-4.

751 Andy Hayler, "AI Use Cases – the Good, the Bad and the Ugly," Bloor Research, May 23, 2025, https://www.bloorresearch.com/ai-use-cases-the-good-the-bad-and-the-ugly.

752 Danny Bradbury, "One in six US workers pretends to use AI to please the bosses," The Register, July 22, 2025, https://www.theregister.com/2025/07/22/ai_anxiety_us_workers/?utm_source=dlvr.it&utm_medium=twitter.

753 Thor Olavsrud, "11 Famous AI Disasters," CIO, August 7, 2025, https://www.cio.com/article/190888/5-famous-analytics-and-ai-disasters.html.

754 Imran Rahman-Jones, "AI Means Google's Greenhouse Gas Emissions up 48% in 5 Years," BBC News, July 3, 2024, https://bbc.co.uk/news/articles/c51yvz51k2xo.

755 Chris Baraniuk, "Electricity Grids Creak as AI Demands Soar," BBC News, May 21, 2024, https://bbc.co.uk/news/articles/cj5ll89dy2mo.

756 Khalid Alaamer, "This is the state of play in the global data centre gold rush," World Economic Forum, April 22, 2025, https://www.weforum.org/stories/2025/04/data-centre-gold-rush-ai.

757 Goldman Sachs, "Is Nuclear Energy the Answer to AI Data Centers' Power Consumption?" Goldman Sachs, January 23, 2025, https://www.goldmansachs.com/insights/articles/is-nuclear-energy-the-answer-to-ai-data-centers-power-consumption.

758 Zoe Kleinman and Brian Wheeler, "Concern the UK's AI Ambitions Could Lead to Water Shortages," BBC News, February 6, 2025, https://bbc.co.uk/news/articles/ce85wx9jjndo

759 Imran Rahman-Jones, "AI Means Google's Greenhouse Gas Emissions up 48% in 5 Years," BBC News, July 3, 2024, https://www.bbc.com/news/articles/c51yvz51k2xo.

760 Ben Dickson, "New AI architecture delivers 100x faster reasoning than LLMs with just 1,000 training examples," Venture Beat, July 25, 2025, https://venturebeat.com/ai/new-ai-architecture-delivers-100x-faster-reasoning-than-llms-with-just-1000-training-examples.

761 Fisher Phillips, "European Industry Pushes Back on the EU AI Act – Key Takeaways for Employers," Fisher Phillips, September 7, 2025, https://www.fisherphillips.com/en/news-insights/european-industry-pushes-back-on-the-eu-ai-act.html.

762 National Conference of State Legislatures, "Artificial Intelligence 2025 Legislation," National Conference of State Legislatures, Last updated July 10, 2025, https://www.ncsl.org/technology-and-communication/artificial-intelligence-2025-legislation.

763 "AI Congressional Mandates, Executive Orders and Actions," NIST, January 21, 2025, Last updated July 30, 2025, https://www.nist.gov/artificial-intelligence/ai-congressional-mandates-executive-orders-and-actions.

764 American National Standards Institute, "China Announces Action Plan for Global AI Governance," American National Standards Institute, August 1, 2025, https://www.ansi.org/standards-news/all-news/8-1-25-china-announces-action-plan-for-global-ai-governance; Amy Yang and Bob Li, "AI Watch: Global Regulatory Tracker - China," White & Case LLP International Law Firm, Global Law Practice, September 22, 2025, https://www.whitecase.com/insight-our-thinking/ai-watch-global-regulatory-tracker-china.

765 Alex Roberts Jerry Wang, "Korea's Won? South Korea's AI Basic Act: Asia's First Comprehensive AI Legislation," Passle, December 31, 2024, https://techinsights.linklaters.com/post/102js56/koreas-wonsouth-koreas-ai-basic-act-asias-first-comprehensive-ai-legislatio.

766 AI Impacts, "2022 Expert Survey on Progress in AI," AI Impacts, October 31, 2023, https://aiimpacts.org/2022-expert-survey-on-progress-in-ai/#Existential_risk.

767 Severin Field, "Why do Experts Disagree on Existential Risk and P(doom)? A Survey of AI Experts," arXiv:2502.14870v1, January 25, 2025, https://arxiv.org/html/2502.14870v1.

768 "Alignment Research Center" (home page), https://www.alignment.org.

769 Peter S. Park, Simon Goldstein, Aidan O'Gara, Michael Chen, and Dan Hendrycks, "AI deception: A survey of examples, risks, and potential solutions," Patterns 5, vol. 5 (May 10, 2024): 100988.

770 Joel Lehman, Jeff Clune, Dusan Misevic, Christoph Adami, Lee Altenberg, Julie Beaulieu et al., "The Surprising Creativity of Digital Evolution: A Collection of Anecdotes from the Evolutionary Computation and Artificial Life Research Communities," Artificial Life 26, vol. 2 (2020): 274–306. https://doi.org/10.1162/artl_a_00319.

771 Zoe Kleinman, "US Air Force Denies AI Drone Attacked Operator in Test," BBC News, June 2, 2023, https://www.bbc.co.uk/news/technology-65789916.

772 "Autonomous Ride-Hailing - Get a Ride in San Francisco, CA," Waymo, n.d., https://waymo.com/rides/san-francisco.

773 Naval Research Laboratory, "DARPA's Robots to the Rescue: Transforming Satellite Maintenance in Space," SciTechDaily, November 17, 2024, https://scitechdaily.com/darpas-robots-to-the-rescue-transforming-satellite-maintenance-in-space.

774 NASA, "Autonomous Systems Help NASA's Perseverance Do More Science on Mars," NASA Jet Propulsion Laboratory, September 21, 2023, https://www.jpl.nasa.gov/news/autonomous-systems-help-nasas-perseverance-do-more-science-on-mars.

775 Bryan Young, "The First 'Killer Robot' Was Around Back in 1979," HowStuffWorks, August 15, 2023, https://science.howstuffworks.com/first-killer-robot-was-around-back-in-1979.htm.

776 Bruce Schneier and Davi Ottenheimer, "Robots Are Already Killing People," The Atlantic, September 6, 2023, https://www.theatlantic.com/technology/archive/2023/09/robot-safety-standards-regulation-human-fatalities/675231.

777 Nick Robins-Early, "AI's 'Oppenheimer Moment': Autonomous Weapons Enter the Battlefield," The Guardian, July 14, 2024, https://www.theguardian.com/technology/article/2024/jul/14/ais-oppenheimer-moment-autonomous-weapons-enter-the-battlefield.

778 Michael J.D. Vermeer, "Could AI Really Kill off Humans?" Scientific American, May 6, 2025, https://www.scientificamerican.com/article/could-ai-really-kill-off-humans.

779 The Editors of Encyclopaedia Britannica, "Three Laws of Robotics," Encyclopedia Britannica, n.d., https://www.britannica.com/topic/Three-Laws-of-Robotics.

780 Dan Milmo, "Company Worker in Hong Kong Pays Out £20m in Deepfake Video Call Scam," The Guardian, February 5, 2024, https://www.theguardian.com/world/2024/feb/05/hong-kong-company-deepfake-video-conference-call-scam.

781 David Trigano and Alex Kozodoy, "The Rise of AI-Driven Cyber Attacks: How LLMs Are Reshaping the Threat Landscape," Deep Instinct, March 12, 2025, https://www.deepinstinct.com/blog/the-rise-of-ai-driven-cyber-attacks-how-llms-are-reshaping-the-threat-landscape.

782 "AI Safety Initiative: Pioneering AI Compliance & Safety," Cloud Security Alliance, n.d., https://cloudsecurityalliance.org/ai-safety-initiative.

783 Department for Science, Innovation and Technology, "AI Safety Institute," GOV.UK, February 9, 2024, https://www.gov.uk/government/organisations/ai-safety-institute.

784 Andy Hayler, "AI Alignment and Safety – Pandora's Bot," The Information Difference, August 6, 2025, https://www.informationdifference.com/ai-alignment-and-safety-pandoras-bot.

785 Meg Risdal, "Introducing Kaggle Game Arena," Kaggle, August 5, 2025, https://www.kaggle.com/blog/introducing-game-arena.

786 Cade Metz and Karen Weise. "A.I. Is Getting More Powerful, but Its Hallucinations Are Getting Worse," The New York Times, May 5, 2025. https://www.nytimes.com/2025/05/05/technology/ai-hallucinations-chatgpt-google.html.

787 Carl Franzen, "OpenAI's GPT-5 rollout is not going smoothly," Venture Beat, August 8, 2025, https://venturebeat.com/ai/openais-gpt-5-rollout-is-not-going-smoothly.

788 Livemint, "'They Ruined ChatGPT': OpenAI Faces Backlash as GPT-5 Reaches All Users," Mint, August 8, 2025, https://www.livemint.com/technology/tech-news/

they-ruined-chatgpt-openai-faces-backlash-as-gpt-5-reaches-all-users-sam-altman-11754632387517.html.

789 Cem Dilmegani and Sıla Ermut, "When Will AGI/Singularity Happen? 8,590 Predictions Analyzed," AIMultiple, Last updated October 28, 2025, https://research.aimultiple.com/artificial-general-intelligence-singularity-timing.

790 Ibid.

791 Gary Marcus, "CONFIRMED: LLMs Have Indeed Reached a Point of Diminishing Returns," Marcus on AI, November 9, 2024, https://garymarcus.substack.com/p/confirmed-llms-have-indeed-reached.

792 DataCamp Team, "What is Symbolic AI?" DataCamp, May 12, 2023, https://www.datacamp.com/blog/what-is-symbolic-ai.

793 Andy Hayler, "Drifting Away? AI Model Performance Over Time," The Information Difference, May 21, 2025, https://www.informationdifference.com/ai-model-performance.

794 Charlie Guo, "LLMs Are Getting Dumber and We Have No Idea Why," Artificial Ignorance, September 5, 2024, https://www.ignorance.ai/p/llms-are-getting-dumber-and-we-have.

795 Lexin Zhou, Wout Schellaert, Fernando Martínez-Plumed, Yael Moros-Daval, Cèsar Ferri, José Hernández-Orallo, et al., "Larger and More Instructable Language Models Become Less Reliable," Nature 634 (25 September 2024): 61–68.

796 Andy Hayler, "When Algorithms Dream: AI Hallucinations in Depth," The Information Difference, August 19, 2025, https://www.informationdifference.com/when-algorithms-dream-ai-hallucinations-in-depth.

797 Cem Dilmegani and Aleyna Daldal, "AI Hallucination: Comparison of the Popular LLMs," AIMultiple, October 1, 2025, https://research.aimultiple.com/ai-hallucination.

798 Maxwell Zeff, "OpenAI's New Reasoning AI Models Hallucinate More," TechCrunch, April 18, 2025, https://techcrunch.com/2025/04/18/openais-new-reasoning-ai-models-hallucinate-more.

799 Andy Hayler, "Reality Check: Do AI Projects Deliver Return on Investment?" The Information Difference, August 23, 2025, https://www.informationdifference.com/reality-check-do-ai-projects-deliver-return-on-investment.

800 Sheryl Estrada, "MIT Report: 95% of Generative AI Pilots at Companies Are Failing," Fortune, August 18, 2025, https://fortune.com/2025/08/18/mit-report-95-percent-generative-ai-pilots-at-companies-failing-cfo.

801 nilkanth ahire, "🧠 "LLMs Are Basically Obsolete"—Why AI Pioneer Yann LeCun Thinks the Real AI Revolution Hasn't Even Started," Medium, April 5, 2025, https://nilkanthahire.medium.com/llms-are-basically-obsolete-why-ai-pioneer-yann-lecun-thinks-the-real-ai-revolution-hasnt-16112d9d0809.

802 Ben Turner, "Current AI Models a 'Dead End' for Human-level Intelligence, Scientists Agree," Live Science, March 27, 2025, https://www.livescience.com/technology/artificial-intelligence/current-ai-models-a-dead-end-for-human-level-intelligence-expert-survey-claims.

803 Gary Marcus, "GPT-5: Overdue, Overhyped and Underwhelming. And That's Not the Worst of It," Marcus on AI, August 10, 2025, https://garymarcus.substack.com/p/gpt-5-overdue-overhyped-and-underwhelming.

804 John Werner, "The Big AI Slowdown," Forbes, November 15, 2024, https://www.forbes.com/sites/johnwerner/2024/11/15/the-big-ai-slowdown.

805 Artur Garcez, "Neurosymbolic AI is the answer to large language models' inability to stop hallucinating," The Conversation, May 30, 2025, https://theconversation.com/neurosymbolic-ai-is-the-answer-to-large-language-models-inability-to-stop-hallucinating-257752.

806 Imandra, "Imandra Unveils CodeLogician: A Groundbreaking Neurosymbolic AI Agent for Mathematical Code Reasoning," PR Newswire, March 26, 2025, https://www.prnewswire.com/news-releases/imandra-unveils-codelogician-a-groundbreaking-neurosymbolic-ai-agent-for-mathematical-code-reasoning-302411440.html; Private Equity Wire, "Imandra completes USD5m seed round led by AlbionVC, IQ Capital and LiveOak Venture Partners," Private Equity Wire, April 18, 2019, https://www.privateequitywire.co.uk/imandra-completes-usd5m-seed-round-led-albionvc-iq-capital-and-liveoak-venture/; "Imandra" (home page), n.d., https://www.imandra.ai/

807 VentureRadar, "Top Symbolic AI Companies," VentureRadar, n.d., https://www.ventureradar.com/keyword/symbolic%20AI.

808 Microsoft Research team, "Frontiers of Multimodal Learning: A Responsible AI Approach," Microsoft Research, February 5, 2024, https://www.microsoft.com/en-us/research/blog/frontiers-of-multimodal-learning-a-responsible-ai-approach.

809 Jacob Mural and Eda Kavlakoglu, "What is reinforcement learning?" IBM, n.d., http://ibm.com/think/topics/reinforcement-learning.

810 Om Kshirsagar, Aman Maurya, and Fatima Shaikh, "AlphaZero Vs StockFish – a Review of Chess Engines," journal-article, by Journal of Emerging Technologies and Innovative Research (JETIR) and JETIR, Journal of Emerging Technologies and Innovative Research (JETIR) 9, no. 4 (2022): b451–b457, https://www.jetir.org/papers/JETIR2204161.pdf.

811 Steven Borowiec, "AlphaGo Seals 4-1 Victory Over Go Grandmaster Lee Sedol," The Guardian, March 15, 2016, https://www.theguardian.com/technology/2016/mar/15/googles-alphago-seals-4-1-victory-over-grandmaster-lee-sedol.

812 The Royal Swedish Academy of Sciences, "Press release: Nobel Prize in Chemistry 2024," NobelPrize.org, October 9, 2024, https://www.nobelprize.org/prizes/chemistry/2024/press-release.

813 Darko Matovski, "Causal AI: the revolution uncovering the 'why' of decision-making," World Economic Forum, April 11, 2024, https://www.weforum.org/stories/2024/04/causal-ai-decision-making.

814 David Anker, "Forecasting – Prediction Is Very Difficult, Especially if It's About the Future!," Cranfield University Blogs, July 10, 2017, https://blogs.cranfield.ac.uk/cbp/forecasting-prediction-is-very-difficult-especially-if-its-about-the-future.

815 See Gary Marcus' Substack, Marcus on AI, https://garymarcus.substack.com.

816 Quoteresearch, "Quote Origin: May You Live in Interesting Times," Quote Investigator, December 18, 2015, https://quoteinvestigator.com/2015/12/18/live.

www.ingramcontent.com/pod-product-compliance
Lightning Source LLC
LaVergne TN
LVHW022153200926
848481LV00006B/1736
* 9 7 8 1 9 1 9 2 4 1 9 2 0 *